wild plants
of Greater Brisbane

Cover: *Banksia aemula*, (Wallum Banksia), JW
Inside front cover: *Drynaria rigidula*, (Basket fern), BC
Inside back cover: *Angophora subvelutina* (Broadleaf Apple), BC

wild plants
of Greater Brisbane

Queensland **Museum**
Queensland Government

A Queensland Museum Guide

Published by the Queensland Museum
in partnership with the
Environment and Parks Branch
of the Brisbane City Council,
and the generous assistance of
the Queensland Herbarium
and Greening Australia

© Queensland Museum 2003

This book may not be reproduced in whole or in part, in any form except for research, individual study and educational purposes. Properly acknowledged quotations may be made, but queries regarding the republication of any material should be addressed to the Director of the Queensland Museum.

Requests for this book should be made to:

Queensland Museum
PO Box 3300
SOUTH BRISBANE QLD 4101
AUSTRALIA
Phone: (07) 3840 7555
Fax: (07) 3846 1918
International Fax: +617 3846 1918

www.qmuseum.qld.gov.au

ISBN 0-9751116-2-0

General Editor: Michelle Ryan
Photography: Bruce Cowell, Gary Cranitch and Jeff Wright, QM; and Glenn Leiper
Design: Janice Watson with special thanks to Baden Phillips and Diane Yeo
Administration Assistant: Marie Vandenberg
With special thanks to Myra Givans and Bronwen Humphries
Illustrations: Roberta Moynihan and courtesy of the Queensland Herbarium.

Set in Stone Serif 8/9.5pt

Printed on 130gsm Sapphire Dull

Published by the Queensland Museum
First printed 2003
Second printing (amended) 2005

All photographs not otherwise acknowledged are the property of the Queensland Museum.

Queensland Museum photographs are available for sale through the Queensland Museum Image Library

Phone: (07) 3840 7614 or (07) 3840 7645

foreword

Wild Plants of Greater Brisbane is the fifth volume in the Museum's best-selling series of environmental guides and is the first book to document the diverse landscapes and flora of the Greater Brisbane region.

It was created in response to the enormous public demand that followed the release of *Wildlife of Greater Brisbane* several years ago. Just as ordinary citizens wish to learn more about the amazingly diverse animal life that surrounds us, they have an equally strong curiosity about the native plants that are a critical component of our local environment.

The Queensland Museum is an internationally-acknowledged centre for conservation, biodiversity research and education and is committed to increasing the public's awareness of the natural environment. Drawing on the expertise of our scientific, photographic and publications staff as well as the botanical expertise of other leading scientific and environmental organisations, this much-awaited publication is sure to become an essential companion for every Brisbane household.

The Museum is indebted to:

- the Brisbane City Council for its generous support and on-going sponsorship of the *Wild Guide* series;
- the Queensland Herbarium for its role in identifying several hundred species of plants; and
- Greening Australia for its support and assistance.

The Museum is also indebted to the authors — all specialists in their fields — whose extensive botanical knowledge and personal goodwill towards the project ensured its successful completion: Alan Barton, Robert Coutts, Paul Donatiu, Glenn Leiper, Bill McDonald, Kathy Stephens, David Barnes, Janet Hauser and Lyndal Plant. Emeritus Professor Trevor Clifford provided planning advice.

This book is the culmination of many countless hours of effort by these authors and by Queensland Museum staff.

The book describes a broad range of plants within the major ecosystems, setting each species within its community and, in the process, helping to demonstrate its links to the wider environment and its significance to ourselves and our lives.

I hope that this book will help us rediscover our connections to the natural world and inspire us to continue to explore, appreciate, understand and preserve the wild plants of the Greater Brisbane Region.

Ian Galloway

Dr Ian Galloway
Director, Queensland Museum

Brachychiton bidwillii (Little Kurrajong), BC

Contents

Foreword v

About This Book ix

Introduction 1

Plants of the Coastal Dunes	**19**
Plants of the Wetlands	**31**
Tidal Wetlands — saltmarshes and mangroves	35
Freshwater Wetlands — lakes, lagoons and swamps	47
Plants of the Wallum Heath	**61**
Plants of the Eucalypt Forests	**87**
Dry Eucalypt Forest	93
Wet Eucalypt Forest	199
Plants of the Rainforests	**211**
Plants of the Mountain Heath	**303**
Plants of City Streets and Parks	**323**
Weeds	**335**

References 347

Authors 350

Acknowledgements 351

Glossary 356

Index 360

    Scientific Names 360

    Common Names 364

List of Wildlife Species 368

Dendrobium kingianum (Pink Rock Orchid), BC

About this book

This book provides an introduction to the flora of the Greater Brisbane Region It is written for the non-specialist and for all those with an interest in wild plants.

The plant species within these pages represent only a small sample of the botanical diversity of the Greater Brisbane Region and the wider South-east Queensland area. Most were chosen because they are familiar and easily located in our natural reserves, parks, streets and gardens. There will be few people who are not acquainted with the majestic Forest Red Gum (the most widespread eucalypt in the region), even if they do not know its scientific name, *Eucalyptus tereticornis*. Other species were included because of their rarity or environmental significance.

The book is arranged in broad general categories that reflect the way that people might encounter wild plants — walking along the beach, bushwalking in our national parks, or simply driving around the city. The plants have been grouped under the following natural habitats:
- Coastal Dunes
- Wetlands — Saltmarshes and Mangroves; Lakes, Lagoons and Swamps
- Wallum Heath
- Eucalypt Forests
- Rainforests
- Mountain Heath
- Streets and Parks

A final category covers weeds, plants that may occur across all habitats and which may pose a significant threat to the native species that are the focus of this book.

Selection was further refined by considering which plants species are most obvious at different times of the year. Our wild plants are so much a part of our everyday lives that they are easily overlooked or ignored, but when we do become aware of them, it is usually because we have noticed an outstanding or unusual characteristic such as, the colour of leaves, flowers, fruit or seeds. Sometimes it is sheer numbers of a single species growing in one place that attracts our attention or a single dominant plant in an otherwise apparently nondescript patch of bushland.

Queensland Museum photographers spent almost two years, working through one of the region's worst droughts to capture the beautiful images that accompany the species accounts. Even so, coverage may not be as complete as some enthusiasts would wish. It would take several volumes of a book this size to adequately capture the diversity of the 3300 native plant species that occur within the Greater Brisbane Region.

The species accounts are intended as a brief guide to the most important physical and biological aspects of a plant. They include:

Scientific Name: The Latin-based name by which a species can be universally recognised and which assigns the plant to a particular grouping. Species are presented in alphabetical order of scientific name. Most home gardeners and nurserymen are familiar with the scientific names of plants.

Common Name: The name by which a plant is most widely known to the general community. Plants, like animals, may have more than one common name. This can cause confusion and is the principal reason for the use of scientific names.

Description — A brief, but meaningful description of the physical aspects of a plant. Every attempt has been made to

Amylotheca dictyophleba (Brush Mistletoe), BC

simplify this information, but it is not always possible to replace formal botanical terms. Readers are urged to consult the glossary at the back of the book for further explanation. Some species, such as the eucalypts, are so closely related and so similar that they cannot be easily distinguished without reference to very fine detail.

Habitat and Range — Broad general information about the type of environment in which a plant might occur and where it might be found within the Greater Brisbane Region and beyond.

Notes — Any other interesting biological or general information, such as comparisons with similar species and Indigenous and European use of plants.

Wildlife — Native plants are critical to the survival of Australia's unique animals. The lists of animals that accompany some species accounts are not comprehensive, but are intended as a guide to increase awareness of the relationship between our wild plants and animals. Many more species of animals may use the same plant. The Museum would be pleased to hear of possible additions to the lists.

This field guide is a first step to identification. Readers are encouraged to consult other books or to use the services of the Queensland Herbarium to further their knowledge of wild plants in the Greater Brisbane Region

The information in this book was correct at the time of printing. However research into native plant species is continuing all the time and changes to scientific names do occur. The Queensland Museum would appreciate notification of any updates, changes, omissions or errors. Please phone (07) 3840 7602 or fax (07) 3846 1918. Updates will be listed on the Queensland Museum website www.Qmuseum.qld.gov.au.

THE GREATER BRISBANE REGION

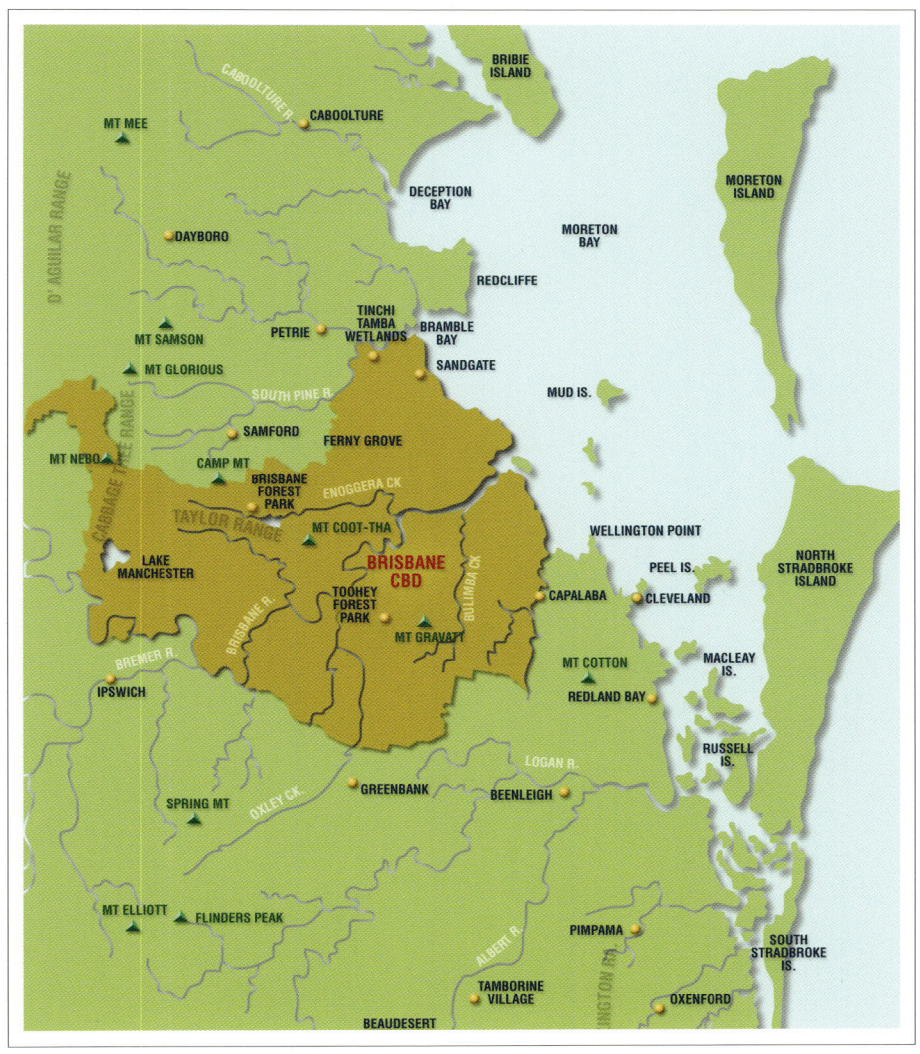

Brisbane Metropolitan area

Introduction

The city of Brisbane and its surrounding region lies in one of Australia's most outstanding natural environments. To the west, the hills and mountains of the Great Dividing Range sweep southward in a great arc. To the east, the azure waters of Moreton Bay are framed by a chain of spectacular sand islands. Hills and fertile valleys abut a narrow coastal plain that encompasses a patchwork of freshwater wetlands tucked behind ribbons of mangroves and deep green estuaries.

These complex interlinking habitats underpin one of the most botanically rich areas in Australia, surpassed only by the Wet Tropics of Far North Queensland and the South-west corner of Western Australia. More than 3300 species of wild (native) plants drape the Greater Brisbane landscape in a riotous abundance of size, shape and colour. From delicate forest ferns to soaring eucalypt giants, the region's native plants have developed over many millions of years of environmental change and all capitalise on a landscape of great age and a climate that varies from sub-tropical to temperate.

However, the most significant changes to the distribution and diversity of our flora have occurred in the relatively short period since European settlement in the early 19th century. An understanding of these changes is a valuable start to learning about our native plants and increasing appreciation of our local environment.

A Plant Paradise

The foundation for this richly diverse vegetation is a climatic zone known as the Macleay-McPherson Overlap, an area where a combination of topography and climate has created tolerable conditions for a wide range of plant and animal species. South-east Queensland lies within the Overlap and plants, commonly found either further north (tropical) or south (temperate) are able to survive and flourish here.

The resulting vegetation communities provide habitats that are critical to sustaining the region's equally diverse fauna. More than 800 species of vertebrate animals and countless invertebrates rely on wild plants for food, shelter and nesting materials.

Agathis robusta (Kauri Pine), BC

Nothofagus moorei (Antarctic Beech), GC

ENVIRONMENTAL DIARY

Ancient Brisbane

The evolution of our wild plants is closely linked to vast changes in geology, climate and environment that have occurred over many hundreds of millions of years. The geological history of the Greater Brisbane Region is shorter than other parts of Queensland but, even so, the oldest rocks in the region may extend back nearly 500 million years.

Fossils from the Triassic to Early Jurassic Periods (approx. 200 million years ago) are the earliest record of the region's plant life and they include conifers, cycads, ferns and ginkgoes, which thrived in the temperate climates of the time.

Australia was then part of the supercontinent of Gondwanaland, and the flora and fauna from this period reflect ties to South America, Africa, Antarctica and India.

In the Triassic to early Jurassic Periods, the Greater Brisbane Region was a large open river plain with abundant swamps, lakes and streams. Uplands, to the north and northwest, and the lowland plains were well vegetated with conifer forest. None of the

Brisbane City now covers 135,000 ha, including Moreton Island. The vegetation on the mainland comprises:
- Total vegetation 55,341 ha (46%),
- Remnant vegetation 39,010 ha (32.9%),
- Non-remnant vegetation 16,331 ha (13.5%)

Within the city boundaries, there are 63 vegetation communities which support 2500 species of native plants (123 Significant), 550 species of vertebrate animals and countless thousands of invertebrates (171 Significant).

flowering plants had yet appeared and the landscape would have looked quite different without the grasses of today. Relicts of this era persist around the world and in Australia, many conifers had their origins in this time. Cycads, which still dot areas of Queensland, were common and Hoop and Bunya Pines are remnants of the Gondwana flora.

The rise of the flowering plants which eventually came to dominate flora worldwide began at the closing of the Cretaceous Period, some 65 million years ago. When Gondwanaland broke up at the end of the Mesozoic and early Tertiary eras, the

Sterculia quadrifida (Native peanut), JW

Woombye, north of Brisbane, c1914 neg no. 45131 courtesy of the John Oxley Library

Australian continent began a long drift northwards and it was during this time that our flora and fauna began to develop in isolation from the rest of the world. This is linked to the major extinction event that led to the demise of the dinosaurs, but which also created opportunities for other life forms to flourish.

At this time, the landscape would have started to assemble its modern features. Plants like *Brachychitons* are known from the fossil deposits of the Oxley Basin. The Antarctic Beech Trees (*Nothofagus* spp.) also date to this period, but they are now restricted to isolated pockets on the Lamington Plateau. Grasses became dominant later in the Tertiary Period, and it was not until the continent started to dry out that eucalypts and acacias became the typical flora of the Australian landscape.

Isolation, climatic variation, and the continuing northern migration and gradual drying of the continent over the past few millions of years have all strongly influenced the development of our native plant communities. For example, rainforest areas have fluctuated in size and distribution, as have arid and semi-arid areas.

It is clear that even before human settlement, dynamic change in response to global conditions was part of the Australian environment.

Discovery

The first humans came to what is now the Greater Brisbane Region more than 40,000 years ago in the late Pleistocene Period. Moreton Bay would have been a large dry land coastal plain. The environmental implications of discovery and settlement by Aboriginal Australians are poorly understood because our information is limited. It is known that Indigenous use of plant resources was not just a simple case of random collection or harvesting, but involved an intimate knowledge and stewardship of the land.

Human settlement is believed to have reinforced the shift towards eucalypt-dominated vegetation, primarily due to

The Aboriginal people of the Greater Brisbane Region have a long and intimate relationship with the environment. More than 20 Traditional Owner Groups have their ancestral homelands in the region. Their extensive knowledge and use of wild plants was developed over thousands of years. Plants provided Aboriginal people with food, medicine, transport, shelter and with everyday utensils and weapons of war. In his journal, European settler Tom Petrie wrote that the Aboriginal people used a wide range of native plants to sustain their lives. Flowers, leaves, seeds, berries and tuberous roots provided important food supplements, while timber and bark were used to make huts, canoes, boomerangs, shields and spears. Twine and fibrous bark were used to fashion string for woven dilli bags.

Syzygium crebrinerve (Purple Cherry), GC

increased fire frequency. Aboriginal people had a sophisticated regime of burning, which promoted the spread of grasslands and eucalypt species and, in turn, encouraged the proliferation of game animals. Indigenous people used the region's native plants to sustain them in their daily lives as sources of food and materials and this was part of a deeper, spiritual connection with the land that was disrupted by the arrival of the British in the late 18th century.

It is important to note that the impact of Indigenous land practices does not compare to the magnitude of environmental changes, such as land clearing for urban development and agriculture, that have occurred in the Greater Brisbane Region since European settlement in 1824.

Rediscovered

After the re-discovery of the east coast of Australia by Captain James Cook in 1770, Mathew Flinders (then a young lieutenant) was the first European to land in Moreton Bay. His explorations in 1799 and 1802 improved knowledge of the area's plant life. In his log, Flinders specifically mentions mangroves, Bribie Island Pine, pandanus, rushes, grass trees, and the presence of 'the Blue Gum' (known from Sydney) she-oaks and the 'Cherry tree of Port Jackson'.

John Oxley, 1823

In 1823, the Surveyor–General of New South Wales John Oxley was given the task of investigating the suitability of Moreton Bay for a penal settlement. By incredible chance, Oxley met three marooned convicts who provided critical information leading to the formal discovery of the Brisbane River, which Oxley navigated as far as the modern suburb of Mt Ommaney. Oxley's log and formal report gave glowing accounts of the area, its beauty and agricultural potential and he made special mention of a 'magnificent Species of Pine' and their potential:

> *if they should prove of good quality, were of a Scantling (size) Sufficient for the topmasts of large Ships …*

Fig tree buttresses, date unknown neg no. 40203, courtesy of the John Oxley Library

Fish and Fern-root

Three convicts, Thomas Pamphlet, John Finnegan and Richard Parsons were the lucky survivors of a shipwreck, initially planned as a Red Cedar collecting trip south of Sydney. Stormy weather and strong inshore currents pushed their boat northward and the three were marooned on Moreton Island in April 1823. Their survival for more than seven months was undoubtedly due to the care and support of the local Aboriginal people they encountered, who provided them with food, taught them to fish and to use native plants, mainly fern roots, for food. The Europeans also gained first-hand, but unwanted, experience of the difficulty of traversing estuaries thickly lined by mangroves.

'The Monarch of these woods'

Within a year, Oxley was back in Moreton Bay, this time with an advance party of soldiers and convicts to establish a penal settlement. On the voyage was Allan Cunningham, a botanical collector for the Royal Gardens at Kew in England. His task was to assist the settlers to achieve self-sufficiency and this was made easier by the extensive provision of plants and seeds from the Government gardens in Sydney. With the introduction of these species, the flora of the Greater Brisbane Region was to be irrevocably changed. Cunningham also accompanied Oxley on his explorations up the Brisbane River during the later half of 1824.

In his journal, Cunningham wrote with great botanical confidence, identifying many of the plants he encountered, often expressing his pleasure in these discoveries. From the moment he sighted the mangrove-fringed estuaries of the Brisbane River, he is able to put scientific names to the species he sees. He mentions numerous plants that are either already familiar to him through previous contact, or through his knowledge of the botanical work of others elsewhere in Australia and South America. On one occasion he is able to give scientific names to more than 25 species. He particularly mentions the large pine described by Oxley, but it remained difficult to inspect as it towered over patches of thick forests along inaccessible riverbanks.

Pultenaea villosa (Hairy Bush Pea), BC

Mt Mee State Forest, BC

By 21 September 1824, Oxley and Cunningham were forced to proceed on foot. They made for a 'Pine Ridge' to gain a better view of the western extremities of the area and had to contend with very thick 'brushes'. Eventually they found themselves in a 'stupendous forest' where Cunningham was able to identify several species that occur commonly in dry vine forests today. But it is his record of 'the pine' that stands out:

> Hitherto in our examination of this River, we have been only gratified with a distant view of the Pine; immediately we approached one of magnificent stature, the Monarch of these woods. It was a healthy well grown Tree, exceeding 120 feet in height with a trunk 3.6 (feet) diam., clear of branches exceeding 80 feet. It was totally impossible not to halt a few moments to admire this noble tree which had all the habits of ramification of the Araucaria braziliensis. (now Araucaria angustifolia)

Cunningham was able to confirm that the pine was a member of the *Araucaria* genus through examination of some fallen fruit and he named the tree *Araucaria brisbanii* but it has been renamed *Araucaria cunninghamii* in his honour and, today, is commonly referred to as Hoop Pine, due to the hoop-like strips of bark that shed in circular horizontal bands around the trunk and branches.

At the time of Cunningham's explorations, dense rainforests covered the highest slopes and mountains of the Moreton Bay district and these were buffered from the drier vegetation below by towering wet eucalypt

> Since European settlement an estimated 67,000 ha or two-thirds of the original 98,000 ha of woody vegetation in Brisbane have been cleared. This includes approximately 90% of lowland forests and more than 80% of all lowland vegetation (below 100 metres).
>
> Around Brisbane only 600 ha of the original 6000 ha of rainforest, and only 450 ha of an original 13,000 ha of *Melaleuca* forest remain. The rate of clearing has decreased from 558 ha/year in 1990 to a current rate of 209 ha/year in 2001 and further declines are expected.

forests. Eucalypt woodlands and forests grew on the dry lowland ridges, hills and alluvial coastal plains. The rich loamy banks of the Brisbane River were fringed by open forest and rainforest characterised by emergent Hoop Pines, some of which were more than 45 m tall. Vegetation along the coastline included freshwater *melaleuca* wetlands and estuarine wetlands of mangroves and samphire flats.

VEGETATION CHANGE
1840 to 1950

The penal colony of Moreton Bay was opened to free settlement in 1839. Although they considered it an alien landscape, European settlers regarded the lush vegetation that surrounded the colony as an endless resource to be exploited.

Early settler Tom Petrie recorded that the vegetation and trees in the region were noted mostly for their commercial potential and value. Government prisoners working on the Brisbane, Albert and Logan Rivers cut cedar and burned mangrove trees to create ash for soap-making.

By 1900, less than 60 years after settlement, the natural landscape of what is now the Greater Brisbane Region had been transformed by agricultural and population expansion. The need for food meant that agriculture, particularly grazing, drove the rapid vegetation loss. The extensive tracts of lowland rainforest and eucalypt forest bore the brunt of the settlers' need for land and were almost totally cleared from the landscape and certainly *Toona australis* (Red Cedar), a fine timber species, was gone.

There were some early attempts to protect the landscape. In 1893 the Colonial Government created a recreational reserve on Mt Gravatt and a group of active local citizens became responsible for the 132 acres (52.8 ha). Later, in 1915, 130 acres (52 ha) were added to the original reserve. But it was not until the 1920s that tangible progress began.

William Jolly (Mayor of Brisbane 1925–1934) initiated a program to set aside 650 ha of land for park and recreational purposes and commented that:

> *In the interests of the citizens of today, but more especially for the future, we should not lose the opportunity of retaining all these beautiful spots around Brisbane. It must be manifestly clear to every thoughtful citizen that if the trees and foliage now growing on most of these hills are cut down, it would destroy to a very great extent the natural beauty of the city.*

Sticherus flabellatus (Shiny fan fern), JW

Syzygium luehmannii (Small Leafed Lilly-pilly), BC

The Aboriginal names for several native plant species have been used to name modern suburbs created as the city grew. The suburbs were named for the plants that either characterised an area or that had important cultural links to local Indigenous communities. Among them are:

Bellbowrie	Paperbark tree
Boondall	Cunjevoi Lily
Booroodabin	She-oak tree
Doolandella	Persoonia (Geebung) tree
Doomben	Tree fern
Geebung	Persoonia tree
Wynnum	Pandanus
Fig Tree Pocket	Fig tree

J. B Chandler (Mayor of Brisbane 1940–1949) considered the idea of planning for a green belt or a 'ring of green' encompassing the city. The idea was to limit urban sprawl by having a large tract of land, six to eight miles in depth, around existing residential areas. William Jolly supported the idea, noting:

it would be a sacrilege to allow the beautiful mantle which surrounds our city to be destroyed…

In the years that followed up to the 1950s, land use in the Greater Brisbane Region was still predominantly agricultural. Land clearing remained focussed on the fertile alluvial plains and gently undulating hills and rises. Areas cleared for agriculture that were allowed to recover came to be dominated by eucalypt forest, particularly if they were frequently burnt (a change that mirrored Indigenous land management).

1950 to 1990

In the four decades from the 1950s to the end of the 1980s, agriculture gave way to urbanisation as the most demanding land use activity in Brisbane and South-east Queensland coastal areas. In some places, land that had not previously been used for agriculture was now cleared for housing and industry. The period from 1974 to1989 was characterised by large scale clearing of bushland. Thirty-three percent of existing bushland cover on the South-east Queensland mainland was cleared during this time and another 17 % in Brisbane City was cleared in the 8 years to 1990.

The prevailing paradigm over at least the past 50 years has been to foster development and urbanisation to capitalise on rapid population growth without examining or considering the implications for the environment.

In general, before 1980 vegetation protection initiatives were minimal and not particularly successful. While rapid vegetation loss continued into the 1980s, this was also a time when government and individuals began to make active attempts to describe bushland values and to explore options to

Fig, *Ficus* sp. North Pine River, JW

protect native bushland for future generations. Growing community and scientific concerns about habitat loss precipitated a sense of urgency to arrest and reverse environmental impacts and caused a sea change in political thinking. As a result, the 1990s became a 'decade of transition'.

1990 to 2003

The 1990s were a period of increasing effort by governments to address community concerns about vegetation clearing and this has been mirrored by raised public expectations for government at all levels to protect the environment.

There are a number of ways that governments have sought to protect biodiversity and prevent habitat loss. This has been done through: town plans, local laws, establishing and managing natural area networks and encouraging conservation on private lands. Levies for 'buying back the bushland' have provided the necessary funds for some councils to build a bushland reserve network and support its management. For example, Brisbane has aquired a substantial conservation reserve network, paid for by the ratepayers. 'Voluntary Conservation Agreements' and 'Land for Wildlife' programs have also been successful initiatives that have enabled local governments to protect the environment in partnership with willing private landowners.

Many people are actively involved in community programs aimed at preserving and regenerating bushland. For example, in 2003 Brisbane City had 119 'Habitat Brisbane' groups and more than 2000 people involved in bushcare, devoting more than 50,000 volunteer hours annually.

> Comparison of present day vegetation with descriptions by the earliest explorers indicates that while the character of the area has been dramatically altered, species composition remains essentially the same. Some native plant species appear to have increased their local range, but there is a threat of gradual replacement of some native species by exotics. Despite the changes that have occurred, examples of pre-European vegetation survive in many localities along the Brisbane River.

Waterhousea floribunda (Weeping Lilly-pilly), JW

Vegetation protection laws have also been steadily improving with some councils able to expand the amount of land under protection. This has been reinforced by the adoption in 2000 of the *Queensland Vegetation Management Act 1999*, which deals with vegetation management on freehold land across all of Queensland. There is also a wonderful array of national parks and other reserves in the Greater Brisbane Region managed by the State Government (see *Wild Places of Greater Brisbane*).

Although there are legitimate reasons for concern and considerable work ahead there are many reasons to be optimistic and hopeful. Overall, people now have more knowledge, respect and appreciation of the environment. In the past decade there has been a growing interest and desire to use native plants and to learn more about them.

The Future

The task of protection does not stop with the regulation of clearing or the acquisition of land for a reserve network. As we halt the loss of natural vegetation and habitats, the priority shifts to enhancing what we have left and making sure that it is well managed, including the threats posed by wildfire, feral species and weeds.

It is important that we address these issues across the whole landscape — fires, feral animals and weeds don't stop at fences.

The need for more locally relevant science and information cannot be understated. There needs to be an improvement in mapping and describing the natural environment across the Greater Brisbane Region. We also need to better understand the way our ecosystems work and more importantly what to do when they aren't working and need help. There is an important role for the collection and interpretation of historical ecological knowledge, so that we can make decisions with a clearer understanding of the health of the remaining patches of natural vegetation.

Inevitably, with increasing population pressures in South-east Queensland, it is expected that there will be threats of further loss or change in the remaining native vegetation, and with this comes increasing concerns for the future. It is imperative that the last remaining natural 'gems' are protected and enhanced. It is possible to turn a 'wasteland' into a much more natural setting. Everyone has the power to make a difference, and this can begin right near you — in your own backyard. You can create a better future by planting trees, shrubs and groundcovers that are native to your area, volunteer a little time to your local community or bushcare group and help out with revegetation, catchment projects or education awareness.

As the region's remnant vegetation figure falls to the 30% threshold — beyond which species extinctions of our wild plants and animals are inevitable — the urgency increases in tempo. It is this generation that must make the tough decisions. — **Alan Barton with thanks to Kristen Sinden**

The '*Cool It! Project*' (a Brisbane City Council initiative) is just one example of how ordinary people can make a difference. The project was carried out through community planting of street trees in the suburbs of Enoggera, Alderley, Gaythorne and Sparkes Hill from July 2002 to July 2003. It aimed to improve shade and beauty of these areas, while increasing unity between residential and industrial citizens and increasing a sense of community pride and ownership. This was made possible through weekend street tree plantings, free plant giveaways and 120 volunteers who contributed more than 7700 hours of their time. Overall, 1150 new street trees were planted and 1500 native plants were distributed to local residents and businesses for use in local gardens.

BOTANICAL 'GEMS'

The following species represent just a few of the botanical 'gems' to be found in the Greater Brisbane Region. They include species that are significant, unique or special for a variety of reasons such as their abundance or rarity, their historical significance or, simply, because of their beauty. Of course there are many more and this selection is used just to remind us of the floral wonders that surround us.

Hoop Pine (Araucaria cunninghamii), BC

Araucaria cunninghamii — Hoop Pine

Araucaria — from *Araucanos* the name the Spanish Conquistadors gave to a tribe in the Chico Sur area of Chile, South America.

cunninghamii — Allan Cunningham, the botanical collector and explorer who recorded the species during his time in Brisbane in 1824.

The *Araucanians* may have existed right at the start of the development of seed-bearing trees some 240 million years ago. Based on fossil discoveries, it is thought that the genus dominated forests across the globe at different times. They are now confined to the Pacific Rim. This wide distribution signifies the links to the common stock that forested the supercontinent Gondwanaland. *Araucanians* are now spread from Patagonia to eastern Australia. These conifers hark back to ancient environments that were hotter and wetter than today and were populated for at least part of that time by large plant-eating dinosaurs.

Hoop Pine has adapted well to modern environments and has a broad climatic range, from northern New South Wales through to New Guinea. With a mature height of up to 60 m, Hoop Pines usually tower over the dry vine forest they inhabit. Most araucarias are thought to have a complex reproductive strategy. In their youth, they have only male flowers, in middle age both male (lower branches) and female parts (upper branches), and in old age when the lower branches have been shed, they carry only female flowers. This may be in response to their ability to produce copious pollen in youth, whereas in old age they focus on the production of cones with fertilised seeds.

Aboriginal people are thought to have used the sap of Hoop Pine as a cement or glue (eg. for fixing axe heads to handles).

Originally European explorers envisaged that the Hoop Pine would make excellent spars for sailing ships. Nevertheless, the primary use of this softwood was for mouldings, flooring, panelling in railway carriages and plywood. A unique use of the timber by early European settlers has been for making boxes to transport butter as the timber did not taint the butter.

Hoop Pine is still a commercial timber tree in Queensland with 45,000 ha in plantations.

Banksia aemula — **Wallum Banksia**

Aemula — from the Greek *aemulus* meaning 'competing with, emulative'. In the case of *Banksia aemula*, the tree emulates the growth habit of its close relative *Banksia serrata* (also Wallum Banksia), which grows further south.

Banksias are named after Joseph Banks, the eminent botanist who accompanied Captain Cook on his voyages to the Pacific and discovery of Australia in 1770. They were first collected by Banks during a field trip with Daniel Solander and the botanical illustrator Sydney Parkinson in bushland near the area later named Botany Bay by Captain Cook. The first Banksias to be formally named were done so by Carl Linnaeus the Younger, son of the man who developed modern botanical naming. *Banksia aemula* is a woody green shrub of the island sand dunes (see p.63). Its spectacular flower, a fine example of the genus, contains a dense profusion of tiny individual flowers all tightly arranged, in a dense spike. As is usual for banksias this plant is capable of surviving bushfires, regrowing from the underground part of the plant.

Banksia aemula (Wallum Banksia), JW

Castanospermum australe (Black Bean), GC

Eucalyptus tereticornis (Forest Red Gum), GC

Castanospermum australe — Black Bean, Moreton Bay Chestnut

Castana — from the Spanish word meaning chestnut and *spermum* meaning seed. This refers to the similarity of the large Black Bean seeds to those of the chestnut tree.

The Black Bean is a spectacular member of the Fabaceae family (the pea family) and has one of the largest flowers of the family. The flowers sprout from last years' wood, not at the tips of the branches, so they can often be hard to see at first glance.

Black Bean seeds were a food source for Aboriginal people, but were only eaten after extensive preparation because they are toxic if eaten raw. The seed pods are very light and durable and make a simple toy boat. Both the broken leaf base and the bark smell distinctly of cucumber.

The timber is sought after for detailed woodwork. Though hard and heavy, Black Bean timber polishes and dresses well, leaving an appearance akin to teak. It also has high electrical resistance and was once commonly used for switchboards.

Eucalyptus tereticornis — Forest Red Gum

Eucalyptus — from the Greek *eu* for 'well' and *calyptos* for 'covered'. The eucalyptus flower is well covered in the bud stage by a cap.

tereticornis — from two Latin words, *terere* meaning 'imperfectly cylindrical' and *cornu* meaning 'horn'. The Blue Gum has a flower bud cap that is long and bent on the end like a horn.

The cap of all eucalypts is actually a fusion of the sepals and petals found in more typical flowers. In the case of eucalypts they have become a tough cap. This was first described by Robert Brown, who travelled with Mathew Flinders in 1805. The cap protects the rest of the flowering parts until it is shed, revealing a brush of numerous showy stamens.

Honey from *Eucalyptus tereticornis* is a pale amber colour. During the late winter and early spring period, bees regularly obtain valuable pollen and nectar supplies. While never a great producer of honey, it flowers at such an important time of the year that the tree is a valuable food source for a broad range of fauna, including flying foxes, honeyeaters, gliders, possums and insects. The gums become an ecosystem all to themselves and after about 100 years of age they are literally a 'tree house' for the same fauna that feed on the tree, by providing shelter and nesting places, particularly hollow limbs.

Toona ciliata — Red Cedar

Toona — from the Indian name for a tree of this genus, Toon.

ciliata — from Latin meaning 'eye lash', having the edges fringed with hair.

Toona ciliata is a large tree of the subtropical rainforests and riparian gallery forests, reaching upwards to 70 m in height and can develop a well buttressed trunk up to 3 m wide. It was never as abundant as other species and it is said that one great tree per hectare was a good stand. *Toona ciliata* is one of the few native rainforest trees that is deciduous and this leads to distinct, fresh red leaves in early spring. This species is also renowned for its life span, some being 2000 years old. The timber was highly prized in the early period of European settlement because it is fragrant, soft and light but also durable and beautifully marked. Its use in furniture, especially ornamental woodwork, allows the rich red colour of the timber to be displayed.

Tragically, Red Cedar was an early focus of European settlers looking for income. By the mid 1840s 'cedar-cutters' were active throughout the region and into Northern New South Wales. The sparseness of the trees quickly led to its exhaustion as a resource and the species has yet to recover from this period.

Toona ciliata (Red Cedar), BC

Moreton Island, BC

Plants of the Coastal dunes

The frontal dunes that are the focus of this chapter are wind-deposited sand formations that occur between the high tide mark and a stable hind-dune. In South-east Queensland, frontal dunes are a narrow ridge parallel to the shore along most of the coast. Anyone who has visited Bribie or the Stradbroke Islands will have walked through, or along, a frontal dune to reach the beach beyond.

There are two main categories of frontal dunes. Initial or early frontal dunes develop when pioneer species trap and hold wind-borne sand. Established frontal dunes are older dunes dominated by shrubs and trees and sheltered by a more recently formed frontal dune

The form and character of both types are affected by natural events such as storm waves, fire, weather cycles, wind and animal movement and human disturbance, including 4WD vehicles, camping, public access and sand mining.

The shape of frontal dunes results from the interaction between plant colonisation and growth and the constant deposition of wind-borne sand. Many of the plants found on frontal dunes have adaptations that enable them to withstand varying levels of exposure to salt spray, sun, wind and a moving sand surface. Some of these plants are actually able to 'ride above' the mobile seaward face of frontal dunes, which are regularly eroded by wave action, and then replenished by offshore sand movement.

Shallow and deep root systems, succulent moisture-retaining stems and leaves, and an ability to cope with high temperatures and salt exposure enable these plants to compete for meagre resources in a very harsh environment. Dune plant species are dispersed primarily by wind and water. These 'dispersal mechanisms' highlight the colonising capability of dune plants and their reliance on wave action, tides, currents and the wind to transport and deposit their seeds.

Although more than 50 plant species can be found on the seaward and landward profiles of frontal dunes, the plants described in the following accounts occur mainly on seaward slopes. The most common seaward species are *Spinifex sericeus* (Beach Spinifex), *Ipomoea pes-capre* (Beach Morning Glory), *Sporobolus virginicus* (Marine Couch), *Carpobrotus glaucescens* (Coastal Pigface), *Casuarina equisetifolia* (Horse-tail She-oak) and *Banksia integrifolia* (Coastal Banksia).

Plants that grow on the landward face of the frontal dunes, such as *Canthium*

Pandanus (*Pandanus tectorius*), BC

Moreton Island

coprosmoides (Coastal Canthium), *Cupaniopsis anacardioides* (Tuckeroo) and *Alphitonia excelsa* (Red Ash) are also found in other plant communities and are described elsewhere in this book.

The very location of dune plants, especially on the seaward face, reflects their role in the stabilisation and protection of an environment adapted quite literally to shifting sands. Beach Spinifex is well equipped to intercept wind-blown sand and will root opportunistically from its nodes. Vines such as Beach Morning Glory and Pigface are also excellent dune stabilisers, often forming a cross-hatch pattern on the upper slope of the seaward profile. Horse-tail She-oak, Coastal Banksia and *Pandanus tectorius* (Pandanus) cement ridge lines and act as a screen for the less salt tolerant species behind. The reasonably high number of vines and creepers that occupy this habitat is evidence of the cyclical pattern of erosion and replenishment of frontal dunes. It is not uncommon to find the pioneering growth of Spinifex and Beach Morning Glory

Bribie Island Pine *(Callitris columellaris)*

hanging vertically over the eroded face of a frontal dune.

Frontal dunes have a protective role for adjacent coastal heath and rainforest communities by providing protection from sand movement and salt spray. Any loss of vegetation from frontal dunes will reduce the amount of sand deposited, and may exposure neighbouring plant communities to sand and saltwater intrusions. If plants are damaged or removed, less sand will be deposited. It is important to reinstate native vegetation in areas degraded by human disturbance so that the functions of frontal dunes are maintained and losses in the range of plants that grow there are prevented.

Frontal dune plant communities are under immense pressure from urban development and recreational use. Wherever possible, these fragile habitats and the associated interactions between water, wind, sand and vegetation should be retained and protected. The connection between dune vegetation and the sea must be maintained because this allows plants to move around and colonise degraded or damaged areas. It is also important to grasp, and work with, the tension between competing ecological, social and economic interests, rather than allow economic considerations to dominate the fate of our dune communities. — **Paul Donatiu**

Plant species accounts
Paul Donatiu

Information on Indigenous usage
Glenn Leiper

Wildlife information
David Barnes

Coastal She-oak (*Casuarina equisetifolia* var. *incana*), JW

HERBS, GRASSES AND GROUNDCOVERS

Carpobrotus glaucescens
Angular Pigface

Description: Prostrate creeping herb to 2 m long. Fleshy, greyish-green leaves and stems; leaves triangular in cross-section. Pinkish-purple flowers with yellow anthers; 4–6 cm wide; September–May. Succulent reddish-purple fruits; 2–3 cm long.

Habitat and Range: Common. Exposed areas on frontal dunes; mainland and coastal sand islands. Vic., NSW, Qld and Lord Howe I.

Notes: Edible salty leaves; fruit pulp tastes like salty apples. Used as emergency food by Aboriginal people who steamed leaves. Juice from fresh leaves used to relieve midge bites and blue bottle stings. *Carpobrotus* means 'edible' (*brotos*) 'fruit' (*karpos*). Important dune stabilizing species.

Wildlife: Fruit — crows and wallabies.

Family: Aizoaceae

Dianella congesta
Blue Flax Lily

Description: Perennial herb to 50 cm tall. Tufted growth. Drooping linear leaves; dark green; 45 cm long. Raceme of blue flowers; all year. Fruit a bright purple-blue berry; 2 cm wide.

Habitat and Range: Coastal dune communities near ridge lines and on hind dunes. NSW to Southern Qld.

Notes: Similar to, but with fewer flowers than other *Dianella* species (see p. 97).

Family: Phormiaceae

Oenothera drummondii subsp. *drummondii*
Beach Primrose

Description: Spreading perennial herb, prostrate but can reach 30 cm tall. Broad leaves alternate; medium to dark green; soft and hairy; oval to 7.5 cm long. Yellow flowers with 4 petals; 4 cm wide; 8 stamens and branching style; mainly September–February, also other months.

Habitat and Range: Frontal dunes on Moreton Bay sand islands. Native to Texas, USA, and South America.

Notes: Exotic, but effective dune stabiliser.

Family: Onagraceae

Scaevola calendulacea
Scented Fan Flower

Description: Succulent sprawling herb to less than 30 cm. Leaves alternate; thick, fleshy; 5 cm long. Purple-blue flowers; 10–17 cm long; flowers year-round. Green berry-like fruits turn purple then black when mature; 10–15 cm long; ripe August to November.

Habitat and Range: Can cover large areas on frontal dunes. On all major sand islands in Moreton Bay. Vic., NSW and Qld.

Notes: Important dune stabilising species that allows sand to accumulate and form mounds. Edible fruit juicy and mildly sweet-salty.

Wildlife: Fruit eaten and dispersed by birds, including Lewin's Honeyeater.

Family: Goodeniaceae

Spinifex sericeus
Beach Spinifex

Description: Robust grass, 30–40 cm tall. Sometimes forms dense mats. Leaves grey-green. Flower inflorescence yellow-brown; separate male and female flowers; September to February. Large seed heads soft, spidery, readily dispersed by wind; mid-January to February.

Habitat and Range: Moreton Bay sand islands. Australia-wide; also New Zealand and Pacific islands.

Notes: Aboriginal people used yellowish stems to make sieves and dilly bags; seed head a toy for children. *Spinifex* means 'thorn-maker' from an Asian species that has sharp leaves.

Family: Poaceae

VINES AND CLIMBERS

Canavalia rosea
Coastal Jack Bean

Description: Trailing perennial plant. Stems 2–3 m long; also forms large intertwined mats. Each 'leaf' consists of three round, dark green leaflets; 11.5 cm long by 10 cm wide. Purplish-pink flowers in racemes; December to February. Pale brown woody pods to 15 cm long; each with several brown to yellow-brown, oval seeds.

Habitat and Range: Beach and coastal dune habitats. Sydney, NSW, to Qld and NT.

Wildlife: Leaves — caterpillar of Purple Cerulean Butterfly.

Notes: Seeds are thought to remain viable after drifting long distances and have been found on remote offshore reefs.

Family: Fabaceae

Hibbertia scandens
Snake Vine, Climbing Guinea Flower

Description: Vigorous scrambling vine that climbs over other plants. Large shiny leaves alternate; tough, often hairy below; obovate; edges entire or toothed. Masses of golden-yellow flowers; 5 petals; 9 cm wide; September–February. Bright red flesh-covered seeds.

Habitat and Range: Along coastal dunes, in heath and eucalypt forest, also edges of rainforest. Bribie and North Stradbroke Is. NSW to Qld.

Notes: New leaf growth looks like it is covered in cotton wool. *Scandens* means 'climbing'.

Family: Dilleniaceae

Ipomoea pes-caprae
Beach Morning Glory

Description: Scrambling vine. Large leathery, notched leaves allegedly shaped liked 'footprint' of a goat; alternate; 3–10 cm long by 3–10.5 cm wide. Single mauve flowers with deep pink or purple throat; 3–5.5 cm long; flowers year-round. Papery fruit capsules contain large brown, bean-like seeds.

Habitat and Range: Frontal dunes on large sand islands and coastal beaches, also secondary dunes. Sydney, NSW, to Cape York, Qld, also NT and Shark Bay, WA.

Notes: Important dune stabilising species; able to cope with seasonal changes in size and shape of frontal dunes.

Family: Convolvulaceae

SHRUBS AND TREES

Acacia sophorae
Coastal Wattle

Description: Spreading shrub to 2 m. Prostrate stems. Firm, flattened phyllodes; grey-green; 5–10 cm long by 1–2 cm wide; tips blunt; indistinct gland on upper edge of stalk near leaf base. Bright yellow flowers in spikes; flowers 2–3 cm; June–November. Twisted, curved seed pods.

Habitat and Range: On dunes and in coastal areas; can form dense thickets. All eastern states and SA.

Notes: Used extensively as dune stabilising species.

Wildlife: Seeds — Variegated Fairy Wren, Red Wattlebird, Spiny-cheeked Honeyeater, Noisy Miner; sap — New Holland Honeyeater, Noisy Friarbird; leaves — caterpillar of Small-tailed Line-blue Butterfly.

Family: Mimosaceae

Banksia integrifolia subsp. *integrifolia*
Coast Banksia

Description: Tree to 25 m. Light grey roughened bark. Leaves scattered, or in irregular whorls, forming dense clusters at branch ends; deep green above, pale or white below; sometimes serrated; 4–20 cm long by 6–35 mm wide. Yellow flower spikes; 12– 20 cm long; December–February, June–August. Oblong to cylindrical seed cone brownish-black; twice as long as broad; thin woody seed capsules gape widely when split.

Habitat and Range: On sandy soils in coastal districts, also on granite soils, coastal dunes on Moreton Bay sand islands. Vic. to Bundaberg, Qld.

Notes: Aboriginal people ate nectar or blossoms soaked in water. Used in wood-turning; bushmen used flower cones as base for candles made of fat. Useful cut flower.

Family: Proteaceae

Callitris columellaris
Bribie Island Pine, Coast Cypress Pine

Description: Small tree 5–20 m. Dark green spreading canopy, cometimes conical with upright branches. Mature leaves scale-like; in whorls of 3 running along branchlet; juvenile leaves in whorls of 4; tip triangular. Male cones cylindricalm 3–5 mm long. Female cones woody, solitary; ovoid to globular; 1.2–2 cm wide; divided into 6 thin segments, outer surface smooth or wrinled, sometimes with fine point below tip; drop when mature. Numerous winged seeds.

Habitat and Range: On deep sands or sandy soils close to sea in Greater Brisbane Region. Angourie, NSW, to Mackay, Qld.

Notes: Although this species does not grow on frontal dunes, it can form thickets on revegetating sand blows and other disturbed areas close to sea. Planted as ornamental. Timber durable, resistant to termites, marine borers and decay. Similar to *Callitris rhomboidea* (Dune Cypress Pine) — shrub or small tree to 12 m; darkish green canopy; thick cone scales; raised point on bark; on sandy soils in coastal eucalypt forests.

Several other species of *Callitris* in Greater Brisbane Region; distinguished by female woody cones. *Callitris baileyi* — small, slender tree to 15 m; green canopy; rare, drier mountain ranges from Burnett district to Qld border. *Callitris endlicheri* (Black Cypress Pine) — tree to 15 m; green or sometimes bluish-green canopy; stony and rocky hills west of Brisbane. *Callitris glaucophylla* (White Cypress Pine) — small tree to 20 m; bluish-grey canopy; on sandy soils inland. *Callitris macleayna* (Brush Cypress Pine) — tree to more than 20 m; green canopy; often with stringy fibrous or scaly bark; edges of rainforest or in wet eucalypt forest; Lamington, Tamborine and D'Aguilar Range. *Callitris monticola* (Dwarf Cypress Pine) — shrub or small tree to 5 m; bluish-grey canopy; rare, exposed shallow stony soils of mountain heaths and eucalypt forest of Border Ranges.

Wildlife: Seed — Crimson Rosella; fruit — Spiny-cheeked Honeyeater.

Family: Cupressaceae

Casuarina equisetifolia var. *incana*
Coastal She-oak, Horse-tail She-oak

Description: Small tree to 10 m. Graceful drooping branches. Fine rigid, twig-like needles (branchlets); true leaves reduced to 6 to 8 teeth. Male and female flowers on same tree, male brown, female red; March–May. Fruit a short, globular cone; 15 mm wide.

Habitat and Range: On ridge tops of frontal dunes. On most Moreton Bay sand islands and along mainland at places such as Scarborough Point. Northern NSW to Gulf of Carpentaria, Qld.

Notes: Aboriginal people used bark as treatment for diarrhoea and dysentery. Branchlets eaten by cattle.

Wildlife: Flowers — Rainbow Lorikeet; seeds — Red-tailed Black-Cockatoo; useful pollen source for honey.

Family: Casuarinaceae

Hibiscus tiliaceus
Cotton Tree

Description: Spreading tree to 10 m. Dense foliage. Large soft leaves alternate; rounded; 10–15 cm. Yellow flowers with 5 lobes; deep purple or crimson throat; 8–15 cm wide; September–May. Globular hairy capsules; 2–2.5 cm long; light brown seeds.

Habitat and Range: Near beaches or along estuaries. Northern NSW to Qld and NT.

Notes: Ornamental species; also used for shade. Aboriginal people used an infusion made from inner bark and sapwood as an antiseptic on wounds, which were then covered with bark from same plant.

Wildlife: Leaves — Hibiscus Harlequin Bug.

Family: Malvaceae

Pandanus tectorius
Pandanus, Coastal Screw-Pine

Description: Small tree to 5 m. Branching prop roots often exposed by wind or wave action; thick, but weak limbs. Linear leaves to more than 1 m long; edges serrated. Insignificant green flowers. Large orange fruit 40 cm wide; breaks into wedge-shaped segments.

Habitat and Range: On coastal dunes and headlands; Bribie I. and Noosa Heads National Parks. Sydney, NSW, to Cape York, Qld.

Notes: Important dune stabilising species. Aboriginal people in Nth Qld used leaves for dillybags, sieves, baskets, mat-cloaks and armlets. Slender seeds eaten raw or cooked; white leaf bases also edible; fruit should not be eaten. Logs roped together to make rafts.

Wildlife: Fruit dispersed by rats, crabs, fruit bats and water.

Family: Pandanaceae

Bribie Island, BC

Plants of the Wetlands

A wetland is essentially an area of land that is either permanently or temporarily inundated by water and it is typically low-lying and swampy. There are two major types of wetlands:

- **Tidal** — those coastal areas which are inundated by seawater at least occasionally; and
- **Freshwater** — areas that are fed by rainfall run-off and river systems.

This chapter focuses on plants that grow in the saltmarsh and mangrove areas of tidal wetlands and those of freshwater lakes, lagoons and swamps but, as always, there is some overlap.

Wetlands and the plant species that they support are a critical part of the total ecosystem. They are known to act as biological filters for pollution and can reduce contamination of the ocean through the breakdown of pollutants such as sewage, nutrients and chemicals. They also trap sediment run-off and help prevent siltation of rivers and estuaries.

Red Mangrove (*Rhizophora stylosa*), GC

TIDAL WETLANDS

Saltmarshes and Mangroves

The wetlands of Moreton Bay include mudflats (which are not covered in this book), mangrove communities and saltmarshes. Mudflats are bare expanses of mud and pools surrounding the coastline. They are covered by the high tide and exposed at low tide.

Mangroves are trees, which are able to flourish in saline conditions and are partially submerged at high tide. Along enclosed or protected shorelines, such as Moreton Bay and Pumicestone Passage, mangroves may form dense stands up to the high water mark. They also form large, continuous stands or fringing forests along tidal creeks and rivers in South-east Queensland.

In the past, mangroves and mudflats were perceived as breeding grounds for mosquitoes and were targeted for land reclamation. Today, their importance as nurseries for fish, crustaceans and other marine life is widely recognised. Mangroves are now protected by law and clearing is illegal.

One of the most common characteristics of mangrove communities are the aerial roots of the trees. These roots are specialised adaptations that not only stabilise and support the plants in the saturated silt in which they grow, but also help them to obtain oxygen.

Aerial roots that arc downwards from the trunk are called stilt or prop roots. These are most obvious in *Rhizophora stylosa*, (Red Mangrove). Pencil-like roots which stick up out of the mud are called pneumatophores and are characteristic of *Avicennia marina* subsp. *australasica*, the Grey Mangrove, the most abundant species in the Greater Brisbane Region.

Many terrestrial animals also utilise mangroves. Stands of *Avicennia marina* subsp. *australasica* (Grey Mangrove) in the Greater Brisbane Region support several large roosts of flying foxes. At flowering time, honeyeaters are frequent mangrove visitors.

Saltmarshes are usually found just inland from mangroves and they vary in extent, with some areas being inundated at each high tide and others remaining above water except for very high tides. The plants that grow in saltmarshes are extremely salt-resistant and are typically low stunted shrubs. They include, *Sarcocornia quinqueflora* (Samphire), *Suaeda australis* (Seablite) and *Enchylaena tormentosa* (Berry Salt Bush). Among these shrubs grow grasses and sedges such as, *Sporobolus virginicus* (Saltwater Couch) and the rush *Juncus kraussii*.

FRESHWATER WETLANDS

Lakes, Lagoons and Swamps

The Greater Brisbane Region has lost many of its original lake, lagoon and swamp systems due to land clearance and filling, but those that survive support unique vegetation communities.

The best examples of freshwater lakes in the region are to be found on Stradbroke and Moreton Islands, where 'perched' lakes have formed in the depressions among the higher sand dunes. Perched lakes lay well above the watertable and water has difficulty draining away because of an almost impervious layer of accumulated decaying organic matter. (Traditional lakes are also formed in depressions but, in this case, the watertable is very close to the surface). Blakesley and Black Snake Lagoons on North Stradbroke Island are examples of perched lakes.

Lagoon systems (which include billabongs) form along watercourses through dry

Swamp Banksia (*Banksia robur*), BC

eucalypt forest. They fill after rain and only occasionally dry out. Among those that survive are the Illaweena Lagoons at Karawatha Forest and the lagoons of Upper Buhot Creek.

The edges of lakes and lagoons often have dense covers of ferns, rushes and sedges, interspersed with paperbark trees. Eucalypt forest may also grow to the water's edge. Like swamps, they may also support several species of aquatic plants.

Freshwater swamps are inundated for much of the year. Some swamps in the Greater Brisbane Region have a base of peat formed over thousands of years by decaying vegetation and animal matter. This makes the water brackish and reduces the oxygen content of the water.

Rushes, sedges and grasses, again dominate the vegetation, particularly at the edges. *Baumea rubiginosa* (Twigrush), and sedges such as *Lepironia articulata* (Grey Sedge) are common throughout the region. Eucalypts, paperbark trees and ferns may border swamps and, in some cases, form the dominant vegetation community.

Eighteen Mile Swamp and Flinders Swamp on Stradbroke Island and Bulwer Swamp on Moreton Island are some of the largest freshwater swamps in the region and there are also small swamps on Bribie Island and a few on the mainland.

Along the eastern fringes of the Greater Brisbane Region, much of the land is flat and composed of alluvial sediment. After heavy rain, this soil becomes saturated and swamps form. These areas are known as 'paperbark swamps' and take their name from *Melaleuca quinquenervia*, the Paperbark Tea-trees that thrive there.

Although these areas may be only inundated for relatively short periods on a seasonal basis, there is usually a high water table, which keeps the subsoil waterlogged. Depending on the degree of soil saturation, few other plant species may grow in paperbark communities. *Melaleuca quinquenervia* can grow as a tall or short tree depending on the soil conditions.

Bribie Island, BC

Swamp Box (*Lophostemon suaveolens*), JW

Two eucalypts sometimes found growing among the paperbarks are *Eucalyptus robusta* (Swamp Mahogany) in the wetter areas and, in drier soils, *Eucalyptus tereticornis* (Forest Red Gum) occurs with the related species *Lophostemon suaveolens* (Swamp Box).

'Wet heaths' are a special type of wetland similar to the paperbark swamps, but occurring on low nutrient soils of the coastal sand plains or black peat, rather than fertile alluvium. Wet heaths have high species diversity and are characterised by dense sedges and low shrubs such as *Banksia robur* (Swamp Banksia) and *Xanthorrhoea fulva* (Swamp Grass Tree). Taller trees do not occur in these wetlands. These wet heaths form part of the larger wallum heath communities that are covered in the next chapter.

Paperbark forests and woodlands were important to Aboriginal people yielding supplies of Bungwall Fern, of which the starchy underground stems were a staple food. Bark stripped from the tea-trees provided roofing for shelters. Early European settlers cleared the paperbarks for pasture and agriculture. More recently, the dwindling paperbark stands have come under threat of development for housing.

Although scattered paperbarks often grow along the edges of waterways, only small areas of forest and woodland now remain at the Deagon Wetlands, Serpentine and Native Dog Creeks (which overlap the boundaries of Logan City and Redland Shire) and at Boondall and Tinchi Tamba Wetlands north of Brisbane.

Melaleuca quinquenervia is not the only paperbark to form a distinctive habitat. Around Boonah, south-west of Ipswich, there are very small stands of *Melaleuca irbyana* (Swamp Tea-tree) forest. — **Kathy Stephens (with Stephen Poole).**

Plant species accounts
Kathy Stephens and Paul Donatiu

Information on Indigenous usage
Glenn Leiper

Wildlife Information
David Barnes

Tidal Wetlands —
saltmarshes and mangroves

Nudgee Beach, BC

HERBS, GRASSES AND GROUNDCOVERS

Crinum pedunculatum
Swamp Lily, Spider Lily

Description: Perennial herb with thick green, strap-like leaves up to 2 m long. Leaves channelled above; to 20 cm wide. Large white, lily-like flowers in clusters; December–January. Large, shiny green bulbous fruits, brown when mature; several grey-green, wedge-shaped or rounded seeds about 3 cm wide.

Habitat and Range: Along riverbanks, near beaches and in wetlands. East coast of Qld.

Notes: Flowers aromatic. Seeds dispersed by water. Aboriginal people may have used sap or crushed leaves to treat marine stings.

Family: Amaryllidaceae

Einadia hastata
Berry Saltbush

Description: Small ascending herb to 75 cm tall. Leaves opposite; soft and thin, dark green; blunt tip and lobes; to 40 mm long and 25 mm wide; turn red before falling. Tiny green flowers unisexual; December–February. Small bright red fruits throughout year.

Habitat and Range: In saltmarsh adjacent to paperbark wetlands. Occurs locally at Tinchi Tamba and Boondall Wetlands.

Notes: *Hastata* means 'triangular with spreading lobes at base' and refers to shape of leaves.

Wildlife: Leaves — caterpillars of Saltbush Blue Butterfly

Family: Chenopodiaceae

Einadia nutans
Native Seaberry

Description: Weak prostrate herb to 1 m. Small leaves opposite; pointed and shaped like arrow heads. Tiny green flowers; December–February.

Habitat and Range: In saltmarsh, occurs locally at Boondall Wetlands. Australia-wide; also New Zealand.

Notes: *Nutans* means 'nodding' and refers to fruiting spikes.

Wildlife: Flowers — Eastern Spinebill; leaves — caterpillars of Saltbush Blue Butterfly.

Family: Chenopodiaceae

Halosarcia indica
Samphire

Description: Perennial herb with shrub-like habit; arching and spreading branches. Cylindrical cream flower spikes. Triangular fruits; smooth whitish seeds.

Habitat and Range: In saltmarsh adjacent to she-oak and paperbark wetlands, occurs locally at Boondall Wetlands with *Sporobolus virginicus*, see p. 40.

Notes: *Halosarcia* means 'salt-skinned'. Similar to *Sarcocornia quinqueflora*, see p. 39.

Wildlife: Leaves — caterpillars of Samphire Blue Butterfly.

Family: Chenopodiaceae

Isolepis inundata
Swamp Club Rush

Description: Perennial herb with tufted, slender, upright stems to 30 cm tall. Leaves reduced to sheathing bracts. Inflorescence consists of 3–12 angular spikelets, each about 4 mm long. Pale yellow, smooth and ovoid nuts.

Habitat and Range: In wetlands and along creek banks near high tide mark, occurs locally at Tinchi Tamba Wetlands.

Family: Cyperaceae

Juncus kraussii
Sea Rush

Description: Clumping erect rush to 1.2 m tall. Leaves reduced to dark sheaths at stem base; leaf blades absent. Pale brown panicles, with scattered flowers, on stiff stems. Fruit a small capsule.

Habitat and Range: In wetlands, along edges of saltmarsh, occurs locally at Boondall Wetlands.

Notes: Stems contain a continuous white pith.

Family: Juncaceae

Portulaca oleracea
Pigweed, Purslane

Description: Prostrate herb. Succulent green leaves alternate; oblong or obovate, 2 cm long and 1 cm wide. Small yellow solitary flowers, but not always open; December–February. Ovoid fruits with glossy small black seeds.

Habitat and Range: In disturbed areas; can be a common garden weed.

Notes: Oily seeds highly nutritious with flavour like linseed. Aboriginal people ground seeds to a paste and cooked them; roots and stems also eaten raw or cooked. Thought to be poisonous to stock.

Wildlife: Leaves — caterpillars of Meadow Argus Butterfly.

Family: Portulacaceae

Sarcocornia quinqueflora
Beadweed, Samphire

Description: Small erect herb to 40 cm. Leaves reduced to membranous edges on succulent jointed stems to 30 cm. Tiny circlets of flowers; December–February.

Habitat and Range: In saltmarsh; can form carpet-like groundcover, occurs locally at Boondall and Tinchi Tamba wetlands. Can form large colonies.

Notes: Often grows with *Halosarcia indica*, see p. 37. *Sarcocornia* means 'flesh horn' and refers to upright nature of branches; *quinqueflora* means '5-flowered' however this species is usually 7-flowered, Fruiting spike dispersed by tide. Stems edible raw, good for pickling.

Wildlife: Leaves — caterpillars of Samphire Blue Butterfly

Family: Chenopodiaceae

Sesuvium portulacastrum
Sea Purslane

Description: Herb with sprawling reddish-green stems. Fleshy leaves opposite; glossy green; linear, to 7 cm long. Pink flowers with five lobes; September–February.

Habitat and Range: In wetlands and along coastal dunes, occurs locally on most Moreton Bay sand islands and at Boondall Wetlands.

Notes: Leaves and stems edible, raw or cooked; used by Captain James Cook and his crew while at Endeavour River, North Qld, as a much-needed vegetable to prevent scurvy; however, after 1–2 minutes a throat irritation develops.

Family: Aizoaceae

Sporobolus virginicus
Saltwater Couch

Description: Coarse perennial grass to 40 cm tall. Forms dense carpets. Short narrow leaves greyish-green, inrolled. Flowering panicle narrow and composed of many small spikelets. Very tiny black seeds.

Habitat and Range: Common near high water mark in saltmarshes and on sand dunes.

Family: Poaceae

Suaeda australis
Seablite

Description: Low dense, spreading herb to 75 cm tall. Erect slender leaves alternate; hairless, fleshy, often reddish; to 55 mm long and 2.5 mm wide. Green flowers in tiny clusters September–December. Globular fruits to 2 mm wide; black seeds.

Habitat and Range: In saltmarsh, wetlands and mangrove flats.

Notes: Similar to *Suaeda arbusculoides* — shorter, wider leaves to 25 mm long and 4 mm wide; fewer flowers. Both young leaves and stem tips edible, either raw or steamed; if boiled, leaves taste like salty beans. Young shoots can be used as a pickle.

Wildlife: Leaves — caterpillars of Samphire Blue Butterfly.

Family: Chenopodiaceae

Tetragonia tetragonioides
New Zealand Spinach

Description: Sprawling succulent herb. Crisp stems to 10 mm wide. Succulent robust leaves light green; triangular or arrow-shaped to 12 cm long; raised veins below; leaf stems to 25 mm long. Plant covered with tiny watery protuberances. Small solitary, pale yellow flowers with 4 lobes; September–February, but also as early as June. Fruit top-shaped; red-crimson when ripe.

Habitat and Range: In saltmarshes and on edges of mangrove forest, occurs locally at Boondall and Tinchi Tamba Wetlands, and Bribie I.

Notes: Edible leaves, although bitter and unsafe unless cooked; served by Captain Cook to his crew. Thought by botanist Sir Joseph Banks to be almost as good as real spinach.

Wildlife: Eaten by native rats.

Family: Aizoaceae

FERNS

Acrostichum speciosum
Mangrove Fern

Description: Large robust fern with clumping habit. Erect fronds to 2 m long; underside of fertile fronds covered in rust-coloured sporangia; raised mid-vein below.

Habitat and Range: In mangrove forests, tidal creeks and swamps. East coast of Qld.

Notes: Aboriginal people roasted stems. In South Pacific, fronds have been woven into thatching material.

Wildlife: Provides valuable habitat for ground dwelling mammals that forage in mangrove swamps.

Family: Pteridaceae

SHRUBS AND TREES

Aegiceras corniculatum
River Mangrove

Description: Shrub or small tree to 4 m. Smooth grey bark and no obvious above-ground roots. Leaves alternate; glossy green; oval, about 7 cm long; contain glands for secreting salt. Small white flowers with 5 petals; 5 creamy stamens; June–September. Fruit pencil-thick, somewhat curved and pointed; red when mature; 5 cm long; ripe December–March.

Habitat and Range: On riverbanks and coasts; sometimes forms thickets. East coast of Qld.

Notes: Flowers smell like old bananas.
Wildlife: Flowers — Mangrove and Brown Dusky Honeyeaters; leaves — caterpillar of White-banded Line-Blue Butterfly.

Family: Myrsinaceae

Avicennia marina subsp. *australasica*
Grey Mangrove

Description: Small tree to 15 m. Characteristic grey trunk and peg or snorkel pneumatophores. Leathery leaves opposite; shiny above, grey below; 9–12 cm long. Gold or creamy-brown flowers in dense clusters; February–June. Flattened capsule fruits to 3 cm; seeds germinate on host plant and fall in December.

Habitat and Range: Locally common in Moreton Bay. Tolerates wide range of soils, muds, salinity levels and exposure; will colonize shallow tidal waters and grow almost as a monoculture. Tas. to Qld.

Notes: Flowers aromatic. Aboriginal people used wood for shields; bitter fruits eaten after soaking and baking; inner bark rubbed on stingray and stonefish stings.

Family: Avicenniaceae

Bruguiera gymnorhiza
Orange Mangrove

Description: Medium-sized tree to 10 m. Buttressed trunk; distinctive 'knee roots'; dark, mottled rough bark. Large leaves 15–20 cm long clumped at the branch ends. Red flowers January–March; flower or calyx remains attached to buoyant fruit after it falls. Green, cigar-shaped fruits 10–20 cm long; ripe April–July.

Habitat and Range: On riverbanks and coasts; predominantly in landward areas on better draining soils with higher levels of organic matter and some freshwater input. East coast of Qld.

Notes: Flowers heavily scented. Aboriginal people ate fruits after washing, pounding and baking.

Wildlife: Flowers — Little Friarbird and Brown Honeyeater; leaves — caterpillar of Copper Jewel Butterfly.

Family: Rhizophoraceae

Ceriops tagal
Yellow Mangrove

Description: Small shrub or tree to 5 m. Base buttressed, marked by lenticels; height determined by salinity levels. Smooth to fissured grey bark on trunk; often rough on base 'knee' roots. Leaves opposite; shiny yellowish-green; to 8 cm long; often pointed upwards. Small white to cream flowers in clusters; December–February. Seedlings to 20 cm long produced on parent plant and have club-shaped root.

Habitat and Range: On well drained soils and muds inundated by highest tides. Local distribution patchy; some extensive stands in Moreton Bay, such as at mouth of Brisbane River.

Notes: High tannin content in leaves and bark. Strong durable timber.

Family: Rhizophoraceae

Excoecaria agallocha
Milky Mangrove, Blind-your-eye

Description: Tree to 6 m. Trunk with rough grey bark; no above ground roots. Leaves alternate; elliptical or ovate, 6–10 cm long by 2–5 cm wide; tip pointed; edges sometimes lightly serrated; older orange-red leaves often found on tree; two distinct glands at base of leaf blades. Cream flowers; November–February. Fruit a capsule with 3 valves; January–March.

Habitat and Range: Often around high tide mark in sandy soils. Not as salt tolerant as other mangrove species.

Notes: Leaves release caustic or irritant white sap if broken. Aboriginal people used milky latex to treat ulcers; in North Qld latex used as a spear poison. In severe drought, leaf loss can be complete.

Wildlife: Thought to be poisonous to animals.

Family: Euphorbiaceae

Enchylaena tomentosa
Ruby Saltbush

Description: Spreading shrub to 1.2 m. Small leaves linear; to 20 mm long and 2 mm wide; on twiggy stems. Tiny solitary flowers, September–December. Succulent flattish, red berry-like fruit, 5–8 mm wide.

Habitat and Range: In saltmarsh adjacent to paperbark wetlands, occurs locally at Boondall Wetlands.

Notes: Sweet fruits were eaten by Aboriginal people. Can be used as green vegetable.

Family: Chenopodiaceae

Lumnitzera racemosa
Black Mangrove

Description: Small tree to 7 m. Spreading habitat with contorted stems and scaly, almost black bark. Leaves arranged in spirals; obovate to 9 cm long and 3 cm wide; distinct notch at tip. White tubular flowers in short spikes; December–May. Short flattened fruits.

Habitat and Range: Uncommon. At high water mark in littoral zone, occurs locally on western side of some Moreton Bay islands and Pumicestone Passage.

Wildlife: Flowers — Brown Honeyeater; leaves — caterpillars of Copper Jewel Butterfly.

Family: Combretaceae

Myoporum acuminatum
Coastal Boobialla, Water Bush

Description: Bushy shrub or small tree to 6 m. Bark pale, corky and fissured. Thick fleshy leaves alternate; light green; to 10 cm long; drawn out to pointed tip. White tubular flowers, some with purple spots in throat; to 15 mm wide; June–October. Purplish fruits contain one hard seed.

Habitat and Range: Behind mangroves in *Casuarina glauca* (Swamp She-oak) wetlands (see p. 58), and coastal scrubs. Occurs locally at Tinchi Tamba Wetlands.

Notes: *Myoporum* means 'closed-pore' and refers to closed appearance of leaf glands. *Acuminatum* means 'drawn out to a point'. Aboriginal people ate small ripe fruit, which are salty-sweet.

Wildlife: Fruit eaten by many species of birds.

Family: Myoporaceae

Rhizophora stylosa
Red Mangrove, Spotted Mangrove

Description: Shrub or small tree to 6 m. Arching stilt and aerial prop roots. Leaves opposite, clustered at end of branches; conspicuous brown spots on underside of leaves; ovate to obovate, to 10 cm long. White flowers to 20 mm wide; flowers year-round. Pear-shaped fruits.

Habitat and Range: At lower tidal level on well-drained, unconsolidated muds that are regularly inundated, often grows wirth *Avicennia marina* subsp. *australasica* (Grey Mangrove) see p. 43.

Notes: Common name taken from reddish trunk. This species is able to lessen impact of boat wash in tidal areas.

Family: Rhizophoraceae

Section Author: **Paul Donatiu**

Freshwater Wetlands —
lakes, lagoons and swamps

Poona Lake, BC

AQUATIC PLANTS

Nymphoides indica
Water Snowflake

Description: Perennial aquatic plant. Smooth green floating leaves; often purplish below; ovate to round, to 20 cm wide. White flowers 2 cm wide; on slender stems 6–10 cm long; petals with delicate fringed edges; in clusters just below point where leaf blade meets stem; October–May. Fruit a capsule with numerous small seeds.

Habitat and Range: Common and widespread. Edges of still water, usually to 20 cm deep, often in drying edges of lagoons or creeks. Sunshine Coast, Petrie, Sandgate, Pine River, Brisbane Valley, Stradbroke I., Beenleigh–Beaudesert, Gold Coast. Northern areas of WA, NT, Qld and Northern NSW.

Wildlife: Plumed and Wandering Whistling Ducks

Family: Menyanthaceae

HERBS, GRASSES AND GROUNDCOVERS

Baloskion pallens

Description: Wiry bright green erect stems to 60 cm. Rusty-brown sheaths at regular intervals along stems give striped appearance. Inflorescence consists of several short brown, cylindrical flower heads at top of stem; flowers year-round.

Habitat and Range: In moist areas in sandy soils and dark sandy peat. In small patches, Sunshine Coast, Beerwah, Moreton Bay sand islands, Geebung, Sunnybank, Stretton and Gold Coast. Coastal Qld south of Port Curtis, including Fraser I. and NSW.

Notes: Previously known as *Restio pallens*.

Family: Restionaceae

Baloskion tetraphyllum

Description: Stems erect, bright green and shiny, reflecting light, 80–100 cm tall. Many curved branching segments towards top; weight often causes stems to droop. Male and female inflorescences different, borne on separate plants. Male flowers narrow, elongated brown spikes to 0.3 cm long; female flowers compact brown miniature cones to 0.5 cm long with spreading overlapping bracts; December to May.

Habitat and Range: Sandy soils on lower slopes as understorey of eucalypt habitats. Sunshine Coast and hinterland (Mapleton), Glasshouse Mountains, Bribie, Moreton and Stradbroke Is, Gold Coast. Coastal Qld south of Cape York to northern NSW.

Notes: Previously known as *Restio tetraphyllus*. Similar to *Caustis blakei* subsp. *blakei*, see p. 94.

Family: Restionaceae

Baumea rubiginosa
Soft Twigrush

Description: Clumping erect smooth green stems to 1 m tall. Stems slightly flattened on one side; tips sharply pointed, but soft to touch. Leaves with reddish-brown sheath at base of plant. Inflorescence several short, fluffy brown to reddish-brown, rounded flower heads on tips of stems 5–8 cm long; supporting sheath below each flower head; flowers year-round.

Habitat and Range: Wet heathland and swampy areas; Sunshine Coast, Glasshouse Mountains, Bribie, Moreton and Stradbroke Is, Petrie-Lawnton, Sunnybank, Tingalpa, Logan, Pimpama and Daves Ck. Qld, WA, NT, NSW and SA.

Family: Cyperaceae

Bolboschoenus caldwellii

Description: Erect grass-like herb to 1 m. Inflorescence a cluster of brown cylindrical spikes, radiating from central point on top of stems; mainly March–September.

Habitat and Range: Waterlogged, closed sedgelands in depressions of river floodplains. Bribie I., Redcliffe, Tinchi Tamba Wetlands, Pinkenba. Inland and coastal Qld south of Cloncurry, also NSW, Vic., Tas., SA and WA.

Notes: Similar to *Bolboschoenus fluviatilis* — to 1–2 m tall; flowers September–February; edges of still water and water-logged depressions; coastal Qld south of Townsville, also NSW and Vic.

Family: Cyperaceae

Cladium procerum
Leafy Twigrush

Description: Tall, robust, cane-like sedge to 2 m. Leaves tufted, as long as stems; edges and lower midribs serrated, can cut skin. Infloresences large with several slender stalks arising from same point at top of stem. Each stalk with cluster of 5–7 light brown spikelets. Stalks may divide further so that all spikelets are at same level, giving a flattened outline to whole structure.

Habitat and Range: In swamps on peat or sand substrate. Coolum Ck, Buderim, Bribie, Moreton, Peel and Stradbroke Is, Oxley Ck, Serpentine Ck, Redland Bay.

Wildlife: Leaves — Caterpillar of Southern Sedge-darter Butterfly.

Family: Cyperaceae

Drosera binata
Forked Sundew

Description: Reddish plant to 20 cm tall. Forked green leaves 15–20 cm long; covered in sticky red, glandular hairs. White flowers to 2 cm wide; in clusters at top of slender red stem; December–February.

Habitat and Range: Uncommon. Wet heathlands on peaty sand and wet acidic sandy soils. Sunshine Coast, Glasshouse Mountains, Bribie, Moreton and Stradbroke Is, Sunnybank. Coastal Qld south of Rockhampton, also NSW, Vic. and Tas.

Notes: Insectivorous plant; sticky hairs trap insects, which die and add nutrients to poor soils.

Family: Droseraceae

Drosera peltata
Tall Sundew

Description: Delicate herb to 25 cm. Slender stems. Dainty round leaves, yellowish; fringed edges and sticky red glandular hairs; regularly spaced along stem. Flowers white, to 0.8 cm wide; most of year.

Habitat and Range: On peaty sand and wet acidic, sandy soils in wet heathlands; also in mountain heaths on rhyolite and sandstone soils. Sunshine Coast, Moreton and Bribie Is, Glasshouse Mountains, Stradbroke I., Esk, Crows Nest, Petrie, Enoggera, Dinmore, Springwood, Capalaba, Logan, Plunkett, Jacobs Well, Mt Edwards, Mt Maroon, Lamington National Park and McPherson Range. Coastal Qld south of Cape York, also NSW, Vic., Tas. and SA.

Notes: Insectivorous plant; sticky hairs trap insects, which die and add nutrients to poor soils.

Family: Droseraceae

Drosera spatulata
Spoon-leaf Sundew

Description: Small red rosette of overlapping, spoon-shaped, red leaves 1–3 cm long; covered with sticky red hairs. Slender leafless stem growing from centre of rosette; 15 cm tall; several pink flowers to 0.8 cm wide at top; flowers March–November, also other months.

Habitat and Range: Common. Wet heathlands on peaty sand and wet acidic, sandy soils. Sunshine Coast, Glasshouse Mountains, Bribie, Moreton and Stradbroke Is, Caboolture, Redcliffe, Kedron, Capalaba, Sunnybank, Daisy Hill State Forest and Binna Burra. Coastal Qld south of Cape York to Northern NSW.

Notes: Insectivorous plant; sticky hairs trap insects, which die and add nutrients to poor soils.

Family: Droseraceae

Lepironia articulata
Grey Sedge

Description: Perennial clumping sedge to 2 m. Forms dense thickets. Stiff, erect stems blue-grey; sharp tips; thickened bands (bumps) at regular intervals support hollow stem. Leaves not obvious. Inflorescence a reddish-brown cylindrical flower head that points sideways, about 5 cm below stem tip; flowers year-round. Fruit a smooth brown nut with spine at tip.

Habitat and Range: Common and widespread. Edges of deep pools with water to 2 m deep; coastal lowland swamps and banks of lakes and lagoons. Moreton Bay islands, Qld, NSW and NT.

Notes: Aboriginal people in North Qld baked and ate woody underground stems.

Wildlife: Seed — Grey Teal.

Family: Cyperaceae

Ludwigia octovalvis
Willow Primrose

Description: Robust, perennial herb to 1.5 m. Erect; branched from base; stems often reddish. Plants densely hairy to smooth. Leaves alternate; narrowly linear to almost ovate, 1–15 cm long; fine tapering tip; rounded base; leaf stalk varies from very short to 2 cm long. Showy, bright yellow flowers; solitary, to 4 cm wide; 4 petals that fall readily when picked; September–May.

Habitat and Range: Edges of lagoons and watercourses, also in dry creek beds; Sunshine Coast, Brisbane waterways, Moreton Bay islands and Gold Coast. Northern areas of WA, NT, Qld and Northern NSW.

Notes: Can become a weed in some areas

Family: Onagraceae

Olearia hygrophila
Swamp Daisy

Description: Straggling, sprawling plant with herbaceous, woody stems to 2 m long. Inconspicuous when not flowering. Leaves alternate; dark green; 7 cm long and 0.5 cm wide; tapered at both ends; edges sometimes with teeth. White flowers; 4–5 cm wide; September–November.

Habitat and Range: Wet gutter drainage lines of peaty swamps on North Stradbroke Island. Understorey plant in wet *Melaleuca* swamps. Known only from this location.

Notes: Endangered; cannot be collected from wild.

Family: Asteraceae

Persicaria decipiens
Slender Knotweed

Description: Herbaceous sprawling shrub to 60 cm. Leaves green, often with dark patch in centre, hairless; 15 cm long by 2 cm wide; tapered at both ends; short stalk. Flowers form narrow pink spikes, 10 cm long by 0.5 cm wide at top of plant; December–February.

Habitat and Range: Common and widespread. Edges of creeks and waterways, often appears weedy in dried-up inundation areas. Eumundi, Sunshine Coast, Nambour, Bribie, Morayfield, Moreton and Stradbroke Is, Sandgate, Wellington Point, Wynnum, Oxley Ck, Colleges Crossing, Gold Ck, Laidley, Gatton, Ipswich, Enoggera, Zillmere, Cleveland, Mt Cotton, Springfield, Daisy Hill State Forest, Beenleigh, Mt Tamborine, Nerang, Rathdowney, Christmas Ck. Coastal Qld, also NSW, Vic., Tas. and SA.

Family: Polygonaceae

Schoenoplectus validus
River Clubrush

Description: Sedge to 1–2 m tall. Stout triangular green stems; inflorescence brown, somewhat drooping; flowers September–May.

Habitat and Range: Common and widespread. Edges of freshwater swamps and dams and along creek lines, also in swales behind coastal dunes. Sunshine Coast, Nambour, Bribie, Moreton and Stradbroke Is, North Pine, Wivenhoe, Long Pocket, Moggill Ck, Woolston, Oxley Ck, Coomera, Palm Beach, Canungra. Qld, NSW, Vic. and SA.

Notes: Aboriginal people in North Qld ate underground stems after roasting and pounding.

Wildlife: Habitat for waterfowl

Family: Cyperaceae

Viola hederacea
Ivy-leaved Violet, Native Violet

Description: Fast growing perennial herb to 15 cm. Often forms dense mat. Leaves light green, paler below; kidney-shaped, toothed, to 30 mm long. White 5-lobed flowers streaked with violet towards centre; mainly July–September, but also at other times.

Habitat and Range: On moist to wet soils, heath and wetlands, also coastal wet eucalypt forests and river banks. All states (except WA); also Malaya.

Notes: Flowers reportedly strongly fragrant on warm days. Similar to *Viola betonicifolia* subsp. *betonicifolia*, see p.109. Aboriginal people ate flowers.

Family: Violaceae

Xyris complanata
Hatpins, Feathered Yellow-eye

Description: Erect, grass-like perennial herb. Tufted growth. Flat leaves with rough edges. Flowering stems to 70 cm; leafless or almost leafless, with rough ribs along edges. Yellow 3-lobed flowers arise from common head 10–25 mm long; December–February. Small knob-like fruit.

Habitat and Range: In sandy moist heath and wetlands along coast. Sydney, NSW, to NT and WA; also tropical Asia.

Notes: *Xyris* means 'cutting knife' or 'shears' and refers to the sword-shaped leaves; *complanata* means 'flattened'. Similar to *Xyris juncea* — cylindrical leaves.

Family: Xyridaceae

FERNS

Blechnum indicum
Bungwall Fern, Swamp Water Fern

Description: Tufted fern to 0.5–1 m tall. Stiff shiny, erect fronds; leaflets with serrated edges. New fronds pink to bronze

Habitat and Range: Common in *Melaleuca* swamps and waterlogged peaty soils. Sunshine Coast, Nambour, Glasshouse Mountains, Bribie, Moreton and Stradbroke Is, Nudgee, Keperra, Mt Cotton, Greenbank, Jacobs Well. Coastal Qld south of Cape York to NSW border, also NSW Central Coast and islands off NT.

Notes: Plants sometimes form hummocky mounds as soil builds up around base. Resistant to fire. Rhizome staple plant food of Moreton Bay Aboriginal people; roasted and eaten as 'biscuit' with fish, crabs and oysters.

Family: Blechnaceae

ORCHIDS

Phaius australis
Swamp Orchid

Description: Ground orchid 50–80 cm tall. Thin broad leaves light green; grow from underground bulb. Showy flower spike 1–1.5 m tall; large white flowers with maroon streaks in throat; petals darken to wine-coloured with age; September to December.

Habitat and Range: Edges of swamps on Moreton Bay islands; also known from isolated locations on mainland including Wide Bay District, Qld.

Notes: Endangered; cannot be collected from the wild.

Family: Orchidaceae

VINES AND CLIMBERS

Parsonsia straminea
Monkey Rope

Description: Stout, twining vine. Older, thicker stems can form hanging twisted 'ropes' to 2 cm or more wide, hanging from canopy; clear sap. Spade-shaped leaves; underside of young leaves purplish. Clusters of cream or pinkish, tubular flowers; 3 mm long; September–May. Long cylindrical, woody pods release numerous seeds with silky hairs.

Habitat and Range: Widespread and common. Variety of moist habitats. Sunshine Coast to Gold Coast and inland, also Moreton Bay islands. Coastal Qld south of Cape York, also NSW. Often grows on trunk of *Melaleuca quinquenervia*, see p. 59.

Notes: Flowers perfumed.

Family: Apocynaceae

SHRUBS AND TREES

Banksia robur
Swamp Banksia, Broad-leaved Banksia

Description: Low spreading shrub 1–1.5 m, but can reach 3 m. Large velvety leaves stiff; dark green above, white below, covered in rusty hairs; 20-30 cm long; edges serrated with irregular teeth. Flower spikes broad 10–20 cm long; rich aquamarine when young, fading to greenish-yellow and eventually brown; December–May. Cones with large, woody seed cases; 2 small winged seeds.

Habitat and Range: Swamps and wet heaths on coastal sands and peat soils, sometimes in dense stands, also in closed sedgelands. Sunshine Coast, Stradbroke I., Beerwah, Karawatha Forest, Gold Coast. Sydney, NSW, to Qld.

Notes: *Robur* means 'strong' and refers to tough leaves.

Family: Proteaceae

Casuarina glauca
Swamp She-oak

Description: Small green tree to 6–16 m. Stiff twig-like 'needles' (branchlets) in segments; true leaves reduced to rows of small teeth at segment joints. Male and female flowers on separate trees; July–November. Male flowers — masses of small brown anthers at tips of branches. Female flowers — tufts of red styles on short stem, develop into short brown, bumpy cones; each cone contains shiny black seed with transparent wing.

Habitat and Range: Saline soils, in the zone where saline and freshwater meet, usually in low lying areas. Sometimes grows with mangroves and marine couch. Bribie and Stradbroke Is, Petrie, Serpentine Ck, Enoggera, Ipswich, Sunnybank, Wellington Point, Redland Bay, Beenleigh, Jacobs Well, Southport, Nerang, Tallebudgera, Currumbin. Coastal Qld south of Townsville, also NSW and WA.

Notes: Able to colonise or stabilise saline areas and estuary banks. Timber valued. Grown as ornamental garden plant.

Wildlife: Flowers — Rainbow and Scaly-breasted Lorikeets; seeds — Pale-headed Rosellas; cones — Black Cockatoos.

Family: Casuarinaceae

Eucalyptus robusta
Swamp Mahogany
See p. 165

Lophostemon suaveolens
Swamp Box
See p. 180

Eucalyptus tereticornis
Forest Red Gum
See p. 168

Melaleuca linariifolia
Snow-in-Summer
See p. 183

Melaleuca quinquenervia
Paperbark Tea-tree, Broad-leaved Paperbark

Description: Small tree 12–14 m, but can reach 18 m. White papery bark. Stiff leaves bluish; small point at tip; usually 5 main longitudinal veins. Profusion of cream bottlebrush flowers; September–May.

Habitat and Range: Common and widespread. Swamps and low depressions of coastal floodplains, on sands and alluvial soils inundated by water; also in dry upper gullies of watercourses and lower slopes of undulating terrain. Sunshine Coast and hinterland, Bribie, Caboolture, Brighton, Strathpine, Moreton and Stradbroke Is, Wellington Point, Bulimba, Indooroopilly, Capalaba, Mt Gravatt, Ipswich, Wacol, Sunnybank, Daisy Hill State Forest, Logan and Gold Coast. Coastal Qld south of Cape York, also NSW.

Notes: Often most conspicuous plant of swamp, but habitat extensively filled and cleared for canal developments, rubbish dumps, sporting fields and pine plantations. Many remaining swamps heavily invaded by weeds and garden plants. Similar to *Callistemon salignus* — see p.138.

Aboriginal people may have soaked nectar-rich flowers in drinking water; papery bark had many uses including building shelters and wrapping food for cooking. In parts of NSW, tree known as *bellbowrie*; name given to Brisbane western suburb.

Wildlife: Flowers — Rainbow and Scaly-breasted Lorikeets, Little Friarbirds, Lewin's, Yellow-faced, White-cheeked, Scarlet and Brown Honeyeaters, Eastern Spinebills Grey-headed and Little Red Flying Foxes and adult butterflies; flowers and bark — Squirrel Gliders; leaves — Koalas.

Family: Myrtaceae

Section Author: **Kathy Stephens**

Moreton Island, BC

Plants of the Wallum heath

Heathlands are areas of stunted vegetation, which occur on low nutrient soils. The plants that grow in heathlands have special adaptations that allow them to exist in a harsh, exposed environment.

In the Greater Brisbane Region, the heaths are distributed across the coastal lowlands (wallum) and on mountainous peaks (montane heath, see p. 303). The main difference between wallum and montane heath is that although the soils of both communities are low in nutrients (particularly phosphorous and nitrogen), the soils of the wallum are usually very deep, extremely porous or completely waterlogged, whereas montane heaths have shallow, skeletal soils overlying bedrock.

The sandy coastal areas of the Greater Brisbane Region were once covered by extensive wallum heath which, in the short period since European settlement, has greatly diminished. The wallum heaths occur on the coastal lowlands of the Sunshine Coast, Gold Coast and the offshore sand islands (Moreton, Bribie and Stradbroke), and on infertile soils derived from rhyolite (Glasshouse Mountains) and sandstone (around Greenbank and Tingalpa). Low nutrient soils are also found in other areas where the parent material is poor, such as sandstone, quartzite, acid granite and wind-distributed sands. Heathland soils are often leached and acidic with a pH between 3.5 and 6.5.

There are certain forms of plant growth that are better suited to wallum heath than other vegetation communities. One of the ways in which heath plants overcome adverse soil conditions is to stop growing in times of stress. This enables the plants to conserve nutrients until conditions improve.

Heath plants usually have extra roots that are close to the soil surface, thereby maximising the plant's root surface area and its ability to absorb nutrients before they become unavailable, either through deep drainage (white sands) or waterlogging (dark peats).

Specialized rootlets to absorb phosphorous form in plants belonging to the Proteaceae, Restionaceae and Cyperaceae families and nitrogen-fixing root nodules form in plants belonging to the families Fabaceae, Casuarinaceae, Mimosaceae and Zamiaceae.

In dry heaths, plants have to adapt to drought conditions. Being evergreen, rather than deciduous, allows plant growth to take place at any time of the year when conditions are favorable. Small thick, pointed leaves enable heath plants to minimise water loss. The leaves may have thick cuticles and sunken pores that enable the plants to control water loss and withstand desiccation. They may also contain tannin, resins and essential oils.

Low shrubs 1–2 m tall and 'sub-shrubs' 0.25–1 m tall are the most common plant forms in a heathland community. By presenting a canopy with a uniform height, the community becomes light and wind reflective and individual plants are not exposed to these harsh factors. Annual herbs or grasses are rare.

Wallum was the Aboriginal name for *Banksia aemula* (Wallum Banksia), which is often the tallest growing plant in heath communities. It is the 'old man banksia' of the popular children's stories by Australian author May Gibbs. The term *wallum* has since been generalised to refer to all the lowland heath communities, whether *Banksia aemula* is present or not.

Bribie Island, GC

Perennial sedges that reshoot from underground stems and terrestrial orchids resprouting from bulbs and tubers are more common. Most wallum heathland plants have fleshy underground stems or organs such as lignotubers, rhizomes, bulbs or tubers.

There are a number of other ecological factors that determine the nature of heath communities such as water, fire and salt spray. In wallum heathland, there is either too much water, or too little. Heathlands can be 'wet' or 'dry', depending on the depth of the water table below the surface. Where there is too much water and the soil is waterlogged, 'wet heaths' occur; areas where water drains freely to deeper levels are 'dry heaths'.

Wet heath communities (see p. 33) grow on a substrate of poorly drained sand or peat. Characteristic species include *Boronia falcifolia* (Wallum Boronia), *Leptospermum* species (tea-trees), *Melaleuca thymifolia* (Thyme Honeymyrtle) and *Xanthorrhoea fulva* (Swamp Grass Tree).

Like the wet heaths, dry heath communities are floristically very rich assemblages of plants and typically include species such as *Persoonia virgata* (Geebung), *Woollsia pungens* and Leucopogons and Acacias. Some of the drier heaths also have an overstorey of taller species such as *Corymbia intermedia* (Pink Bloodwood), *Banksia integrifolia* (Coast Banksia) and *Eucalyptus racemosa* (Scribbly Gum).

The diversity and abundance of plants in heathlands is strongly related to fire. Fire is a major disturbance that stimulates germination and regeneration in heathlands. Plants have responded to fire by:

- developing woody fruits that insulate seed;
- buds able to produce epicormic growth; and
- the development of underground organs and heat-resistant bark.

The timing of fire in relation to flowering and seed-set is critical. Many species, such as Banksias and Hakeas, have woody pods, which retain seed for years and only release seed after fire. Smoke treating the seed of heathland plants to increase germination rates is common practice in plant nurseries. If heathlands are burned during flowering and before seed is formed on the plants, no seed will be released into the soil. If this happens several years in succession, the species richness of a heathland community will be severely reduced. Once seed has been formed the fire triggers seed dispersal and germination.

Many of the heathland plants do release their seed either from capsules which split or as succulent berries that drop. However, if fires occur too frequently and the seed bank in the soil is depleted, plants that resprout from regenerative organs buried in the soil (such as lignotubers), are likely to succeed over those that do not have this adaptive ability.

The leaves of heath plants also contain tannins, resins and essential oils that increase their flammability. Standing litter, slow decomposition rates and reliable periods of dry weather also contribute to the susceptibility of heathlands to fire. Most heath species are well adapted to fire and new growth often sprouts from trunks, the base of plants and underground tubers, rhizomes and bulbs within a week of being burnt.

For thousands of years, this interaction between fires and species diversity in heathland has been manipulated by human intervention. Heaths are often sites of conflict between protection (hazard reduction, habitat manipulation and fire suppression) and ecological fire management objectives (population enhancement and the maintenance of diversity). In the light of the highly fragmented nature of remnant heaths in South-east Queensland and the land uses that impact on them, this conflict will not be resolved easily. Unfortunately, while the prescription for 'protection management' is clear, the ecological information required to manage fire to maintain diversity in heathlands is largely incomplete and further research is essential.

Once scorned as infertile and useless, it is now recognised that the wallum heaths are a critical part of our environment. The heaths are home to many small birds and mammals, including the rare Ground Parrot (*Pezoporus wallicus*) and the Wallum Froglet (*Crinia tinula*) and they contain some of the most beautiful wildflowers in the region. It is disappointing to see so much of this community lost to development on the coastal lowlands. — **Kathy Stephens**

Wallum Boronia (Boronia falcifolia), BC

Plant species accounts
Kathy Stephens

Information on Indigenous usage
Glenn Leiper

Wildlife information
David Barnes

HERBS, GRASSES AND GROUNDCOVERS

Baloskion tetraphyllum
See p. 49

Blandfordia grandiflora
Christmas Bells

Description: Small herbaceous plant, 30–50 cm tall. Leaves a basal tuft, so plant is inconspicuous when not in flower. Clusters of showy, drooping, orange bell-shaped flowers at tops of leafless stems; December–February. Flowers usually orange with yellow petal tips, but some all yellow forms. Dry papery seed pods remain on plants for some time after flowering.

Habitat and Range: On sandy soils, wet heathlands, *Melaleuca* swamps. Sunshine Coast, Buderim, Stradbroke and Russell Is, Gold Coast, Bilinga, also Wide Bay District, Qld, and NSW.

Notes: Rare. Protected plant, cannot be collected from wild. Much habitat lost to development on coastal lowland plains.

Family: Blandfordiaceae

Burchardia umbellata
Milk Maids

Description: Small, slender tufted herb to 60 cm tall. Leaves tufted from base; round with pointed tip, slightly shorter than flowering stems. Small lily-like flowers radiate from top of slender stems; 6 spreading white petals with reddish centre; 6 purple-black anthers appear as dots from a distance; September–February.

Habitat and Range: In wet heath areas on sandy coastal plains. Sunshine Coast, Bribie, Beerwah, Glasshouse Mountains, Stradbroke and Peel Is, Karawatha; also Wide Bay District, Qld. Australia-wide, except NT.

Notes: Aboriginal people ate crisp tubers.

Family: Colchicaceae

Caustis recurvata
Curly Wig

Description: Wiry, herbaceous sedge, 0.5–1 m tall. Stems erect with masses of leaves at top; light green leaves rolled tightly inward; weight of leaves often causes plant to sprawl. Brown sheathing bands on stem where leaves emerge in clusters.

Habitat and Range: On coastal well drained sands in a variety of communities. Sunshine Coast, Beerwah, Bribie, Moreton and Stradbroke Is, Coolangatta, also Wide Bay and Port Curtis Districts, Qld, and NSW.

Notes: Three species of *Caustis* used in cut flower industry.

Family: Cyperaceae

Patersonia sericea var. *sericea*

Description: Grass-like plant. Basal tuft of narrow flat leaves; bluish-green; smooth to touch; young plants with hairy edges. One to several, iris-like violet flowers on stems above leaves; 3 large petals spreading from a tube, surrounded by toughened dark bracts covered in white silky hairs.

Habitat and Range: Uncommon. Sandy wallum heath and understorey of eucalypt woodlands, also on rhyolite, sandstone and granite soils. Coastal Qld south of Rockhampton, and NSW.

Notes: Similar to *Patersonia glabrata* —leaves occur up stem rather than at base; taller. Also similar to *Patersonia fragilis* — smaller; greenish bracts, not thick; in swampy habitats.

Family: Iridaceae

Sowerbaea juncea
Vanilla Lily, Rush Lily

Description: Tufted herb with round hollow, bluish leaves, 30–50 cm tall. Masses of lilac, pink or sometimes white flower heads on long stems 50–75 cm tall; September–February.

Habitat and Range: Common. In ground layer of sandy coastal wallum and wet heath communities. Sunshine Coast, Beerwah, Bribie, Moreton, Peel and Stradbroke Is, Burpengary, Hayes Inlet, Tugun; also Wide Bay and Port Curtis Districts, Qld, and NSW, Vic. and WA.

Notes: Fragrant vanilla perfume. Showy wildflower display over large areas.

Family: Anthericaceae

FERNS

Dicranopteris linearis var. *linearis*

Description: Creeping fern to 30 cm tall. Leathery fronds forked 2–3 times with two branches at each fork being equal. Leaflets on each frond at right angles to stem. Lower surfaces of fronds pale bluish-green.

Habitat and Range: In damp organic loam soils in *Melaleuca* swamps, riverbanks and forests. Sunshine Coast, Beerwah, Boonah, Stradbroke and Russell Is; also coastal Qld south of Cape York, NT and NSW.

Notes: Similar to *Sticherus flabellatus* var. *flabellatus*, see p. 201.

Family: Gleicheniaceae

Gleichenia dicarpa
Pouched Coral Fern

Description: Creeping fern to 50 cm. Upright fronds forking and layered. Edges of frond leaflets turns under to form pouches, appears scalloped. Underside of leaflets often hidden by pouching, or if visible, pale green.

Habitat and Range: In peaty loams and wetlands on peat, on shady freshwater stream banks. Glasshouse Mountains, Mt Mee, Bribie and Stradbroke Is, Wellington Point, Bellbowrie, Sunnybank, Daisy Hill, Plunkett, Lamington National Park; also coastal Qld south of Cape York, NSW, Vic. and Tas.

Notes: Similar to *Gleichenia mendellii* — occurs in same habitat, but underside of frond is white.

Family: Gleicheniaceae

Lycopodiella cernua
Coral Fern

Description: Trailing fern that roots where stem touches ground; fronds 15–30 cm tall. Stiff, upright branches; looks like miniature pine tree or branched coral. Crowded overlapping fertile leaves cause tips of branches to bend downward. Leaves lower on stem more widely spaced and spreading; pale green, stiff, triangular; broad base clasps stem, tapers to a sharp point.

Habitat and Range: Damp areas in coastal sands. Eumundi, Buderim, Palmerston, Sunshine Coast, Moreton and Stradbroke Is, Mt Glorious, Burbank, Carole Park, Currumbin; also coastal and inland areas of Qld south of Cape York to NSW border and NT.

Family: Lycopodiaceae

VINES AND CLIMBERS

Cassytha pubescens
Dodder Laurel

Description: Densely twining parasitic-vine. Attaches to host with small suckers. Short reddish hairs on new growth. Inconspicuous white flowers on spikes or shortly branched stems. Fruit round, greenish; about 5 mm wide.

Habitat and Range: Widespread. In heath, coastal foredunes and swales, also eucalypt forests with heath understorey. Beerwah, Bribie, Moreton and Stradbroke Is, Mt Barney; Qld, NSW, Vic., Tas., SA and WA.

Notes: Sometimes almost smothers other small shrubs. Aboriginal people ate small fruit; sometimes used stems as twine.

Family: Lauraceae

SHRUBS AND TREES

Acacia baueri subsp. *baueri*

Description: Tiny shrub 10–15 cm tall. Green leaves whorled around stem; slightly down-turned tip; covered with bumps. Golden-yellow ball flowers on long stalks, followed by flattened seed pod; June–November.

Habitat and Range: Wet heathlands on sandy coastal plains. Sunshine Coast, Bribie, Beerwah, Moreton and Stradbroke Is, Gold Coast; also Wide Bay District, Qld, and NSW.

Notes: Vulnerable. Protected plant, cannot be collected from the wild. Much habitat lost to development on coastal lowlands.

Family: Mimosaceae

Acacia suaveolens
Sweet Wattle

Description: Spindly upright shrub, 1–2 m tall. Few branches. Stiff bluish leaves with one central vein; oblong, with small pointed tip. Stems also often bluish; sharply angular. Very pale cream flower balls on stalks; May–November. Seed pods violet to blue-black; flattened with bumps over seeds.

Habitat and Range: Widespread and common, but always in small numbers. On sands in wallum heath, also heath understorey of eucalypt forest and on shallow, infertile soils of mountains. Sunshine Coast, Glasshouse Mountains, Beerwah, Mt Mee State Forest, Bribie, Moreton and Stradbroke Is, Sunnybank, Canungra, Gold Coast and Lamington National Park; also Wide Bay, Port Curtis and Mitchell Districts, Qld, and NSW, Vic., Tas. and SA.

Notes: Sweet honey perfume to flowers.

Family: Mimosaceae

Acacia ulicifolia
Prickly Moses, Juniper Wattle

Description: Low, branched prickly shrub, 0.5–1.0 m high, but may reach 2 m. Small scattered leaves; green to yellow-green; narrow, end in spiny tip, widest near base. Flowers form white balls on stem to 1 cm long; June–September. Seed pods rough, long and narrow; seeds arranged vertically along pod length.

Habitat and Range: Widespread and common. On shallow or infertile soils in wallum heath, also mountain heaths. Sunshine Coast, Beerwah, Woodford, Moreton and Stradbroke Is, D'Aguilar Range, Crows Nest, Springwood, Plunkett, Gold Coast, Lamington National Park; also coastal Qld, NSW, Vic., Tas. and SA.

Family: Mimosaceae

Aotus lanigera

Description: Upright herbaceous shrub, 1–1.5 m tall. Plant branches sparingly close to ground; series of upright single stems densely covered with long soft hairs. Leaves green; upright, parallel to stem. Showy yellow pea flowers on upper portion of stem; June–November; often with leafy extension above flowering part.

Habitat and Range: Common in wallum heath of coastal lowlands and Moreton Bay sand islands; prefers wet areas. Sunshine Coast, Bribie, Moreton and Stradbroke Is, Gold Coast; also coastal Qld south of Rockhampton, and NSW.

Notes: Forms nitrogen-fixing nodules on roots. Similar to *Aotus ericoides* — lacks hairy stems; spreading leaves; small red spot of colour at base of petals. Collected by Alan Cunningham from Maroochy in 1874.

Family: Fabaceae

Astrotricha longifolia

Description: Spindly woody shrub to 2 m tall. Stems and underside of leaves covered with masses of white woolly hairs, giving plant whitish appearance. Leaves to 10 cm long by 1 cm wide; tip tapered; base rounded; edges entire; leaves tend to hang downwards from short stalk to 2 cm long. Creamy-white flowers in clusters on large, open branched inflorescence at end of branches; September–November. Fruit a flattened berry.

Habitat and Range: Occasional occurrence in sandy areas and slopes with skeletal soils. Cooyar, Moreton and Stradbroke Is, Mt Gravatt, Plunkett; also coastal Qld south of Rockhampton and NSW.

Family: Araliaceae

Austromyrtus dulcis
Midyim Berry, Midgen Berry

see p. 132

Baeckea frutescens
Weeping Baeckea

Description: Woody shrub 1–3 m tall. Sprawling to drooping branches. Tiny green, needle-like, leaves opposite or in clusters; to 1 cm long. Masses of small white flowers along stems; mid-October–November. Seed capsule with 3 segments; sheds numerous small chaffy seeds.

Habitat and Range: Sandy soils of coastal wallum. Coolum, Buderim, Beerwah, Bribie and Stradbroke Is, Carole Park; also coastal Qld south of Townsville, and NSW.

Notes: Nectar attractive to bees and other insects. Cultivated as ornamental garden plant.

Family: Myrtaceae

Banksia aemula
Wallum Banksia

Description: Small tree to 8 m tall. Chunky brown bark; branches and trunk often gnarled. Stiff flat leaves; green above, paler and often with rusty hairs below; 2–20 cm long; edges serrated. Flowers cream to golden, becoming brown with age; in large spikes 8–15 cm long at ends of branches; tip of flower style triangular, shaped like arrowhead, 1 mm long; mainly March–August. Cylindrical fruiting 'cone' contains large woody seed cases embedded in brown, velvety core; single dark seed with papery wing.

Habitat and Range: On sand in coastal wallum communities. Sunshine Coast, Bribie, Moreton and Stradbroke Is, Gold Coast; also Wide Bay and Port Curtis District, Qld and NSW.

Notes: Characteristic plant that gives wallum heath its name. Similar to *Banksia serrata* — to 16 m; straight trunk; tip of flower style spear-shaped 2.5–3 mm long; less widespread.

Family: Proteaceae

Banksia oblongifolia
Dwarf Banksia

Description: Low woody shrub, 0.5–1.0 m tall. Multi-stemmed. Stiff leaves dark green above, white below; 3–7 cm long; tip truncated; edges serrated and blunt. Pale yellow flower spikes at ends of branches; 5–15 cm long; mainly December–May. Fruiting cones usually with many tightly packed, densely hairy seed cases.

Habitat and Range: On sandy soils and steep upper slopes on shallow soils in damp areas of wallum. Sunshine Coast, Glasshouse Mountains, Bribie, Moreton and Stradbroke Is, Downfall Ck, Mt Mee State Forest, Crows Nest, Gold Coast; also coastal Qld, south of Rockhampton, and NSW.

Family: Proteaceae

Boronia falcifolia
Wallum Boronia

Description: Upright branching shrub, 1–1.5 m tall. Stems reddish. Succulent green, needle-like leaves consist of three leaflets. Bright magenta pink flowers; 4 spreading petals; wax-like appearance; mainly September–February.

Habitat and Range: In wet patches of heath and sedgelands of sandy coastal plains. Sunshine Coast, Beerwah, Bribie, Moreton, Peel and Stradbroke Is, Toorbul, Gold Coast; also Wide Bay and Port Curtis Districts, Qld, and NSW.

Notes: Other *Boronia* species occur in wallum, such as *Boronia rosmarinifolia*, see p. 135.

Family: Rutaceae

Callitris columellaris
Coast Cypress Pine, Bribie Island Pine

See p. 27

Conospermum taxifolium
Devil's Rice

Description: Herbaceous shrub 1–1.5 m tall. Usually occurs as single upright dark green stem. Narrow leaves also dark green; covered with dense soft white hairs; 2–3 cm long; point upwards around stem. Flattened cluster of dainty white flowers at top of stem; September–November.

Habitat and Range: Common. On sand plains and heath understorey on coastal dune slopes. Sunshine Coast, Beerwah, Bribie, Moreton and Stradbroke Is, Sunnybank, Gold Coast; coastal Qld south of Rockhampton and NSW and Tas.

Family: Proteaceae

Dillwynia retorta var. *retorta*

Description: Straggling woody shrub 0.5–2.0 m tall. Short green linear leaves at right angles to stem; each leaf with spiral twist at base where it attaches to stem. Yellow pea flowers on slender stems along upper stems; red semi-circular marking at centre of largest petal. Purple-black pods.

Habitat and Range: On white to grey sandy soils, also on sandstone slopes in coastal lowland heaths. Sunshine Coast, Beerwah, Caboolture, Bribie, Moreton and Stradbroke Is, Tingalpa, Plunkett, Gold Coast; coastal and inland Qld, south of Bundaberg, also NSW and Vic.

Family: Fabaceae

Drosera peltata
See p. 51

Elaeocarpus reticulatus
Blueberry Ash

Description: Small upright tree, 2–4 m tall. Elongated leathery leaves grey-green; edges serrated; obvious veins; 8–10 cm long and 2–3 cm wide. Masses of small frilled, white or pink, bell-shaped flowers; resemble ballerina skirts. Elongated blue fruits 2 cm long.

Habitat and Range: On more fertile sandy soils enriched by humus. In dry eucalypt forests with heath understorey; also in wet eucalypt forest. Sunshine Coast, Blackall Range, D'Aguilar Range, Glasshouse Mountains, Bribie, Moreton and Stradbroke Is, Aspley, Wellington Point, Murphy's Creek, Gold Coast, Numinbah Valley, Lamington National Park, Main Range; coastal Qld south of Rockhampton and NSW and Vic.

Notes: Flowers fragrant. Cultivated as ornamental.

Family: Elaeocarpaceae

Epacris pulchella
Wallum Heath

Description: Straggly shrub to 1 m tall. Several unbranched stems. Prickly erect, leaves; green, triangular; tip sharp; base heart-shaped, overlaps stem. Buds and showy tubular flowers pink, fade to white with age; clustered around tops of stems; look like a bracelet; September–May.

Habitat and Range: On sandy coastal soils in wallum heath. Sunshine Coast, Glasshouse Mountains, Bribie, Moreton and Stradbroke Is, Crows Nest, Gold Coast; Wide Bay District, Qld, and NSW.

Notes: Weight of flowers can cause stems to sprawl. Similar to *Epacris microphylla* — smaller, less prickly leaves; white flowers; in wetter areas. Also similar to *Epacris obtusifolia* — narrow, non-prickly leaves, rounded tip; white flowers twice as long as *Epacris pulchella*.

Family: Epacridaceae

Gompholobium virgatum var. virgatum
Wallum Wedge Pea

Description: Rounded spreading shrub, 1–1.2 m tall. Stems often reddish. Leaves consist of 3 flat, leaflets; bluish; spreading, elongated. Large bright yellow pea flowers; usually single; near ends of branches. Fruit a globular pod.

Habitat and Range: Common and widespread. On sandy soils in heath, also in heath understorey of dry eucalypt forests. Sunshine Coast, Moreton and Stradbroke Is, Beerwah, Bribie, Crows Nest, Sunnybank, Eight Mile Plains, Plunkett, Gold Coast, Lamington National Park; also Wide Bay and Port Curtis Districts, Qld, and NSW.

Notes: Seed pod pops audibly when mature.

Family: Fabaceae

Homoranthus virgatus

Description: Erect shrub 0.5–1 m tall. Viewed from above, plant has squarish appearance due to leaf arrangement. Stiff leaves opposite; usually dull bluish; linear. Cream to greenish-white tubular flowers in compact clusters at ends of branches; protruding styles; September–February.

Habitat and Range: On coastal sands in heath communities. Sunshine Coast, Bribie, Moreton and Stradbroke Is; also Wide Bay and Port Curtis Districts, Qld, and NSW.

Family: Myrtaceae

Jacksonia stackhousii
Wallum Dogwood

Description: Erect low shrub to 25 cm tall. Multi-branched, appears leafless. Stems often whitish, bluish or yellowish. Large pea flowers, 1 cm across, vary from deep orange-yellow to white; June–November.

Habitat and Range: Uncommon. In heath on sandy soil. Sunshine Coast, Moreton and Stradbroke Is, Bribie, Gold Coast; also Wide Bay and Port Curtis Districts, Qld, and NSW.

Notes: Similar to *Jacksonia scoparia*, see p. 177.

Family: Fabaceae

Leptomeria acida
Currant Bush

Description: Rounded shrub to 2 m tall, often slightly above other heath plants. Multi-branched. Leaves inconspicuous, reduced to small scales. Small red flowers; mainly June–August. Shining, succulent fruits, green turning yellow and then plum with age.

Habitat and Range: Widespread and common. On sands and shallow soils on ridges in heath and eucalypt communities Moreton and Stradbroke Is, Mt Mee, Diana's Bath, Coolangatta Airport; also Wide Bay District, Qld, and NSW.

Notes: Root parasite. Aboriginal people ate acidic fruit; women often carried large amounts for later use; vitamin C content half that of oranges.

Family: Santalaceae

Leptospermum liversidgei

Description: Shrub to 3 m tall. Small rounded green leaves pressed close to stem; point upwards; lemon-scented. White, or sometimes pink open flowers; December–February. Top of immature fruit hairless; 5 rounded segments immediately after petals are shed; fruit becomes woody and remains on branches for many years.

Habitat and Range: In wallum heathland and swamps. Sunshine Coast, Beerwah, Bribie, Moreton, Peel and Stradbroke Is, Gold Coast; also Wide Bay District, Qld, and NSW.

Notes: Cultivated as ornamental plant.

Family: Myrtaceae

Leptospermum polygalifolium
Wild May, Tea-tree

Description: Shrub to 4 m tall. Scaly bark; often multi-stemmed in wallum due to fire. Soft green leaves with rounded tip. White flowers with 5 spreading petals; September–November. Woody seed capsules about 1 cm wide; remain on stems.

Habitat and Range: Common and widespread. In well drained, sandy wallum areas and as a dense shrub layer in dry eucalypt forest, also common in sandstone, granite and rhyolite heaths. Sunshine Coast and hinterland, Glasshouse Mountains, Bribie, Moreton and Stradbroke Is, northern, southern and western Brisbane suburbs, Springbrook and west to Main Range; coastal and inland Qld, except far west, and NSW.

Notes: Round galls sometimes form along twigs and branches.

Wildlife: Fruit — Crimson Rosella.

Family: Myrtaceae

Leptospermum semibaccatum
Tea-Tree

Description: Low shrub to 2 m. Similar to *Leptospermum liversidgei*. Leaves rounded on tips; curve outwards from stem. Fruit are not held on plant, but shed soon after formation; not as woody or large as previous two species.

Habitat and Range: In wallum heath. Sunshine Coast, Beerwah, Moreton, Bribie, Peel and Stradbroke Is, Tugun.

Family: Myrtaceae

Leucopogon biflorus

See p. 178

Leucopogon margarodes
Pink-bearded Heath

See p. 179

Leucopogon juniperinus
Prickly Bearded Heath

See p. 178

Leucopogon pimeleoides

Description: Shrub to 2 m tall. Slender branches. Leaves green; sharply pointed; 1.5 cm long by 0.3 cm wide. Sprays of tiny white tubular flowers in widely spaced spikes at tips of branches; flowers with white woolly hairs on inside; July–November. Weight of flower masses often causes branches to droop. Tiny fruit.

Habitat and Range: In wallum heath and heath understorey in eucalypt communities. Sunshine Coast, Landsborough, Moreton, Bribie and Stradbroke Is, Sunnybank, Tugun; also Wide Bay district, Qld, and NSW.

Notes: Several *Leucopogon* species in South east Queensland; characteristic plant of wallum heaths. All have tubular white flowers with woolly hairs in throat.

Family: Epacridaceae

Melaleuca thymifolia
Thyme Honeymyrtle

Description: Small twiggy shrub to 1 m tall. Flaky bark. Leaves darker above, paler below; more or less evenly tapered at both ends. Showy pink or purple flowers in spikes 2 cm long; September–February. Tiny fruit about 2 mm wide; thickened teeth on edges.

Habitat and Range: Wet sandy wallum heath. Sunshine Coast, Elimbah, Burpengary, Sunnybank, Rochedale, Karawatha Reserve, Ipswich, Stradbroke I., Gold Coast; also coastal Qld south of Rockhampton, and NSW.

Family: Myrtaceae

Persoonia virgata
Geebung

Description: Spreading shrub 2–3 m tall. Fine narrow leaves. Narrow yellow tubular flowers with long petal lobes that curl sharply outwards; flowers hang from slender stems; July–November. Fruit a firm, short inflated pod; green, turning purple; fine hair-like extension at tip; contains single seed.

Habitat and Range: Common and widespread in wallum and heath shrub understorey of eucalypt communities on sandy soils, also on rhyolite. Yandina, Mt Coolum, Sunshine Coast, Landsborough, Mapleton, Beerwah, Glasshouse Mountains, Moreton, Bribie and Stradbroke Is, Mt Tamborine, Southport, Coolangatta; also coastal Qld south of Rockhampton, and NSW.

Wildlife: Leaves — Swamp Wallaby.

Family: Proteacea

Notes: Fruit edible when soft and fallen.

Petrophile canescens
Conesticks

Description: Stiff erect shrub, 1–1.5 m tall. Stiff divided leaves; blue-green and hairy. Short upright inflorescence; creamy compacted flower spike 4 cm long at tips of mature branches. Fruit resembles miniature pine cone.

Habitat and Range: On coastal sands and sandstone and rhyolite soils. Mt Mee, Moreton and Stradbroke Is, Crows Nest, Chermside, Helidon, Lamington National Park; coastal Qld south of Rockhampton, and NSW.

Family: Proteaceae

Phebalium woombye

Description: Shrub to 2 m tall. Firm leaves alternate; dark green above, silver-green with obvious rusty dots below; midvein indented. Trusses of several white (rarely pink) flowers at tips of branches; 5 spreading petals; long stamens hang down from centre; June–November.

Habitat and Range: Wallum and heath areas of coastal lowlands and rhyolitic ranges. Noosa National Park, Mt Coolum, Pt Arkwright, Sunshine Coast, Woombye, Moreton and Bribie Is, Toorbul, Canungra, Springbrook; coastal Qld south of Rockhampton, and NSW.

Notes: Pink flowered form known from areas like Woodgate, Canungra and Mt Walsh.

Family: Rutaceae

Phyllota phylicoides

Description: Erect shrub, 1–1.5 m tall, usually with yellow stems. Narrow light green leaves spread out from stem or sometimes point downwards; often with small hook on tip. Single, showy yellow flowers; usually crowded just below tip of branch; resemble elongated spike; June–November.

Habitat and Range: On sand soils of coastal lowlands and sandstone ranges, also dry eucalypt forest. Mt Coolum, Sunshine Coast, Moreton, Bribie and Stradbroke Is, Chermside, Aspley, Tingalpa, Bundamba, Sunnybank, Karawatha, Carole Park, Plunkett; also coastal Qld south of Rockhampton, and NSW.

Family: Fabaceae

Platysace ericoides

Description: Dwarf branching shrub to 30 cm tall. Tips of branches hairy. Short green leaves; finely pointed and stumpy. Tiny white flowers with 5 petals arranged in compact clusters at end of slender stems on branch tips; flowers year-round.

Habitat and Range: In coastal sands and sandstone areas. Sunshine Coast, Glasshouse Mountains, Bribie, Moreton Peel and Stradbroke Is, Crows Nest, Wellington Point, Tingalpa, Oxley, Kuraby, Ipswich, Daisy Hill, Jacobs Well, Camira, Beenleigh, Plunkett, Mt Tamborine, Southport, Burleigh, Currumbin; also coastal Qld south of Rockhampton, and NSW.

Wildlife: Flowers — adult butterflies

Family: Apiaceae

Pomax umbellata
see p. 105

Pultenaea myrtoides

Description: Woody shrub 1–1.5 m tall. Young stems with white silky hairs. Leaves green and smooth above, white silky hairs below; edges curved under. Clusters of yellow and red pea flowers on tips of branches; June–November. Short flattened seed pods.

Habitat and Range: On well-drained sandy and shallow soils. Sunshine Coast, Beerwah, Bribie Moreton, Stradbroke and Russell Is Tingalpa, Glasshouse Mountains, Donnybrook, Lawnton, Mt Cotton, Sunnybank, Mt Gravatt; also Wide Bay District, Qld, and NSW.

Notes: Forms nitrogen-fixing root nodules. Several *Pultenaea* species in wallum and heathlands. *Pultenaea retusa* — has indentation at midvein in upper leaf tip, see p. 194. *Pultenaea villosa* — see p. 193. *Pultenaea petiolaris* — see p. 192. Most similar to *Pultenaea paleacea* — leaves more crowded at branch tips and bracts drawn out to a long fine point.

Family: Fabaceae

Ricinocarpos pinifolius
Wedding Bush

Description: Woody spreading shrub, 2–4 m tall. Very narrow leaves; glossy dark green above, white star-shaped hairs below; edges rolled under. Masses of showy pure white flowers; 5 or 6 large spreading petals; yellow central stamens; June–November. Fruit a rounded, lobed green capsule with lumpy surface.

Habitat and Range: On sandy soils. Sunshine Coast, Beerwah, Moreton, Bribie and Stradbroke Is, Toorbul, Rochedale, Sunnybank, Gold Coast; coastal Qld south of Townsville, and NSW, Vic., Tas., WA and NT.

Notes: Once common, now becoming less frequent due to habitat destruction.

Family: Euphorbiaceae

Sprengelia sprengelioides

Description: Prickly upright herbaceous shrub to 1 m tall. Leaves dark glossy green, densely overlapping; concave up stem; base heart-shaped and clasps stem; tip tapers to sharp point; upper tips often turn brown. Large white flowers not numerous; in short cluster or single; 5 spreading petals. which do not open completely flat; July–November.

Habitat and Range: Common. On moist sands in wallum heath. Buderim, Sunshine Coast, Beerwah, Moreton, Bribie and Stradbroke Is, Gold Coast; also Wide Bay and Port Curtis Districts, Qld, and NSW.

Family: Epacridaceae

Strangea linearis

Description: Low shrub to 30 cm tall. Numerous erect stems growing from woody rootstock. Leaves slightly curved, thick and leathery; held stiffly upright. Inconspicuous white-cream flowers on slender stems; petals curve back. Drooping elongated, woody seed capsules; longitudinal ridges; remain on stem unopened for some time; release single flat seed with papery wing.

Habitat and Range: Sandy coastal soils, in moist wallum and understorey of eucalypt woodlands. Beerwah, Gold Coast, Sunshine Coast, Moreton, Peel and Stradbroke Is, Tugun; also Wide Bay District, Qld, and NSW.

Notes: Fragrant flowers. Fire needed for seed release.

Family: Proteaceae

Woollsia pungens

Description: Very prickly erect shrub to 1 m tall. Young stems with white woolly hairs. Stiff overlapping leaves; dark glossy green; concave, often spreading or curved downwards; sharp spiny tip; base heart-shaped, clasps stem. Single white tubular flowers borne some distance below end of stem; 5 spreading petals; mainly September–May.

Habitat and Range: Common. On sandy soils in coastal wallum, also in heath understorey of eucalypt woodlands and in montane heaths. Mt Mee, Moreton and Stradbroke Is, Mt Greville, Mt Maroon, Mt May, Mt Minto, Lamington National Park, Mt Ernest, Mt Barney, Mt Lindesay; also Wide Bay District, Qld, and NSW.

Notes: Flowers fragrant.

Wildlife: Flowers — Brown Honeyeater; leaves — Swamp Wallaby

Family: Epacridaceae

Xanthorrhoea fulva
Swamp Grass Tree

Description: Tufted herbaceous plant to 2.2 m tall when flowering. Grows from woody rootstock; lacks trunk; characterised by long stiff leaves that resemble a clump of grass. Leaves blue-green; triangular to flat. Cream flower spike 10–60 cm; grows at top of stout woody stem; June–November, Protruding seed cases embedded in woody spike (flowerbase).

Habitat and Range: Occurs only in wet heathlands and swamps of coastal wallum; does not occur on well-drained soils or slopes. Sunshine Coast, Beerwah, Moreton, Stradbroke and Russell Is, Hollywell; also Wide Bay and Port Curtis Districts, Qld.

Notes: Germinates readily after fire.

Wildlife: Flowers — White-cheeked Honeyeater and adult butterflies.

Family: Xanthorrhoeaceae

BC

Xanthorrhoea latifolia
Grass Tree

See p. 198

Brisbane Forest Park, BC

Plants of the Eucalypt forests

The Greater Brisbane Region is one of the most botanically rich areas in Australia and the number of eucalypt species that grow here reflect this diversity.

Eucalypts forests grow on many different soils from deep sands, alluvium, sandy loams or shallow sandy and stony soils to the more fertile basaltic soils. They also occur across a range of habitats from the coastal lowlands to the steep upper mountain slopes.

Unfortunately, the once extensive eucalypt forests of the coastal lowlands have either been cleared or thinned for forestry, agriculture or urbanisation. Forests on particular soil types, such as red soils of the Redland Bay, were initially cleared for cultivation and are now gradually being lost to residential use. Most of the remaining forested areas in the region have been modified to some extent by logging and /or firing.

Continued disturbance has resulted in increased soil erosion, raising of water tables and increased potential for salination problems, as well as the loss of animal habitat.

A eucalypt forest is generally composed of a grass layer, a shrub layer and sometimes a tall shrub/small tree layer that includes species such as wattles and she-oaks. The tree layer is usually made up of eucalypts with two or three species growing together, but other closely related species like *Lophostemon confertus* (Brush Box) or *Angophoras* (smooth and rough bark apples) may sometimes be more prevalent.

In some of the larger remaining eucalypt forests, small areas of other vegetation communities, such as paperbark swamps and rainforest-like patches, may be found along drainage lines and in moist gullies or small gorge-like areas where conditions are suitable.

Eucalypt forests can be divided into wet and dry communities. Drier forests can be further defined as woodland and open forest. Wet eucalypt forest, sometimes called 'tall forest', is generally found in higher rainfall areas on moister, more fertile soils and often borders rainforest. The remaining wet forests in the Brisbane region are now mostly confined to alluvial or volcanic soils on the slopes of ranges, such as at Tamborine Mountain. *Eucalyptus grandis* (Flooded Gum), *Eucalyptus saligna* (Sydney Blue Gum), *Eucalyptus acmenoides* (White Mahogany) and *Eucalyptus propinqua* (Grey Gum) are typical tall forest species.

In open dry forest, the tree crowns just touch or slightly overlap. This type of forest now grows only on the coastal hills and mountain slopes around Brisbane, with some of the more natural areas protected in reserves such as, Toohey Forest Park, Brisbane Forest Park, Karawatha Park, Springwood Conservation Park, Daisy Hill State Forest, Bunya State Forest, and Freshwater National Park.

In eucalypt woodland, the trees are separated from one another creating a park-like effect. Sometimes, when trees are widely separated, the forest is called 'open' woodland. Many woodland areas in the Greater Brisbane Region are due to disturbance, but they may also be the natural result of shallow, infertile soils on a rocky substrate. Generally, many more species grow in the shrub layer of woodland areas.

On the Moreton Bay sand islands and on some sandstone-derived soils close to the coast, eucalypt forests are described as having a 'heathy understorey'. These forests are characterised by shrub species that are also found in heath areas, particularly grass trees (*Xanthorrhoea* spp.), members of the heath family, such as white beards (*Leucopogon* spp.) and ground berry (*Acrotriche aggregata*), and Protea species, including banksias (*Banksia* spp.) and peas (*Daviesia* spp., *Dillwynia* spp. and *Pultenaea* spp.).

On the deep sands and sandy soils of the coastal lowlands, *Eucalyptus racemosa* (Scribbly Gum) is often the dominant tree, growing with *Corymbia* spp. (pink or red bloodwoods), *Eucalyptus tindaliae* (Queensland white stringybark) and *Eucalyptus microcorys* (Tallowwood). On the younger more fertile soils in high rainfall areas, *Eucalyptus pilularis* (Blackbutt) may be the dominant tree.

At higher elevations on coastal hills, stringybarks such as, *Eucalyptus carnea* (Broad-leaved White Mahogany) and *Eucalyptus resinifera* (Red Mahogany) are more dominant, again growing with *Corymbia* species and sometimes *Angophora woodsiana* (Smudgee).

The alluvial flats of streams, creeks and rivers, and valley floors support a different suite of species including *Eucalyptus tereticornis* (Forest Red Gum) and *Eucalyptus siderophloia* (Grey Ironbark) and *Eucalyptus moluccana* (Gum-topped Box), particularly on clay soils.

Eucalyptus tereticornis is probably the most common eucalypt in the Greater Brisbane Region and has often been left as remnant forest along streams and rivers in rural areas. Unfortunately, very few natural areas of this species remain. *Eucalyptus microcorys* (Tallowwood) is another common eucalypt that is widespread on a range of soil types.

On the stony soils of hills and mountain slopes, *Corymbia citriodora* subsp. *variegata* (Spotted Gum) becomes more common with species such as *Angophora leiocarpa* (Smooth-barked Apple) and *Eucalyptus siderophloia* or *Eucalyptus crebra*.

There is fossil evidence of eucalypts from the Oligocene Epoch 22-38 million years ago and at the present time more than 800 species are recognised. The eucalypts are a botanically complex group that can even be difficult for botanists to distinguish. For example, some eucalypt species are very similar and closely related species appear to hybridise when they grow together. To cope with the complexities within the group, botanists have introduced many separate divisions in an attempt to come up with a meaningful classification of the species in Australia. In recent times, for example, the bloodwoods have been placed in a separate group, *Corymbia* and a number of other eucalypts in the Brisbane region have been re-named and classed as separate species.

The eucalypts and many of the shrubs that occur in forests and woodlands have developed life strategies that allow survival of the species after drought, fire and grazing damage. One of these strategies is the presence of dormant epicormic buds that are protected by the outer bark of stems and branches. If the crown of the tree is damaged by fire, drought, grazing animals or by storm then the buds are stimulated to produce juvenile leaves giving the fire-damaged eucalypts a characteristic brush-like appearance in the regrowth period.

Another survival adaptation is the lignotuber (underground stem), which is common in many eucalypts. It is best seen by examining a seedling — the two bumps above the root eventually come together to form a large woody tuber. (This is sometimes difficult to observe in older specimens as it is overtaken by stem growth). The lignotuber contains numerous buds and vascular tissue and food reserves. If seedling growth is damaged, then buds are stimulated to grow and produce several new stems, one of which eventually dominates the plant. Some eucalypt species do not have lignotubers, so these species rely on abundant seed production after a disturbance such as fire.

Fire is a critical factor in the survival of many Australian plants because it stimulates regeneration — by sprouting from underground stems, by the development of buds at the base of the tree, or by increased seed/seedling production immediately after fire when there is less competition and fewer seed predators.

Corymbia gummifera (Red Bloodwood), BC

Other mechanisms to promote fire include: flammable oils in the leaves; the retention of dead material such as grass tree skirts; loose bark or heavy litter drop; and some eucalypts have a growth habit that promotes up-draughts. *Pultenaea villosa* (Kerosene Bush) is aptly named because it burns rapidly with a blue flame. In the case of grass trees, old tightly packed, leaf bases act as efficient insulators to protect the growing part of the plant.

The seeds of many species may lay dormant in the soil for extended periods, sometimes for years. The high temperatures of fires break the hard coating surrounding the seeds and this results in much higher germination rates. So, while the parent shrub may die, its progeny are given a good opportunity of becoming established in its place. The grass tree *Xanthorrhoea johnsonii* shows enhanced flowering and consequently a potentially higher seed set in the flowering season following a fire. This may lead to an increased number of offspring in the following growing seasons.

The overall effect of fire on species' richness depends on a number of different factors such as fire frequency, in what season the fire occurs, and intensity of the fire. The species composition of many eucalypt communities after fire is determined largely by which species existed previously. The specialised traits that allow survival during a succession of fires also enable survival and reproduction to occur under the stresses imposed by factors such as drought and low nutrient soils.

Although often forming attractive trees, the ultimate size of most eucalypts does not recommend them for the normal sized urban block. The possible exception is *Eucalyptus curtisii* (Plunkett Mallee), which grows naturally in a few places around the Greater Brisbane Region.

Eucalyptus trees can be identified by their distinctive flower capsules or 'gum nuts' as they are commonly called. In eucalypts, the sepals and petals of the plant are fused together, forming a protective cap over the stamens. The shape of the cap or *operculum*, which forms the top half of the bud, differs according to the species. The lower half is called the hypanthium and its shape and size is also a useful aid to identification. When a eucalyptus tree flowers, the cap falls off and numerous prominent stamens (the 'flower') are exposed. The seeds are contained in the hypanthium which becomes woody and dry. — **Robert Coutts**

Hovea acutifolia (Pointed-Leaved Hovea), BC

Plant species accounts
Robert Coutts

Information on Indigenous usage
Glenn Leiper

Wildlife information
David Barnes

A useful first step in identifying eucalypts is to look closely at the bark of the tree. The following convenient classification is based on bark types:

Gum or Smooth Barks

These usually feel smooth to grainy. Bark colour tends to be lighter in shades of white and grey to pink, but often with darker patches. The outer bark is shed annually revealing yellow or orange new bark, which soon fades to shades of light white to grey.

Stringybarks

The persistent fibrous bark of stringybarks is rough to touch and can be pulled off in long to short fibres. The bark may be furrowed and sometimes crosshatched or flaky in the furrows. Colour is usually shades of brown to grey with an underbark of red to brown. The bark may continue onto the twigs or small branches, depending on the species.

Bloodwood Bark

Bloodwoods have a persistent bark with short fibres. It is rough to touch and usually broken up into rectangular to squarish scales (like a crocodile or snake skin). Some scales are closely attached to the trunk and some are easily detached. The outer bark is usually grey to brown and the underbark is reddish to light brown. The bark may persist only to the smaller branches or twigs, depending on the species.

Note: *Corymbia citriodora* and *Corymbia henryi* and *Corymbia tessellaris* (Moreton Bay Ash) are in the bloodwood group, but all have a smooth bark. The barks of *Angophora woodsiana* (Smudgee) and *Angophora subvelutina* (Broad-leaf Apple) sometimes appear similar to bloodwood bark.

Gum or Smooth Barks, *Eucalyptus grandis* (Flooded Gum), BC

Eucalyptus baileyana (Bailey's Stringybark), GC

Corymbia intermedia (Pink Bloodwood), GC

Box bark

Box bark is rough and persistent and divided into close-fitting scales that are not easily detached. The scales are fibrous and rectangular to squarish. Species described in this book, which have a box-like bark, are *Eucalyptus moluccana* (Gum-topped Box) and *Lophostemon confertus* (Brush Box), but they also have a smooth upper bark. Colour is usually brown to dark grey with the upper surface smooth grey or sometimes pink as in the case of *Lophostemon confertus*.

Halfbarks

Halfbark eucalypts have a smooth upper bark and a variable sized stocking of rough, persistent bark that may be stringy, scaly or box-like in texture. The colour of smooth bark is usually shades of white to grey. Rough bark may be brown or dark grey to nearly black.

Ironbarks

Ironbark eucalypts have a rough bark that is often deeply furrowed and usually difficult to remove from the trunk. The exceptions are *Eucalyptus dura* (Gum-topped Ironbark) and *Eucalyptus fibrosa* (Broad-leaved Ironbark), which have slightly separated, layered crests between the furrows. Bark colour is usually dark grey-brown to almost black with the exposed under bark light reddish-brown. Bark may persist only to smaller branches or to twigs depending on species. — **Robert Coutts**

Box Bark, *Lophostemon confertus* (Brush Box), GC

Half Barks, *Corymbia tessellaris* (Moreton Bay Ash), GC

Eucalyptus melanophloia (Silver Leaf Ironbark), BC

Dry Eucalypt forest

Karawatha Forest, JW

HERBS, GRASSES AND GROUNDCOVERS

Calotis lappulacea
Yellow Burr Daisy

Description: Hairy perennial herb to 50 cm. Woody base, but young plants with rosette of leaves that soon wither. Leaves alternate; shape varies, linear, or narrow and obovate, sometimes toothed or deeply lobed; 5–25 mm by 1–4 mm; usually no leaf stalk. Numerous yellow, daisy-like flowers grouped in heads, 5–7 mm wide; solitary or in leafy groups; mainly September–November and March–May. Fruit a minute, wedge-shaped burr.

Habitat and Range: On heavier clay soils on coastal hills in Greater Brisbane Region. Australia-wide.

Notes: Often in disturbed and cleared areas

Family: Asteraceae

Caustis blakei subsp. *blakei*
Foxtails

Description: Perennial herb to 1.5 m tall. Stems rigid with many nodes; leaves reduced to dark red-brown scales at each node. Brush-like inflorescence resembles fox or horse's tail; 20–50 cm long; many non-flowering branches, each with clusters of 10–20 branchlets. Tiny flower spikes 6–7 mm; 4–5 dark brown glumes each containing 1 flower. Fruit a nut about 4 mm long.

Habitat and Range: On deep sands and dry sandy soils in Greater Brisbane Region. Taree, NSW, to Bundaberg, Qld; also Helidon west of Brisbane.

Notes: Often dominates grass layer in Scribbly Gum or Blackbutt forests on sand islands. Much habitat in coastal lowlands cleared. Similar to *Baloskion tetraphyllum*, see p. 49).

Family: Cyperaceae

Chrysocephalum apiculatum
Yellow Buttons

Description: Perennial herb to 60 cm. Woody rootstock; often with mat-like growth. Soft greyish-green, hairy leaves; sometimes hairless above; narrow, obovate to oblong; 1–7 cm by 0.2–1.5 cm; tip pointed; base tapered. Yellow flower heads at ends of branchlets; each head at about same height; July–September, also year-round. Fruits small, angular with minute bristles and barbs

Habitat and Range: Common. On deep sands and sandy and stony soils, in grass layer of open or disturbed forests in Greater Brisbane Region. Australia-wide.

Notes: Variable species; previously known as *Helichrysum ramosissimum* and *Helichrysum apiculatum*. Often on edges of paths.

Wildlife: Leaves — caterpillars of Australian Painted Lady Butterfly.

Family: Asteraceae

Commelina diffusa
Wandering Jew, Scurvy Weed

Description: Creeping, grass-like herb. Weak stems; plant spreads by rooting at stem nodes. Leaves narrowly ovate; 6–10 cm by 0.4–1.5 cm; tip usually pointed; base of leaf encloses stem. Delicate flowers, outer 3 segments green, inner 3 segments blue; September–May. Fruit a small capsule; 5 brown to black, pitted or veined seeds.

Habitat and Range: Common. Often in moist or shaded, disturbed sites, sometimes on rainforest edges in Greater Brisbane Region. Narooma, NSW, to Nth Qld; also Melanesia and Pacific islands.

Notes: Cosmopolitan; will grow anywhere, including suburban gardens. Previously known as *Commelina cyanea*.

Family: Commelinaceae

Cymbopogon refractus
Barbed Wire Grass

Description: Perennial clumped grass to about 1.5 m. Bluish-green leaves; narrow, linear; underside rough to touch; 40 cm by 1–4 mm; tip tapered; faintly lemon-scented when crushed; Red-brown flower spikelets turned back like ties on barbwire fencing; pair of spikelets, partially enclosed by leafy sheath; Spikelets dissimilar — one attached to stem, 5–6.5 mm long; other with stalk; February–April. Flowering stem reddish-green.

Habitat and Range: Common. On poor sandy and stony soil, often on edge of disturbed areas. Vic. to Qld and NT.

Notes: Similar to *Themeda triandra,* see p.107.

Wildlife: Habitat for small, ground-dwelling mammals and frogs. Seed — rosellas.

Family: Poaceae

Desmodium rhytidophyllum
Rusty Tic-trefoil, Native Desmodium

Description: Twining perennial herb to 1 m long. Rusty hairs on stems. Leaves consist of three smaller leaflets; alternate; green above, paler below; short silky hairs; oval to rhombic; 1.5–7 cm by 1–3.5 cm. Leaf tip obtuse or pointed; base rounded; edges sometimes wavy. Pink-purple flowers in racemes to 25 cm long; December–May, also year-round. Fruit pod with minute hooked hairs; 15–25 mm long.

Habitat and Range: On deep sands and sandy and stony soils, also disturbed areas. Bega, NSW, to Nth Qld; also New Guinea.

Family: Fabaceae.

Dianella caerulea var. *producta*
Blue Flax Lily

Description: Tufted perennial, lily-like plant. Extended scaly stems to nearly 1.8 m tall when flowering, but often much less. Linear leaves alternate; in 2 distinct rows; dark green to bluish-green above, paler below; 10–75 cm by 3–25 mm; prominent midrib, veins usually more obvious below. Leaf merges into sheath at base; 2 sides almost closed together near tip; Midrib, leaf edges and base of sheath with minute sharp teeth. Whitish flowers in groups 3-6 in racemes, on stem taller than foliage; 6 stamens with enlarged stalks, yellow towards top, pollen sacs pale yellow-brown; September–February. Fruit a succulent blue berry; more-or-less spherical; 7–12 mm; black shiny seeds.

Habitat and Range: In shaded, often-moister areas on coastal hills and mountain slopes in Greater Brisbane Region. Nowra, NSW, to Bundaberg, Qld.

Notes: Six varieties of *Dianella caerulea* in South-east Queensland; difficult to identify in field. Extended stem and whitish flowers separates this variety from others. Similar to *Dianella caerulea* var. *caerulea* (Blue Flax Lily, Paroo Lily, Blueberry Lily) — To 50 cm; tufted or mat-like growth; leaves dark green above, paler below; groups of of 3–25 blue flowers; Tas. and Vic. to South-east Qld. Aboriginal people reputedly ate ripe fruit; roots pounded to flour and roasted; leaves used to weave baskets.

Wildlife: Fruit — Lewin's Honeyeater and Silvereye.

Family: Phormiaceae

Dianella revoluta var. *revoluta*
Flax Lily

Description: Perennial lily-like herb. Tufted or mat-like growth. Linear leaves in two rows; alternate; stiff, sometimes twisted; bluish to grey-green above, paler below; prominent midvein; edges slightly to distinctly rolled under, 15–80 cm by 4–12 mm. Leaf merges into a sheath at base. Groups of 2–9 dark blue to violet flowers; 6 stamens with enlarged stalks, orange-yellow towards top, pollen sacs pale-brown to almost black; September–February. Fruit a succulent, pale to dark blue spherical berry; black shiny seeds.

Habitat and Range: Common. On deep sands and dry, shallow sandy or stony soils around Brisbane. Tas., Vic., SA, WA and Qld

Notes: Variable species. Four varieties in South-east Qld; but this is only one likely to be encountered near Brisbane.

Family: Phormiaceae

Gahnia aspera
Sword Grass, Saw Sedge, Saw-leaf

Description: Tufted grass-like sedge, 40–80 cm tall. Solid stems 3–8 mm thick. Long leaves light green to yellow-green; edges rolled under, but sharp enough to cut skin; tip with fine point. Flower spikes 10–25 cm long; in clusters of 7–10; each spikelet consists of single flower surrounded by 7–8 blackish-brown glumes; flowers year-round. Fruit a shiny, dark red-brown nut.

Habitat and Range: Common. On sandy soils in shaded areas, on hill slopes and close to streams, also in dry rainforest. Southern NSW to Nth Qld; also Polynesia and Malasia.

Notes: Aborigines pounded nuts to flour.

Wildlife: Seed — Pied Currawong, Brown Cuckoo-dove; leaves — caterpillars of Spotted, Flame and Varied Sedge-Skippers and Green Darter Butterflies.

Family: Cyperaceae

Goodenia hederacea

Description: Creeping or climbing herb to 80 cm. Multiple stems, often with cotton-like hairs. Leaves alternate, can also form rosette at base; green to silvery-green above, sometimes with short woolly hairs on one surface or both; variable shapes, linear to elliptical; 1–8 cm by 3–40 mm; edges sometimes with teeth; leaf stalk 2–65 mm. Yellow flowers in groups of 1–4 on leafy racemes to 80 cm long; underside of petals hairy; August–March. Fruit a small oval capsule, 8–10 mm long; seeds pale brown.

Habitat and Range: On shallow sandy or stony soils on coastal hills and ranges west of Brisbane. Vic. to Caloundra, Qld, also Springbrook and Ipswich

Notes: Similar to *Goodenia rotundifolia*, see below.

Family: Goodeniaceae

Goodenia rotundifolia
Star Goodenia

Description: Perennial herb — sometimes prostrate with runners; also nearly erect to 50 cm. Leaves alternate; dark green above, paler below, hairy; kidney to almost circular shaped with blunt teeth; 0.8–4.5 cm by 8–45 mm; blunt lobes; tip blunt; base wedge to heart-shaped; leaf stalk 2–25 mm long. Solitary bright yellow flowers, often with dark reddish-brown throat; underside of petals hairy; September–May. Fruit a small, spherical capsule, 4–8 mm long; seeds pale brown.

Habitat and Range: On sandy soils on coastal hills and ranges, often in disturbed areas. Hunter River, NSW, to Rockhampton, Qld, also west to Central Qld and eastern Darling Downs

Notes: Similar to *Goodenia hederacea*, see above.

Family: Goodeniaceae

Haemodorum austroqueenslandicum
Bloodroot

Description: Perennial herb 60–150 cm tall, less when in flower. Bulbous orange-red rootstock. Green sword-like leaves radiating around stem base; 35–70 cm by 1.5–7 mm; numerous longitudinal veins; a few leaves alternate up stem. Flowers dark red-brown to black. Fruit a blackish, 3-lobed capsule.

Habitat and Range: Uncommon. On older dune sands and shallow sandy soils, also in heath. Hat Head, NSW, to Rockhampton and west to Central Qld.

Notes: Similar to *Haemodorum tenuifolium* — nearly cylindrical, slightly flattened leaves, 30–55 cm by 1–2 mm wide; flowers brown or grey, bluish-white lustre outside, red inside; swampy soils and wet heath, Evans Head, NSW, to Fraser I., Qld.

Family: Haemodoraceae

Hybanthus stellarioides
Spade Flower

Description: Perennial herb to 30 cm. Slender wiry stems. Leaves alternate; green above, paler below; narrow and linear; 1–8 cm by 2–8 mm, tip pointed, edges sometimes rolled under; scattered short soft hairs. Solitary orange or yellow, spade-like flowers; September–February. Fruit a small ribbed capsule; pitted seeds.

Habitat and Range: Common. On sandy soils in grass layer of forest, also disturbed areas. Illawarra District, NSW, to Bundaberg, Qld.

Notes: Previously known as *Hybanthus enneaspermus* subsp. *stellarioides*. Similar to *Hybanthus monopetalus* (Ladies' Slipper) — leaves alternate on lower stem, opposite towards top; blue spade-like flowers; favours moist shaded sites, wide distribution.

Family: Violaceae

Imperata cylindrica
Blady Grass

Description: Perennial tufted grass. Stiff erect leaves; linear to ovate; edges with minute sharp teeth; 3–100 cm by 2–20 mm; tip pointed with tuft of long hairs. Flower spikes enclosed by hairy glumes; September–February. Fruit a minute grain 1–1.3 mm long.

Habitat and Range: Widespread. On shallow sandy and sandy-stony soils, also in disturbed areas in Greater Brisbane Region. Australia-wide; also South-east Asia.

Notes: Weedy; a good indicator of recent fires and other disturbance. Spreads by means of an underground stem and less commonly from seed. Aboriginal people in Nth Qld used leaves for dilly bags and for thatching huts.

Family: Poaceae

Laxmannia gracilis
Wire Lily

Description: Tufted erect, perennial herb to 40 cm. Often with stilt-like, fibrous roots. Leaves alternate; dark green; linear and cylindrical, to triangular in cross section; 4–75 mm by 1–2 mm; leaves merge into sheath at base; tip with sharp point; edges hairy. Small lily-like, pink and white flowers in groups of 4–17; surrounded by ring of rough, red-brown outer bracts; flowers tend to open at dusk; August–November. Fruit a minute capsule, ovoid to globular; 2–3 mm.

Habitat and Range: Widespread. On moist sandy soils in open stony areas, also alongside paths in moist places and heath. SA, Vic. and NSW to Nth Qld.

Notes: Variable species. Similar to *Laxmannia compacta* — prostrate or stilted spreading herb to about 10 cm; occurs in heath and shrubland.

Family: Anthericaceae

Lepidosperma laterale var. *laterale*
Variable Swordsedge

Description: Sparsely clumped, grass-like plant to 90 cm. Short rhizome; arching sharp-edged flowering stems and leaves look similar. Leaves arranged around base; shorter than stems, linear, flat or slightly convex, 40–90 cm by 2–6 mm; tip pointed. Brown flower spikelets in panicle 6–30 cm long; surrounded by 6 pointed glumes; brown leaf-like bract at base. Fruit an oblong to egg-shaped nut, 2.5–3 mm long.

Habitat and Range: Widespread. On deep sands and sandy and stony soils SA, Tas., NSW to Nth Qld.

Notes: Several similar species. *Lepidosperma laterale* var. *angustum* — flat stems 2–2.5 mm wide; sometimes in eucalypt woodland. *Lepidosperma laterale* var. *majus* — flat stems 5–10 mm wide; sometimes in mountain areas.

Family: Cyperaceae

Lobelia gibbosa

Description: Small erect herb to 50 cm. Reddish stems. Few leaves; alternate; linear to lanceolate, 1–7 cm long by 1–6 mm; tip with sharp point; base wedge-shaped; edges entire or sometimes with a few irregular teeth; usually no stalk. Mauve-blue flowers in groups of 1–3 on one side of a raceme 3–8 mm long; October–March. Deep blue fruit; seed capsule asymmetrical and ovoid; 4–7 mm by 4–6 mm.

Habitat and Range: Common. In rocky areas, or on shallow sandy and stony soils. Most states to North Qld.

Notes: Seven species of *Lobelia* in region. *Lobelia purpurascens* (White Root) — sometimes troublesome weed of lawns and gardens; sharply-toothed, stalked leaves, green above, purple below; small white flowers.

Family: Campanulaceae

Lomandra confertifolia subsp. *confertifolia*
Mat Rush

Description: Tufted grass-like, perennial herb, slightly leaning, to 30 cm. Leaves light green; flat or slightly rounded in cross-section; 3.5–25 cm by 0.5–1.5 cm; 2–3 fine teeth at tip, middle tooth often shortest; area below teeth sometimes light brown. Small yellow-purple flowers inside leaves; September–May. Fruit a dark brown capsule to 5 mm long; splits along back.

Habitat and Range: Rare. Confined to rocky crevices on mountain tops in Greater Brisbane Region, also north to Rockhampton.

Notes: Similar to *Lomandra confertifolia* subsp. *pallida* — leaves 30–70 cm by 1–2.5 mm; flowers July–November; common in coastal areas on deep sands and sandy or stony soils in rocky areas around Brisbane.

Family: Xanthorrhoeaceae

Lomandra longifolia
Spiny-headed Mat Rush

Description: Tufted, perennial grass-like herb, forms clumps to 1 m tall. Leaves green, flat; 50–100 cm by 4–8 mm; tip shaped like a 'W' with 2–3 teeth; central tooth above or below 2 outside teeth; area below teeth light brown. Small yellow-purple flowers in clusters; September–February. Dark brown seed capsules about 5 mm long.

Habitat and Range: Common and widespread. In most forest types around Brisbane, but mainly in moist or shaded positions along drainage lines. Tas., SA and Vic. to Nth Qld.

Notes: Planted as ornamental. Similar to *Lomandra hystrix* — more robust; flowering stems with 4 branches; leaves to 5–11 mm wide; often has 2–4 minute teeth well below tip; riverine habitat.

Family: Xanthorrhoeaceae

Lomandra multiflora
Many-flowered Mat Rush

Description: Perennial grass-like herb, forms sparse clumps to 90 cm tall. Leaves thick, semi-circular in cross-section; blue to grey-green; lighter longitudinal veins; 25–90 cm by 1.5–4 mm; tip rounded, lacks teeth. Creamy-yellow flowers in clusters; June–January. Male and female flowers on separate plants; male — on stalks, drooping; female — lack stalks. Dark brown seed capsule to 5 mm long.

Habitat and Range: Common. On sandy soils on coast, hills and ranges in Greater Brisbane Region. Vic. to Nth Qld and NT.

Notes: Attractive when in flower, but not obvious at other times.

Wildlife: Leaves — caterpillars of Heath Ochre, Black-ringed Ochre, Brown Ochre and Orange Ochre Butterflies.

Family: Xanthorrhoeaceae

Murdannia graminea
Slug Herb, Blue Murdannia

Description: Slender grass-like perennial herb 10–60 cm tall. Roots thick and tuberous. Leaves with sheath at base of blade; a few smaller leaves on flowering stems; roughly hairy; linear, 5–30 cm by 2–11 mm; tip pointed, sometimes purplish and hairy; short leaf sheath at base. Small flowers — outer segments sepal-like, greenish, 6–8 mm long; 3 inner segments petal-like, blue or lavender, rarely white; 3 stamens; December–April. Fruit ellipsoid, 6–10 mm long; seeds grey-brown, angular and pitted.

Habitat and Range: Common. On moist sandy soils around Brisbane. Gundagai, NSW, to Nth Qld, also NT and WA.

Notes: Blue flowers more common west of coastal lowlands.

Family: Campanulaceae

Poa labillardieri var. *labillardieri*
Tussock Grass

Description: Fine tufted grass to 1.2 m tall. Leaf blades slightly rigid; linear; 0–80 cm by 1–3.5 mm; flat or rolled under at edges; covered with rough to soft hairs, rough to touch; minute hairs at tip of blade; leaf sheath open, pale at base; Flower spikelets in narrow panicle 10–25 cm long; flowers most of year. Glumes of spikelets with 1–3 veins; upper glume slightly longer, 2–3.5 mm, with rough hairs. Fruit a minute grain 1–2 mm long.

Habitat and Range: Mainly confined to mountain areas at moderate to high altitudes, often in moist soils along drainage lines and soaks, also in wet eucalypt forest. Vic. to Townsville, Qld.

Wildlife: Habitat for ground-dwelling frogs. Leaves – caterpillars of Chequered Grass-skipper and Marbled Xenica Butterflies.

Family: Poaceae

Pomax umbellata
Pomax

Description: Perennial dense small shrub, 10–40 cm. Multi-branched with hairy stems, often more obvious when in flower and fruit. Leaves opposite; dull green above, paler and often hairy below; ovate to lanceolate, 4–30 mm by 2–13 mm; tip pointed; base wedge-shaped to tapered; edges sometimes wavy and rolled inwards above. Minute dull red flowers; 2–4 joined at base and surrounded by calyx-like cup, 2–3 mm long; September–May. Flowers bisexual. Fruit a top-shaped capsule with 2 valves.

Habitat and Range: Often on deep sand, sandy and stony soils in eucalypt forest or in heath understorey, often in disturbed areas on edges of paths in Greater Brisbane Region. Australia-wide.

Notes: Persistent calyx-like, lobed cup and opposite leaves help identify this plant.

Family: Rubiacaeae

Stylidium debile
Frail Trigger Plant

Description: Small herb to 40 cm. Leaves in rosette and also alternate up stem; spoon-shaped, obovate, 5–30 mm by 2–15 mm; tip blunt, sometimes with short fine point; edges entire and hairless. Whitish to mauve, pink, or reddish, orchid-like flowers in slender raceme or panicle; sparse glandular hairs; 2 stamens and stigma fused into single red column; September–May. Fruit a cylindrical capsule; smooth brownish seeds.

Habitat and Range: Widespread. In swampy areas or permanently moist soaks, on deep sands or sandy and stony soils in shaded areas or along drainage lines. Tuggerah Lakes, NSW, to Rockhampton and west to Central Qld.

Notes: Red column bent down until feeding insect 'triggers' pollen release. One of five trigger plants in region.

Family: Stylidiaceae

Stylidium graminifolium
Grass Trigger Plant

Description: Grass-like herb to 80 cm. Leaves linear to elliptical, 5–40 cm by 1–6 mm; tip pointed; longitudinal veins; edges entire or with minute teeth, usually hairless; lack stalks. Pink orchid-like flowers in slender raceme that is up to half length of flowering stalk; 5-lobed corolla, one lobe shorter, narrows to rounded point, often curved down; 2 stamens and stigma fused into single red column; flower stalk 20–75 cm long; August–January. Fruit an egg-shaped to oblong capsule 5–12 mm long; seeds smooth, brownish.

Habitat and Range: Widespread. Mainly in moist soaks on deep sands, sandy and stony soils in shaded areas. SA, Tas., Vic. and NSW to Nth Qld.

Notes: Red column bent down until feeding insect 'triggers' pollen release.

Family: Stylidiaceae

Themeda triandra
Kangaroo Grass

Description: Tufted perennial grass to about 1 m. Leaves clustered around base, alternate up stems; blue-green or bright green; older leaves persistent, fading to light brown; linear 50 cm by 2–5 mm; tip flattened; edges rough to touch; open leaf sheath at base of blade. Flower spikelets reddish-brown; resemble kangaroo paws; July–February. Fruit a minute grain.

Habitat and Range: Widespread and common. On more fertile deeps sands, on sandy soils. Australia-wide; also New Guinea.

Notes: Previously known as *Themeda australis*. Sometimes planted as ornamental.

Wildlife: Leaves — caterpillars of Evening Brown, Orange Ringlet, Ringed Xenica and Common Brown Butterflies; Grey Kangaroo.

Family: Poaceae

Thysanotus tuberosus
Fringed Lily

Description: Perennial herb to 30 cm. Tuberous root system. Leaves linear to more-or-less cylindrical towards tip; 20–60 cm long; fluted below with membranous wings at base that are sometimes lost by flowering time. Groups of 1–8, mauve lily-like flowers in panicle 20–60 cm long; flower stalks equally long, 6–22 mm, jointed at middle; two whorls of 6 petals; inner whorl fringed along edges; September– February. Fruit a capsule 3–7 mm wide; seeds black.

Habitat and Range: Widespread. On sandy and stony soils in eucalypt communities, also in heath in Greater Brisbane Region. SA, Vic, NSW, to Nth Qld.

Notes: Previously included in family Liliaceae. Aboriginal people reputedly ate tuberous roots.

Family: Anthericaceae

Tricoryne anceps subsp. *pterocaulon*

Description: Wiry perennial, lily-like plant to 70 cm long. Often in clumps or mat-like thickets. Short rhizome and fibrous roots. Dark shiny green, winged branches function as leaves; grass-like leaves only present at seedling stage. Minute yellow, lily-like flowers; in groups of 3–22 in clusters; winged flowering stems 1–5 mm wide, with longitudinal ridges; September–February. Fruit divided into 3 segments, obovoid; 5–7 mm long.

Habitat and Range: Sometimes locally common. On sandy soils on slopes, often in shaded areas along edges of drainage lines in Greater Brisbane Region. Coffs Harbour, NSW, to Nth Qld; also New Guinea.

Notes: Similar to *Tricoryne elatior,* see below. Previously included in family Liliaceae

Family: Anthericaceae

Tricoryne elatior
Yellow Rush Lily

Description: Fine, wiry perennial plant, 10–40 cm. Short rhizome and fibrous roots. Leaves basal; blue-green; linear 5–10 cm by 2–4 mm; reduced to scales on upper flowering branches. Light yellow, lily-like flowers; in groups of 2–10 in umbels; flowering stems, cylindrical, slightly striped with longitudinal ridges sometimes with rough hairs at base; September–February. Fruit divided into 3 segments, ellipsoid; 4–6 mm long.

Habitat and Range: Widespread and common. On deep sands, sandy loams and lateritic soils, also sometimes in heath or on edges of swampland. WA, SA, NT Vic., and NSW to Nth Qld.

Notes: Similar to *Tricoryne anceps* subsp. *pterocaulon*, see above. Previously included in the family Liliaceae

Family: Anthericaceae

Viola betonicifolia subsp. *betonicifolia*
Purple Violet

Description: Erect perennial herb. Very short stem. Leaves form clumps around base; narrowly ovate to spade-shaped, 1–7.5 cm by 5–30 mm; tip pointed or blunt; edges entire or sometimes with shallow, rounded teeth; leaf stalk to 12 cm long. Dark purple to violet flowers, lowest petal with white markings; occasionally all-white flowers; solitary; flower stalks to 20 cm; September–February. Fruit a 3-valved capsule.

Habitat and Range: Widespread. Usually in moist areas, coast to mountain ranges. SA, Vic., Tas. and NSW to Mackay, Qld.

Notes: Similar to *Viola hederacea* (Ivy-leaved Violet), see p. 55.

Wildlife: Leaves — caterpillar of Laced Fritillary Butterfly (Rare and Threatened).

Family: Violaceae

Wahlenbergia gracilis
Australian Bluebell

Description: Sprawling or sometimes tufted perennial herb to 50 cm. Lower leaves alternate; elliptical to obovate; 0.5–3.5 cm by 3–10 mm; tip usually rounded; base wedge-shaped; edges often wavy; leaf stalk 0–15 mm long. Upper stem leaves lack stalk; linear to narrow and elliptical, 1–6.5 cm by 1.5–7 mm; edges wavy or with small hard teeth. Blue flowers; calyx with 5-lobes; September–May. Seed capsule like an upside-down cone.

Habitat: Widespread. On sandy and stony soils in Greater Brisbane Region, often in lawns, gardens and in cleared or disturbed areas. All states except WA; also New Guinea, New Caledonia and New Zealand.

Notes: Similar to *Wahlenbergia stricta* (Tall Bluebell) — hairy; leaves mostly opposite; lack stalk; blue flower; in range of habitats and disturbed areas.

Family: Campanulaceae

FERNS

Calochlaena dubia
Mountain Bracken

Description: Ground fern forming dense thickets to about 1.5 m tall. Creeping rhizome with soft silvery, silky brown hairs. Stalks of frond woody, covered with knotty protuberances; hairs towards darkish base. Foliage lacy, leathery to herbaceous texture. Fronds light yellow-green, paler below; drooping at tips, broadly triangular; 30–80 cm long. Sori on underside edges of frond lobes.

Habitat and Range: Sometimes locally common. On shallow sandy and stony soils in moist gullies and along drainage lines and watercourses on coastal hills and ranges, also in wet eucalypt forest and sometimes riverine rainforest. Tas., Vic. and NSW to Townsville, Qld.

Notes: Previously known as *Culcita dubia*.

Family: Dicksoniaceae

Drynaria rigidula
Basket Fern

Description: Hardy fern, creeping or in clumps, sometimes an epiphyte. Creeping rhizome with dense red hairy scales; fronds often with hairy scales and star-shaped hairs. Two types of fronds — short, oval 'nest-leaves', brown and paper-like, catch soil and litter, 10–30 cm by 6–8 cm, no stalks; large green fronds, leathery or paper-like on short winged stalks, 6–150 cm long, occasionally to 2 m, tip pointed, base wedge-shaped, edges with teeth. Sori in single row either side of midrib on underside of frond, but visible as rounded bumps on upper surface.

Habitat and Range: Mainly in rocky areas on hillsides; also shaded positions and in dry rainforest in Greater Brisbane Region. Clarence River, NSW, to Nth Qld; also Malasia and Polynesia. Rare in NSW.

Family: Polypodiaceae

Psilotum nudum

Description: Terrestrial, or less commonly epiphytic primitive plant. Rhizome short, creeping and much branched, with minute, root-like growths and buds. Yellow-green aerial stems; much branched towards ends to about 75 cm long, then open and drooping. Aerial stems repeatedly divided into two more-or-less equal branches; ridged to nearly circular or triangular in cross-section. Minute scale-like appendages spiralling around stem represent 'leaves'.

Habitat and Range: In sandstone and other rock crevices, or sometimes as an epiphyte on trees, also in rainforest in Greater Brisbane Region. Vic. and NSW, to Nth Qld, NT, WA, NZ; widespread in tropics and subtropics world-wide.

Notes: Sometimes planted as ornamental. Member of *Psilophyta* group of plants; sometimes considered ancestors of true ferns; fossils found in rocks of Devonian Period, 350–400 million-years-old.

Family: Psilotaceae

LILIES

Dianella caerulea* var. *producta
Blue Flax Lily

See p. 97

Dianella revoluta* var. *revoluta
Flax Lily

See p. 98

Thysanotus tuberosus
Fringed lily

See p. 107

Tricoryne elatior
See p. 108

ORCHIDS

Dipodium variegatum
Hyacinth Orchid

Description: Leafless ground orchid 25–60 cm tall. Flowering stems greenish to purplish-red. Flowers in racemes; creamy white to pink with deep maroon blotches; labellum mauve to maroon; petal-like segments narrow, ovate and slightly curved, 1.2–1.7 cm long; August–January. Flower stalks with maroon spots. Fruit a capsule.

Habitat and Range: On deep sands and moist sandy soils, sometimes in heath around Brisbane. Vic. to Rockhampton, Qld.

Notes: Similar to *Dipodium punctatum* — pink flower and stalk, December–April. Also similar to *Dipodium hamiltonianum* (Yellow Hyacinth Orchid) — yellow-green petals with red or mauve spots; coastal wallum, September–December. Edible stalks taste like asparagus.

Family: Orchidaceae

Dockrillia linguiformis
Tick Orchid, Tongue Orchid. Thumbnail Orchid

Description: Orchid with wiry prostrate stems, grows on tree trunks and rocks. Stems root along length. Leaves alternate; thick, flattened, succulent with longitudinal furrows above; oblong to obovate, 2–4 cm by 7–15 mm wide. Cream to white flowers in groups of 6–20 in racemes; labellum cream with pale purple markings; August–October. Fruit a capsule.

Habitat and Range: In rocky exposed sites in open forest and sometimes rainforest in Greater Brisbane Region. Ulladulla, NSW, to Bundaberg, Qld, also west to Burnett and Darling Downs Districts.

Notes: Previously known as *Dendrobium linguiforme*.

Family: Orchidaceae

VINES AND CLIMBERS

Cayratia clematidea
Slender Grapefruit

Description: Weak climbing plant to 2 m. Climbs by means of tendrils; underground stem forms small tubers. Stems and flower parts sometimes covered with short dense hairs. Leaves alternate; usually divided into five leaflets, arranged like fingers of hand; end leaflet largest; toothed edges, oval or elliptical, 1–8.5 cm by 0.5–4 cm. Small greenish flowers grouped on common stalk. September–February. Fruit a blackish globular berry; 5–7 mm wide; 2–4 seeds.

Habitat and Range: Sometimes common. In moist alluvial soils, sandy or rocky areas and rainforest edges. Shoalhaven, NSW, to Nth Qld.

Wildlife: Fruit — Lewin's Honeyeater, Wompoo Fruit-dove; leaves — caterpillar of Joseph's Coat Moth.

Family: Vitaceae

Eustrephus latifolius
Wombat Berry

Description: Wiry twinning, climber to 1 m; often scrambles over itself. Dark green stem initially leafless, but soon develops many branches and leaves in two rows. Leaves bright green above, paler below; linear to ovate, 3–12 cm by 1–45 mm; no obvious midrib above, several raised, parallel longitudinal veins below; tiny leaf stalk. Pink or white flowers in drooping clusters. Flower segments in two whorls; inner 3 segments fringed with hairs. Fruit an orange globular berry; 1–2 cm wide; black seeds.

Habitat and Range: Common in most habitats. On sandy soils; more common in moist shaded areas; also rainforest. Vic. to Qld; also Pacific Is. and Melanesia.

Notes: Similar to *Geitonoplesium cymosum* (Scrambling Lily) see p.114.

Family: Philesiaceae

Geitonoplesium cymosum
Scrambling Lily

Description: Wiry, twining climber; often scrambles over itself. Dark green stem initially leafless, but soon develops many branches and leaves in two rows. Leaves alternate; shiny dark green above, paler below; linear to ovate; 1.5–13 cm by 2–40 mm; distinct midrib above, several parallel longitudinal veins; leaf stalk 1–5 mm long. Drooping white flowers in clusters; flower segments in 2 whorls; inner segments lack hairs; September– February. Buds with green tips. Fruit a black berry to 2 cm wide.

Habitat and Range: Common, but confined to moist shaded areas along drainage lines, also on edges of all types of rainforest in Greater Brisbane Region. Vic. to Qld; also Pacific Is. and Malaysia

Notes: Similar to *Eustrephus latifolius* (Wombat Berry) see p. 113.

Family: Philesiaceae

Hardenbergia violacea
Native Sarsaparilla

Description: Small, scrambling or prostrate, plant to 2 m long. Leathery leaves alternate; dark green above, paler bluish-green below; ovate to narrow and lanceolate, 3–12 cm by 1–5 cm; tip blunt or with sharp point; base heart-shaped; prominent net veins; leaf stalk 1 cm long with 2 scale-like leaflets 1 mm from blade. Attractive bright purple pea flower in groups of 20–30 in a raceme or panicle; September–November. Oblong, flattish seed pod, 20–45 mm long,

Habitat and Range: Widespread. On sandy or stony soils in Greater Brisbane Region. All states, except WA.

Notes: Often grows with *Corymbia* spp. (Spotted Gums), see pp.141-143. Planted as ornamental.

Wildlife: Flowers — Eastern Spinebill; leaves — caterpillar of Common Grass-blue Butterfly.

Family: Fabaceae

Kennedia rubicunda
Red Kennedy Pea, Running Postman

Description: Scrambling twining or prostrate plant. Often forms dense mats; rusty stems to 4 m long, with silky hairs. Leaves alternate; in groups of 3; green above, paler below; often covered in rusty, silky hairs; rounded to ovate, 3–15 cm by 1–8 cm; edges often wavy. Dark red or purple flowers in groups of 2–12 in raceme 4–5 cm long; calyx with dense silky hairs 10–15 mm long; August–November. Flat seed pods also with dense silky hairs; 5–10 cm by 8–10 mm.

Habitat and Range: Common. On sandy and stony soils, also disturbed areas in Greater Brisbane Region. Vic. to Nth Qld.

Wildlife: Flowers — Lewin's, Brown and New Holland Honeyeaters, Eastern Spinebill.

Family: Fabaceae

Smilax australis
Austral Sarsaparilla

Description: Scrambling climber with spiny stems and paired tendrils. Leathery leaves alternate; dark shiny green above, paler below; ovate to broadly lanceolate, 4–15 cm by 2–10 cm; tip rounded or with fine point; base heart-shaped or rounded; 5 longitudinal veins. Creamy-green flowers in clusters; male and female flowers on separate plants; July–November. Fruit a globular black berry, 6–10 mm wide.

Habitat and Range: Fairly common on sandy and stony soils, often along drainage lines or in more shaded areas, also edges of rainforest. Vic. and NSW to North Qld and NT.

Notes: Similar to *Smilax glyciphylla*, see p. 309. Aborigines reputedly ate raw ripe fruit, which has a pleasant, slightly hot taste.

Family: Smilacaceae

SHRUBS AND TREES

Acacia complanata
Flat-stemmed Wattle

Description: Arching shrub 2–5 m tall. Multi-stemmed. New branchlets are flattened with darker green 'wings' along edge and tend to grow in a slightly zig-zag pattern. Older stems brownish-grey, more cylindrical, lose wings. Phyllodes alternate; light yellowish-green to dark green; elliptical to oval, slightly curved towards blunt tip; 5–12 cm by 1.5–4.5 cm; 9 longitudinal veins. Phyllode stalk 2–3 mm long. Small volcano-like gland on upper edge, 0.2–1.2 cm from base. Yellow puffball flowers in clusters of 4–8 globular heads; each head 40–45 flowers; November–May. Fruit a flattish pod.

Habitat and Range: Uncommon. On shallow sandy and stony soils in forest understorey, sometimes forms thickets. Coffs Harbour, NSW, to Bundaberg, Qld.

Notes: Aboriginal people used wood for boomerangs, shields and clubs; inner bark used for twine. This species sometimes shoots from underground stem around base after fire has killed above-ground stems; this results in mallee-like growth; allows species survival by vegetative reproduction rather than just seed.

Wildlife: Gum and seeds — Squirrel Glider; seeds — Pale-headed Rosella.

Family: Mimosaceae

Acacia concurrens
Black Wattle, Curracabah

Description: Tall shrub 2–10 m. Bark grey to brown; slightly furrowed; new growth and buds with dust-like covering; new branches angular. Phyllodes alternate; greyish-green; slightly curved; tip blunt; 10–16 cm by 1–3 cm; 3–4 longitudinal veins linked by cross-veins, lower 2 run together to edge. Minute volcano-like gland at phyllode base. Phyllode stalk brownish-green; 5–9 mm long. Light yellow flowers in dense paired spikes 5–10 cm long; July–August. Fruit a narrow coiled pod.

Habitat and Range: Common. On sandy and stony soils in forest understorey; also in regrowth areas and roadside verges in drier areas. Swansea, NSW, to Pialba, Qld, also west to Burnett and Darling Downs Districts.

Notes: Previously known as *Acacia cunninghamii*. Similar to *Acacia leiocalyx*, see p. 121, and *Acacia disparrima* subsp. *disparrima*, see p. 118. Like all adult acacias which lack 'true leaves', when seeds of *Acacia concurrens* germinate, first few phyllodes on seedling are narrow and sometimes topped with a few leaflets that are soon lost. Acacia seeds have hard seed case; high temperatures of bush fires break case and increase germination rates of seeds stored in soil. Ability to fix nitrogen gives Acacias and other plants like she-oaks a competitive edge in nitrogen poor soils after fires or removal of topsoil. Aboriginal people used wood and bark, ate seeds and roots. Infusion made from bark to treat coughs and colds.

Wildlife: Medium pollen source for honey.

Family: Mimosaceae

Acacia disparrima subsp. *disparrima*
Hickory Wattle

Description: Small tree. 2–15 m. Dark bluish-grey scaly bark. Phyllodes alternate; blue to grey-green; curved; 5–15 cm by 0.6 cm; tip pointed; 1–3 fine, prominent longitudinal veins, many finer veins running parallel, no cross veins. Small volcano-like gland at base. Greenish phyllode stalk with dust-like covering; 2–5 mm long. Cream or yellow flowers in single or paired spikes; January–May. Fruit a flat woody pod; straight or curved; thickened edges.

Habitat and Range: On deep sands behind foredunes, sandy and stony soils in moist areas in Greater Brisbane Region. Grows best on alluvial soils along watercourses and edges of rainforest. Bellingen River, NSW, to Bundaberg and Burnett District, Qld.

Notes: Previously known as *Acacia aulacocarpa*. Similar to *Acacia concurrens*, see p. 117, but lacks dust-like covering on new phyllodes. Used as an ornamental, but may grow to a small to medium-sized tree, not suited to a suburban block. Aboriginal people used wood for boomerangs and clubs.

Wildlife: Seeds — Australian King Parrot; leaves — caterpillars of Imperial Hairstreak Butterfly; pollen source for bees.

Family: Mimosaceae

Acacia fimbriata
Brisbane Golden Wattle, Fringed Wattle

Description: Often crooked tall shrub to 6 m. Smooth grey-brown bark; branches angular or flattened, sometimes hairy along ridges. Phyllodes alternate; dark-green; straight or slightly curved; linear to narrow and elliptical; 2–6.5 cm by 2–5 mm; tip with short sharp point; single midvein, faint lateral veins; fringe of fine white hairs around edge. Prominent volcano-like gland on upper edge 1–6 mm from base. Profuse bright yellow flowers in globular heads; each head 10–20 flowers; June–November. Fruit a flat pod; whitish-blue lustre.

Habitat and Range: In moist gullies and along watercourses on sand and stony soils sometimes on hillsides and edges of dry rainforest in Greater Brisbane Region. Nerriga, NSW, to Bundaberg, Qld, also Stanthorpe District.

Notes: Similar to *Acacia perangusta*, see p. 122. Aboriginal people probably used gum and seeds after treatment. Planted as ornamental. Attractive growth habit, but like all acacias has a relatively short life span, around 10 years.

Wildlife: Seeds — King Parrot and Crimson Rosella; leaves — caterpillar of Imperial Hairstreak Butterfly; medium pollen source for bees.

Family: Mimosaceae

Acacia implexa
Lightwood

Description: Tall shrub 2–12 m tall. Bark grey. Drooping branches; smaller branches nearly cylindrical or slightly angular; whitish-blue lustre. Phyllodes alternate; green to dark green; narrow, elliptical, slightly curved; 7–18 cm by 6–25 mm; tip blunt or sharp, sometimes with short fine point; base tapers to stalk; 3–7 prominent longitudinal veins, numerous cross veins. Inconspicuous volcano-like gland at phyllode base. Phyllode stalk 2–7 mm long. Creamy flowers in globular heads on raceme; each raceme 4–8 heads; December. Fruit a narrow flat pod, but coiled and twisted; seeds on whitish folded stalk.

Habitat and Range: On sandy and shallow stony soils in southern and western areas of Greater Brisbane Region. Vic. and NSW to eastern Darling Downs, Qld.

Notes: Often forms suckers.

Wildlife: Seeds — Emerald Dove, Wonga Pigeon, Australian King Parrot and Eastern Rosella. Leaves — caterpillars of Moonlight Jewel, Stencilled Hairstreak and Two-spotted Line Blue Butterflies.

Family: Mimosaceae

Acacia irrorata subsp. *irrorata*
Green Wattle

Description: Shrub or small tree, 2–14 m tall. Smooth or slightly fissured bark; new growth often yellowish-green; branchlets ribbed with dense yellow hairs. Feathery green leaves consist of 9–pairs of leaflets; alternate; hairy. Prominent volcano-like gland on main stem near upper 1–4 pairs of leaflets. Creamy globular heads of about 30 flowers on soft hairy racemes; September–February. Fruit a narrow flat pod, straight or slightly curved.

Habitat and Range: In moist gullies and along creeks, also on hills and ranges and edges of rainforest. Bermagui, NSW, to Bundaberg, Qld, also eastern Darling Downs.

Notes: Unlike most other wattles around Brisbane, retains true leaves.

Family: Mimosaceae

Acacia leiocalyx
Black Wattle

Description: Shrub or small tree, 2–10 m. Grey to brown, slightly furrowed bark on older specimens; branchlets sharply angled or flattened, often reddish; new growth sometimes bronze-green with a slight dust-like covering. Phyllodes alternate; light to dark green; slightly curved; 8–16 cm by 10–30 mm; tip sharp to blunt; 3 prominent longitudinal veins running together towards base, linked by cross veins. Minute volcano-like gland at phyllode base. Phyllode stalk 3–4 mm long. Yellow flowers in paired spikes 3–7 cm long; May–August. Fruit a loosely coiled pod.

Habitat and Range: Common. On deep sands, on sandy and stony soils in forest understorey, also in regrowth areas and along roadside verges. Mittagong NSW, to Bundaberg, Qld.

Notes: Previously known as *A. cunninghamii*. Similar to *A. concurrens*, see p. 117.

Family: Mimosaceae

Acacia penninervis var. *longiracemosa*
Mountain Hickory

Description: Erect or spreading tall shrub, 2–8 m tall. Bark greyish, furrowed; branchlets cylindrical. Leathery phyllodes alternate; dark green; narrow, elliptical and slightly curved; 5–15 cm by 0.7–4 cm; prominent light green midvein (sometimes looped) with finer side veins; tip blunt or sharp; base sometimes asymmetrical. Small volcano-like gland 5–30 mm above phyllode base. Phyllode stalk sometimes hairy. Creamy globular heads of 10–30 flowers in racemes; July–September. Fruit a straight, flat pod.

Habitat and Range: On deep sands, on sandy and shallow stony soils, usually in higher rainfall areas on hills and mountains in Greater Brisbane Region. Grafton, NSW, to Bundaberg, Qld; also Burnett District.

Family: Mimosaceae

Acacia perangusta
Eprapah Wattle

Description: Shrub or small, often crooked, tree to about 6 m. Smooth grey-brown bark on older specimens. Branches angular or flattened but not hairy. Phyllodes alternate; green; straight or slightly curved, usually linear, 3–7.5 cm by 1–2 mm; tip with sharp point; single fine, but prominent midvein, faint lateral veins. Volcano-like gland on upper edge of phyllode, 7–14 mm from base. Bright yellow globular heads of 9-12 flowers, June–September. Fruit a flat pod, slightly raised over seeds; whitish blue lustre.

Habitat and Range: Rare. Confined to moist gullies and along watercourses on sandy and stony soils to south and south-east of Brisbane, also along Burrum River, north of Maryborough, Qld.

Notes: Habitat under threat from urbanisation. Similar to *Acacia fimbriata*, see p.119.

Family: Mimosaceae

Acacia podalyriifolia
Queensland Silver Wattle

Description: Spreading shrub to 5 m. Phyllodes alternate; silvery-grey to whitish-blue; elliptical to oval; 2–5 cm by 1–2.5 cm; edges wavy with fine hairs; prominent midvein slightly offset towards upper edge. Inconspicuous volcano-like gland 0.5–2 cm from phyllode base. Phyllode stalk 1–2 mm long. Bright yellow globular heads of 10–20 flowers in racemes; June–September. Fruit a flat pod; straight or twisted with thick edge; whitish-blue lustre and velvety hairs.

Habitat and Range: On shallow stony hills and ridges in Greater Brisbane Region. Endemic. Legume, NSW, to Brisbane, also Crows Nest and Stanthorpe, Qld

Notes: Popular cultivated species, but often develops sooty mould.

Family: Mimosaceae

Acrotriche aggregata
Ground Berry

Description: Spreading, sprawling shrub to about 1 m tall, sometimes 2–3 m. Mat-like growth. Multi-stemmed; new growth hairy. Prickly leaves alternate; dark green above, whitish-green below; variable shape and size, flat or concave above; sometimes minute teeth on edge towards sharp tip; base blunt; longitudinal veins on underside. Minute green to creamish flowers in clusters of 5–10 or on short spikes; sometimes below leaves. Fruit a succulent red drupe.

Habitat and Range: On deep sands, in rocky areas and on shallow sandy soils in forest understorey, also in dry rainforest. Yerranderie, NSW, to Cairns, Qld.

Notes: Often common with *Xanthorrhoea* spp. (Grass Trees). Similar to *Monotoca scoparia,* see p. 185. Fruit edible, but tasteless.

Family: Epacridaceae

Allocasuarina littoralis
Black She-oak

Description: Small tree 2–15 m. Dark grey, furrowed bark; smaller branches light grey, point upwards. Dark green twig-like 'needles' (branchlets); each branchlet with segments 4–10 mm, easily broken at joints. True leaves a whorl of 6–8 minute, whitish 'teeth' at tip of each segment. Male and female flowers on separate trees. Male — masses of rusty brown flower spikes at ends of branchlets; June–August. Female — bright red flowers lack petals and sepals; clustered on branches; April–October. Dark grey woody cones; cylindrical; 10–30 mm by 8–21 mm; dark brown to black winged seeds.

Habitat and Range: Common. On deep sands and sandy-stony soils in forest understorey in coastal areas, also in regrowth areas and along roadside verges in Greater Brisbane Region. Tas. to Vic., NSW and Nth Qld.

Notes: Sometimes forms thickets with dense mat of shed branchlets covering ground; regrowth of other species may be retarded. Early coloniser of sandblows in places like Moreton I. or Fraser I. Previously known as *Casuarina littoralis*. Similar to *Allocasuarina torulosa*, see opposite. Timber once used as fuel in bread ovens; also suitable for cabinetwork. Sometimes planted as ornamental.

Wildlife: Seeds — black cockatoos.

Family: Casuarinaceae

Allocasuarinas and closely related *Casuarinas* are separated by following general characteristics:

- *Allocasuarina* — red-brown to black, shiny winged seeds; small bracts of woody cone thick, extend only slightly beyond cone body, have separate angular or divided protuberance on back; teeth 4–14; occur mainly on nutrient-deficient soils (except *Allocasuarina torulosa*).

- *Casuarina* — dull grey to yellow-brown winged seeds; small thin bracts of woody cone enclosing seeds extend beyond cone body; lack protuberance; 6–20 teeth; occur mainly on more fertile soils.

Allocasuarina torulosa
Forest She-oak, Rose She-oak

Description: Slender tree 2–30 m tall. Corky, light brown to grey furrowed bark; new growth often plum red. Drooping green, twig-like 'needles' (branchlets); each branchlet with segments 4–7 mm, easily broken at joints. True leaves a whorl of 4–5 minute whitish teeth at tip of each segment. Male and female flowers on separate trees. Male — rusty brown flower spikes at ends of branchlets; June–November. Female — dark red flowers, lack petals and sepals; clustered on branches April–October. Brownish woody and warty cones; 15–35 mm by 12–25 mm; shiny, brown winged seeds.

Habitat and Range: On fertile deep sands, sandy loams and volcanic soils on hillsides and mountain slopes, sometimes on edge of rainforest in wetter areas in Greater Brisbane Region. Nowra, NSW, to Coen, Nth Qld.

Notes: Previously known as *Casuarina torulosa*. Timber burns well; used for veneer and wood turning. Sometimes planted as ornamental. Similar to *Allocasuarina littoralis*, see opposite.

Wildlife: Important food source for Glossy Black Cockatoo.

Family: Casuarinaceae

Alphitonia excelsa
Red Ash, Soap Tree, Soapy Ash

Description: Small tree 2–10 m. Mottled smooth light grey bark becomes darker and furrowed with age; older specimens sometimes covered with encrusting lichens. New shoots golden-brown with velvety hairs. Leaves alternate; dark glossy green above, white with velvety hairs below; lighter green lateral veins in raised loop towards edge of underside, covered with brown hairs. Leaf shape varies, elliptical to oval, 3–15 cm by 1.5–5 cm; tip blunt or pointed; base wedge-shaped; edges rolled under. Tiny cream flowers in panicles; February– June. Fruit a round black berry; red seeds.

Habitat and Range: On deep sands and moist sandy soils, also dry rainforest and rainforest edges in Greater Brisbane Region. Mt Dromedary, NSW, to South-east Qld; also NT and WA.

Notes: New shoots smell of sarsaparilla when crushed. Leaves contain saponin, a chemical released by soaking or crushing leaves in water; useful for washing hands; Aborigines used leaves to catch fish. Opportunistic species of disturbed areas; sometimes regenerating from underground stem.

Wildlife: Leaves — caterpillars of Small Green-banded Blue Butterfly; flattened, whitish caterpillars feed on undersides of leaves sometimes leaving much ravaged plant with few intact leaves.

Family: Rhamnaceae

Amyema congener
Mistletoe

Description: Semi-parasitic shrub. New growth often has dense brownish or whitish matted hairs. Leathery leaves opposite or in whorls; lanceolate to oval, 3–10 cm by 1–5.5 cm; Club-shaped flowers; red and yellow with green tips, in clusters of three on common stalk, 1–3.5 cm long; flowers all year. Fruit elliptical to globular; 8 mm long.

Habitat and Range: Found mostly on *Allocasuarina* or *Casuarina* spp. (She-oaks) or *Acacia* spp. (Wattles) and exotic trees in Greater Brisbane Region. Merimbula, NSW, to Nth Qld.

Notes: Gains some nutrients from host plant. Twenty-five species of mistletoe in South-east Qld; often mimic leaf shape of host plant. Fruit has sweet gelatinous pulp, may be eaten raw.

Wildlife: Flowers — Mistletoe Bird, Lewin's and White-cheeked Honeyeaters, Eastern Spinebill; leaves — caterpillars of Imperial Jezebel, Black Jezebel, Dark Purple Azure, Satin Azure, Southern Purple Azure and Trident Pencilled-blue Butterflies.

Family: Loranthaceae

Angophora floribunda
Rough-barked Apple

Description: Tree 12–20 m. Rough, often-furrowed bark. New buds, branches and stalks velvety hairy, sometimes with long reddish hairs. Leaves opposite; bright green above, paler below; lanceolate to oval, 5–18 cm by 1–4.5 cm; tip tapers to point; base wedge-shaped; leaf stalk to 1 cm. White flowers in dense clusters at end of twigs; prominent stamens in whorls to about 10 mm long; July–January, often flowers better in dry years. Flower bud with wedge-shaped base. Fruit a thin woody capsule with 5 ribs; 6–10 mm by 6–8 mm; ageing to dark grey-brown.

Habitat and Range: Common in drier areas and on ranges to west; often along watercourses on deeper alluvial sandy soils; also along flats and terraces west of Brisbane. Vic. but mainly NSW to Rockhampton, Qld, also west to Goondiwindi, isolated occurrence near Atherton, Nth Qld.

Notes: Opposite leaves, ribbed seed capsule and buds without operculum distinguish this species from most eucalypts in Greater Brisbane Region. Similar to *Angophora subvelutina*, see p. 130 and *Angophora woodsiana* see p 131. Flowers have honey-like scent.

Wildlife: Sap — Sugar Glider; flowers — Rainbow Lorikeet, Noisy Friarbird, Yellow-faced, Yellow-tufted and White-throated Honeyeaters; leaves — caterpillar of Copper Jewel Butterfly; good pollen source for bees.

Family: Myrtaceae

Angophora leiocarpa
Rusty Gum

Description: Tree to 25 m. Often not upright; moderately dense canopy, sometimes with twisted branches. Dimpled, smooth bark; colour variable, pink or grey to whitish cream. Leaves opposite; green above, paler below; lanceolate to oval, 4–16 cm by 1.0–2.5 cm; tip pointed; base wedge-shaped, leaf stalk 10–15 mm. Juvenile leaves usually narrower. White flowers in dense clusters at ends of twigs; prominent stamens to 10 mm long; December–January. Flower buds sometimes hairy; on stalks, to about 1 cm long. Fruit a thin woody capsule; usually smooth or with 5 slight ribs; 0.8–1.2 cm long; often narrowed towards top; ageing to dark brownish-grey.

Habitat and Range: On deep sands and sandy soils of coastal lowlands and stony hills in Greater Brisbane Region. Grafton and Narrabri, NSW, to Qld and NT.

Notes: Opposite leaves separates this species from most eucalypts. Grows with *Eucalyptus racemosa*, see p. 163 and with *Corymbia* spp. on hill slopes. Similar to *Corymbia citriodora* subsp. *variegata*, see p. 141. Previously known as *Angophora costata* —broader leaves; larger capsule 9–15 mm long with 5 distinct ribs; occurs on deep sands or sandy soils in coastal lowlands and hills; Coffs Harbour to Bodalla, NSW. Both species planted as ornamentals.

Wildlife: Flowers — Grey-headed Flying Fox, Crimson Rosella, Noisy Friarbird, White-cheeked Honeyeaters; adult butterflies; leaves — caterpillar of Cyane Jewel Butterfly; koalas; good pollen source for bees.

Family: Myrtaceae

Angophora subvelutina
Broadleaf Apple

Description: Tree to 20 m, often less. Dark grey bark; rough flaky, brittle; sometimes similar to bloodwood or stringybark eucalypts. Small branches often drooping; new growth and flowers with scattered, long reddish hairs and dense, shorter white hairs. Leaves opposite; bright green or with whitish-blue lustre; broadly oval, 6–14 cm by 2–6 cm; tip blunt or acute; base heart-shaped; edges wavy; no stalk. Profuse white flowers in bundles at end of twigs; prominent stamens to 10 mm long; December– January. Flower stalk to 1.5 cm long. Fruit a thin woody capsule; 5 ribs; 6–10 mm by 6–100 mm; brownish, ageing to darker brownish-grey.

Habitat and Range: On alluvial soils, on flats and along watercourses, more common west of Brisbane. Bega, NSW, to Maryborough, Qld, also west to eastern Darling Downs and south-eastern Burnett District.

Notes: Opposite leaves, ribbed capsule and bark texture separates this species from most eucalypts. Similar to *Angophora woodsiana* see opposite. Flowers have pleasant smell. Sometimes planted as ornamental.

Wildlife: Flowers — Queensland Blossom Bat, adult butterflies; good pollen source for bees

Family: Myrtaceae

Angophora woodsiana
Smudgee

Description: Tree 10–20 m, often less. Open canopy. Rough greyish bark; reddish-brown patches sometimes exposed along trunk; sometimes similar to bloodwood or stringybark eucalypts. Fibrous bark varies from slightly flaky to scaly. Long curved leaves opposite; dark green above, paler below; oval, 6–16 cm by 1.5–4.5 cm; red midrib and leaf stalk, particularly on regrowth or young plants. Juvenile leaves larger. Masses of whitish flowers in large bundles at ends of twigs; prominent stamens to about 10 mm; Flower stalks 1–3 cm long. December–January. Fruit a thin woody capsule; 5 ribs; 1–1.8 cm by 1–1.5 cm; ageing to dark brownish-grey.

Habitat and Range: Common. On sandy soils derived from sandstone in forest understorey, coastal lowlands and ranges in Greater Brisbane Region. Coffs Harbour, NSW, to Noosa River, Qld.

Notes: Opposite leaves, ribbed capsule and bark texture separate this species from most eucalypts. Sometimes flowers as a shrub 1–2 m tall; flowers with pleasant honey-like smell. Similar to *Angophora floribunda*, see p. 128.

Wildlife: Good pollen source for bees.

Family: Myrtaceae

Astrotricha latifolia

Description: Shrub or small tree 2–4 m, sometimes taller. New growth, parts of inflorescence and undersides of leaves covered with a tangled mass of loose soft white hairs. Leaves alternate; green to shiny green above, paler and whitish-green below; ovate to elliptical; 8–22 cm by 2–10 cm; tip tapers to fine point; base rounded to slightly heart-shaped; leaf edges sometimes finely wavy. Leaf stalk 2–8 cm long. Yellowish-green flowers densely hairy outside; September–January. Fruit a flattened dry capsule, separates into 2 segments.

Habitat and Range: Sometimes locally common on fertile volcanic soils in wet eucalypt forest, but also on shallow sandy or stony soils of coastal hills and mountain ranges. Bundaberg, Qld, to Narooma, NSW

Notes: Previously known as *Astrotricha floccosa*, — occurs at Binna Burra.

Family: Araliaceae

Austromyrtus dulcis
Midgin, Midyim

Description: Semi-prostrate small shrub, 0.5–1.5 m. Sometimes with mat-like growth; young shoots covered with long hairs. Leaves opposite; dull to shiny green above, paler with white to grey hairs below; ovate, 0.9–3 cm by 3–18 mm; tip tapers to point; base wedge-shaped; leaf stalk 1–3 mm long. New leaves often bronze-green with oil dots visible below (hands lens a help). White flowers solitary or in racemes; sometimes with soft hairs; September–May. Lower half of flower bud with dense hairs. Fruits white to grey with black spots; sometimes with silky hairs.

Habitat: Common. On deep sands on Stradbroke I. and on sandy soil elsewhere, sometimes in montane heath. Urunga, NSW, to Fraser I., Qld.

Notes: Fruit pleasant tasting. Often used as ground cover in native gardens. Some habitat lost to development.

Family: Myrtaceae

Banksia integrifolia subsp. *compar*
Coast Banksia

Description: Tree 2–25 m. Rough, flaky or fissured grey bark; twisted branches; new branches soft and hairy. Leathery leaves alternate; in whorls of 3–5 at end of branches; dark shiny green above, white with short matted hairs below; obovate to oblong, 5–20 cm by 0.6–3.5 cm; edges wavy, sometimes with teeth. Leaves on juvenile plants more sharply toothed. Stiff, pale yellow flower spike on ends of branches; December–July. Woody cones 5–20 cm by 5.5–7.5 cm; each woody follicle along cone contains several winged seeds.

Habitat and Range: On deep sands and sandy loams on coastal lowlands and hills in Greater Brisbane Region. Northern NSW to Proserpine, Nth Qld.

Notes: Two other subspecies in region. *Banksia integrifolia* subsp. *integrifolia*, see p. 26. *Banksia integrifolia* subsp. *monticola* — leaves 10–13 cm, with wavy edges; mainly confined to exposed mountain heath areas, but extends to Darling Downs and Moreton Districts; also to Blue Mountains, NSW.

Wildlife: Flowers — Grey-headed Flying Fox, Queensland Blossom Bat, Eastern Tube-nosed Fruit Bat; Rainbow and Scaly-breasted Lorikeets, Noisy Miner, Noisy Friarbird, Eastern Spinebill, Blue-faced, Lewin's, Scarlet, Yellow-faced, White-naped and Brown Honeyeaters; seed — Yellow-tailed Black-Cockatoo, good pollen source for bees.

Family: Proteaceae

Banksia spinulosa var. *collina*
Golden Candlesticks

Description: Shrub to 2 m tall. Multi-stemmed; smooth to scaly grey-brown bark; branchlets usually hairy. Leaves dark green; whorled at ends of branchlets, alternate below; linear to obovate; 2–12 cm by 0.1–10 mm; base wedge-shaped with white matted hairs below, flat or slightly turned under. Mature leaves below current year's growth, flatter and with edges sharply toothed for more than half length. Stiff brush-like, orange-yellow flower spikes; style hook-shaped, either yellow or deep red to purple-black on upper half; April–August. Woody cone with about 100 woody follicles that contain winged seeds.

Habitat and Range: On deep sands and sandy loam soils, also in heath in Greater Brisbane Region. Hawkesbury River, NSW, to Nambour, Qld.

Notes: Often planted as ornamental. Two other varieties near Brisbane. *Banksia spinulosa* var. *spinulosa* — narrow leaves 1–2 mm wide, toothed near tip, edges rolled under; south-east of Brisbane, east of Gympie in Noosa River catchment. *Banksia spinulosa* var. *cunninghamii* see p. 311.

Wildlife: Flowers — Sugar Glider, Brown Antechinus, Lewin's, Yellow-faced, White-naped, White-cheeked and Scarlet Honey-eaters, Eastern Spinebill; seed — Yellow-tailed Black Cockatoo.

Family: Proteaceae

Banksia spinulosa var. *cunninghamii*
Hairpin Banksia

See p. 311

Boronia polygalifolia
Dwarf Boronia

Description: Semi-prostrate, small shrub 10–60 cm tall. Hairless. Leaves opposite; green above, paler below; narrow and elliptical, 6–30 mm by 1–6 mm; tip narrowed to point or blunt; base tapered; obvious oil dots; each edge of leaf stalk extends down branchlets to form 2 ridges. Solitary light pink or white flowers, sometimes tipped with red or purple; September–January. Fruit flattened, oblong 3.5–5 mm long; petals persistent around fruit.

Habitat and Range: Uncommon. On sandy soils in heathy forest understorey or on rocky outcrops in mountain areas. Moruya, NSW, to Rockhampton, Qld.

Notes: Similar to *Boronia parviflora* (Swamp Boronia) —pink or white flowers in groups of 3 uncommon, swampy coastal heath; Vic. to Maryborough, Qld, also SA and Tas.

Family: Rutaceae

Boronia rosmarinifolia
Forest Boronia

Description: Shrub 0.5–2 m. Leaves opposite; shiny dark green above, sometimes with star-shaped hairs, paler below with dense soft hairs; linear or oblong; 6–40 mm by 1–7 mm; edges rolled under; raised oil glands on upper surface. Flowers with 4 pink petals (occasionally white); 8–10 stamens; July–October. Fruit oblong, slightly flattened segments to about 6 mm.

Habitat and Range: On deep sands and sandy soils; also in dry heath in Greater Brisbane Region. Coffs Harbour, NSW, to Bundaberg, Qld, in Burnett and Darling Downs Districts.

Notes: Species varies across range. Aborigines reputedly used oils from leaves as protection from mosquitoes and leeches.

Family: Rutaceae

Brachychiton populneus
Kurrajong

Description: Evergreen tree to 20 m. Trunk cylindrical to bottle-shaped; dark grey bark; slightly furrowed with fine cracks. Leaves alternate; yellowish, particularly when dry; oval or with 3–5 deep lobes; 4–14 cm by 1–8 cm (to 12.5 cm when lobed); tip tapers to bristle-like point; edge thick; blunt teeth. Flowers creamy-white with speckled dark red throat; bell-shaped calyx with 5–6 petal-like lobes covered with dense short hairs; October–December. Boat-shaped woody fruit; brownish-grey; 4–10 cm long; 4–18 seeds, outer layer with irritant hairs on lower surface.

Habitat and Range: On sandy soils, also in dry rainforest around Brisbane, more common west of region. Eastern and western sides of Great Dividing Range; Vic. and NSW to inland from Townsville, Qld.

Notes: Seeds nutritious, but irritating hairs need to be removed before eating raw or toasted. Aboriginal people made string and rope from inner bark fibre; firesticks and shields from wood. Tuberous roots eaten when young and provided reliable water source in drier areas. Ornamental street tree. Known to form hybrids in the Boonah district with *Brachychiton discolor*, see p. 249 and *Brachychiton rupestris*, see p. 326.

Family: Sterculiaceae

Breynia oblongifolia
Coffee Bush

Description: Shrub 1–2 m. Spreading, sparsely branched. Leaves alternate; in two rows along stem; bluish-green above, paler below; elliptical to oval; 1–4 cm by 0.7–1.5 cm; tip and base rounded. Minute greenish flowers; male and female flowers on same plant; male with 3 stamens fused in a column; female with three short styles; September–December. Fruit a bright red berry turning black; 6 mm wide.

Habitat and range: Widespread, but uncommon. On deep sands, and moist sandy and stony soils, also in dry rainforest and sometimes disturbed areas. Merimbula, NSW, to South-east Qld.

Notes: Sometimes planted as ornamental.

Wildlife: Flowers — White-cheeked Honeyeater; leaves — caterpillars of Large Grass-yellow Butterfly.

Family: Euphorbiaceae

Bursaria spinosa
Prickly Pine

Description: Thorny shrub 1–3 m tall. Small leaves clustered, or in small groups, or alternate; shape varies; 0.5–4.5 cm by 0.4–1.8 cm; tip blunt; base tapered, sometimes with a few hairs. Flowers white or cream in panicle, sometimes only a few; petals narrow; September–May. Fruit a stalked, kidney-shaped capsule; opens around edge to reveal two valves.

Habitat and Range: Can be locally common. On sandy and stony soils in drier forest, sometimes in disturbed areas. WA, SA, Vic., Tas. NSW and South-east Qld.

Notes: Similar to *Bursaria incana* — small tree to 6 m, dark grey slightly furrowed bark; leaves hoary-white below, occurs inland.

Wildlife: Flowers — Eastern Spinebill; leaves — caterpillars of Fiery Copper and Bright Copper Butterflies.

Family: Pittosporaceae

Callistemon salignus
White Bottlebrush

Description: Small tree 2–15 m. Whitish, peeling, papery bark; often with brownish fibres on surface and pinkish bark below. New shoots pink-red with silky hairs, but quickly turn green and lose hairs. Stiff leaves alternate; greyish-green above, slightly darker and glossy below; conspicuous oil glands; elliptical, 3–11 cm by 0.5–2 cm; tip and base tapered; single midrib, lateral veins obvious above; leaf stalk 2–3 mm. Creamy-white bottlebrush flowers in spikes at ends of branchlets; 3–8 cm by 2.5–3 cm; September–November. Fruit a rounded capsule; 4–5 mm wide.

Habitat and Range: On moist sandy and alluvial soils, also edges of rainforest, but mainly along watercourses in Greater Brisbane Region. North-eastern Vic. to Nth Qld.

Notes: Similar to *Melaleuca quinquenervia* see p. 59. Planted as an ornamental and street tree.

Wildlife: Medium source of pollen for bees.

Family: Myrtaceae

Callitris columellaris
Bribie Island Pine

See p. 27

Casuarina cunninghamiana
River She-oak

Description: Tree 10–35 m. Dull green canopy. Dark grey fissured bark. Spreading to slightly drooping, twig-like 'needles' (branchlets); each branchlet segmented, 6–9 mm by 0.4–0.6 mm; easily broken at joints; slightly ridged. Branchlets and fruiting cones covered in minute hairs. True leaves a whorl of 8–10 minute, whitish teeth at tip of each segments; tend to wither over time. Male and female flowers on separate trees. Male — rusty brown flowers grouped in spikes at end of branchlets; June–November. Female — clusters of dark red flowers on branches below current year's growth; lack petals and sepals; April–October. Woody grey globular cone; 5–14 mm by 6–8 mm; numerous winged, grey to yellow-brown seeds.

Habitat and Range: Common on alluvial flats and terraces of permanent freshwater rivers and creeks in Greater Brisbane Region. NSW to Nth Qld.

Notes: Similar to *Casuarina glauca* (Swamp She-oak), see p.58; hybridises with *Casuarina glauca* where ranges meet. Sometimes planted as ornamental. Timber used for casks, axe handles and ornamental turnery; previously used for shingles and bullock yokes; good fuel. Name *she-oak* relates to oak-like look of timber to English Oak, although early settlers considered it inferior. Various insects form distinctive galls on branchlets of she-oak species, may be mistaken for woody cones.

Wildlife: Good pollen source for bees.

Family: Casuarinaceae

Clerodendrum floribundum
Lolly Bush

Description: Shrub or tree, 2–10 m. New growth sometimes with matted hairs; young stems almost square in cross-section. Leaves opposite; shiny green; shape varies, broadly oval to elliptical, 4–18 cm by 2–10 cm; tip blunt or pointed; base rounded, acute or heart-shaped; leaf stalk purplish, 2–7 cm long. White tubular flowers; number varies, sometimes clustered together forming panicle; sometimes with minute hairs; 5-lobed, green calyx; stamens about 2.5 cm long; August–December. Fruit a black berry about 1 cm long, grows on enlarged red, fleshy calyx.

Habitat and Range: Common. On sandy and stony moist soils, also edges of dry rainforest in Greater Brisbane Region. Taree NSW, to Qld and NT.

Notes: Similar to *Clerodendrum tomentosum* — leaves and inflorescences covered in soft dense hairs. Also *Clerodendrum inerme* (Scrambling Clerodendrum) — calyx does not spread under fruit; sometimes in coastal forests inland of mangrove communities. Aborigines reputedly used wood as fire sticks; leaves and inner bark soaked in water and liquid drunk or rubbed on body to relieve colds and other aches.

Wildlife: Leaves — caterpillar of Fiery Jewel Butterfly

Family: Verbenaceae

Corymbia citriodora subsp. *variegata*
Spotted Gum

Description: Erect tree 10–40 m. Fairly open canopy. Smooth 'dimpled' bark; spotted pinkish to silver-grey; sometimes darker or lighter patches along trunk; shed in small sheets or scales, leaves slight depressions ('dimples'). Sometimes drooping, narrow leaves alternate; darkish grey-green above, slightly paler below; lanceolate; 10–23 cm by 1–2.8 cm; tip tapered; base wedge-shaped; leaf stalk 1–3.5 cm long. Seedling and juvenile leaves with stiff hairs; usually broader; sometimes stalks come into leaf blade from below. Cream flowers in raceme or in groups of 2–5 on common stalk; July–September and November–December. Flower buds top to pear-shaped; operculum hemispherical with beak; half as long as hypanthium. Fruit a slightly warty, usually urn-shaped woody capsule; 1–2 cm by 0.8–1.3 cm; 3 enclosed valves.

Habitat and Range: On shallow stony soils on coastal hills, ridges and mountain slopes in Greater Brisbane Region. Coffs Harbour, NSW, to Maryborough, Qld, also west to Carnarvon and Dawes Ranges, north of Monto, and near Warwick on Darling Downs.

Notes: Flowering inconsistent and irregular. Previously known as *Eucalyptus maculata* and *Eucalyptus variegata*. Similar to *Corymbia citriodora* subsp. *citriodora* — trunk often less spotted; leaves with strong lemon scent; planted as ornamental. Also similar to *Angophora leiocarpa*, see p. 129. Timber grey-brown, hard, strong and moderately durable.

Wildlife: Flowers — Grey-headed Flying Fox, Yellow-bellied Glider (+sap), Squirrel Glider (+bark), Scaly-breasted and Little Lorikeets, Noisy Friarbird, Brown and White-cheeked Honeyeaters (in winter when food is scarce); leaves — Koalas, Brushtail Possum, Greater Glider; medium source of pollen for bees; seed — Yellow-tailed Black Cockatoos, Pale-headed Rosella.

Family: Myrtaceae

Corymbia gummifera
Red Bloodwood

Description: Tree 2–40 m. Moderately dense canopy. Rough grey scaly bark; brown to reddish-brown underneath; smaller upper branches smooth, pink-grey. Bark scales rectangular, adhere closely to trunk; sometimes much longer than wide on young trees and saplings. Broad leaves alternate: dark green above, paler below; ovate, 7.5–19 cm by 1–5 cm; tip pointed or tapered; base wedge-shaped; leaf stalk flattened, 1.2–2.5 cm long. Seedling and juvenile leaves with stiff hairs, usually broader than adult leaves; sometimes stalk comes into blade from below. White flowers in groups of 4–8 in umbel on long stalk; December–April. Flower buds ellipsoidal to obovoid; 0.7–1.3 cm long; operculum sometimes pointed, much shorter than rest of bud. Seed capsule usually urn-shaped with lip at top; faintly ridged; sometimes shiny brown; 1–1.8 cm by 0.8–1.5 cm.

Habitat and Range: On deep less fertile sands and shallow sandy or stony soils in Greater Brisbane Region. Eastern Vic. to Fraser I., Qld.

Notes: Often adopts a mallee-like growth on older less fertile sands. Similar to *Corymbia intermedia*, see p. 144. Grows with *Eucalyptus racemosa*, see p. 163 and sometimes *Banksia aemula*, see p. 71, on deep sands. Previously known as *Eucalyptus gummifera*. Aborigines reputedly used flowers for nectar; ate sweet evaporated insect exudate (manna) on leaves; used gum for treating venereal sores. Timber red and durable, but gum veins restrict use to poles, house stumps, mining timber, fencing and hardboard manufacture.

Wildlife: Flowers — Grey-headed Flying Fox, Little Lorikeet, Noisy Friarbird, New Holland and White-cheeked Honeyeaters, Eastern Spinebill; sap — Yellow-bellied Glider, Sugar Glider (+ flowers, manna); fruit — Crimson Rosella.

Family: Myrtaceae

Corymbia henryi
Large-leaved Spotted Gum

Description: Tree 10–30 m. Moderately dense canopy. Smooth 'dimpled' trunk; spotted light pink to grey; colour fairly consistent, but sometimes slightly darker or lighter patches along trunk. Bark shed in small sheets or scales leaving slight depressions ('dimples') in surface. Broad leaves alternate to almost opposite; green above, slightly paler below; lanceolate, 11.5–30 cm by 2–8.5cm; tip tapered; base wedge-shaped or asymmetrical; leaf stalk 1–3 cm long. Seedling and juvenile leaves with stiff hairs, broader than adult leaves; sometimes with stalk coming into blade from below. Whitish flowers in groups of 3 in racemes or panicles; December–February. Flower buds ellipsoidal to top-shaped; 1.2–1.5 cm long; operculum hemispherical to cone-shaped, sometimes with short beak toward tip; as long as, or shorter than, hypanthium. Fruit a woody capsule, often warty; ovoid to urn-shaped; 1.2–2 cm by 1.2–1.5 cm.

Habitat and Range: On shallow sandy or sandy-clay soils in moister sites along drainage lines on coastal hills and ranges in Greater Brisbane Region. Grafton, NSW, to north of Brisbane, Qld.

Notes: Previously known as *Eucalyptus henryi*. Similar to *Corymbia citriodora*, subsp. *variegata*, see p. 141.

Family: Myrtaceae

Corymbia intermedia
Pink Bloodwood

Description: Tree 2–40 m tall. Moderately dense canopy. Rough scaly bark; light brown to brown underneath; smaller branches also with rough bark. Bark scales broad, rectangular, adhere closely to trunk; sometimes much longer than wide on younger trees and saplings. Broad leaves alternate to almost opposite; darkish green above, paler below; ovate; 6–16 cm by 1–4.0 cm, tip tapered or pointed; base wedge-shaped or asymmetrical; leaf stalk 1–2.5 cm long. Seedling and juvenile leaves with stiff hairs; broader than adult leaves; some with stalk coming into blade from below. Whitish flowers in groups of 5–8 in panicles; December–May. Flower buds ellipsoidal to ovoid; 0.7–1.5 cm long; operculum hemispherical to cone-shaped with short beak; shorter than hypanthium. Fruit a woody capsule; ovoid to urn-shaped; 1.2–2 cm by 1–1.8 cm; tip tapered; often with dull, white-spotted, scaly surface; winged seeds.

Habitat and Range: On deep sands, on more fertile sandy or clay loams and moist alluvial soils, sometimes on edge of rainforest in Greater Brisbane Region. Gloucester, NSW, to Cape York, Qld, less common in drier areas between Rockhampton and Townsville.

Notes: Previously known as *Eucalyptus intermedia*. Grows with *Eucalyptus racemosa*, see p. 163, on more fertile soils and sometimes in exposed places close to sea. Similar to *Corymbia gummifera*, see p. 142. Timber pink, strong and durable, but gum veins restrict use to bridgework, railway sleepers, fencing and mining timber.

Wildlife: Flowers — Grey-headed Flying Fox, Rainbow and Scaly-breasted Lorikeets; seed — black cockatoos, Pale-headed Rosella; leaves — Koalas; medium source of honey and pollen for bees.

Family: Myrtaceae

Corymbia tessellaris
Carabeen, Moreton Bay Ash

Description: Tree 10–30 m. Dark grey to black, scaly lower bark to 1–4 m from base of trunk; changes abruptly to smooth white to greyish-white on upper trunk. Bark scales in square to rectangular segments; yellowish when first shed. Narrow leaves alternate; dull grey to blue-green; linear to lanceolate, 6–25 cm by 0.5–2.5 cm; drooping almost vertical, sometimes slightly curved; tip finely pointed; base tapered or wedge-shaped; leaf stalk 0.5–1.2 cm long. Whitish flowers in groups of 2–7 in racemes or panicles; November–February. Flower buds top-shaped; operculum hemispherical with short point, much shorter than hypanthium. Fruit a thin-walled, easily crushed capsule; cup to slightly urn-shaped; 0.9–1.2 cm by 0.5–0.8 cm.

Habitat and Range: On sandy loam and alluvial soils on coastal hills and valleys in Greater Brisbane Region. Woodenbong, west to Narrabri, NSW, north to Cape York, Qld; also south-west Papua New Guinea.

Notes: Previously known as *Eucalyptus tessellaris*. Often grows with *Eucalyptus tereticornis*, see p. 168. Planted as ornamental in parks, not suitable for suburban yards. Timber hard and tough, but subject to borers; used for general construction not in contact with ground.

Wildlife: Flowers — Rainbow, Scaly-breasted, Musk and Little Lorikeets; minor pollen source for honey bees

Family: Myrtaceae

Corymbia trachyphloia subsp. *trachyphloia*
Brown Bloodwood

Description: Tree 2–25 m tall. Rough brown to grey scaly bark on main branches; flaky and loose; smooth grey to whitish on smaller branches. Bark scales in squarish segments that tend to curl outwards at ends, giving a flaky appearance; easily detached revealing light brown bark underneath. Narrow leaves alternate; dark green above, paler below; ovate, 7.5–13+ cm by 0.5–2.5 cm; tip tapered; base wedge-shaped; leaf stalk 0.9–1.6 cm long. Whitish flowers in groups of 3–6 in panicles; December–April. Flower buds obovoid to top-shaped; 3–5 mm long; operculum with short point; much shorter than hypanthium. Fruit a small woody, but thin-walled capsule; ovoid to urn-shaped; 5–10 mm by 4–7 mm.

Habitat and Range: On shallow sandy and stony soils on coastal hills and mountains in Greater Brisbane Region. Grafton, NSW, to Nth Qld.

Notes: Previously known as *Eucalyptus trachyphloia*. Similar to *Corymbia gummifera* and *Corymbia intermedia*, see pp. 142, 144. Timber light brown, moderately strong and durable; used for construction, mine props, fencing and fuel.

Wildlife: Leaves — Koalas; medium source of pollen for bees.

Family: Myrtaceae

Daviesia umbellulata
Northern Bitter Pea

Description: Multi-stemmed shrub 1–2 m. Arching branches; new branches hairy, ridged and angular, sometimes clustered or fairly close together on stem. Stiff leaves alternate; light green; oval, narrow and flattened; 0.7–2.5 cm by 2–4 mm; often hairy on edges and along prominent midrib; tip with sharp spine; lack stalk. Orange-yellow pea flowers, single or multiple in racemes; largest petal with dark red marks at base; August–October. Fruit a flattened triangular pod.

Habitat and Range: On shallow sandy or stony soils, also deep sands of coastal wallum. Sydney, NSW, to Bundaberg, Qld.

Notes: Similar to *Daviesia ulicifolia* (Native Gorse) — branches end in spines; rigid, prickly leaves to 2 mm wide.

Family: Fabaceae.

Daviesia villifera
Bitter Pea

Description: Spiny shrub 1–3 m. New branches with long hairs; sometimes clustered on stem; arch downwards. Stiff twisted leaves alternate; dark green; ovate; 5–9 mm by 2–4 mm; prominent midrib; tip with sharp rigid spine; base heart-shaped, with short hairs; lacks leaf stalk. Orange-yellow pea flowers on stalks; largest petal with reddish-brown markings at base; July to December. Fruit a flattened triangular pod, often tinged red when young; seeds kidney-shaped.

Habitat and Range: On shallow, sandy soils on coastal hills and slopes. Bateman's Bay, NSW, to northern Brisbane, Qld, also ranges of Central Qld and Stanthorpe District.

Notes: Often in understorey of spotted gum forests (*Corymbia* spp.), see p. 142–144. Previously known as *Daviesia squarrosa*, which does not occur in Qld.

Family: Fabaceae

Daviesia wyattiana
Long-leaved Bitter Pea

Description: Sparsely branched shrub 1–3 m. New stems triangular in cross-section, ridged. Long, strap-like leaves alternate; bluish-green; linear, 5–30 cm by 1.5–6 mm; tip obtuse or pointed; prominent midrib. Orange-yellow pea flowers, single or multiple in racemes; largest petal with dark red markings towards base; July–December. Fruit a flattened triangular pod, 8–11 mm long.

Habitat and Range: Sometimes common. On sandy and stony soils on coastal hills and mountain slopes. Southern NSW to Bundaberg, Qld, also west to ranges of Central Qld and Stanthorpe District.

Notes: Differs from other Bitter Peas in Brisbane region because it lacks spiny leaves

Family: Fabaceae

Dodonaea triquetra
Forest Hop Bush

Description: Sparsely branched shrub 2–3 m. Leaves alternate; light to dark glossy green above, paler below; oblong to lanceolate; 3.5–15 cm by 1–4 cm; tip tapered or with short point; base tapered along leaf stalk; edges sometimes wavy. Minute, yellowish-green flowers; lack petals. Male flowers a tuft of 8–10 stamens; May–June. Female flowers with thread-like style; June–September. Papery seed capsule; 1.8–2 cm by 1.6–1.8 cm; 3 wings; purplish-brown towards wings at maturity; often in clusters of about 12.

Habitat and Range: On deep sands and sandy soils around Brisbane; often in disturbed places and along edges of paths in Greater Brisbane Region. Vic. to Rockhampton, Qld.

Notes: Similar to subspecies of *Dodonaea viscosa* — all have sticky leaves; difficult to identify in field.

Family: Sapindaceae

Eucalyptus acmenoides
White Mahogany, Yellow Stringybark

Description: Tree to 30–40 m, often taller. Moderately dense canopy. Finely fibrous, light grey-brown bark, slightly furrowed, stringy; dark brown beneath, smooth on small upper branches. Drooping narrow leaves alternate; dark green above, paler below; fairly thin in cross-section; lanceolate to ovate, 7–15 cm by 7–2.5 mm; tip tapered; base wedge-shaped or sometimes oblique; veins just visible or conspicuous; leaf stalk 0.8–1.8 cm long. Seedling and juvenile leaves opposite for first few pairs then alternate; broader than adult leaves. White flowers on common stalk in groups of 4, 7 or 20 in umbels; September–December. Flower buds ovoid, 5–7 mm long; operculum cone-shaped with beak, about as long as hypanthium. Woody seed capsule wineglass or cup-shaped; top slightly curved inward; 4–6 mm by 4–7 mm; 4 valves level with rim.

Habitat and Range: On sandy loams and stony soils in higher rainfall areas on hillsides and ranges, also close to rainforest in Greater Brisbane Region. Sydney, NSW, to Rockhampton, Qld, also further north to Atherton Tableland.

Notes: Previously known as *Eucalyptus triantha*. Similar to *Eucalyptus helidonica* — narrow blue-green leaves, paler below; on shallow stony soils in Greater Brisbane Region. Timber yellowish-brown or brown; hard, strong, durable and termite resistant; considered one of best eucalypt timbers to use and work in general construction. Common name may refer to colour of timber. Aboriginal people used bark for shelters and to make twine and containers.

Wildlife: Leaves — caterpillar of Coral Jewel Butterfly; source of pollen for honey and bees.

Family: Myrtaceae

Eucalyptus baileyana
Bailey's Stringybark

Description: Tall erect tree, 10–40 m. Fine to moderately dense canopy. Fibrous, dark grey to almost black bark; furrowed, stringy; distinct regular cross-hatched pattern of bark fibres with small reddish-brown to black flakes in furrows; sometimes exudes small blobs of gum (kino). Narrow, drooping leaves; dark green above, paler below; ovate and sometimes curved, 8–18 cm by 1–3 cm; tip tapers to point; base wedge-shaped. Seedling leaves and juvenile leaves opposite for first few pairs, then alternate on reddish twigs; broadly ovate; almost white below and covered with star-shaped hairs (hand lens helpful). White flowers in groups of 4–8 on common stalk in umbels; October–January. Flower buds pear-shaped or obovoid; operculum hemispherical, often with short beak, shorter than hypanthium; stamens joined in 4 bundles. Woody seed capsules globular to urn-shaped; 0.8–1.4 cm by 1–1.5 cm; faint longitudinal ridges; often a warty texture on outside; 3 valves at, or slightly above, rim.

Habitat and Range: On stony sandy soils on sandstone on hillsides and ridges to south of Brisbane. Limited distribution area, habitat under threat; preserved in parks like Toohey Forest and Karawatha. Patchy distribution; Coffs Harbour, NSW, to Brisbane, Qld, also on ranges of Central Qld and Darling Downs.

Notes: Sometimes confused with ironbarks at a distance, but closer inspection reveals differences. Timber light grey, but darkening; strong and durable, used for fencing, poles and general construction work

Wildlife: Flowers and bark — Squirrel Glider.

Family: Myrtaceae

Eucalyptus biturbinata
Grey Gum

Description: Tree 10–30 m. Fine to moderately dense canopy. Smooth white, grey to light grey bark with darker, sometimes brownish granular patches; bark shed in large plates or flakes; new bark orange-yellow. Slightly drooping, spreading leaves alternate; dark green above, paler below; ovate, 8.5–19 cm by 1–4 cm; tip tapered; base wedge-shaped; veins usually visible; leaf stalk 1–2.8 cm. Seedling and juvenile leaves with first few pairs opposite, then alternate; grey-green; narrow, lanceolate. White flowers in groups of 6–10 in umbels; December–February. Flower buds ovoid to elliptical; 7–15 mm long; operculum wrinkled and conical, about as long as hypanthium. Woody seed capsule top or bell-shaped; 7–10 mm by 6–10 mm; flat or raised disc; 4 spreading valves curving outward.

Habitat and Range: On moderately fertile soils; mainly confined to hill slopes and mountain ranges in Greater Brisbane Region. Gloucester, NSW, to Bundaberg, Qld, also west to Burnett and Darling Downs Districts.

Notes: Previously known as *Eucalyptus punctata* var. *didyma*. Bark colour varies, but similar to *Eucalyptus major*, see p. 155 and *Eucalyptus propinqua*, see p. 161; can be distinguished from the other grey gums by much larger capsules and habitat preference. Often grows with *Corymbia citriodora* subsp. *variegata*, see p. 141, *Eucalyptus acmenoides*, see p. 149, or *Eucalyptus tereticornis*, see p. 168, on steep slopes. Timber heavy, strong and durable, good for construction, but difficult to work.

Wildlife: Leaves — koalas; probably a minor source of pollen.

Family: Myrtaceae

Eucalyptus carnea
Broad-leaved White Mahogany, Queensland White Mahogany

Description: Tree 10–30 m. Moderately dense canopy. Light grey-brown, fibrous stringy bark; brown underneath; bark on younger trees and saplings sometimes with cross-hatching. Thick leaves alternate; sometimes spreading to drooping; dull shiny blue to dark blue-green above, slightly paler below; lanceolate-ovate, often curved, 5–15 cm by 1–4.2 cm; tip pointed; base wedge-shaped or slightly asymmetrical; leaf stalk 1–2 cm long. Seedling and juvenile leaves dull light green above, paler below; opposite for a few pairs, then alternate; more spreading; broad and lanceolate, wider than adult leaves; becoming blue-green on older saplings (less than 2 m) or on trunks of mature fire damaged trees. Whitish flowers in groups of 7 or more in umbels; often clustered towards ends of branchlets; September–February. Flower buds ovoid to ellipsoid; 7–11 mm long; operculum conical, usually with beak, as long as, or longer than, hypanthium. Woody seed capsule hemispherical to cup-shaped; 4–7 mm by 5–10 mm, disc flat; 3–5 valves at about rim level.

Habitat and Range: Locally common. On shallow sandy loams and stony soils on coastal hills and ranges in Greater Brisbane Region. Hunter River, NSW, to Bundaberg Qld.

Notes: Previously known as *Eucalyptus umbra* subsp. *carnea*. Closely related to *Eucalyptus acmenoides*, see p. 149; *Eucalyptus helidonica*, see p. 149; and *Eucalyptus psammitica*, see p. 162.

Wildlife: Leaves — Greater Glider; minor source of pollen and honey for bees.

Family: Myrtaceae

Eucalyptus crebra
Narrow-leaved Ironbark, Red Ironbark

Description: Tall tree 10–30 m. Fine, fairly open canopy. Bark dark grey or almost black; rough deeply furrowed; very hard ironbark. Narrow drooping leaves alternate; bluish to grey-green, almost same colour both sides; linear to ovate, 5–18 cm by 6–15 mm; tip tapers to point; base tapered to wedge-shaped; veins fairly faint; leaf stalk 1–2 cm long. Seedling and juvenile leaves opposite for first few pairs, then alternate; narrower than adult leaves. Flowers on common stalk in groups of 4–9 in racemes or panicles; mainly August–February, but sometimes also March–May. Flower buds club to diamond-shaped; 4–6 mm long; operculum conical, and often with beak, shorter than hypanthium. Woody seed capsules shortened egg-shaped to cup-shaped; 3–6 mm by 3–6 mm; 3–4 valves below or slightly above rim.

Habitat and Range: Common. On well drained, shallow stony soils of hills, ridges and mountain slopes in Greater Brisbane Region. South of Sydney, NSW, to Cape York, Qld.

Notes: Often grows with *Corymbia citriodora* subsp. *variegata,* see p. 141, near Brisbane. Similar to *Eucalyptus siderophloia*, see p. 167, but leaves are narrower and more consistently drooping, woody seed capsules smaller; difficult to distinguish in field. Timber dark red; very hard and durable; used for poles, railway sleepers and heavy timber constructions. Aboriginal people used wood for spear and clubs.

Wildlife: Flowers — Little Lorikeet, Crimson Rosella, Noisy Friarbird; leaves — koalas; major source of pollen for bees, less so for honey.

Family: Myrtaceae

Eucalyptus dura
Gum-topped Ironbark

Description: Tree 10–30 m. Sometimes drooping canopy. Dark brownish to black, hard ironbark; deeply furrowed; edges of crests between furrows layered slightly scaly; each layer slightly separated (by 0–1 mm) at edges, slightly reddish-brown; upper branches smooth, silvery-grey with lighter patches. Leathery leaves alternate; dull grey-green above, slightly paler below; lanceolate to ovate, 6–15 cm by 8–35 mm; tip tapers to point; base wedge-shaped; veins faint; leaf stalks 0.8–2 cm long. Seedling and juvenile leaves opposite for a few pairs, then alternate; broad, ovate and larger than adult leaves. Whitish flowers in groups of 3–9 in racemes or panicles; June–November. Flower buds obovoid to diamond-shaped; ribbed 5–11 mm long; operculum conical, slightly shorter and narrower than hypanthium. Woody seed capsule pear-shaped to almost cylindrical; 7–9 mm by 5–8 mm; curves inwards towards tip, usually ribbed; disc flat and narrow; 4 valves, usually just below rim.

Habitat and Range: Rare. On well-drained, shallow sandy or stony soils, but confined to hills, exposed ridges and mountain slopes in Greater Brisbane Region. Moreton and Darling Downs Districts, Mt French and near Crow's Nest, South-east Qld.

Notes: Previously known as *Eucalyptus* sp.2. Similar to *Eucalyptus fibrosa* (Broad-leaved Ironbark) — bark texture similar, but ironbark continues onto smaller branches; operculum up to twice as long as hypanthium; seed capsule fairly smooth; 4–5 valves curve slightly outwards; on shallow stony soils on coastal hills and ridges around Brisbane.

Family: Myrtaceae

Eucalyptus major
Grey Gum

Description: Tree 10–30 m. Moderately dense, spreading and drooping canopy. Smooth greyish bark with darker greenish or brownish-grey patches formed by small, finely cracked granular segments; bark shed in large, irregular patches; orange when first exposed, becoming grey with time. Leaves alternate; dark green above, paler below; ovate, 7–21 cm by 1–4.5 cm; tip pointed; base wedge-shaped; veins usually visible; leaf stalk 1–3 cm long. Seedling and juvenile leaves opposite for a few pairs, then alternate; broader than adult leaves and spreading from twigs. Flowers in groups of 5–10 in umbels; December– February. Flower buds angular with distinct rib; ovoid to ellipsoid; 4–8 mm long; operculum conical with short beak, about as long as hypanthium. Woody seed capsule hemispherical to top-shaped; 4–5 mm by 5–7 mm; sometimes with faint rib; in clusters; size varies; disc narrow and slightly raised; 3–4 valves curve outwards.

Habitat and Range: On stony soils on hills and slopes and in moist gullies in lower rainfall areas in Greater Brisbane Region. Casino, NSW, to Port Curtis, Qld, also west to ranges of Central Qld.

Notes: Previously described as a variety of *Eucalyptus propinqua*, see p. 161; difficult to separate in field; tends to replace *Eucalyptus propinqua* on drier sites. Often grows with *Corymbia citriodora* or *Corymbia henryi,* see pp. 141 and 143, *Eucalyptus microcorys* see p. 157, or *Lophostemon confertus* (Brush Box), see p. 206, in moist gullies or along drainage lines.

Wildlife: Often shows evidence of possums; leaves — koalas.

Family: Myrtaceae

Eucalyptus melanophloia
Silver Leaf Ironbark

Description: Tree 10–20 m, often of poor form. Moderately dense canopy. Brownish to dark grey to almost black ironbark; hard, rough, deeply furrowed. Rounded leaves mostly opposite; silvery bluish-grey, almost same colour both sides; broad, ovate, 2.5–10 cm by 1.5–6 cm; tip blunt; base heart-shaped to rounded; veins faint; lacks leaf stalk. Seedling and juvenile leaves ovate to almost circular or heart-shaped; sometimes with short stalk. Whitish flowers in groups of 3–7 in panicles; December–February. Flower buds ellipsoidal; 5–7 mm long; silver-green; operculum conical with small beak, about as long as hypanthium. Woody seed capsule top-shaped to hemispherical; 3–7 mm by 3.5–7 mm; disc depressed, narrow; 3 valves slightly below or above rim.

Habitat and Range: More common in drier western parts of Greater Brisbane Region, on gently sloping stony ridges and hills; best development on more fertile soils. Dubbo, NSW, to Nth Qld.

Wildlife: Flowers — Queensland Blossom Bat; leaves — caterpillar of Emerald Hairstreak Butterfly; medium source of pollen for honey and bees.

Family: Myrtaceae

Eucalyptus microcorys
Tallowwood

Description: Tree 10–50 m. Moderately dense canopy. Brownish-orange bark; often spongy and slightly furrowed; stringy with very small cork plates and volcano-like pores on outer bark; orange-brown beneath. Drooping and spreading leaves alternate; dark green above, paler below; lanceolate to ovate, 5–14 cm by 1–3.5 cm; tip pointed; base wedge-shaped; veins visible; leaf stalk 8–18 mm long. Seedling and juvenile leaves opposite for a few pairs, then alternate; usually shorter, but wider, than adult leaves. White flowers in groups of 4–7 in racemes or panicles; July–November. Flower buds club-shaped, tapering to stalk; operculum hemispherical, top marked like a hot cross bun, much shorter than hypanthium. Seed capsules narrow, conical to pear-shaped; 5–9 mm by 4–6 mm; disc nearly flat, narrow; 3 valves enclosed or just protruding.

Habitat and Range: Common. On deep sands and sandy-loam soils and in moist gullies, also in wet eucalypt forest in Greater Brisbane Region. More common on moderately fertile soils with regular moisture. Cooranbong, NSW, to Maryborough and Fraser I., Qld.

Notes: Found on more protected and/or southerly slopes and alluvial flats of creeks and rivers that may have supported a community of dry rainforest species in past. Volcano-like pores may be due to insect activity. Timber yellowish-brown; greasy, heavy, hard and durable; used for many purposes including flooring, decking, poles and supports, but subject to borer attack.

Wildlife: Flowers — Grey-headed Flying Fox, Scaly-breasted Lorikeet, Squirrel Glider (+ bark); leaves — koalas; source of pollen for honey and bees.

Family: Myrtaceae

Eucalyptus moluccana
Gum-topped Box

Description: Tall erect tree 25–30 m. Fine to moderately dense, sometimes drooping canopy. Halfbark — rough, light to dark grey bark on lower trunk and often up to base of larger branches; smooth silver-grey, sometimes with darker patches on branches on upper half of tree. Lower bark in long thin scales that adhere closely to trunk, sometimes in a cross-hatched pattern; smooth bark shed in strips that hang down over rough bark. Leaves alternate; dull grey-green above, slightly paler below; lanceolate to ovate, 10–20 cm by 2–8 cm, tip pointed; base wedge-shaped; leaf stalk 1–2.8 cm. Seedling and juvenile leaves opposite for a few pairs, then alternate; almost circular to ovate. Whitish flowers in groups of 5–15 in raceme or panicle; February–May. Flower buds obovoid or narrow and ellipsoid; 7–9 mm long; operculum conical, usually with beak, about as long as or slightly shorter than, hypanthium which tapers to stalk. Woody seed capsules cylindrical to barrel-shaped; 5–9 mm by 5–6 mm long; disc depressed; usually 4 valves well below rim.

Habitat and Range: On heavier clay soils and alluvial slopes in some southern parts of Brisbane and further west. Nowra, NSW, to Atherton Tableland, Nth Qld.

Notes: May occur in pure stands; sometimes grows with *Eucalyptus tereticornis*, see p. 168, on alluvial flats, or with *Corymbia citriodora* var. *variegata*, see p. 141, on drier sites. Apparently tolerant of slightly saline soils. Timber light brown; fine grained; hard, strong and very durable; resistant to termite attack; good for structures such as bridges and wharves; good fuel.

Wildlife: Leaves — koala; pollen source for honey and bees.

Family: Myrtaceae

Eucalyptus pilularis
Blackbutt

Description: Tall tree, 10–60 m. Fairly dense, spreading and drooping canopy. Grey or grey-brown, stringy rough bark extending well up trunk; upper trunk and branches smooth, white to light grey, often marked by insect larvae; bark shed in long strips revealing white to yellowish-grey surface. Leaves alternate; glossy dark green above, paler below; lanceolate, sometimes curved, 7–19 cm by 1–4 cm; tip pointed; base wedge-shaped and rounded; visible veins; leaf stalk 1–2 cm long. Seedling and juvenile leaves opposite; much paler below; lack stalk; often broader than adult leaves. Whitish flowers in groups of 6–12 in umbels; December–May. Flower buds diamond to club-shaped; 7–11 mm long; operculum conical with beak, as long as, or longer than, hypanthium. Woody seed capsules globular to hemispherical; 6–11 mm by 7–11 mm; disc flat or sloping downwards; usually 4 valves level with the rim.

Habitat and Range: On deep sands, sandy loams and red sandy soils on coastal hills and ranges, also in wet eucalypt forest in Greater Brisbane Region. Eden, NSW, to Maryborough and Fraser I. Qld, also North Stradbroke and Moreton Is.

Notes: Generally considered to lack a ligno-tuber and so regenerates from seed after fire. Timber light yellow-brown; hard, strong, moderately durable; usually straight-grained and easy to work; used in house and general construction.

Wildlife: Flowers — Sugar and Feathertail Gliders, Grey-headed Flying Fox, Rainbow, Scaly-breasted and Little Lorikeets, Noisy Friarbird, Yellow-faced, White-naped, New Holland and Scarlet Honeyeaters, Eastern Spinebill; leaves — koala; good source of pollen, but nectar supply variable for honey.

Family: Myrtaceae

Eucalyptus planchoniana
Planchon's Stringybark

Description: Large-stemmed tree, 2–30 m, or sometimes with a mallee-like growth habit on Moreton Bay islands. Fairly open to moderately dense, drooping canopy. Rough, slightly furrowed, brown-orange stringy bark; shed in prickly short fibres; small patches of dark red-brown sometimes exposed; smaller branches smooth. Drooping leaves alternate; blue-green; curved, lanceolate to ovate, 11–20 cm by 1.5–4 cm, tip tapers to point; base wedge-shaped and sometimes asymmetrical; veins visible; leaf stalk 1–3 cm long. Whitish flowers in groups of 4–7 in umbels; December–February. Flower buds diamond-shaped, ridged; operculum narrow and conical, slightly shorter than hypanthium. Large woody seed capsules globular; 1.5–2.5 cm by 1.6–2.5 cm; longitudinal ribs; disc wide and depressed, 4 valves below rim.

Habitat and Range: Uncommon. On deep sands and shallow infertile sandy soils on low ridges and gentle slopes south of Brisbane. Laurieton, NSW, to south of Brisbane, Qld, also on sandstones near Helidon on eastern Darling Downs.

Notes: Bark colour and texture similar to *Eucalyptus microcorys,* see p. 157. Timber light to dark brown; sometimes greasy, heavy and durable; suitable for general construction.

Wildlife: Flowers and bark — Squirrel Glider

Family: Myrtaceae

Eucalyptus propinqua
Grey Gum

Description: Tree 10–30 m. Moderately dense, spreading and drooping canopy. Smooth light grey bark with darker grey-brown patches formed by small, finely cracked granular segments; bark shed in large, irregular patches; orange when exposed, becoming grey with time. Leaves alternate; dark green above, paler below; lanceolate to ovate, 7–16 cm by 1–2.5 cm, tip pointed; base wedge-shaped, veins usually visible; leaf stalk 1–3 cm long. Seedling and juvenile leaves opposite for a few pairs, then alternate; seedling leaves smaller, ovate; juvenile leaves similar to adult. Whitish flowers in groups of 5–10 in umbels; December–May. Flower buds rounded to ovoid; 4–6.5 mm long; operculum hemispherical to conical, about as long as hypanthium. Small woody capsule, hemispherical to top-shaped; 3–4 mm by 4–6 mm; disc flat to slightly raised, 3 or 4 valves curved outwards.

Habitat and Range: On sandy loams or stony soils in higher rainfall areas on coastal hills near ranges, also in wet eucalypt forest or edge of rainforest in Greater Brisbane Region. Wyong, NSW, to Bundaberg, Qld, also west to ranges of Central Qld and on Darling Downs.

Notes: Previously known as *Eucalyptus propinqua* var. *propinqua*. Similar to *Eucalyptus major*, see p. 155.

Wildlife: Flowers — Rainbow and Scaly-breasted Lorikeets; seed — Pale-headed Rosella; leaves — koala, Yellow-bellied Glider (+flowers, sap, manna); medium pollen source for honey.

Family: Myrtaceae

Eucalyptus psammitica
Sandstone Mahogany

Description: Tree 10–30 m tall. Moderately dense drooping canopy. Rough, stringy light grey-brown bark; slightly furrowed; brown to dark brown underneath. Narrow, thick leaves alternate; spreading and drooping; green-grey above, slightly paler below; slightly curved, lanceolate, 9–15 cm by 1.5–3 cm: tip pointed; base wedge-shaped usually asymmetrical; lateral veins faint; leaf stalk 1–2 cm long. Seedling and juvenile leaves with first few pairs opposite, then alternate; darkish green above, paler below; usually wider than adult leaves. White flowers in groups of 7–11 in umbels; July–December. Flower buds ovoid; 7–8 mm long; operculum conical, often with beak shorter than hypanthium. Woody seed capsules cup-shaped to hemispherical; 6–9 mm by 6–9 mm; disc flat or slightly raised to 1 mm wide, usually at rim level, 4 valves curved outwards or level with rim.

Habitat and Range: Rare; limited distribution. On shallow, infertile sandy soils on sandstone. Coffs Harbour to Grafton District, NSW, and Toohey Forest, Brisbane, in Qld.

Notes: Similar to *Eucalyptus carnea,* see p. 152; difficult to separate in field. Immature capsules picked up off ground may lack broad disc and may be mistaken for *Eucalyptus carnea* capsules.

Family: Myrtaceae

Eucalyptus racemosa
Scribbly Gum

Description: Erect or crooked tree, 2–25 m; characteristic insect larvae 'scribbles' on trunk. Smooth, shiny bark varies white to whitish or silver-grey, with darker bluish-grey to brownish patches; new bark yellow but soon fades. Narrow drooping leaves alternate; spreading and drooping; dull blue-green, slightly paler below; ovate and often curved, 7–18.5 cm by 1–3.5 cm; tip pointed; base wedge-shaped and often asymmetrical; veins obvious. Seedling and juvenile leaves opposite for a few pairs, then alternate; usually larger and broader than adult leaves. Whitish flowers in groups of 5–12 in umbels; July–October. Flower buds club-shaped; 3–5 mm long; operculum hemispherical with fine point; much shorter than hypanthium. Seed capsules hemispherical to pear-shaped; 5–7 mm by 4–6 mm; disc slightly convex reddish-brown; 4 valves level or below rim.

Habitat and Range: On deep sands on younger dune systems near sea and older leached sands; on sandy soils of coastal lowlands and on edges of swampy areas, but sometimes on hills around Brisbane. Morisset, NSW, to Rockhampton Qld.

Notes: Previously known as *Eucalyptus signata*. Larvae of wood-boring moth, *Endoxylon cinerea*, cause scribbly lines. Much natural habitat lost to development. On less fertile sands, tree has mallee-like growth, possibly due to soil infertility, frequent fires and drought. On edges of swamps this species apparently tolerates periodic inundation of roots. Often grows with *Corymbia intermedia*, see p. 144 and *Corymbia gummifera*, see p. 142. Aboriginal people used gum to treat diarrhoea and as an astringent.

Wildlife: Seed — Pale-headed Rosella; sap — Yellow-bellied Glider; leaves — koalas.

Family: Myrtaceae

Eucalyptus resinifera
Red Mahogany

Description: Erect tree 10–45 m. Moderately dense spreading and drooping canopy. Bark grey-brown; slightly furrowed, fibrous and stringy; in slightly raised narrow strips; colour and texture variable, faint reddish tinge on older trunks, reddish-brown underneath. Narrow leathery leaves alternate; dark green above, paler below; ovate, 7–18 cm by 1.2–2.5 cm; tip pointed; base wedge-shaped, symmetrical; some lateral veins more distinct than others; leaf stalk 1–2.5 cm long. Seedling and juvenile leaves opposite for a few pairs, then alternate; usually broader and wider than adult leaves. Whitish flowers in groups of 5–11 in umbels; September–February. Flower buds ovoid; 1.2 – 2 cm long; operculum elongated and conical, 2–4 times as long as hypanthium. Woody seed capsules cup-shaped to hemispherical; 5–9 mm by 5–7 mm; disc raised; 3–4 prominent valves curve outwards.

Habitat and Range: On deep sands in higher rainfall areas and well-drained sandy loams, also wet eucalypt forest on coastal hills and ranges in Greater Brisbane Region. Huskisson, NSW, to Bundaberg, Qld, also isolated occurrences Nth Qld.

Notes: Bark and prominent operculum separate this species from other stringy barks. Sometimes occurs as emergent on edges of rainforest. Timber red-brown; strong, tough, moderately durable; used for house construction, ship-building and general construction.

Wildlife: Flowers — Yellow-bellied Glider (+ leaves, sap), Sugar Glider (+sap, manna), Yellow-faced Honeyeater, Rainbow Lorikeets; medium source of honey and good source of pollen for bees.

Family: Myrtaceae

Eucalyptus robusta
Swamp Mahogany

Description: Tree 2–25 m. Dense drooping canopy. Dark brown, fibrous stringy bark; furrowed, often forms thick spongy strips. Large thick leaves alternate; spreading and drooping; glossy dark green above, paler below; broad, ovate, 8–16 cm by 3–5 cm; tip pointed, base wedge-shaped, rounded or asymmetrical; veins visible; leaf stalk 2–3.5 cm long. Seedling and juvenile leaves opposite for a few pairs, then alternate; broad and ovate to nearly twice as wide as adult leaves. Whitish flowers in groups of 5–10 in umbels; March–August. Flower bud ovoid; 15–25 mm long; operculum conical or pointed, usually with strong beak, as long as, or longer than, hypanthium. Large seed capsules cylindrical to bell-shaped; 0.9–1.6 cm by 0.8–1.1 cm; disc flat or depressed; usually 3 valves joined together, below or slightly above rim level.

Habitat and Range: Uncommon. Mainly near swampy areas and sand lakes in coastal lowlands and Moreton Bay islands, also edges of heath and saltwater estuaries and lagoons. Moruya, NSW, to Rockhampton, Qld.

Notes: Much natural habitat lost to development. Sometimes planted as ornamental. Timber light red to reddish-brown; light, but moderately hard, strong and durable. Known to form hybrids with *Eucalyptus tereticornis* when the two species grow close together.

Wildlife: Flowers — Queensland Blossom Bat, Rainbow, Scaly-breasted and Little Lorikeets, Bell Miner, Noisy Miner, Lewin's, Yellow-faced, Scarlet and Striped Honeyeaters, Noisy Friarbird, Eastern Spinebill; leaves — koala.

Family: Myrtaceae

Eucalyptus seeana
Narrow-leaved Red Gum

Description: Often crooked tree 10–35 m, but can be much shorter. Fine, open, drooping canopy. Grey to brownish-grey smooth bark; darker granular patches and sometimes rough bark at base; pale orange when first exposed. Narrow drooping leaves alternate; dull bluish-grey green, slightly paler below; linear to ovate, sometimes curved, 7–20 cm by 0.7–2 cm; tip pointed; base wedge-shaped; leaf stalk 1–3 cm long. Seedling and juvenile leaves opposite for a few pairs, then alternate; lanceolate; wider than adult leaves. White flowers in groups of 4–11 in umbels; September–December. Flower buds ovoid; 1–1.5 cm long; operculum 2–4 times longer than hypanthium. Woody seed capsules top-shaped to hemispherical; 4–8 mm by 5–8 mm; disc ring-like; 3–4 valves curved outwards above rim.

Habitat and Range: Uncommon to rare. Mainly in swampy sands and clays, sometimes near moist soaks, on coastal hills and slopes around Brisbane. Telegraph Point, NSW, to Caloundra, Qld, also Stanthorpe.

Notes: Most habitat lost to development. Similar to *Eucalyptus bancroftii* (Orange Gum) — previously known as *Eucalyptus seeana* var. *constricta*; new bark bright orange fading to grey with darker patches; leaves thicker, 1.5–4. cm wide; slightly larger woody seed capsule with single ridge, 6–9 mm by 7–9 mm; operculum sometimes blunt and 2-3 times longer than hypanthium; swampy sands and low ridges of coastal lowland, often on edges of heaths; patchy distribution from Bundaberg, Qld, to Kew, NSW. Bark also similar to *Eucalyptus major*, see p.155 and *Eucalyptus tereticornis*, see p.168. Timber heavy and hard; does not split or saw readily; mainly used for fence posts.

Wildlife: Flowers — Sugar, Yellow-bellied and Squirrel Gliders (+sap); Rainbow and Scaly-breasted Lorikeets; leaves — koalas.

Family: Myrtaceae

Eucalyptus siderophloia
Grey Ironbark

Description: Tree to 30 m. Sometimes drooping, moderately dense canopy. Hard rough, dark grey to nearly black ironbark; furrowed. Narrow leaves alternate; light grey to darkish green, slightly paler below; ovate, 7–22 cm by 1–4 cm; tip pointed; base tapered to wedge-shaped; veins faint; leaf stalk 0.8–3 cm long. Seedling and juvenile leaves opposite for a few pairs, then alternate; broader than adult leaves. Whitish flowers in groups of 4–7 in raceme or panicle; June–September. Flower buds spindle-shaped; 6–9 mm long; operculum with beak, as long as, or shorter than, hypanthium. Woody seed capsules top-shaped; 4–6 mm by 4.5–7.5 mm; disc flat or depressed below rim; 3-5 valves at, or curved outward, above rim.

Habitat and Range: On deep sands and sandy-stony soils on hillsides, ridges and sometimes along drainage lines, often in exposed areas close to coast in Greater Brisbane Region. Sydney, NSW, to Bundaberg, Qld; also west to ranges of Central Qld.

Notes: Previously known as *Eucalyptus drepanophylla*. Similar to *Eucalyptus crebra* see p.153 — difficult to separate in field; leaves much wider, less drooping; flowers and seed capsules usually larger. Timber red; hard, heavy, tough and durable; strength makes it suitable for bridge construction, poles and other building, also a good fuel. Aboriginal people used wood to make shields.

Wildlife: Flowers — Squirrel Glider; Rainbow and Scaly-breasted Lorikeets, Eastern Rosella; leaves — koalas, Greater Glider; important source of honey, but not pollen for bees.

Family: Myrtaceae

Eucalyptus tereticornis
Forest Red Gum

Description: Tall tree to 50 m. Moderately dense, sometimes drooping canopy. Smooth often shiny bark; sometimes a short 'stocking' of rough bark at base of trunk; Bark colour varies, commonly white to silver-grey with darker, brownish shiny patches; shed in large plates or flakes. Narrow leaves alternate; greyish-green above, slightly paler below; ovate and curved, 8–24 cm by 1–4 cm; tip pointed; base wedge-shaped; conspicuous veins; leaf stalk 1–3.5 cm long. Seedling and juvenile leaves opposite for a few pairs, then alternate; often bluish-green and very broad; usually wider, but not as long as adult leaves. Creamy white (occasionally pink) flowers in groups of 5–12 in umbels; June–November. Flower buds ovate; 1–2 cm long; operculum conical, 2–5 times as long as hypanthium. Woody seed capsule top-shaped to globular; 4–8 mm by 5–10 mm; wide raised disc; usually 4 valves curving outward.

Habitat and Range: Widespread. On deep sands and on moist sandy loams of alluvial flats and terraces, or fertile soils derived from basalt; but also on hills and mountain ridges in Greater Brisbane Region. Eastern Australia; southern Papua New Guinea.

Notes: One of most common eucalypts in region. Often remains after clearing along drainage lines and rivers in rural areas; few natural forests, except in some reserves. Similar to *Eucalyptus seeana* see p.166. Aborigines reputedly used wood for shields and drank nectar.

Wildlife: Flowers — Rainbow, Scaly-breasted and Little Lorikeets, Pale-headed Rosella (+seed), Yellow-faced, White-throated and Scarlet Honeyeaters (in winter when food is scarce); leaves — koalas (major food source), Brushtail Possum; important source of pollen for bees and of medium importance for honey.

Family: Myrtaceae

Eucalyptus tindaliae
Queensland White Stringybark,
Queensland White Mahogany

Description: Tall erect tree, 10–30 m. Fine canopy. Fibrous grey-brown stringybark; finely wavy and furrowed; sometimes cross-hatched around base, may appear pinkish-brown on surface, red-brown underneath. Narrow leaves alternate; bluish to grey-green above, slightly paler below; fairly thick, oval and often curved, 7–15 cm by 1–4 cm; tip pointed; base asymmetrical; visible veins; leaf stalk 8–16 mm long. Seedling and juvenile leaves opposite for first few pairs, then alternate; paler below; often very small and rough to touch with star-shaped hairs; edges wavy, sometimes with minute blunt teeth. Whitish flowers in groups of 11 or more in umbels; December–May. Flower buds obovoid; 6–7 mm long; minute warty oil glands; operculum bluntly conical to rounded, much shorter than hypanthium; buds below leaves of current year's growth. Woody seed capsules hemispherical, can be broader than long; 4–8 mm by 6–11 mm; disc reddish-brown to 2 mm wide; 3–4 valves level or slightly curving outwards just above rim; clustered together on very short stalks.

Habitat and Range: Widespread. On deep sands and sandy soils, coastal hills and lower slopes in Greater Brisbane Region. Coffs Harbour, NSW, to Maryborough, Qld.

Notes: Some habitat north of Brisbane cleared for pine plantations. Previously known as *Eucalyptus phaeotricha*, and *Eucalyptus nigra*. Similar to *Eucalyptus eugenioides* (Thin-leaved Stringybark) — thin leaves; stalked buds lacks warty oil glands; mainly mountain areas, McPherson Range to Bunya Mountains. Timber pale, strong and durable; used for house frames, general construction and flooring.

Wildlife: Leaves — koalas, Squirrel Glider (+ flowers, bark); minor source of pollen and honey for bees.

Family: Myrtaceae

Exocarpos cupressiformis
Native Cherry

Description: Semi-parasitic shrub 2–8 m. Yellow-green, erect or drooping branches lined with narrow ridges. New growth usually covered with minute dust-like particles. Leaves reduced to minute, alternate scales on growing tips, but soon fall off older stems. Very small creamy-green flowers in groups of up to 20 in minute racemes; October–May. Single succulent egg-shaped berry on each raceme; 5–6 mm by 4–5 mm.

Habitat and Range: Common. On deep sands and sandy soils of coastal lowlands, hills and ranges in Greater Brisbane Region. SA, Tas. and NSW to Nth Qld.

Notes: Root parasite. Edible, but astringent fruit; stalk sweet and palatable when deep red. Similar to *Exocarpos latifolius* (Broad-leaved Native Cherry) — small tree 2–10 m; ovate leaves; also in drier areas and dry rainforest. Aborigines reputedly ate fruit when ripe.

Wildlife: Fruit — Wonga Pigeon, Australian King Parrot, Crimson Rosella, Noisy Friarbird; leaves — caterpillars of Spotted Jezebel and Fiery Jewel Butterflies.

Family: Santalaceae

Gompholobium latifolium
Golden Glory Pea

Description: Sparsely branched shrub, 1–2 m tall. Leaves consist of 3 leaflets on common stalk; alternate; dark green above, paler below; leaflets wedge-shaped; 2–5 cm by 1.5–5 mm; tip pointed, sometimes cut off; edges sometime slightly rolled under. Large yellow pea flowers; solitary or 2–3 together; largest petal to 3 cm wide; July–December. Globular seed pod, 1.2–1.8 cm long.

Habitat and Range: Common. On sandy and stony soils on coastal hills and ranges in Greater Brisbane Region. Vic. to Bundaberg, also Stanthorpe and Wallangarra Districts of Darling Downs.

Notes: Seed pods pop audibly when mature. Similar to *Gompholobium virgatum* — see p. 75.

Family: Fabaceae

Gompholobium pinnatum
Poor-man's Gold, Wedge Pea

Description: Wiry small shrub 10–30 cm tall. Erect to leaning growth; thin, flexible stems. Fine leaves, consist of up to 19 leaflets; alternate; leaflets linear or narrow and elliptical; 8–12 mm by 0.5–1.5 mm; tip with minute point; edges bent or rolled under; pair of minute bristle-like bracts at base of each leaflet. Yellow pea flowers in groups of 2–3 in racemes; September–February. Black globular seed pods, 6–12 mm long;

Habitat and Range: On deep sands and moist sandy soils of coastal lowland and hillsides in Greater Brisbane Region. Ulladulla, NSW, to Nth Qld.

Notes: Seed pods pop audibly when mature.

Family: Fabaceae

Hakea florulenta

Description: Slender shrub 1–3 m, often less. Underground stem; young shoots often with silky hairs. Leaves alternate; light blue to grey-green; elliptical; 4–15 cm by 1–3 cm; tip blunt or rounded; base wedge-shaped; prominent midrib; veins feint, usually 2 broadly spaced lateral veins extending along nearly 3/4 of leaf blade; leaf stalks 3–12 mm long. Creamy white flowers in clusters of 16–20 around short reddish, hairy stalk; September–November. Fruit a woody follicle; ovoid, but lower surface more curved; warty surface 2–2.5 cm by 0.9–1.2 cm; splits into 2 halves to release 2 winged seeds.

Habitat and Range: On less fertile deep sands, sandy or shallow stony soils often near drainage lines and on moist or swampy soils in Greater Brisbane Region. Clarence River, NSW, to Rockhampton, Qld, also Granite Belt of Darling Downs.

Notes: Similar to *Hakea salicifolia,* see p. 314 — smaller narrow leaves; 11 cm by 2 cm; blunt, raised warts on woody follicle; mainly in mountain areas. Regenerates from underground stem after plant is burnt; fruits will open at ambient temperature or after a fire.

Family: Proteaceae

Hakea plurinervia
Queensland Hakea

Description: Multi-stemmed shrub 2–3 m. Leaves alternate; light grey-green to yellow-green; obovate to elliptical and often curved, 7–20 cm by 4–35 mm; tip blunt or with sharp point; base wedge-shaped; 5–9 parallel veins, net veins visible; leaf stalk 3–7 mm long. Numerous creamy-white flowers on common short stalk covered with long white hairs; June–November. Fruit a woody follicle; ovoid, but lower surface more curved; 2.5–3.5 cm by 1.2–1.5 cm; tip sometimes with short horn-like point; splits into 2 halves to release 2 winged seeds.

Habitat and Range: On sandy or stony soils on coastal hills and ranges in Greater Brisbane Region. South of Brisbane to Nth Qld.

Notes: Similar to *Acacia* spp. (Wattles), but has a true leaf not a phyllode.

Family: Proteaceae

Hibbertia aspera
Trailing Guinea Flower

Description: Small spreading shrub to 50 cm, often less. Multi-stemmed, semi-erect; rough star-shaped hairs on branches and leaves. Leaves alternate; shiny green; spoon-shaped to reversed lanceolate, 4–20 mm by 2–7 mm; tip blunt; base tapered; edges rolled under; upper surface becomes less hairy over time; leaf stalk 1 mm long. Fragile yellow flowers; solitary on fine stalk; 5–15 mm long; 5 bi-lobed petals; December–February. Fruit minute.

Habitat and Range: Widespread. On sandy and stony soils in moist, shaded areas on coastal lowlands, hills and ranges, also mountain heath. in Greater Brisbane Region; SA and NSW to Nth Qld

Family: Dilleniaceae

Hibbertia stricta
Guinea Flower

Description: Small shrub to 60 cm, often less. Multi-stemmed, mat-like growth. Stems rough and hairy. Leaves alternate; glossy dark green; linear to oblong, 5–28 mm by 1–15 mm; often with warty swellings on upper surface; tip rounded or pointed sometimes hairy; leaf edges rolled under to raised midrib below; leaf stalk 1 mm long. Fragile yellow flowers; solitary with 5 bi-lobed petals; September–February. Fruit minute.

Habitat and Range: Widespread. On deep sands and sandy soils in Greater Brisbane Region. SA, Vic. and NSW to Nth Qld. Similar to *Hibbertia vestita*, see below.

Notes: Size and shape of leaves varies.

Family: Dilleniaceae

Hibbertia vestita

Description: Small shrub to 30 cm. Multi-stemmed, mat-like growth. Stems and leaves often with silky hairs. Leaves alternate; dark green above, paler below; linear to oblong, 4–7 mm by 1–2 mm; tip and base blunt; leaf edges rolled under, but not to midrib; leaf stalk to 1 mm. Large, fragile yellow flowers; 5 bi-lobed petals, paler underneath; June–November.

Habitat and Range: On swampy and shallow sandy soils in Greater Brisbane Region. Wyong, NSW, to Rockhampton, Qld.

Notes: Similar to *Hibbertia stricta*, see above.

Family: Dilleniaceae

Hibiscus heterophyllus
Native Rosella

Description: Shrub or small tree to 10 m. Dark green stem often prickly. Leaves alternate, shape varies, ovate to elliptical, sometimes with 3 lobes; 5–20 cm by 0.5–11 cm; tip with sharp point; base wedge-shaped to tapered; edges slightly to distinctly saw-toothed; sometimes sparse hairs; gland at base of midrib on underside, midrib with minute hooked spines; leaf stalk 0.5–6 cm long. Large solitary flowers on thick hairy stalks; petals white, pale pink or yellow with purplish-red throat; September–November. Seed capsule ovate with a beak; 1.5–2 cm long; covered with straw-coloured hairs.

Habitat and Range: Often found along drainage lines in coastal hills and ranges, also sometimes in remnant or edges of dry rainforest in Greater Brisbane Region. Illawarra District, NSW, to Nth Qld.

Notes: Two other species of *Hibiscus* in Greater Brisbane Region. Similar to *Hibiscus diversifolius* (Swamp Hibiscus) — spreading prickly shrub; 1–2 m with hairy stems; leaf edges with blunt rounded teeth; flower light yellow with dark red-purple throat, September–November and March–May; in swampy areas on coastal lowlands, Southern NSW to North Qld; also New Guinea, Philippines, Pacific Is and Central and Southern America. *Hibiscus splendens* — shrub to 7 m; branches and leaves with dense velvety hairs and prickles; leaves with 3–5 lobes; edges saw-toothed; flowers pink with reddish throat, June–November; fruit with straw-coloured hairs; on more fertile and sometimes stony soils, hills and ranges, Illawarra District, NSW to North Qld; sometimes planted as ornamental. Aborigines reportedly ate young shoots, leaves and roots; flowers eaten raw or cooked. Bark fibre used to make dilly bags or hunting nets.

Family: Malvaceae

Hovea acutifolia
Pointed-leaved Hovea

Description: Upright shrub 2–5 m. Branches and flower calyx have long dense, grey or rusty hairs. Leaves alternate; glossy dark green above, rusty hairs below; elliptical, 2–9 cm by 5–18 mm; tip with sharp point; base short and tapered or rounded; edges slightly rolled under; net veins usually faint above, raised below; leaf stalk 3–5 mm long. Blue or light purple (rarely white) pea flowers in clusters of 1–4; largest petal with light cream-green splash at base; June–November. Inflated hairy seed pod.

Habitat and Range: Common. On sandy and stony soils on coastal lowlands and hills, often on slopes near drainage lines and moist gullies in Greater Brisbane Region. Manning River, NSW, to Bundaberg, Qld.

Notes: Seed pod pops audibly when ready to expel seeds. Sometimes planted as ornamental. Life span 6–10 years; regenerates from seed after fire. Several *Hovea* species in region. *Hovea heterophylla* (Common Hovea) — scrambling small shrub 10–40 cm, rarely to 1 m; semi-prostrate, multi-stemmed; leaves dark green above, paler and often sparsely hairy below; narrow and ovate to linear, 1–7 cm by 2–6 mm; tip rounded or with sharp point; net veins distinct on upper surface; leaf stalk 1–3 mm long; leaves on young plants particularly variable, lower leaves ovate, upper leaves narrow; purplish pea flowers in pairs, August–October; inflated seed pod to 1 cm; Tas., SA, Vic. and NSW to Nth Qld.

Family: Fabaceae

Jacksonia scoparia
Dogwood

Description: Twiggy shrub 2–5 m. Usually leafless, but with grey-green angular or winged stems; new growth sometimes with a few obovate leaves. Taller specimens with rough dark grey, furrowed bark, branches sometimes drooping; new growth silvery to blue-green. Orange-yellow pea flowers in small groups in racemes; calyx silky hairy; August–October. Seed pods flat with silky hairs; 6–12 mm long.

Habitat and Range: Common. On deep sands and sandy or stony soils, extending to drier areas west of Brisbane. Bega, NSW, north to Rockhampton, Qld.

Notes: Sometimes grows in very exposed places such as, headlands and along edges of sand blows on sand islands. Aboriginal people reputedly ate gum and pollen of flowers. Similar species *Jacksonia stackhousii* (Wallum Dogwood) — rarely erect shrub to 50 cm high; cylindrical grey-green branches; heathland and woodland near sea, see p. 76.

Wildlife: Leaves — caterpillars of Fiery Jewel and Copper Pencilled-blue Butterflies; minor source of honey and medium source of pollen for bees.

Family: Fabaceae

Leucopogon biflorus
Twin-flowered Bearded Heath

Description: Prickly, tangled shrub 0.5–1.5 m with many branches. Leaves alternate; bluish to grey-green above, paler below; rigid and spreading out from stems; oblong, 7–21 mm by 1.5–4 mm; tip with needle-like point; base shortly tapered or slightly rounded; several longitudinal veins; lacks leaf stalk. Pendulous white, tubular flowers with curly white hairs on inside; usually in pairs, but sometimes solitary or three together; July–October. Fruits a greenish drupe, ovoid 3–4 mm long.

Habitat and Range: On shallow sandy or stony soils, often on sandstone in woodland on hills and ranges. Dunedoo, NSW, to Rockhampton, and west to ranges of Central Qld.

Notes: Several species of *Leucopogon* in region; all identified by white tubular flowers with white curly hairs and berry-like fruit.

Family: Epacridaceae

Leucopogon juniperinus
Prickly Bearded Heath

Description: Spreading, densely branched shrub to 1 m. Branchlets with soft hairs. Prickly leaves alternate; spread all around stems; dark green above, paler below; linear to lanceolate, broadest just below tip; 6–16 mm by 1–2.5 mm; tip with short sharp, rigid point; base abruptly cut off. White tubular flowers; solitary on short stalks; white curly hairs on inside; May–October. Fruit a dull yellow drupe to 5 mm long.

Habitat and Range: Most common bearded heath in Greater Brisbane Region. On deep sands and sandy or stony soils; also heath, montane heath and wet eucalypt forest. Vic. to Bundaberg, Qld, and west to Carnarvon Ranges.

Notes: Similar to *Leucopogon biflorus*, see above.

Family: Epacridaceae

Leucopogon margarodes
Pink-bearded Heath

Description: Straggly shrub or small tree 2–4 m. Branches usually hairy. Blunt leaves alternate; dark bluish-green above, paler and often hairy below; obovate, convex above, broadest below tip; 4–14 mm by 1–3 mm; tip usually rounded, but with short fine point; edges rolled under; longitudinal veins visible below. White tubular flowers; solitary or paired on very short stalks 1–2 mm long. Fruit a succulent whitish drupe; longitudinal markings; 5–6 mm long

Habitat and Range: Confined to deep sands and sandy soils, common in forest understorey on sand islands of Moreton Bay and further north at Cooloola and Fraser I. Broken Bay, NSW, to Fraser I., Qld.

Family: Epacridaceae

Lomatia silaifolia
Crinkle Bush

Description: Variable shrub, 1–2 m. Leaves alternate, light green above, paler to almost shiny blue-green and sometimes hairy below; divided several times almost to midrib into about 12 lobes; edges of lobes usually with saw-like teeth; lacks stalk; base short, runs along edge of stem. White flowers in racemes to 30 cm long; December–May, but also throughout the year. Fruit a brownish, papery follicle; almost ovoid; 2.5–4 cm long; winged seeds.

Habitat and Range: Common. On sandy or stony soils in forest understorey on coastal hills and montane heath. Jervis Bay, NSW, to Rockhampton, and west to Central Qld ranges, also Darling Downs.

Notes: Species varies in division of leaves, size of lobes, and colour; 3 varieties previously recognised in Qld, now considered one species.

Family: Proteaceae

Lophostemon suaveolens
Swamp Box

Description: Tree 2–25 m. Grey-brown bark; fibrous to papery; light tan flecks underneath. Larger branches often twisted into unusual shapes. Leaves in whorls of 3–4 at ends of branchlets, but alternate lower down stem; dull green above, paler below; ovate to elliptical, 6–15 cm by 3–7 cm; oil glands more visible on lower leaf surface; tip blunt or with short point; base rounded to wedge-shaped; leaf stalk 1–3 cm long. Whitish flowers in groups of 3–8; broad rounded petals, sepals broad and rounded; numerous stamens grouped into 5 feathery bundles; September– February. Flower buds hairy, 3–4 mm long. Woody seed, thin-walled capsule hemispherical; 4–6 mm by 5–8 mm.

Habitat and Range: In moist sandy soils on edge of *Melaleuca* swampland and along creeks and river banks in drier areas, but less commonly on hills and slopes in Greater Brisbane Region. Scotts Head, NSW, to Nth Qld; also New Guinea and Malaysia.

Notes: Timber rot and borer resistant, useful for piles and underground supports; burns to a soft flour-like ash that is favoured for cooking bush damper. Often grows with species such as *Eucalyptus robusta*, see p.165, *Eucalyptus tereticornis* see p.168, *Eucalyptus resinifera* see p.164, *Eucalyptus racemosa*, see p.163, and on moister sites with *Casuarina glauca,* see p.58 and *Melaleuca quinquenervia,* see p.59.

Wildlife: Flowers — Rainbow Lorikeet; leaves — koalas; caterpillars of Ornate Dusk-flat, Coral Jewel and Fiery Jewel Butterflies; medium source of honey for bees.

Family: Myrtaceae

Lysiana maritima

Description: Spreading parasitic mistletoe with aerial stem and several branches. Leaves opposite, sometimes clustered; flat and spoon-shaped, 2–12 cm by 4–20 mm; tip pointed; base tapered; prominent midrib, 2–4 distinct lateral veins; leaf stalk 5–10 mm long. Flowers red (occasionally yellow), sometimes tipped with green or black; in pairs on common stalk 1–3 mm long; 6 petals, 6 stamens; September–February. Fruit berry-like, pale to nearly translucent; ellliptical to pear-shaped, nipple at top; 8–14 mm long.

Habitat and Range: In or near mangrove communities; on *Ceriops tagal*, see p. 44, or *Rhizophora stylosa*, see p. 46, or on adjacent trees such as *Acacia* spp. (Wattles) *Casuarina glauca*, see p.58 or *Myoporum acuminatum*, see p. 46. Southern Qld to NT.

Notes: Previously known as *Lysiana subfalcata* subsp. *maritima*. *Lysiana subfalcata* — has more drooping, sparsely branched stems; narrow and ovate to spoon-shaped leaves; fruit sometimes lacks nipple; drier inland areas in eucalypt forest or dry rainforest on species of *Acacia*, *Atalaya*, *Alectryon* and *Santanlum*.

Wildlife: Mistletoe Bird

Family: Loranthaceae

Maytenus silvestris
Narrow-leaved Orangebark

Description: Shrub 2–5 m. Young branchlets reddish with minute corky spots. Leaves alternate; ovate; often curved towards tip; 1–10 cm by 1.5–18 mm; tip narrowed and topped by short fine point; base wedge-shaped; vein network obvious; edges of adult leaves minutely toothed; juvenile leaves more coarsely toothed; leaf stalk 1–4 mm. Minute pale green flowers in clusters or racemes; October–December. Orange fruit, spherical to obovoid; dries to brown; 2 seeds.

Habitat and Range: Common. On sandy or stony soils in moister areas, also dry rainforest in Greater Brisbane Region. Illawarra District, NSW, to Caloundra, Qld, also Stanthorpe District.

Notes: Similar to *Maytenus bilocularis*, see p. 282.

Family: Celastraceae

Melaleuca bracteata
Black Tea Tree

Description: Tree 2–15 m tall. Hard, dark furrowed bark. Leaves alternate and scattered; dark green; nearly linear to lanceolate, 0.5–2.8 cm by 1–3 mm with 5–11 longitudinal veins; tip tapered or with sharp point; base wedge-shaped; oil glands visible. Young leaves hairy, lack stalk. White bottlebrush flowers on spike to 3.5 cm long; solitary or sometimes grouped in threes; September–November. Hypanthium of flower bud with soft hairs; 1.5–2.5 mm long. Woody seed capsule globular; 2.5–3 mm wide.

Habitat and Range: Common along drier watercourses to west of Brisbane. Macleay River, NSW, to Nth Qld, also SA and WA.

Notes: Several varieties of this species planted as ornamentals around Brisbane, light green leaves.

Family: Myrtaceae

Melaleuca linariifolia
Flax Leaf Paperbark, Snow-in-summer

Description: Tall shrub 2–10 m. Papery layered bark. Leaves opposite; linear to elliptical, 1–3 cm by 1–30 mm; tip tapers to fine point; base tapered, juvenile leaves hairy; oil glands with distinct smell; leaf stalk 0–1 mm long. Numerous fluffy white flower spikes at end of twigs; September–November and February–May. Lower half of flower bud smooth. Woody capsule; cylindrical to nearly globular; 3–4 mm wide.

Habitat and Range: Swampy areas and along sandy watercourses in eastern coastal areas. North of Bateman's Bay, NSW, to Bundaberg, Qld.

Notes: Similar to *Melaleuca trichostachya* — fruit top-shaped; widespread. Walgett, NSW, to Nth Qld; also NT and SA. Both species planted as ornamentals.

Family: Myrtaceae

Melaleuca nodosa
Prickly Leaf Paperbark

Description: Shrub, 1–7 m. White corky to papery bark. Leaves alternate and scattered; dotted with oil glands; fairly rigid, cylindrical, linear or oblong; 10–40 mm by 1–3 mm; tip rigid and sharp; base wedge-shaped. Yellow or white flower heads to 1.5 cm long; sepals minute, 0.5 mm long; petals rounded, 1–1.5 mm long; yellow stamens, in bundles of 3–5; September–February. Fruit in woody clusters 6–10 mm; egg-shaped, 2–3 mm wide.

Habitat and Range: Widespread. On deep sands and moist sandy soils, also in coastal heath. Campbelltown, NSW, to Nth Qld, also SA.

Notes: Sometimes planted as an ornamental.

Wildlife: Medium source of pollen for bees.

Family: Myrtaceae

Melichrus procumbens
Jam Tarts

Description: Semi-prostrate shrub to 30 cm. Spreading mat-like growth; hairy stems and leaves. Soft leaves alternate, crowded around stems; light green above, paler below, with long soft, white hairs; linear to narrow and ovate; 6–27 mm by 1.2–4 mm; tip tapers to point; edges lined with hairs; raised parallel longitudinal veins. Solitary flowers said to resemble 'jam tarts'; cream to almost translucent; face downwards; July–September. Fruit a greenish-red, flattened and globular drupe; 4-5 mm wide; usually with numerous verticle edges.

Habitat and Range: Uncommon. Restricted to shallow sandy soils on sandstone in Greater Brisbane Region. Georges River, NSW, to Brisbane, Qld, also Darling Downs District on granite soils.

Notes: Two other species in region. *Melichrus adpressus* — to 1.5 m; stiff pointed leaves with papery edges; 15–32 mm by 2–6 mm; fruit globular, 4–5 mm wide, sharply divided into smooth greenish-brown top half and darker, wrinkled lower half; also on sandy soils, but sometimes in heath or dry rainforest; Angourie Point, NSW, to Nth Qld. *Melichrus urceolatus* — variable species to 1.5 m; spreading leaves crowded at tips of branches; edges thin, translucent to white; 6–25 mm by 2–6 mm; fruit globular, 4–6 mm wide, same colour as *Melichrus adpressus*, but not as sharply divided; in drier areas on sandy soils; Vic. to Nth Qld.

Family: Epacridaceae

Monotoca scoparia
Prickly Broom Heath

Description: Small shrub to 1 m or less. Leaves alternate, blue to grey-green above, pale whitish–green below; oblong to narrow and lanceolate, convex above; 5–23 mm by 1–3 mm; longitudinal veins visible; edges rolled under slightly; tip rounded, but with fine rigid point. White tubular flowers in clusters of 1–2, or on very short spike; March–June. Fruit a succulent yellow to orange drupe; ellipsoid; 2–3 mm long.

Habitat and Range: Widespread. On infertile deep sands and sandy soils in forest understorey, also in heath in Brisbane region. Vic., SA, Tas. and NSW to Nth Qld.

Notes: Similar to *Monotoca* sp. — 2–10 m tall; wider leaves; occurs on more fertile deep sands in wetter forest north to Fraser I. Also similar to *Acrotriche aggregata*, see p. 123.

Family: Epacridaceae

Ozothamnus diosmifolius
Sago Flower

Description: Branching shrub 2–5 m. Papery bark on older plants; younger branches and stems with dense short hairs. Leaves alternate; dark green and rough above, paler and covered with short dense, white hairs below; linear to narrow and elliptical, 9–30 mm by 1–2.5 mm; tip rounded, sometimes topped with fine bent point; edges usually curved under to midrib; leaf stalks 0–1 mm. White to pink flower heads resemble sago pudding; July–November. Minute fruit 1–2 mm long; topped by fine white hairs

Habitat and Range: Widespread. On sandy and stony shallow soils, often in disturbed areas on edges of heaths, rainforests and paths in Greater Brisbane Region. Eden, NSW, to Bundaberg, Qld, and ranges of Central Qld.

Notes: Previously known as *Helichrysum diosmifolium*.

Family: Asteraceae

Persoonia stradbrokensis
Coastal Geebung

Description: Tall shrub to 4 m. Young branchlets with dense hairs. Leaves alternate; light green to yellow-green, not much paler below; elliptical to ovate, 3–11 cm by 10–40 mm; flat to curved, sometimes with edges slightly rolled under; hairy when immature; 3–4 lateral veins visible; leaf stalk 2–6 mm long. Orange-yellow flowers usually solitary on hairy stalk 1–4 mm long; 4 petal-like segments 10–13 mm long with minute point; hairy on underside; petals rolled back as stamens mature; January-May. Fruit purplish-green; almost ellipsoid; 10–15 mm by 7–10 mm; hairless when ripe.

Habitat and Range: Widespread, but never abundant. On deep sands and on sandy and stony soils on coast and hills of Greater Brisbane Region. Hastings River, NSW, to Bundaberg, Qld.

Notes: Previously known as *Persoonia cornifolia* — broader, shorter leaves; on sandy or stony soils on ranges and western slopes. Several species of *Persoonia* in region. Leaf shape varies, but usually with orange-yellow solitary flowers; also greenish drupe with succulent outer layer and harder inner layer protecting seeds. Some species hybridise with each other. Aboriginal people reputedly ate sweet pulp of fruit when ripe.

Wildlife: Flowers — Brown and White-cheeked Honeyeaters.

Family: Proteaceae

Petalostigma pubescens
Bitter Bark

Description: Shrub or small tree 2–10 m. Bark dark grey becoming slightly furrowed and scaly on older trees. Leaves alternate; usually in two rows; shiny green sometimes hairy above, pale brownish-green with dense long and short hairs below; ovate to nearly circular, 2–6 cm by 1–2.5 cm; tip blunt to pointed; base rounded or tapered; edges wavy; leaf stalk hairy, 3–8 mm long. Flowers cream to light brown; December–May. Male and female flowers on different plants. Male — in clusters of 3–4. Female — solitary, stigma branches petal-like. Fruit orange-yellow; segmented, globular to egg-shaped; 12–17 mm wide; fleshy layer often hairy and slightly lobed.

Habitat and Range: Widespread. On sandy or stony soils, also in dry rainforest in Greater Brisbane Region. Ramornie, NSW, to Nth Qld, also WA and NT; New Guinea.

Notes: Similar to *Petalostigma triloculare* (Long-leaf Bitter Bark) — Shrub or small tree 2–15 m. Leaves alternate; usually in two rows; shiny dark glossy green above, paler light grey-green with fine long hairs below; narrow and elliptical, 2.5–8.5 cm by 1–3.5 cm; tip sharp or tapered to a point; base tapered or blunt; edes sometimes wavy; leaf stalk 5–7 mm long. Flowers green to cream or light brown; December-May. Fruit orange-brown; segmented, globular to egg-shaped; 10–18 mm wide; thin fleshy layer, usually hairless and slightly lobed. Sometimes locally common. On moist sandy and stony soils, often along or near drainage lines, also edges of dry or subtropical rainforest in Greater Brisbane Region. Nymboida, NSW, to Rockhampton, Qld. Aboriginal people of Marlborough area, Qld, used pounded fruits, along with leaves of a different (unidentified) plant as a fish poison. At Lockhart River, Qld, a liquid made from the fruit is used for toothache.

Wildlife: Leaves — caterpillar of Copper Jewel Butterfly.

Family: Euphorbiaceae

Petalostigma triloculare, BC

Pimelea linifolia subsp. *linifolia*
Slender Rice Flower

Description: Small, semi-prostrate to erect shrub to 1 m. Sparsely branched with distinctive leaf arrangement. Leaves opposite; in four rows; each pair at right angles to pair above and below. Leaves green above, paler below; elliptical to obovate, 5–30 mm by 2–7 mm; midrib conspicuous; tip tapered to blunt with short fine point; base wedge-shaped to contracted; leaf stalk 0.5–1 mm long. Numerous white flower heads; surrounded by 4 leaf-like bracts often with reddish tinge;; 2 stamens; flowers year-round. Green fruit 3–5 mm.

Habitat and Range: Widespread. On deep sands and sandy and stony soils, also in heath and disturbed areas near paths and forest edges. Vic. to Nth Qld, also SA and Tas.

Notes: Poisonous to stock; sometimes planted as ornamental.

Family: Thymelaeceae

Pimelea neo-anglica
Poison Pimelea, Scanty Rice Flower

Description: Slender shrub to 3 m. Leaves opposite; blue-green above, paler below; linear to elliptical; 5–40 mm by 1–4 mm, tip tapered; base tapered or wedge-shaped; leaf stalk to 1 mm. Cream to green flower heads; flowers surrounded by 2, (occasionally 4) leaf-like bracts; flowers year-round. Succulent bright orange-red fruit; egg-shaped.

Habitat and Range: Widespread. On sandy or stony soils, often on mountain slopes, also on edges of rainforest on main range west of Brisbane. Condobolin, NSW, to Burnett District, Qld, also ranges of Central Qld.

Notes: Considered poisonous to stock.

Wildlife: Fruit — Lewin's Honeyeater.

Family: Thymelaeaceae

Pittosporum revolutum
Yellow Pittosporum

Description: Sparsely branched shrub 1–4 m. New shoots and flowers with dense rusty brown hairs. Leaves alternate below growing point, or in whorls of 4–6 at ends of branchlets; green above, paler with dense to sparse rusty-brown hairs, particularly on main veins, below; ovate to elliptical, 4–15 cm by 1.5–6 cm; tip short and tapered; base rounded; edges wavy and slightly rolled under; leaf stalk 5–13 mm long. Yellow tubular flowers in raceme; 5 sepals, hairy outside; 5-lobed petals joined in tube 9–12 mm long; 5 stamens; September–November. Fruit a woody orange-yellow capsule; paler inside; egg-shaped; 1.2–2 cm long; thick walled, often rough or warty on outside; seeds reddish, immersed in sticky fluid.

Habitat and Range: Sometimes locally common. On deep sands and on moister soils, often on alluvial soils along drainage lines and watercourses, also in wet forest and on edges of rainforest in Greater Brisbane region. Vic. to Bundaberg, Qld.

Notes: Flowers perfumed. Similar to *Pittosporum undulatum* — see p. 288. Aboriginal people ate bitter-tasting seeds; leaves contain saponin, can be used as soap.

Family: Pittosporaceae

Podolobium aciculiferum
Spiny Shaggy Pea

Description: Spiny shrub 1–2 m tall. Branches hairy and broadly spreading. Leaves opposite or sometimes alternate, or in irregular whorls of 3; dark shiny green above, paler below; lanceolate to ovate, 1–3 cm by 3–9 mm; tip with sharp spine; two spines at base of very short leaf stalk. Orange-yellow pea flowers; solitary or in short raceme; December–May. Seed pod curved, oblong; 1–1.5 cm; sometimes softly hairy; short stalk.

Habitat and Range: Often locally common. On stony soils, sometimes also on edges of wet eucalypt forest or rainforest. Nerrigundah, NSW, to Rockhampton, Qld.

Notes: Previously known as *Oxylobium aciculiferum*. Often on edges of *Corymbia* communities, see pp.142–146 and growing with *Daviesia villifera*, see p.147.

Family: Fabaceae

Podolobium ilicifolium
Native Holly, Prickly Shaggy Pea

Description: Shrub 1–2 m rarely to 3 m. Branches and undersides of leaves sometimes covered with soft short hairs. Holly-like leaves opposite or in irregular whorls of 3; dark shiny green above, paler below; lanceolate to ovate, 2–10 cm by 1–3 cm; tip with sharp spine; base wedge-shaped; edges with deep irregular lobes, each lobe ends in sharp spine; two spines at base of very short leaf stalk. Orange-yellow pea flowers, often with reddish markings in throat; in racemes; July–May. Hairy seed pods egg-shaped to oblong, sometimes curved.

Habitat and Range: Often locally common. On sandy or stony soils on coastal hills and mountain slopes, also sometimes in mountain heath. Vic. to Bundaberg, Qld, also ranges of Central Qld.

Notes: Previously known as *Oxylobium ilicifolium*.

Family: Fabaceae

Pomaderris argyrophylla subsp. *argyrophylla*

Description: Tall shrub to 5 m. Young branchlets with silvery hairs. Leaves green above, paler below, covered with dense, curly silvery hairs; narrow and ovate, 3.5–13 cm by 9–33 mm; tip pointed; base wedge-shaped to tapered; edge slightly rolled under; midrib raised below, impressed on upper surface; lateral veins looping, more-or-less parallel, visible below, usually covered with a few straight hairs; leaf stalk 10–16 mm long. Creamy-yellow flowers in large panicles; with dense soft hairs; 5-lobed, tubular calyx covered with straight and curly grey hairs; September–November. Fruit a capsule protruding above edge of calyx; ellipsoid; to 3 mm long; 3 valves.

Habitat and Range: Confined to rocky and mountainous areas as an understorey shrub. Barrington Tops, NSW, to Nth Qld.

Notes: One of 12 species in South-east Qld. *Pomaderris ferruginea* — new parts with rusty hairs on leaves; curly and rusty hairs below; 4–10 cm by 14–35 mm; petals yellowish, Mt Coot-tha, Taylor Range, Springbrook. Also similar to *Pomaderris lanigera* see p. 320.

Family: Rhamnaceae

Pomax umbellata
See p. 105

Pultenaea euchila
Orange Pultenaea

Description: Shrub 1–2 m tall. Angular branches. Leaves alternate, dark blue-green above, slightly paler below; oblong, 1–2 cm by 2–35 mm; tip rounded, often with minute notch; base tapered; edges flat to slightly rolled under; midrib conspicuous, other veins faint; leaf stalk 1–1.5 mm long. Orange-yellow pea flowers; sometimes with red at base of largest petal; often clustered at ends of branches; June–November. Inflated seed pods egg-shaped to triangular; 7–9 mm long.

Habitat and Range: Uncommon. On sandy or clay soils on coastal hills, sometimes near drainage lines or in disturbed areas. Lake Macquarie, NSW, to Bundaberg and Gayndah Districts, Qld.

Notes: One of 14 species of *Pultenaea* in Moreton Region.

Family: Fabaceae

Pultenaea petiolaris
Rayed Bush Pea

Description: Small, semi-prostrate shrub to about 30 cm. Leaves alternate; crowded at tip of stems; dark glossy green and grooved above, sometimes with coarse hairs; paler and hairy below; linear; 1–3 cm by 1.5–4 mm; tip blunt with slightly bent point; base rounded; edges slightly rolled under; leaf stalk 2.5–12 mm, longest just below flowers. Orange-yellow pea flowers with dark reddish base; in dense heads in uppermost leaves; 5-lobed calyx with dense hairs; June–November. Inflated seed pod hairy; flattened; egg-shaped to triangular; 6–9 mm long.

Habitat and Range: Uncommon, but widespread. On sandy soils on sandstone, sometimes in disturbed areas along edges of pathways in Greater Brisbane Region. Wauchope, NSW, to Nth Qld.

Family: Fabaceae

Pultenaea villosa
Kerosene Bush, Hairy Bush Pea

Description: Shrub to 1–3 m tall. Stems with long spreading, white or rusty hairs; branchlets sometimes arching. Leaves alternate; crowded at tip of stems; green above, sometimes with a few hairs, particularly along edges, often concave; lower surface usually with spreading hairs; shape varies, narrow and obovate, wedge to spoon-shaped; 4–10 mm by 1–3 mm; tip rounded to asymmetrical and bent over; base wedge-shaped to tapered; leaf stalk 0–1 mm long. Orange-yellow pea flowers with red at base of largest petal; 5–12 mm long; calyx with 5 deep lobes, often with spreading hairs; March–November. Inflated seed pod hairy; egg-shaped to triangular, 4–6 mm.

Habitat and Range: Widespread and common. On deep sands on edges of sand blows and sandy soils in forest understorey, often in disturbed, regularly burnt areas. Bega, NSW, to Bundaberg and Gayndah, Qld.

Notes: Good fire indicator with life span of 6–8 years. May dominate shrub layer in frequently burnt areas, but population gradually declines if not burnt after about 6 years, until next fire restarts life cycle.

Family: Fabaceae

Pultenaea retusa

Description: Sparsely branched shrub 1–2 m tall. Upper branches angular, covered with soft short hairs. Leaves alternate; dark green above, paler below; linear to narrowly oblong; 5–15 mm by 1.5–3 mm; tip usually with shallow notch; edges flat to slightly bent under, usually hairless. Orange-yellow pea flowers in small heads; 5–7 mm long; 5-lobed calyx with silky hairs; July– November. Hairy seed pod; flattened, egg-shaped to triangular; 5–7 mm long.

Habitat and Range: Uncommon. On sandy and stony soils or swampy soils on coastal hills and ranges in Greater Brisbane Region. Illawarra, NSW, to Nth Qld.

Family: Fabaceae

Rapanea variabilis
Muttonwood

Description: Shrub to small tree 1–12 m. Terminal buds covered with fawn to brown hairs. Leaves alternate; dark shiny green above, much paler below; shape variable; 3–9 cm by 3–35 mm; tip blunt to pointed; base wedge-shaped to tapered; edges slightly wavy or rolled under, entire or with prickly teeth. Very small white bell-shaped flowers in clusters; Fruit a globular drupe, bluish-purple when ripe; 4–6 mm long

Habitat and Range: Widespread. On deep sands, sandy and stony soils from coast to mountain slopes, also dry, subtropical and remnant rainforest. Illawarra District, NSW, to Nth Qld.

Notes: Sometimes known as *Myrsine variabilis*.

Wildlife: Fruit — Lewin's Honeyeater; leaves — caterpillar of White-banded Line-blue Butterfly.

Family: Myrsinaceae

Swainsona galegifolia
Smooth Darling Pea

Description: Perennial shrub to 1 m. Semi-prostate to erect; multi-stemmed. Leaves alternate; consist of 21–25 leaflets; green to grey-green; leaflets linear to elliptical, lower leaflets 6–20 mm by 1.5–8 mm; tip rounded to notched; base tapered. Groups of 15–20 pink-purple pea flowers in racemes; colour varies, blue to mauve or dark red; flower stalk to 11 mm, hairless; September–February. Inflated seed pods; elliptical and beaked; sometimes with a few hairs.

Habitat and Range: Sometimes locally common. On shallow sandy and stony soils, on hill slopes or along drainage lines, sometimes in disturbed areas in western parts of region. Newcastle, NSW, to Nth Qld.

Notes: Similar to *Swainsona queenslandica* see below.

Family: Fabaceae

Swainsona queenslandica
Darling Pea

Description: Perennial shrub to 1 m. Multi-stemmed. Leaves alternate; consist of 19–25 leaflets; grey-green; ovate, lower leaflets 10–20 mm by 2–3 mm; tip rounded to notched; base tapered. Groups of 20 pink-purple pea flowers in racemes; colour varies, whitish-pink to dark red; flower stalk to 5 mm long with minute hairs. Seed pods elliptical, sometimes with dense hairs,

Habitat and Range: Sometimes locally common. On shallow sandy and stony soils, on hills and ranges in Greater Brisbane Region. Newcastle, NSW, to Rockhampton, Qld and ranges of Central Qld.

Notes: Similar to *Swainsona galegifolia* see above.

Family: Fabaceae

Westringia eremicola
Slender Westringia

Description: Spindly shrub 1–2 m. Stems with 4 ridges, squarish in cross section and like leaves slightly rough to touch because of upright pointing hairs. Leaves in whorls of 3; light to dark green above, paler below; densely hairy; linear to elliptical, 8–25 mm by 0.8–2.5 mm; tip acute or with short fine point; base wedge-shaped; edges often rolled under, almost to midrib; leaf stalk to 1.5 mm long. Mauve-blue flowers solitary or in clusters; orange to brown dots in throat; hairy, green sepals joined in hairy, 5-lobed calyx; flower stalks 1–1.5 mm long; flowers mainly September–February, sometimes March–May. Fruit divided into 4 segments at maturity.

Habitat and Range: On sandy and stony soils. SA, Vic. and NSW to Bundaberg, Qld.

Notes: One of six species in Greater Brisbane region. Four species considered rare and confined to mountainous areas — *Westringia blakeana*, *Westringia grandifolia*, *Westringia rupicola*, and *Westringia sericea*. *Westringia tenuicaulis* — multi-stemmed; leaf edges do not curve under; mainly in heaths. *Westringia fruticosa* (Coastal Rosemary) — leaves in whorls of 4–5; lanceolate, broader, 3–5 mm wide; often planted as ornamental; NSW Central Coast.

Family: Lamiaceae

Xanthorrhoea glauca subsp. *glauca*
Grass Tree

See p. 321

Xanthorrhoea johnsonii
Grass Tree

Description: Grass tree usually 1–3 m, less commonly 4–5 m tall. Single black aerial stem; very occasionally with two branches; woody, covered with old leaf bases. Narrow green leaves in arching upright tufts; light cream-green at base inside crown; diamond-shaped in cross section, 1–2.5 mm wide. Dead leaves form skirt below live leaves. Small white flowers on spike 0.2–2 m long by 20–40 mm wide; flowering stem that supports spike usually as long as or shorter than, spike. April–December. Fruit a 3-lobed capsule embedded in woody spike (flower-base); 3 dull black seeds.

Habitat and Range: Sometimes locally common. On well-drained, shallow and often coarse textured sandy stony soils on hill ridges, or on leached deep sands in Greater Brisbane Region. Singleton, NSW, to Nth Qld.

Notes: Similar to *Xanthorrhoea latifolia*, see p. 198. Flowering increases markedly (up 80%) in areas burnt in previous year, otherwise flowering tends to be inconsistent. Slow growth rate measured at about 8–9 mm per year. Number of juvenile trees low compared to amount of seed produced after fire. Old leaf bases insulate stem and growth point from high temperatures during fires. Aboriginal people soaked flowers in water to produce a thick drink; grubs in trunk resin treated and used as a glue to waterproof bags; dry flower stalks of *Xanthorrhoea* species used as rubbing sticks for fire-making; also as light fishing spears.

Family: Xanthorrhoeaceae

Xanthorrhoea latifolia subsp. *latifolia*
Grass Tree

Description: Grass tree usually without aerial stem, or rarely to 2 m. Yellow-green to green leaves in arching upright tufts; light cream-green at base inside crown; nearly flat, diamond-shaped to triangular in cross section, 2.5–6 mm wide. Small cream to white flowers on spikes 0.5–1.2 m long, 20–35 mm wide; flowering stem that supports spike usually 1–2 times long as spike; April–September. Fruit a 3-lobed capsule embedded in woody spike (flower-base); 3 dark brown seeds.

Habitat and Range: Sometimes locally common, often in thickets. Well drained, shallow sandy and stony soils on ridges and mountain slopes. Wyong, NSW, to Nth Qld.

Notes: Similar to *Xanthorrhoea fulva*, see p. 85.

Family: Xanthorrhoeaceae

Xanthorrhoea macronema
Bottle-brush Grass Tree, Saw-edged Grass Tree

Description: Stemless grass tree to 1 m. Underground stem sometimes branched to produce more than one crown. Yellow green to light green leaves in arching upright tufts; light cream-green at base inside crown; nearly triangular, 2.5–3.5 mm wide; a few whitish longitudinal veins on upper surface, edges rough to touch. Cream-yellow flowers larger than in other species of grass tree; brush-like flower spike, 5–16 cm long, 14–20 mm wide; flowering stem that supports spike nearly 10 times as long as spike; July–January. Fruit a 3-lobed capsule embedded in woody spike (flower-base); 3 dull black seeds.

Habitat and Range: Uncommon. On more fertile deep sands and moist sandy loams, also sometimes in wet eucalypt forest on coastal lowlands and hills. Sydney, NSW, to Bundaberg District, Qld.

Family: Xanthorrhoeaceae

Wet Eucalypt forest

Bellthorpe State Forest, BC

HERBS, GRASSES AND GROUNDCOVERS

Geranium solanderi var. *solanderi*
Native Geranium

Description: Weak-stemmed perennial herb to 50 cm. Coarse stiff hairs on stems and leaves. Leaves deeply divided into 5–7 lobes; each lobe divided again at tip. Flowers with 5 pink petals and yellowish veins; solitary or paired on common stalk; 5 green sepals; flowers year-round, but mainly September–February. Thin fruits with curved awns and stiff hairs, 12–15 mm long; open from base to reveal pitted black seeds.

Habitat and Range: In grass/herb layer of eucalypt forest, sometimes along edges of paths; also in rainforest and on mountains. All states except NT; also NZ.

Notes: Taproot starchy; may have been roasted by Aboriginal people, but probably not very palatable.

Family: Geraniaceae

Pseuderanthemum variabile

Description: Weak-stemmed perennial herb to 30 cm. Hairy branches and creeping rhizome. Leaves opposite; dark green, hairy above, purplish and dotted with glands below; narrow, lanceolate to oval; tip blunt to sharp; base rounded or wedge-shaped; edges sometimes wavy. Groups of 3-5 pink to mauve (sometimes white) flowers; calyx with dense hairs; flowering September–May. Fruit a hairy capsule, 1–1.5 cm long.

Habitat and Range: Widespread. Often in moist shaded areas of eucalypt forests and dry rainforest, also in *Allocasuarina littoralis*, (see p. 124) thickets and semi-evergreen vine thickets to north and west of Brisbane. Bega, NSW, to Qld and NT.

Wildlife: Leaves — caterpillars of Leafwing, Blue-banded Eggfly, Varied Eggfly and Blue Argus Butterflies.

Family: Acanthaceae

FERNS

Blechnum cartilagineum
Gristle Fern

Description: Hardy fern, often with pinkish new growth. Fronds usually 35–90 cm long, but to 135 cm with stalk. Each stalk pale and smooth above, black warty scales at base. Lobes of fronds joined at base; leathery with minute teeth along edge; 10–22 cm by 1–2 cm. Lowermost pair of lobes separated and bent downwards.

Habitat and Range: Widespread in moister gullies and hillsides of eucalypt forest and rainforest. Tas. to Qld; also Phillipines and Melanesia.

Notes: Sori in narrow continuous line either side of midvein on underside of lobe, sometimes covered by protective dark brown tissue; this and minute teeth characteristic of Brisbane species.

Family: Blechnaceae

Sticherus flabellatus var. *flabellatus*
Shiny Fan Fern

Description: Fern to less than 1 m. Long creeping rhizome with scales at tip. Frond stalk to 60 cm, scaly at base, smooth above. Fronds forked 2–3 times, roughly equal branches; 14–30 cm long, narrowed at both ends. Dormant buds between branches covered with scales. Fronds light yellowish-green above, underside paler green or sometimes with whitish-blue lustre. Single row of sori each side of segment midrib.

Habitat and Range: Often grows in thickets; in moist gullies and along creek banks around Brisbane. Eastern Australia from Vic. to Qld; also New Guinea, New Caledonia, NZ.

Notes: Similar to *Dicranopteris linearis*, see p. 66.

Family: Glecheniaceae

PALMS

Livistona australis
Cabbage Tree Palm

Description: Erect palm, 20–30 m. Single stem marked with annual growth scars and furrows, 30–50 cm wide. Large, shiny green fan-shaped leaves in dense crown; stiff, but drooping at ends. Leaf stalks with curved spines towards base. Leaf blade 1–2 m long, divided into 70 folded segments. Inflorescence to 1 m; enclosed by several long hairy spathes. Creamy-white flowers; September–February.

Habitat and Range: In swampy areas or along watercourses in wet eucalypt forest and rainforest. Vic. to Townsville, Nth Qld.

Notes: Aboriginal people cut out and ate cabbage-like heart of leaf-material; this killed plant. Leaves used for making bags, baskets, fishing nets and lines. Cultivated worldwide.

Wildlife: Fruit — Grey-headed Flying Fox (+ flowers), Brush Turkey, Wompoo Fruit-dove, Topknot Pigeon; leaves — caterpillars of Orange Palm-dart and Yellow Palm-dart Butterflies.

Family: Arecaceae

Lepidozamia peroffskyana
Pineapple Palm

See p. 205

SHRUBS AND TREES

Eucalyptus grandis
Flooded Gum

Description: Erect tree to more than 50 m. Canopy dark green. Powdery, smooth light grey to white bark; greenish underneath; shed in long strips, with 1–2 m of thin, scaly brownish bark at base. Leaves alternate; spreading or drooping; dark glossy green above, paler below; 8–16 cm by 1–5 cm. Seedling and juvenile leaves oval to 14 cm. Flowers white; 4–12 originate at common point on singe stalk; March–August. Buds 7–10 mm long with conical top. Mature seed capsules woody; 5–8 mm by 5–7 mm; protruding thickish valves pointed inwards from rim.

Habitat and Range: On moist loamy soils of alluvial or volcanic origin in valleys and slopes close to ranges; often grows with an understorey of rainforest species; common near rainforest or as an emergent in rainforest regrowth. Newcastle, NSW, to Bundaberg, Qld, also isolated populations at Bloomfield, Nth Qld.

Notes: Ornamental in parks, but not as tall and erect and with branches closer to ground. Lacks underground stem found in many eucalypts. Timber used for housing. Closely related to *Eucalyptus saligna* (Sydney Blue Gum), see p. 204; difficult to separate in field without seed capsules.

Wildlife: Flowers — Grey-headed Flying Fox, Little Lorikeet; leaves — koalas; sap — Yellow-bellied Glider.

Family: Myrtaceae

Eucalyptus saligna
Sydney Blue Gum

Description: Erect tree to 50 m. Canopy greyish-green; broad trunk. Smooth bluish-grey to white bark, sometimes with darker patches; shed in long strips, often with up to 4 m of brownish scaly bark at base. Leaves alternate; spreading or drooping; greyish-green above, paler below; 7–17 cm by 1–4.5 cm. Seedling and juvenile leaves lanceolate to oval, to about 14 cm. Flowers white; 7–12 originate at common point on single stalk; December–February. Buds 6–9 cm long with conical top and silvery lustre. Mature seed capsules woody; about 5-8mm by 5-7mm; protruding valves thin, pointed and spreading outwards from rim.

Habitat and Range: On moist, moderately fertile soils in wet eucalypt forest, near rainforest or as an emergent in rainforest regrowth. Mainly confined to higher altitudes and mountain slopes near Brisbane. Southern NSW to Maryborough, Qld, also isolated populations north to Mackay and west to Carnarvon Gorge.

Notes: Similar to *Eucalyptus grandis* (Flooded Gum), see p. 203, but difficult to separate in field without seed capsules. Timber used as general purpose hardwood. Ornamental species in parks.

Wildlife: Leaves — koalas.

Family: Myrtaceae

Lepidozamia peroffskyana
Cycad Flower, Pineapple Palm

Description: Palm-like plant to 6 m tall. Stem covered with old leaf stalks; new growth covered with short, soft hairs. Shiny green leaves alternate; 2–3 m long. Leaf stalks 30–60 cm long with hairy swollen base. About 200 leaflets along upper surface, spreading but drooping down to pointed tip. Leaflets linear and often curved; 7–14 longitudinal veins below; 10–35 cm by 0.7–1.5 cm. Separate male and female plants. Male cones cylindrical 40–60 cm. Female oval to 80 cm long. Cones formed September–December or after fire; seeds red when ripe; in pairs; 4–6 cm by 3–3.5 cm.

Habitat and Range: Confined to mountainous areas near Brisbane, sometimes on rainforest edges. Taree, NSW, to Blackall Range, Qld.

Notes: Cultivated as ornamental. Aboriginal people ate poisonous seeds after prolonged soaking, grinding and cooking.

Family: Zamiaceae

Lomatia arborescens
Tree Lomatia

Description: Shrub or small tree 2–10 m. Multi-stemmed; grey-brown smooth bark; new growth often with rusty hairs. Leaves alternate; elliptical to oblong, 3–14 cm by 1–6 cm; tip blunt or tapered to point; base sharp or blunt; edges entire or toothed; conspicuous veins. White to cream flowers in racemes 4–16 cm long; December–February. Fruit a dark brown to greyish black follicle; almost egg-shaped; winged seeds.

Habitat and Range: Often on mountain ranges, also in rainforest and mountain heath near Brisbane. Barrington Tops, NSW, to Nambour, Qld.

Notes: Leaves larger and more evenly toothed in rainforest, but smaller and sometimes entire in exposed areas.

Family: Proteaceae

Lophostemon confertus
Brush Box

Description: Tree to 30 m. Narrow, but dense crown with leaves in clusters of 4–5 at ends of branchlets. Lower trunk with rough, greyish-brown bark in segments; upper branches smooth pink-grey. New growth covered with fine hairs. Leaves alternate below growing point; dark glossy green above, paler below; elliptical to oval, 9–17.5 cm by 2.5–4.5 cm. White flowers in groups of 3–8 with broad petals, numerous stamens in 5 feathery bundles; December–January. Fruit a bell–shaped capsule 1–1.3 cm long.

Habitat and Range: Various habitats, coastal lowlands to mountain ridges. Grows best on deep alluvial clay soils; but also occurs on deep sands, sandy and stony soils along drainage lines and in moist gullies. Emergent in drier rainforests near Brisbane. Newcastle, NSW, to Fraser I., Qld.

Notes: Sometimes dominant species in wet eucalypt forests and dry rainforest (eg Fraser I., Mt Cordeaux). Often has mallee-like growth in drier areas or is shrub-sized on young dunes or in exposed areas near sea (Moreton and Fraser Is). Naturalised around Sydney. Ornamental street tree; important commercial timber. Rough bark resembles box bark eucalypts.

Wildlife: Flowers — Rainbow and Scaly-breasted Lorikeets, Crimson Rosella, White-naped and Scarlet Honeyeaters; seeds — black cockatoos, Pale-headed Rosella; leaves — koalas, caterpillars of Ornate Dusk-flat, Eastern Dusk-flat, Bronze Flat and Coral Jewel Butterflies; medium pollen source for bees.

Family: Myrtaceae

Macrozamia lucida

Description: Small, palm-like plant to 1 m. Stem usually underground. Dark shiny green crown with 2–15 fronds. Top fronds erect, lower fronds spreading; stalk rounded and sometimes slightly twisted, 25–50 cm long; 3–7 mm wide at bases of lowest leaflets. Each leaflet narrow, curved, twisted at base; sharp tip; whitish, slightly thickened base; 5–11 raised veins on underside. Male and female cones on separate plants. Male cones cylindrical and spiny; 15 cm by 4 cm. Female cones cylindrical; 15–20 cm by 7–9 cm; 2 reddish seeds on each segment, released September–December or sometimes after fires.

Habitat and Range: On coastal hillsides. Pottsville, NSW, to Conondale Ranges, Qld.

Notes: Similar to *Macrozamia macleayi* (Pineapple Zamia) — Palm-like plant to 2 m; denser crown with 50–100 leaves; each leaf 0.5–2 m long with 80–160 leaflets. Lowest leaflets (sometimes up to 28 pairs) reduced to spines. Male cones cylindrical, 15–20 cm by 3.8–6.5 cm. Female cones cylindrical to barrel-shaped, 19–30 cm by 7–10 cm. Coastal districts; Mt Glorious to Port Curtis, Qld.

Aboriginal people ate poisonous seeds after prolonged soaking, grinding and cooking. Member of one of oldest groups of seed plants, Cycadophyta; cycads were dominant component of forests 200 million years ago.

Wildlife: Leaves — caterpillar of Cycad Blue Butterfly.

Family: Zamiaceae

Melastoma affine
Blue Tongue

Description: Spreading shrub 2–3 m tall. Branchlets, leaves and hypanthium covered with short stiff hairs. Leaves opposite; dark green above, paler below; ovate 6–12 cm by 2–4 cm; tip narrowed to a short fine point; base broadly rounded; 5 prominent longitudinal veins, usually 2 finer veins near leaf edges, veins sunken on upper surface and raised below. Flowers light purple, mauve or rarely white on short stalks in groups of 5–11; 10 prominent stamens. September–February. Fruit reddish, globular; 6–8 mm long; develops within greenish, hairy cup-shaped hypanthium; semi-succulent, but eventually dries and splits.

Habitat and Range: Moist sandy soils and in, or on, edges of swamps. Bundaberg, Qld, to Kempsey, NSW; also NT, WA and Malaysia.

Notes: Fruit pulp edible. Attractive ornamental. Similar to closely related, exotic species *Tibouchina urvilleana* (Laisandra).

Family: Melastomataceae

Pilidiostigma rhytispermum
Small–leaved Plum Myrtle

Description: Bushy shrub to 5 m. Fine hairs on younger branchlets. Leaves opposite; dark green, small oil dots on underside and edges (hand lens helpful); narrow, oblong to obovate; tip blunt; 1.5–5 cm by 0.5–2 cm; hairy midrib. Solitary white flowers with 5 petals and sepals; numerous stamens; July–October. Fruit a succulent, purplish-black berry; oblong; 8–10 mm long; ripens March–April; 1–8 seeds.

Habitat and Range: In wet eucalypt forests, edges of rainforest and along watercourses in coastal areas, also in dry rainforest. Brisbane north to Gympie, Qld.

Notes: Similar to *Pilidiostigma glabrum* — hairless, purplish-red leaf stalks; white or pink flowers; larger pear-shaped berries to 1.4 cm long.

Family: Myrtaceae

Trochocarpa laurina
Tree Heath

Description: Shrub or small crooked tree 2–8 m tall. Rough brownish, slightly furrowed bark; soft pinkish new growth. Alternate leaves in clusters; dark green above, paler below; elliptical to oval; edges sometimes turned under; 3–9 cm by 1–3.5 cm; 5–7 longitudinal veins. Tubular white flowers on spike 1–3.5 cm long; mainly January, also other times. Fruit a succulent purplish to black drupe; dimpled or ribbed when dry; 6–8 mm; ripe June–October.

Habitat and Range: On deep sands and sandy soils along moist gullies, also in rainforest near Brisbane. Bermagui, NSW, to Qld; also New Guinea

Notes: Other heath species in region have leaves to 3 cm long and less than 1 cm wide.

Wildlife: Fruit — Lewin's Honeyeater.

Family: Epacridaceae

Wikstroemia indica
Tie Bush

Description: Slender shrub, 1–2 m. Smooth trunk; tough 'bootlace', brownish bark tears off in narrow strips. New growth and flower parts often with sparse rusty hairs; branches become smooth and shiny with age. Leaves opposite; dark green above paler bluish-green below; oval to elliptical; 1.5–6.5 cm by 5–25 mm; tip sharp or sometimes pointed; base wedge-shaped or asymmetrical. Pale green to cream flower heads; each head 1–4 flowers, 2.5 cm long; Fruit a succulent bright red berry; egg-shaped.

Habitat and Range: Widespread. On sandy or stony soils of coastal lowlands, hills and ranges; also rainforest edges in Greater Brisbane Region. Illawarra, NSW, to Nth Qld; also Asia and Pacific Islands

Notes: Fruit and leaves toxic if eaten.

Family: Thymelaeaceae

Mt Tamborine, BC

Plants of the Rainforests

In this reach [Bulimba Reach], *the right or east bank was more particularly clothed with twining plants and a density of brushwood than the opposite or western shore where the open woodland, in forest ridges, was remarked. In the thick and shaded brushes, and towering above the highest trees, were observed the corymbose branched heads of a pine ... After winding up several short bends we at length ... entered a noble reach* [Milton Reach and Toowong Reach] *... bounded by dark densely matted woods in which the new pine was particularly conspicuous.*
— Alan Cunningham, 17 September 1824]

At the time of European settlement, rainforests occupied an estimated 390,000 hectares within the Greater Brisbane Region. Just over half that area — 154,000 ha — now remains, mostly on the steeper ranges. The more accessible rainforests were logged for their valuable timbers, particularly *Toona ciliata* (Red Cedar), *Gmelina leichhardtii* (White Beech) and *Araucaria cunninghamii* (Hoop Pine), and were later cleared for dairying and cropping. Only fragments survive of the once extensive and rich rainforests that existed on the river floodplains and the deep basaltic soils of the Blackall Range and the Beechmont and Mt Tamborine Plateaus.

Rainforest structure and composition vary considerably within the Greater Brisbane Region, reflecting the diversity of landforms, soils and climatic conditions. Four broad rainforest types are recognized, each with its own distinctive structural features and habitat requirements.

Subtropical Rainforest

This is the most widespread, structurally complex and diverse rainforest. It usually has 2–3 tree layers, often with an understorey of palms, tree-ferns and ferns. Strangler figs are common and many of the canopy trees have relatively large leaves and buttressed roots. Large vines and epiphytic ferns and orchids are also common. This type of rainforest occurs on fertile soils, especially those derived from basic volcanic rocks (basalt) and in areas of high rainfall (more than 1500 mm annually.)

Subtropical rainforest is often divided into two main types — warm and cool Warm subtropical rainforest generally occurs at lower altitudes, up to

Freycinetia scandens, BC

600–700 m, and is frequently dominated by *Argyrodendron trifoliolatum* (White Booyong). Other prominent species include *Cryptocarya obovata* (Pepperberry) *Castanospermum australe* (Black Bean), *Syzygium francisii* (Giant Water Gum) and *Ficus macrophylla* (Moreton Bay Fig). Examples of warm subtropical rainforest may be seen at Mount Tamborine, Lamington National Park and around Maleny.

On more exposed, freely-drained hill slopes and crests, there is a drier form of warm subtropical rainforest characterized by large, emergent *Araucaria cunninghamii*. This type of vegetation is common on the northern slopes of the Lamington Plateau in the Coomera and Canungra Creek valleys.

Cool subtropical rainforest generally occurs above 700–800 m and it is the major rainforest type in the Lamington and Border Ranges National Parks and along the Main Range. The main canopy species in this forest type are *Caldcluvia paniculosa* (Rose-leaf Marara), *Geissois benthamii* (Red Carabeen), *Argyrodendron actinophyllum* (Black Booyong), *Dysoxylum fraserianum* (Rose Mahogany) and *Sloanea woollsii* (Yellow Carabeen).

Much of the cool subtropical rainforest along the Main Range carries some emergent *Araucaria cunninghamii*, and on the upper slopes of the Bunya Mountains to the north-west of Brisbane, the rainforest is dominated by *Araucaria bidwillii* (Bunya Pine).

A third subtype is sometimes recognized, mixed subtropical or gully rainforest, which supports both warm and cool subtropical species. It occurs in moist situations on slightly less fertile soils. *Sloanea woollsii*, *Ficus watkinsiana* (Watkins' Fig) and *Pseudoweinmennia lachnocarpa* (Mararie) are prominent in the canopy. The understorey is often dominated by *Archontophoenix cunninghamiana* (Piccabeen or Bangalow Palms). This community is common on the slopes of the Blackall Range and around Springbrook.

Dry rainforest

Dry rainforest occurs on relatively fertile soils in areas of lower rainfall (less than 1100 m) and is widespread in western parts of the Greater Brisbane Region. It has a pronounced dry season during late winter and spring. The canopy of dry rainforest is relatively low (20 m or less) with scattered to dense emergents of *Araucaria cunninghamii* and semi-deciduous species, such as *Brachychiton discolor* (Lacebark) and *Flindersia australis* (Crows Ash). *Olea paniculata* (Native Olive) is a common canopy species on basalt soils (eg Bunya Mountains), while *Dissiliaria baloghioides* (Lancewood) dominates the dry rainforests around Beenleigh and Ormeau. *Araucaria bidwillii* is a common emergent in northern parts of the region around Benarkin and Jimna.

Species richness in dry rainforest is often comparable with that of subtropical rainforest, but palms and tree ferns are absent and the ground layer is often quite sparse. Large vines are common, but plank buttresses are rare. The leaf sizes are relatively small, and many species have spines or prickles.

In parts of the Lockyer and Fassifern Valleys, there are areas of vine thicket (often called softwood scrub). This community is lower and more open and generally lacks emergent *Araucaria cunninghamii*. It is characterized by large specimens of *Brachychiton rupestris* (Narrow-leaved Bottle Tree), which give this community its alternative name of 'bottle-tree scrub'

Warm temperate rainforest

Areas of high rainfall and relatively infertile soils support warm temperate rainforest. This type of rainforest is much simpler structurally and less diverse than subtropical rainforest and it is often dominated by *Ceratopetalum apetalum* (Coachwood). Many species in warm temperate rainforests have toothed leaves and the tree trunks are slender and relatively uniform in size, often with a whitish covering of lichens.

Another form of warm subtropical rainforest occurs along the exposed crest of the eastern McPherson Range. Mosses and tree ferns are common and the canopy includes *Caldcluvia paniculosa*, *Doryphora sassafras* (Sassafras) and *Orites excelsa* (Prickly Ash).

Cool temperate rainforest

This rainforest type occurs at high altitudes (more than 900 m) on the McPherson Range, in areas subject to very high rainfall (more than 2000 mm annually). Frequent low cloud and mist are features of these areas. The commonest and often the only tree is *Nothofagus moorei*, the Antarctic Beech and the understorey is dominated by tree ferns and ground ferns. Mossy epiphytes, filmy ferns and lichens are abundant.

In some of the species descriptions that follow, littoral rainforest is mentioned. This group of vegetation communities is found close to the sea, either on nutrient-enriched deep sand or on soils derived from basalt or metasediments. Littoral rainforest has characteristics of both subtropical and dry rainforests. The canopy is often relatively low and wind-sheared and many of the species tolerate some salt-spray. Characteristic species include *Cupaniopsis anacardioides* (Tuckeroo), *Acronychia imperforata* (Beach Acronychia) *Alectryon coriaceus* (Beach Alectryon) and *Macaranga tanarius* (Macaranga).
— **Bill McDonald**

Plant species accounts
Bill McDonald and Janet Hauser

Information on Indigenous usage
Glenn Leiper and Bill McDonald

Wildlife information
David Barnes and Bill McDonald

HERBS, GRASSES AND GROUNDCOVERS

Alocasia brisbanensis
Cunjevoi, Spoon Lily

Description: Large erect to sprawling herb to 2 m. Stems thick and fleshy; covered in old leaf bases. Very large leaves alternate; purplish-brown to green; 70 cm long by 60 cm across; base heart-shaped; leaf stalk inserted at edge (or rarely within edge), to 110 cm long;. Yellow-green flowers massed together on cylindrical stalk (spadix), enclosed by leafy spathe, about 25 cm long; flowers mainly December. Fruit a red ovoid berry, clustered on spadix; several seeds.

Habitat and Range: Subtropical rainforest at low to mid-altitudes, also on rainforest edges. Qld and NSW.

Notes: Stems and leaves contain calcium oxalate crystals; if eaten raw, cause burning sensation in lips, mouth and tongue, followed by swelling and intense pain.

Family: Araceae

Alpinia caerulea
Native Ginger

Description: Large herb with tuberous rhizomes, forms clumps to 2m high. Leaves alternate; glossy green above and below; oblong-lanceolate, to 40 cm; base of leaf enclosing thick stem. White flower spikes; September–October, but also other times. Fruit a blue ovoid capsule, 1.5 cm long; numerous brown seeds surrounded by fleshy aril; ripe February–May,

Habitat and Range: Subtropical rainforest, also on rainforest edges and in moist eucalypt forest. Qld, NSW and NT.

Notes: Aril edible with ginger taste. Aboriginal people ate fruit and roots; leaves used to roof shelters. Similar to *Alpinia arundelliana* —smaller leaves and flowers; short (3–4 mm) ligule.

Family: Zingiberaceae

Dawsonia longifolia
Giant Moss

Description: Largest species of moss in Australia, to 20 cm or more high. Leaves to 3.5 cm long; characteristic blue-green. Fruit an ovate, flattened capsule on a short stalk.

Habitat and Range: Subtropical and cool temperate rainforest, forming colonies on roadsides, embankments and mounds associated with wind-thrown trees. Qld, NSW, Vic. and Tas.

Notes: Previously known as *Dawsonia superba*, now considered to be restricted to New Zealand. Similar to *Dawsonia polytrichoides*, — leaves less than 1.5 cm long. Mosses are non-vascular plants, so-called because they lack a regular water and food conducting system composed of vascular tissue, which is a characteristic of more complex plants.

Family: Dawsoniaceae

Elatostema reticulatum
Native Spinach

Description: Coarse straggling herb to 50 cm. Stems often root at nodes. Leaves alternate; lower surface hairy; ovate to elliptical, 7–15 cm long; tip drawn out to a point; base strongly asymmetrical; edges regularly toothed. White or yellowish flowers in dense heads; male and female flowers on same plant; male heads 12–25 mm across on 2–8 cm stalk; female heads about 9 mm across, lack stalk.

Habitat and Range: Subtropical and warm temperate rainforest, also wet eucalypt forest, generally along streams or on moist rock faces. Qld and NSW.

Notes: Similar to *Elatostema stipitatum* — smaller; leaves 1–3 cm long; flower heads 5 mm across; female heads with stalks; in cool subtropical and cool temperate rainforest.

Family: Urticaceae

Plectranthus parviflorus

Description: Shrub 10–70 cm high. Fleshy tuberous base to about 3 cm across; branches die away after flowering. Leaves opposite; dense hairs above, sparse below; circular to ovate, 2–6.5 cm long; tip bluntly pointed; edges with shallow to blunt teeth, 4–12 pairs of teeth. Pale blue to violet-blue flowers in dense clusters in 1–5 racemes; flowers year-round.

Habitat and Range: Dry rainforest, more widespread and common in eucalypt forests and woodlands, frequently in rocky areas. Qld, NSW and Vic.; also Malesia and Polynesia.

Notes: Non-aromatic. Similar to *Plectranthus nitidus* — grows on rock outcrops in and adjacent to subtropical rainforest; lacks tuberous base; leaves shiny, purple below.

Family: Lamiaceae

FERNS

Adiantum atroviride
Maidenhair Fern

Description: Ground fern. Creeping, much-branched rhizome with dark brown scales. Fronds erect to spreading, to 75 cm long; leaflets dark green, hairless; outer edge lobed or finely toothed; leaflet stem dark brown to black. Sori to 2 mm across, usually 1–5 per segment.

Habitat and Range: Edges of subtropical rainforest, more common in eucalypt forest.

Notes: Similar to closely related *Adiantum aethiopicum* — stems and fronds lighter in colour.

Family: Adiantaceae

Adiantum silvaticum

Description: Ground fern. Long creeping rhizome, usually on soil surface. Fronds to 80 cm high; leaflets dark green above, slightly blue-green below, hairless; leaflet stem dull reddish-brown to black; main stem somewhat zig-zag. Sori mostly 2–5 per leaflet.

Habitat and Range: Subtropical rainforest and associated moist open forest, often along streams and moist cliff faces, typically on less fertile soils. Qld and NSW.

Notes: Similar to *Adiantum hispidulum* — short creeping rhizomes; short hairs on leaflets.

Family: Adiantaceae

Arthropteris tenella

Description: Terrestrial or epiphytic fern. Very long, creeping rhizome to 6 mm across, densely covered with brown, papery scales. Fronds erect to weeping; bright green, glossy, hairless or with a few scattered white hairs; usually 25–45 cm long, sometimes to 60 cm long; stalk to 8 cm long, yellowish to reddish brown, scaly; leaflets narrowly elliptical, 3–10 cm long; tip of upper leaflets drawn out to point; tip of lower leaflets blunt or pointed; edges entire or crenulate. Sori circular.

Habitat and Range: Most types of rainforest, grows on rocks or trees. Qld and NSW; also New Zealand.

Notes: Similar to *Arthropteris beckleri* — rhizomes more slender with red-brown hairs and brown scales; smaller fronds, leaflets dull green, with numerous long hairs, to 1.7 cm long; in moister, cooler habitats

Family: Davalliaceae

Asplenium australasicum
Crows Nest Fern, Bird's Nest Fern

Description: Ground or epiphytic fern. Stout erect rhizome with even rosettes of radiating fronds. Fronds 60–80 cm long; lack stalks; yellow-green; tip blunt or sharp, narrowing abruptly at base; midvein strongly keeled on lower surface; hairless. Numerous sori, 1 mm across, often 40–60 mm long.

Habitat and Range: Most types of rainforest, common on rocks and as a large epiphyte in trees. Qld, NSW and Vic.; also Pacific Islands.

Notes: Similar to *Asplenium harmanii* — untidy rosettes of large erect fronds; 50–130 cm long; tapering at base; rhizomes sometime produce lateral branches in older plants; grows mostly on rocks, seldom an epiphyte; restricted to Border Ranges.

Family: Aspleniaceae

Blechnum patersoni
Strap Water Fern

Description: Ground fern with erect rhizome. Fronds erect to weeping; dark green and leathery; fertile and sterile fronds different; entire or deeply lobed, often mixed on same plant; mostly 20–50 cm long; sterile fronds 10–25 mm across, broader towards tip; fertile fronds usually shorter, 2–4 mm across.

Habitat and Range: Moist subtropical rainforest, often in clumps along gullies or in rock crevices.

Notes: Similar to *Blechnum cartilagineum* (Gristle Fern), see p.201.

Family: Blechnaceae

Lastreopsis microsora subsp. microsora
Creeping Shield Fern

Description: Ground fern. Long creeping rhizome covered with brown scales. Fronds erect, broad to triangular; 3–4 leaflets; 30–90 cm long; top leaflets blunt tip; edges with sharp teeth; leaflet stalk, main stem and veins often with dense, pale brown hairs. Sori circular pale brown, persistent.

Habitat and Range: Widespread and common. All rainforest types, also wet eucalypt forest. Qld, NSW and Vic.; also New Zealand.

Notes: Similar to *Lastreopsis silvestris* — dense, soft, pale to reddish-brown hairs. Also similar to *Lastreopsis decomposita* — top leaflets with sharp to pointed tip; small dark, triangular scales on leaflet stalk, stem and veins.

Family: Dryopteridaceae

Microsorum scandens
Fragrant Fern

Description: Epiphytic or lithophytic fern. Very long creeping rhizome, tough and wiry, with spreading and persistent scales. Fronds dark green; 20–50 cm long; sometimes divided into leaflets; entire fronds and divided fronds can occur on same plant; stem to 20 cm long. Sori 1–3 mm across; circular or ovate; impressed into leaf surface, in 2 rows either side of midvein.

Habitat and Range: Moist subtropical rainforest, often forms mats on boulders and tree trunks. Qld, NSW and Vic.; also New Zealand.

Notes: Fronds with musk scent when fresh. Similar to *Microsorum pustulatum* (Kangaroo Fern) — fleshy rhizomes with flattened scales; frond leathery and unscented.

Family: Polypodiaceae

Platycerium bifurcatum subsp. *bifurcatum*
Elkhorn

Description: Large bracket epiphyte. Short creeping, much-branched rhizome. Fertile and sterile fronds different; both forms covered with dense star-hairs when young. Sterile 'nest leaves' overlapping, broader than long; cover spongy base of plant; becoming brown and papery with age. Fertile fronds usually 25–90 cm long; more or less erect or weeping; divided 2–5 times; top leaves narrow, sporangia, covering all or most of top leaves.

Habitat and Range: All rainforest types, except dry, also in wet eucalypt forest. Qld and NSW; also New Guinea.

Notes: Plantlets grow from buds on outer lower edge of plant and enable clump to encircle tree trunk.

Family: Polypodiaceae

Platycerium superbum
Staghorn

Description: Large bracket epiphyte. Short creeping rhizome with few branches. Fertile and sterile fonds different. Sterile 'nest leaves' often 60 cm or more across, upper part spreading, wedge-shaped; edge deeply and irregularly lobed; remains green for a number of years. Fertile fronds 75–160 cm long; spreading to weeping; divided 4–6 times; top leaves 1.5–4 cm across; sporangia in single patch, 10–50 cm across, in fork of first division of frond.

Habitat and Range: Subtropical and dry rainforest. Qld and NSW.

Family: Polypodiaceae

Pyrrosia confluens var. *confluens*
Horseshoe Felt Fern

Description: Epiphytic or lithophytic fern with a long creeping, much branched rhizome. Rhizomes covered with flattened red-brown to dark brown scales with fringed edges. Fronds thick and leathery; surfaces covered with star-hairs; narrowly obovate to oblong, usually 3–7 cm long; fertile and sterile fronds similar in size and shape. Sori restricted to top of fertile frond, forming two oblong or ovate patches or a single horseshoe-shaped patch.

Habitat and Range: Subtropical, dry and littoral rainforest, on trunks and branches of trees and on rocks. Qld and NSW: also New Caledonia.

Family: Polypodiaceae

Pyrrosia rupestris
Rock Felt Fern

Description: Epiphytic or lithophytic fern. Long creeping, much-branched rhizome. Rhizomes covered with spreading, papery, pale reddish-brown scales. Fronds thick and leathery; surfaces covered with star-hairs; sterile and fertile fronds different; sterile fronds circular to obovate, 1.5–4 cm long; fertile fronds narowly lanceolate, usually 4–10 cm long. Sori cover most of lower surface of fertile fronds; irregularly arranged in 1–4 rows on each side of midvein, becoming continuous with age.

Habitat and Range: All rainforest types, also in open forests, on trees and rocks, often in exposed situations. Qld and NSW; also New Guinea.

Family: Polypodiaceae

ORCHIDS

Calanthe triplicata
Christmas Orchid

Description: Terrestrial plant to 1.5 m high rising from fleshy conical 'bulb'. Leaves 4–10 per shoot; 25–90 cm long; narrowly obovate to elliptical, pleated; tip sharp to pointed. Groups of 18–40 whitish flowers in 1 or 2 stiff erect racemes, 30–150 cm long; flowers 30 mm across, crowded on top of fleshy green stalk, which elongates as flowers develop; October–January. Fruit a capsule 3–4 cm long.

Habitat and Range: Subtropical, littoral and dry rainforest, also in wet eucalypt forest, coastal lowland and ranges. Qld and NSW; also Asia, Malesia and Melanesia.

Family: Orchidaceae

Dendrobium speciosum
King Orchid, Rock Orchid

Description: Epiphytic or lithophytic orchid with erect to spreading stems to 100 cm long. Stems fleshy, cylindrical and thickest just below middle; tapering slightly towards each end, rooting only at base. Leaves spreading to erect; thick, leathery and smooth; elliptical to oblong, 18–25 cm long. Flowers white to yellowish, with red or purplish marks on labellum; 1.5–5 cm across; in racemes, 10–60 cm long; August–October. Fruit a capsule, 4–5 cm long.

Habitat and Range: Subtropical and dry rainforest and adjacent eucalypt forest, growing on trees and rocks, often in large dense masses. Qld and NSW.

Family: Orchidaceae

Sarcochilus falcatus
Orange Blossom Orchid

Description: Small semi-pendulous, epiphytic orchid. Stems 1–8 cm long, 3–8 leaves. Thick leathery leaves narrowly oblong to elliptical; often with unequal sides; 5–16 cm long. Cream to white flowers, about. 30 mm across; in racemes to 18 cm long; June–October. Old inflorescences dry black. Fruit a cylindrical capsule to 6 cm long.

Habitat and Range: Subtropical, warm temperate and cool temperate rainforest. Epiphytic on trees, rarely growing on rocks. Qld, NSW and eastern Vic.

Notes: Flowers highly fragrant, resemble orange blossom.

Family: Orchidaceae

VINES AND CLIMBERS

Abrus precatorius
Crab's Eye, Gidee Gidee

Description: Slender twining plant growing over shrubs and ground plants. Young stems with white hairs, becoming hairless. Leaves alternate; consist of 7–19 pairs of leaflets; 4–11 cm long; dull green above, paler below; leaflets oblong to ovate, 0.6–2.5 cm long; base of leaf stalk swollen. White, pink or mauve, pea-shaped flowers; 10–12 mm long. Fruit a brown oblong pod, 3–6.5 cm long; splits to reveal 2–6 hard, glossy red and black seeds.

Habitat and Range: Common. On edges of littoral rainforest and in other coastal scrubs. Qld, NT and WA.

Notes: Seeds poisonous, can cause death when chewed and swallowed. Aboriginal people used seeds for necklace beads and to decorate implements.

Family: Fabaceae (Leguminosae)

Austrosteenisia blackii
Blood Vine

Description: Robust vine with stem to 15 cm wide. Small paired scales at base of leaf and leaflets. Damaged stems ooze reddish sap. Deciduous in late spring; new leaves and inflorescences protected by large deciduous bracts. Leaves alternate; consist of 7–11 leaflets; 3–9 cm long by 15–50 mm across, increasing in size along stem; sparsely hairy below; base of leaf stalk swollen. Maroon pea-shaped flowers; September– November. Fruit a thin pod; 2–5 seeds.

Habitat and Range: Common in canopy and on edges of dry and subtropical rainforest. Qld, NSW; also New Guinea.

Notes: Similar to *Derris involuta* — lacks paired scales at base of leaflets. Also *Austrosteenisia glabristyla* (Giant Blood Vine) — narrower leaflets, 7–20 mm wide.

Family: Fabaceae (Leguminosae)

Calamus muelleri
Lawyer Vine, Wait-a-while

Description: Slender climbing palm, scrambles over shrubs and low trees and ascends to rainforest canopy. Stems cane-like, spiny, to 20 m long; hook-like modifications on leaves and sterile inflorescences for climbing. Leaves alternate; leaf blade about 30–50 cm long, consists of 9–12 segments; hooked spines on stem and sheath. Inflorescence of small greenish flowers; December–February. Fruit a creamy-yellow globular berry; about. 12 mm across; covered with scales.

Habitat and Range: Subtropical rainforest on coast and lower ranges. Qld and NSW.

Notes: Aboriginal people used stems for weaving. During early settlement, surveyors used one chain lengths of stems as standard measures.

Family: Arecaceae

Callerya megasperma
Native Wistaria

Description: Tall woody climber ascending to rainforest canopy. Bark at base of large vines flaky and peeling. Stems twining; young growth hairy. Leaves alternate; consist of 7–9 leaflets; green, slightly glossy above, hairless or with sparse fine hairs below; 10–20 cm long; tip with blunt point; leaf stalk swollen at base. Light purple pea-like flowers, in racemes; July–October. Fruit an oblong pod; longitudinal ribs, velvety; 1–4 large seeds with brown papery coat.

Habitat and Range: Lowland subtropical and littoral rainforest, more common on edges. Qld and NSW.

Notes: Previously known as *Millettia megasperma*. Similar to *Callerya australis* — smaller leaves and leaflets (3–6 cm long); shorter, narrower seed pods (20–30 mm wide), lack longitudinal ribs; smaller, hard seeds.

Family: Fabaceae (Leguminosae)

Celastrus australis
Staff Vine

Description: Woody climber or shrub. Branches mostly grey or grey-brown, with numerous raised pale lenticels; young branchlets with small scales. Leaves alternate; lanceolate to elliptical, 3–9 cm long; tip sharp; edges with regular teeth. Small yellowish-green flowers in panicles; October–June. Fruit a yellow, ellipsoid to almost globular capsule; inner surface with scattered red spots; 2–3 seeds enclosed in orange aril.

Habitat and Range: Subtropical and dry rainforest. Qld, NSW and Vic.

Notes: Similar to *Celastrus subspicata* — mostly red-brown or dark brown stems; larger leaves (5–15 cm long).

Family: Celastraceae

Cissus antarctica
Native Grape, Kangaroo Vine, Water Vine

Description: Large woody climber, ascending to rainforest canopy. Young stems with grey or rusty hairs. Tendrils with 1 or 2 branches, opposite leaves. Leaves dark green and hairless above, with rusty hairs and raised domatia below; ovate to oblong, 5–14 cm long; base rounded; edges regularly toothed. Small yellowish flowers in clusters; September–May. Fruit a purplish, globular berry, about 15 mm across.

Habitat and Range: Common. In subtropical, littoral and dry rainforest. Qld and NSW.

Notes: Astringent fruit edible, but sometimes causes throat irritation.

Family: Vitaceae

Cissus hypoglauca
Five-leaf Water Vine, Giant Water Vine

Description: Large woody climber ascending to rainforest canopy. New growth with rusty hairs. Tendrils with 2 branches, opposite leaves. Leaves consist of 5 leaflets, central leaflet largest; dull to glossy green above, lower surface pale green to ashy-grey, densely hairy to hairless; obovate or ovate, 3–15 cm long; edges entire or sparsely toothed (regularly toothed in juvenile plants). Small yellow flowers in panicles; September–February. Fruit a purple globular berry, about 10 mm across; 1 seed.

Habitat and Range: Subtropical, cool temperate and littoral rainforest, also moist eucalypt forest. Qld, NSW and Vic.

Notes: Similar to *Cissus sterculiifolia* — tendrils unbranched; leaflets green, with several prominent domatia. Edible fruit, but often causes throat irritation.

Family: Vitaceae

Clematis glycinoides
Headache Vine

Description: Woody climber with twining stems and leaf stalks. Leaves opposite; consist of 3 leaflets; ovate–oblong, 1.5–2 cm long; tip long and sharp; edges entire or with a few teeth near base; leaf stalk 2–8 cm long; some leaflet stalks extended and act as tendrils. Flowers white to purplish, 2–3.5 cm across, in panicles; separate male and female flowers on same plant; August–November. Fruit an achene, with long feathery appendage, 2–3 cm long; in globular clusters.

Habitat and Range: All types of rainforest, also in eucalypt communities. Qld, NSW and Vic.

Notes: Similar to *Clematis pickeringii* — can only be distinguished by male flowers

Family: Ranunculaceae

Dioscorea transversa
Native Yam, Long Yam

Description: Slender twiner, stems 2–4 m long, arising from underground tuber. Leaves alternate; glossy green, lower surface dull and sometimes purplish; ovate to triangular, 5–12 cm long; tip pointed; base spear-shaped to heart-shaped; 5–9 veins from base; leaf stalk slender, 1–9 cm long, with swelling near tip. Male and female flowers on separate plants; male in spikes 3–6 cm long, female in racemes 10–20 cm long; September–November. Fruit a 3-lobed, papery capsule; 2–3 cm long; flat, winged seeds.

Habitat and Range: Subtropical, littoral and dry rainforest. Qld and NSW.

Notes: Tuber a staple food of coastal Aboriginal people; usually roasted but also eaten raw.

Family: Dioscoreaceae

Fieldia australis
Fieldia

Description: Small climber or epiphyte growing on tree trunks, tree ferns and rocks. Stems, leaf stalks and leaves with rough bristly hairs. Leaves opposite; each pair of leaves unequal in size; both leaf surfaces dull and sparsely hairy; elliptical to oblong, to 7 cm long and 30 mm across, tip pointed; base tapered; edges coarsely toothed. Single, creamy-white, bell-shaped flowers 2.5–3.5 cm long. Fruit an oblong to ovoid berry, 1-3 cm long; whitish, flecked with purple.

Habitat and Range: Cool subtropical and cool temperate rainforest, generally above 1000 m. Qld, NSW and Vic.

Family: Gesneriaceae

Jasminum didymum subsp. *racemosum*
Native Jasmine

Description: Straggly shrub to climber. Young stems sparsely hairy or hairless. Leaves opposite; consist of 3 smaller leaflets; ovate, 1–4 cm long; tip sharp or blunt. White tubular flowers 5–8 mm long, in clusters or panicles of 9 or more flowers. Fruit a black globular berry; about 8 mm across; 1–2 seeds.

Habitat and Range: Subtropical and dry rainforests. Qld, NT and WA.

Notes: Flowers perfumed. Similar to *Jasminum didymum* subsp. *didymum* — larger leaves, terminal leaflet more than 4 cm long; occurs in coastal districts in littoral rainforest; hylerids between two subspecies are common.

Family: Oleaceae

Legnephora moorei
Round-leaf Vine

Description: Woody climber ascending to rainforest canopy. Young stems with bristly hairs, older stems woody. Large leaves alternate; green and hairless above, lower surface ashy-grey, often with fine hairs; almost circular, about 8–20 cm long and wide; base heart-shaped; usually 5 veins from base; leaf stalk longer than leaf blade. Small flowers in racemes 2–5 cm long; mainly December– February. Fruit a dark blue flattened to globular berry; seeds 8–10 mm long with numerous small projections.

Habitat and Range: Subtropical, littoral and dry rainforest. Qld and NSW.

Notes: Often only noticed by fallen grey-black leaves on forest floor.

Wildlife: Fruit – Lewin's Honeyeater, Green Catbird and Rose-crowned Fruit-dove.

Family: Menispermaceae

Marsdenia rostrata
Common Milk Vine

Description: Woody climber to about 10 m. Stems twining; copious milky sap. Leaves opposite; soft and hairless or with scattered hairs below; oblong–elliptical to ovate, 4–13 cm long; tip narrows to blunt point; base rounded or slightly heart-shaped; midvein whitish on upper surface, larger net veins below; 5–20 small glands clustered at base of leaf blade. Creamy-yellow flowers 8–9 mm wide; September–February. Fruit an ovoid capsule, 5–7 cm long.

Habitat and Range: All types of rainforest, also moist eucalypt forest. Qld, NSW and Vic.

Notes: Similar to *Marsdenia longiloba* — rare; clear, slightly yellowish sap; 5–6 basal glands. Also similar to *Parsonsia longipetiolata* — copious milky sap; lacks glands at base of leaves.

Family: Asclepiadaceae

Melodorum leichhardtii
Zig-zag Vine

Description: Woody climber ascending to rainforest canopy. Stems twining; branchlets form coils and knot-like bends around supports. Young shoots covered with brown, star-like scales. Leathery leaves alternate; hairless or sparsely covered with brown star-like scales, narrowly elliptical to oblong, 6–12 cm long; tip blunt or slightly notched; often with minute, translucent dots. Pale creamy-brown flowers 10–15 mm wide, usually in pairs, October–November. Fruit a cluster of stalked orange berries; 1–4-seeds; ripe December–May.

Habitat and Range: Subtropical, littoral and dry rainforest. Qld and NSW.

Notes: Flowers with strong, pleasant banana scent (amyl acetate).

Family: Annonaceae

Morinda jasminoides
Sweet Morinda

Description: Woody climber, sometimes scrambling and shrub-like. Stems straggling or twining. Leaves opposite; soft, hairless; lanceolate to narrowly elliptical, 3–8 cm long; tip with long narrow point, 1–4 pit-like domatia on both surfaces. White to purplish flowers, 4–6 mm long, in heads; September–February. Fruit an orange berry with a single seed.

Habitat and Range: Subtropical and littoral rainforest, also in moist eucalypt forest. Qld, NSW and Vic.

Notes: Flowers perfumed. Similar to *Morinda canthoides* (Veiny Morinda) — leaves with prominent net veins and small, inconspicuous domatia; dry rainforest;

Wildlife: Eaten by many species of birds.

Family: Rubiaceae

Palmeria scandens
Anchor Vine

Description: Woody climber ascending to rainforest canopy. Stem bases in younger plants, often 4-sided. Branchlets and young leaves on leading shoots often resemble flukes of an anchor. Leaves opposite; both surfaces rough with scattered star hairs; elliptical to oblong, 5–12 cm long; edges usually entire, but sometimes with fine shallow rounded teeth; numerous minute, translucent oil dots. Whitish flowers in racemes; male and female flowers on separate plants; June–August. Fruit a red, globular to ellipsoid berry, about 5 mm long; sits on fleshy pinkish-red base.

Habitat and Range: Subtropical, warm temperate and cool temperate rainforest. Qld and NSW.

Notes: Leaves aromatic when crushed.

Family: Monimiaceae

Passiflora herbertiana subsp. herbertiana
Native Passionfruit

Description: Slender climber with twining, finely hairy stems. Tendrils not branched. Leaves alternate; 3 broad shallow lobes; glossy green with fine hairs below; tip sharp; leaf stalk 1.5–4 cm long, with 2 raised glands near tip. Yellow to orange or pinkish flowers, 4–6.5 cm wide. Fruit an almost globular berry; green with pale spots; 2.5–5 cm long.

Habitat and Range: Subtropical and littoral rainforest. Qld and NSW; subspecies on Lord Howe I.

Notes: Leaves similar to *Passiflora suberosa*, see p. 342 — paired glands near middle of leaf stalk. Also similar to *Passiflora aurantia* which is hairless.

Widlife: Leaves — caterpillar of Glasswing Butterfly.

Family: Passifloraceae

Piper novae-hollandiae
Giant Pepper Vine

Description: Large climber, to 30 cm wide at base. Climbs on tree trunks by small roots; stems jointed and enlarged at nodes. Leaves alternate; hairless, dark glossy green above, dull and paler below; ovate, 6–12 cm long; rounded or sharp base in exposed leaves, broadly ovate with heart-shaped base in shaded leaves. Small cream flowers in spikes opposite leaves. Fruit a red ovoid berry; ripe November–January,

Habitat and Range: In moist subtropical rainforest, more common at lower altitudes. Qld and NSW.

Notes: Aboriginal people chewed leaves as a treatment for sore gums. Edible fruit.

Wildlife: Eaten by many species of birds.

Family: Piperaceae

Pothos longipes
Pothos

Description: Slender climber or epiphytic on tree trunks. Vertical climbing shoots root on surface, flowering shoots free-growing. Leaves alternate; variable in size, lanceolate to ovate, 1.5–5 cm long; broadly winged and flattened so that leaves appear to be constricted or jointed in upper part. Flowers massed on cylindrical stalk about 6 cm long; stalk enclosed in dark purple to greenish spathe about 25 mm long; November–December. Fruit a red ovoid berry; single seed; a few to several fruits clustered on flowering stalk.

Habitat and Range: Moist subtropical rainforest in lowlands and on ranges. Qld and NSW.

Notes: Aboriginal people ate flesh around seed raw or roasted.

Wildlife: Eaten by many species of birds.

Family: Araceae

Ripogonum album
White Supplejack

Description: Stout climber with stems to about 15 m long. Sometimes shrub-like when young; stems usually prickly. Leaves opposite, alternate, or more usually in whorls of 3; green above and below, thick, stiff and hairless; elliptical to ovate, 8–17 cm long; tip sharp; 5 prominent veins from base; leaf stalk 5–13 mm long, thick and twisted. Creamish flowers 6–8 mm long, in spikes or racemes; September–December. Fruit a black globular berry; 6–15 mm wide; one or a few seeds.

Habitat and Range: Subtropical, littoral and warm temperate rainforest. Qld, NSW and Vic.

Notes: Similar to *Ripogonum brevifolium* — smaller leaves, 3–8 cm long, usually opposite or alternate (not in whorls).

Family: Ripogonaceae

Ripogonum elseyanum
Hairy Supplejack

Description: Climber with stems to about 8 m long. Sometimes shrub-like when young; stems with rusty hairs, older stems prickly. Leaves opposite; thick and stiff; elliptical to ovate, 6–20 cm long; tip sharp; base rounded or heart-shaped; 3 prominent veins from near base; leaf stalk with thick rusty hairs. Creamish flowers, 5–8 mm long, in spikes or racemes; June–November. Fruit a black globular berry, 6–12 mm wide; one or a few seeds.

Habitat and Range: Subtropical, littoral, warm temperate and cool temperate rainforest. Qld and NSW.

Family: Ripogonaceae

Rubus rosifolius var. *rosifolius*
Rose-leaf Bramble

Description: Scrambling shrub or climber with trailing stems to 2 m long. Mature stems hairy, with stout prickles to 5 mm long. Leaves alternate; rose-like, consist of 5 or 7 leaflets, green with glandular hairs, lanceolate to narrowly elliptical, 3–8 cm long; tip sharp; base rounded to heart-shaped; edges toothed. White flowers with 5 petals; flowers year-round. Clusters of small red succulent berries.

Habitat and Range: Subtropical, warm temperate, cool temperate and dry rain-forest, especially on edges, also in moist eucalypt forest. Qld, NSW and Vic.; also Asia.

Notes: Fruit edible, but insipid. Similar to *Rubus rosifolius* var. *commersonii* — flowers with 9–13 petals.

Family: Rosaceae

Smilax australis
Austral Sarsaparilla

See p. 115

Tetrastigma nitens
Three-leaf Water Vine

Description: Woody climber ascending to rainforest canopy. Stems hairless; tendrils, entire or with 2 opposite branches; Leaves consist of 3 smaller leaflets, central leaflet largest; dark green, glossy above; obovate to broadly elliptical, 4–12 cm long; tip pointed to sharp; edges coarsely and regularly toothed, sometimes teeth are reduced to hard points. Small greenish flowers in clusters; December–February. Fruit a blackish berry, 1–4 wrinkled seeds.

Habitat and Range: Subtropical, littoral and dry rainforest. Qld and NSW.

Notes: Fruit edible, but can irritate throat.

Wildlife: Eaten by many species of birds.

Family: Vitaceae

Trophis scandens subsp. *scandens*
Burny Vine

Description: Woody climber or scandent shrub. Bark on twigs very tough and rough to touch; milky sap often present. Leaves green and hairless above, paler and scabrous below; ovate–oblong to elliptical, mostly 3–8 cm long; edges entire or with a few small teeth towards tip. Cream flowers; male in spikes 1–4 cm long, female clustered in gobular head; September–February. Fruit a red ovoid berry, 5–8 mm long.

Habitat and Range: Subtropical, littoral and dry rainforest. Qld, NSW and NT; also South-east Asia and Pacific Islands.

Notes: Aboriginal people used bark for string to make dilly bags, fish and dugong nets. Edible seed.

Family: Moraceae

Zehneria cunninghamii
Slender Cucumber

Description: Slender delicate, climbing or trailing herb. Stems twining, hairless to scabrous. Tendrils lack branches; spiralling in upper half. Leaves thin, scabrous, occasionally with 3 shallow lobes; triangular to ovate, 2.5–9 cm long; tip pointed to sharp; base heart-shaped to spear-shaped; edges toothed. White flowers 2–4 mm wide; September–February. Fruit a globular berry, 6–12 mm wide; green turning pale yellow; 4–8 seeds; ripe December–May.

Habitat and Range: Subtropical and dry rainforest in coastal lowlands and on ranges. Qld and NSW.

Wildlife: Fruit — Lewin's Honeyeater and Brown Cuckoo-dove.

Family: Cucurbitaceae

PALMS

Archontophoenix cunninghamiana
Piccabeen Palm, Bangalow

Description: Medium to tall feather palm to 25 m. Stem straight and cylindrical, slightly swollen at base; regular circular scars left by large sheathing leaf base. Leaves alternate; consist of 50–80 leaflets on either side of leaf axis; arching, 2–4 m long; leaflets linear, 30–80 cm long, with long thread-like tips; smooth and green on both surfaces. Pinkish-mauve flowers in drooping branched panicles; 10 mm wide; August–December. Fruit a bright red berry; elliptical, 10–15 mm long, single seed; ripe December–May.

Habitat and Range: Subtropical and littoral rainforest and wet eucalypt forest, mostly beside creeks, but also on poorly-drained alluvial flats and on hill slopes, often in dense groves. Qld and NSW.

Notes: Similar to *Archontophoenix alexandrae* (Alexandra Palm) — leaflets greyish on underside; occurs in Central and Nth Qld; planted extensively in and around Brisbane. Aboriginal people of Moreton Bay used leaf sheath as a carrying vessel (*pikki*).

Wildlife: Flowers — Rainbow Lorikeet; fruit — Grey-headed Flying Fox, Wompoo and Rose-crowned Fruit-doves, Australian King Parrot, Crimson Rosella, Common Koel, Lewin's Honeyeater, Pied Currawong, Satin Bowerbird, Brown Cuckoo-dove, Topknot and White-headed Pigeon; leaves — caterpillars of Orange Palm-dart and Yellow Palm-dart Butterflies.

Family: Arecaceae

Linospadix monostachya
Walking-stick Palm, Midgenbil

Description: Small palm to 3 m tall. Trunk slender, with prominent circular leaf scars at short intervals; base of trunk swollen. Leaves consist of 6–30 leaflets; linear to oblong, with a few teeth at tip; upper leaflets wider than lower ones. Greenish flowers in pendulous spikes; separate male and female flowers on same plant; August–October. Fruit a red berry, 10–15 mm long; in long drooping spikes; 1 seed; ripe March–May.

Habitat and Range: Moist subtropical rainforest. Qld and NSW.

Notes: Aboriginal people ate the fruit.

Family: Arecaceae

SHRUBS AND TREES

Abrophyllum ornans
Native Hydrangea

Description: Shrub or small tree to 8 m. Branchlets slender, green, hairy. Large leaves alternate; very soft and thin; elliptical, 10–20 cm long; tip pointed; base tapering into leaf stalk; edges irregularly toothed, each tooth a small blunt, callous projection; main lateral veins indented, thick, raised and fleshy below. Greenish-yellow flowers in short panicles; November–December. Fruit a blackish, globular berry; 4–5 mm wide; numerous small, brown seeds; ripe April–June.

Habitat and Range: Often on poorer soils, in subtropical rainforest, especially in gullies. Qld and NSW.

Notes: Perfumed flowers. Similar to *Cuttsia viburnea*, see p. 258

Family: Grossulariaceae

Acacia melanoxylon
Blackwood

Description: Small tree to 15 m. Branchlets and young shoots hairy. Phyllodes alternate; oblanceolate; 6–10 cm long; rounded, occasionally pointed, at tip; 3–7 main longitudinal veins; raised gland on phyllode edge, 1–10 mm above base. Pale cream globular flower heads in short racemes; November–January. Fruit a coiled or twisted narrow pod; black oval seeds connected to pod by red fleshy thread; ripe March–April.

Habitat and Range: Subtropical rainforest and wet eucalypt forest in coastal and upland areas, often dominates regrowth. Qld, NSW, Vic., Tas. and SA.

Notes: Similar to *Acacia maidenii* (Maiden's Wattle) — numerous pale raised lenticels on branchlets; pale creamy flowers in spikes; twisted rather than coiled pods.

Family: Mimosaceae

Acmena ingens
Red Apple

Description: Medium to large tree to 40 m. Trunk straight and cylindrical; buttressed in large trees. Branchlets angular, smooth, red; new growth bright red. Leaves opposite; thick and tough on adult trees; narrowly oblong to elliptical, 9–19 cm long; tip with fine point; edges rolled under and wavy; numerous lateral veins; oil dots visible in new growth; leaf stalks often red. Small white flowers in panicles; November–December. Fruit a large red globular berry; 25–40 mm across; ripe May–September.

Habitat and Range: On volcanic soils in subtropical rainforest, mainly at higher altitudes. Qld and NSW.

Notes: Fruit sour, but edible.

Wildlife: Fruit eaten by many species and birds.

Family: Myrtaceae

Acmena smithii
Lilly-pilly

Description: Small to medium tree to 20 m. Bark brown, scaly; shed in patches. Leaves opposite; glossy to dull above; shape varies, elliptical to ovate or lanceolate, 4–16 cm long; tip pointed; lateral veins at wide angles to midvein; well-spaced oil dots. Small creamish-white flowers in panicles; November–December. Fruit a pale, whitish-mauve berry; 10–20 mm wide; small round cavity at top, encloses single large seed; ripe May–July.

Habitat and Range: On a range of soils in subtropical rainforest. Qld, NSW and Vic.

Notes: Edible sour fruit. Narrow-leaved form of this species — shrub to small tree; along streams in coastal subtropical rainforest and wet eucalypt forest; leaves 6–9 cm long.

Wildlife: Fruit eaten by many species of birds.

Family: Myrtaceae

Acronychia imperforata
Beach Acronychia

Description: Shrub or small tree to 15 m. Leaves opposite; thick and leathery; dull green above, paler below; obovate, 3–12 cm long; rounded or notched at tip; oil dots rare or absent; little or no scent when crushed. Cream flowers with 4 petals, in clusters; January–March. Fruit a yellow fleshy drupe, 1 cm long; ripe October–November.

Habitat and Range: Littoral and coastal subtropical rainforest. Qld and NSW.

Notes: Salt-tolerant species suitable for planting on sandy beaches. Similar to endangered *Acronychia littoralis* — glossy, mid-green leaves; abundant oil dots; pleasantly aromatic when crushed; relatively large, creamy-white fruit.

Wildlife: Flowers — Rainbow Lorikeets.

Family: Rutaceae

Acronychia laevis
Glossy Acronychia, Hard Aspen

Description: Shrub or small tree to 10 m. Leaves opposite; glossy dark green above and below; 4–7 cm long; dense oil dots; leaf stalks slender, green, 5–10 cm long. Creamy-white flowers with 4 petals, in clusters; November–March. Fruit an attractive pink to purplish drupe; lobed, flattened at top; 6–12 mm across; ripe April–July,

Habitat and Range: Occasionally on edges and within dry and subtropical rainforest. Qld and NSW; also Melanesia.

Notes: Leaves aromatic when crushed. Similar to *Acronychia pauciflora* — fewer, less distinct oil dots; shorter, whitish leaf stalks; white fruit.

Wildlife: Fruit — Green Catbird.

Family: Rutaceae

Acronychia oblongifolia
Common Acronychia, White Acronychia

Description: Tall shrub or small tree, to 15 m. Branchlets reddish-brown with pale distinct leaf scars. Leaves opposite; glossy green; oblong–elliptical, 4–12 cm long; rounded or notched at tip; base tapered; distinct veins on both surfaces, 5–11 pairs of lateral veins; numerous oil dots; strong pleasant smell when crushed. White flowers with 4 petals, in clusters; January–March. Fruit a white fleshy drupe; 4 lobes, each contains 1 or 2 dark brown seeds; ripe July–November.

Habitat and Range: Subtropical and dry rainforests at all altitudes, also common on rainforest edges and in regrowth. Qld, NSW and Vic.

Notes: Fruit edible, but acidic.

Wildlife: Fruit eaten by many species of birds.

Family: Rutaceae

Alchornea ilicifolia
Native Holly

Description: Straggling shrub to 6 m high. Leaves alternate; stiff and leathery; 3–9 cm long; several sharp spines at angles and tip of leaf; minute brown stipules at base of leaves on new growth. Inconspicuous, creamish-green flowers in racemes; November–December. Male and female flowers on separate plants, Fruit a brown, 3-lobed capsule; 5–7 mm wide; ripe September–November.

Habitat and Range: Common in dry rainforest, also in subtropical rainforest. Qld and NSW.

Notes: Grown for attractive, holly-like foliage; easily struck from cuttings.

Family: Euphorbiaceae

Alectryon coriaceus
Beach Alectryon

Description: Shrub or small tree to 6 m. Leaves alternate; consist of 2–4 leaflets; glossy green above, dull grey below; broadly elliptical to obovate, 6–11 cm long; rounded or notched at tip. Small greenish-yellow flowers in panicles; 5 petals; November–December. Fruit a rusty, hairy capsule; 3–4 lobes, each with glossy black seed partly enclosed by red aril; ripe April–June.

Habitat and Range: Littoral rainforest and beach scrub. Qld and NSW.

Wildlife: Fruit eaten by Green Catbird; leaves — caterpillars of Dark Pencilled-Blue, Large Purple Line-blue, Hairy Line-blue, Small-tailed Line Blue and Glistening Blue Butterflies.

Family: Sapindaceae

Alectryon tomentosus
Hairy Alectryon, Hairy Bird's Eye

Description: Small tree to 15 m high. Branchlets, leaf stalks and leaf axes covered with dense short brown hairs. Leaves alternate, consist of 4–8 leaflets; lowest leaflets usually much smaller; leaflets hairy on both sides, more dense below. Small, creamy-pink to reddish flowers in downy panicles; May–August. Fruit a 1 to 3-lobed capsule; about 10 mm across; 1–3 glossy black seeds surrounded by fleshy red aril; ripe May–August.

Habitat and Range: Also in subtropical rainforest. Qld and NSW.

Notes: Attractive, hardy small tree that regenerates freely in suburban gardens. Edible, astringent red aril. Similar to *Alectryon subdentatus* — up to 6 leaflets; mature leaflets more rounded, less hairy below.

Family: Sapindaceae

Alyxia ruscifolia
Chain Fruit

Description: Shrub to 4 m high. Milky sap in stems and leaves. Stiff, glossy leaves in whorls of 3–6; size and shape variable; spine at tip. White flowers in clusters from centres of leaf whorls; 6 mm wide; June–September. Fruit a globular orange to red berry, 5 mm across; singly or in a chain of up to 4; ripe June–December.

Habitat and Range: In most types of rainforest. Qld and NSW.

Notes: Flowers sweetly perfumed. Larger-leaved forms of *Alyxia ruscifolia* are similar to *Alyxia magnifolia*, which occurs mainly north of Brisbane.

Family: Apocynaceae

Anopterus macleayanus
Macleay Laurel

Description: Shrub or small tree to 15 m. Young trees mostly straight and unbranched. Branchlets reddish-green, thick, with prominent leaf scars; leaf buds red, soft and scaly. Leaves alternate; clustered in pseudowhorls; thick and smooth; glossy green above, paler below; narrowly oblanceolate, 18–40 cm long; leaf edges bluntly and often irregularly toothed; leaf stalk red. White, bell-shaped flowers, 10–15 mm across, in racemes; November–December. Fruit a reddish-brown, 2-valved capsule; 3–4 cm long; up to 16 winged seeds; ripe June–August.

Habitat and Range: Subtropical and warm temperate rainforest on rich basaltic and less fertile soils. Qld and NSW.

Family: Grossulariaceae

Aphananthe philippinensis
Rough-leaved Elm, Grey Handlewood

Description: Small to medium tree to 35 m, but generally less than 20 m. Trunk fluted and buttressed. Bark dark brown, scaly; shed in irregular patches. Leaves alternate; ovate or oblong, 3–10 cm long; edges sharply toothed, especially in juveniles; short stiff hairs give rough, sandpapery feel. Small creamish-green flowers; separate male and female flowers, male in short clusters, female single, or rarely two together; September–November. Fruit a small black, fleshy drupe; ripe October–January.

Habitat and Range: Common in riverine rainforest, but also away from watercourses in subtropical and dry rainforest. Qld and NSW; also New Guinea and Malesia and Melanesia.

Notes: Similar to *Streblus brunonianus*, see p. 295

Family: Ulmaceae

Araucaria cunninghamii
Hoop Pine

Description: Tall tree to 50 m. Columnar trunk and distinctive canopy shape. Green leaves curved and scale-like; pointed, veinless, less than 8 mm long; clustered along branchlets. Juvenile leaves longer and straighter. Flowers November–December. Male and female cones on separate trees; male cones cylindrical to 5 cm long; female cones ovoid, 8–10 cm long, consisting of winged scales; seed is retained on scale at shedding; ripe December–January.

Habitat and Range: In most types of rainforest, but common as an emergent tree above dry rainforest. Qld and NSW; also New Guinea.

Notes: Planted as street tree, see p.325

Family: Araucariaceae

Argyrodendron actinophyllum subsp. *actinophyllum*
Black Booyong, Blush Tulip Oak

Description: Large tree to 50 m. Dense, spreading crown. Trunk straight and cylindrical; large, thick buttresses. Bark dark grey to black; rough, scaly. Leaves alternate; consist of 4–9 leaflets; 7–15 mm long; leaflets dark green above, paler below; several domatia in vein angles. White bell-shaped flowers, 3–5 mm long; in panicles; separate male and female flowers on same tree; March–April. Fruit a cluster of 2–4 winged brown seeds, 2–6 cm long; ripe May–August.

Habitat and Range: Common in moist subtropical rainforest, particularly at higher altitudes. Qld and NSW.

Notes: Branches carry large numbers of epiphytic ferns and orchids. In favourable years, abundant fruit blown throughout forest.

Family: Sterculiaceae

Argyrodendron trifoliolatum
White Booyong, Brown Tulip Oak

Description: Medium to large tree to 40 m. Trunk cylindrical, strongly buttressed at base. Bark brown to grey; fissured and often scaly. Branchlets, leaf stalks and underside of leaflets silvery-brown to silvery grey-green, due to covering of minute scales. Leaves alternate; consist of 3, occasionally 5, leaflets; dark green above; leaflets narrowly elliptical to oblong, 7–14 cm long; gradually narrowed to tip and base; edges wavy; midvein raised on both surfaces; leaf stalk 1–5 cm long, prominent swelling at base. Creamy-brown, bell-shaped flowers in branched panicles; about 6 mm wide; July–September. Fruit a cluster of 1–4 brown, scaly seeds attached to thin, silvery-brown wings; 3 cm long; ripe November–January.

Habitat and Range: Common on basalt or alluvial soils in subtropical rainforest below 600 m altitude, but occurring at higher altitudes on McPherson Range. Qld and NSW; also New Guinea and Celebes.

Notes: Similar to *Argyrodendron* sp. Kin Kin (Rusty Tulip Oak) — leaflets a shining reddish-brown below; leaflet stalks longer; midvein sunken on upper surface; common on poorer soils in rainforests in Nambour to Gympie area, Qld.

Wildlife: Seeds — Brush Turkey; leaves — caterpillar of Bronze Flat Butterfly.

Family: Sterculiaceae

Atractocarpus chartaceus
Narrow-leaved Gardenia

Description: Shrub to 6 m. Branchlets with horizontal scars left by fallen stipules. Leaves opposite or in whorls of 3; dark green above, paler below; shape varies, narrow to broadly lanceolate, 5–12 cm long; tip pointed; raised lateral veins on upper surface. Juvenile leaves very long and narrow. White flowers, single or in pairs, on short stalks; May–August. Fruit an orange-red berry; ovoid; numerous triangular seeds; ripe August–November.

Habitat and Range: Common understorey shrub in subtropical and dry rainforest. Qld and NSW.

Notes: Previously known as *Randia chartacea*. Fruit with sweet pulp. Flowers strongly perfumed. Attractive plant for shady positions.

Family: Rubiaceae

Auranticarpa rhombifolia
Holly Wood

Description: Small to medium-sized tree to 25 m high. Terminal buds scaly. Leaves alternate, clustered in whorls; diamond-shaped; edges irregularly toothed in upper half. Dense white flower heads; flowers 12–15 mm across; November–January. Fruit an orange-yellow, pear-shaped capsule; 6–8 mm; 2–3 black seeds; ripe April–May.

Habitat and Range: On fertile soils in dry and subtropical rainforest.

Notes: Previously known as *Pittosporum rhombifolium*. Popular ornamental.

Wildlife: Flowers — Adult butterflies.

Family: Pittosporaceae

Baloghia inophylla
Brush Bloodwood

Description: Small to medium-sized tree to 25 m high. Trunk often fluted; bark pale creamy-brown with raised dark brown areas and rusty streaks. Branchlets with circular scars above each leaf-pair (left by bud scales). Leaves opposite; stiff and leathery; oblong to elliptical, 5–15 cm long; almost transverse lateral veins; paired, slit-like glands on edges near base; numerous fine translucent dots. Creamy-white to pale pink flowers in short racemes; 25 mm across; separate male and female flowers on same plant; August–October. Fruit a brown to black capsule, 12–18 mm wide; splits into 3 segments, each with single brown seed; ripe December–May.

Habitat and Range: Common understorey tree in dry and subtropical rainforest. Qld and NSW; also New Caledonia, Lord Howe and Norfolk Is.

Notes: Leaves not aromatic when crushed. Flowers perfumed. Grown readily from fresh seed or cuttings. Damaged stems exude pale sap that changes rapidly to rusty reddish-brown.

Wildlife: Seeds – King Parrot.

Family: Euphorbiaceae

Brachychiton acerifolius
Flame Tree, Flame Kurrajong, Illawarra Flame Tree

Description: Medium to large tree to 35 m. Partly to completely deciduous in late spring and early summer. Trunk cylindrical; bark grey-brown, fissured. Leaves alternate; glossy green hairs; shape varies, 3-lobed or entire on mature trees (entire leaves narrow and ovate), juvenile leaves with 5–7 deep lobes; 10–30 cm long; veins radiate from base; slender leaf stalk, 7–25 cm long. Smooth red, bell-shaped flowers in panicles; October–January. Fruit a cluster of large dark brown, boat-shaped follicles; each containing numerous seeds enclosed in yellow, hairy covering; ripe May–July.

Habitat and Range: Subtropical and dry rainforest. Qld and NSW.

Notes: Magnificent ornamental tree in full flower, especially when still leafless; flowers infrequently in rainforest; generally at best in drought years

Wildlife: Flowers — Rainbow Lorikeet, Australian King Parrot; leaves — caterpillars of Tailed Emperor, White-banded Plane and Common Pencilled-blue Butterflies.

Family: Sterculiaceae

Brachychiton discolor
Lacebark

Description: Medium tree to 25 m tall. Deciduous. Trunk cylindrical, sometimes swollen at base, bark grey-brown with green vertical fissures. Branchlets with dense brown star-hairs towards tips. Leaves alternate; dark green above, white and downy below; edges with 3 to 5 lobes; major veins radiate from leaf base to tip of each lobe. Pink bell-shaped flowers with 5 lobes; 3–4 cm across; separate male and female flowers; November–February, mostly while still leafless. Clusters of brown, boat-shaped follicles; to 20 cm long; each follicle contains 10–30 pale oval seeds in fine cottony covering; ripe December–July.

Habitat and Range: Common in dry rainforest. Qld and NSW.

Notes: Attractive, hardy ornamental. Aboriginal people ate roasted seeds. Similar to *Brachychiton australis* — leaves hairless; flowers small, white.

Wildlife: Seeds — Regent and Satin Bowerbirds and Paradise Riflebird; leaves — caterpillars of Tailed Emperor and White-banded Plane Butterflies.

Family: Sterculiaceae

Callicarpa pedunculata
Callicarpa

Description: Open, sprawling shrub to 4 m. Branchlets, leaf stalks and terminal buds with dense hairs. Leaves opposite; green with scattered star-hairs above, dense covering of pale brown star-hairs below; 8–16 cm long; edges shortly-toothed. Tiny pinkish-mauve flowers in clusters; October– November. Fruit a glossy deep purple berry; 3–4 mm wide; in dense clusters; ripe February–March.

Habitat and Range: Uncommon. In dry rainforest and on edges of subtropical rainforest. Qld and NSW; also New Guinea.

Notes: Much of this plant's native habitat dominated by exotic shrub, *Lantana camara*, see p. 343, which it superficially resembles.

Wildlife: Fruit — Lewin's Honeyeater and Silvereye birds.

Family: Verbenaceae

Canthium odoratum
Shiny-leaved Canthium, Sweet Susie

Description: Shrub or small tree to 5 m. Distinctive horizontal branches; branchlets with horizontal scars left by fallen stipules. Leaves opposite, glossy dark green above, paler below; ovate to broadly elliptical, 1–4 cm long; a few, barely visible lateral veins; 1–2 domatia sometimes present. Masses of white flowers in clusters; November–February. Fruit a globular black drupe; 6–8 mm wide; ripe March–November.

Habitat and Range: In dry rainforest, and also on edges. Qld only.

Notes: Flowers perfumed.

Family: Rubiaceae

Capparis arborea
Brush Caper Berry

Description: Shrub or small tree to 8 m. Leaves alternate; stiff and tough; elliptical to oblong-ovate, 5–12 cm long; paired spines to 12 mm long at base; tip bluntly rounded; prominent veins, leaf stalk 6–15 mm long. Juvenile leaves ovate to heart-shaped; spine at tip. Single white flowers with numerous stamens; December–January. Fruit a dark green globular berry; 3–4 cm across; long stalk; numerous seeds; ripe December–March.

Habitat and Range: Subtropical and dry rainforest. Common in regrowth vegetation.

Notes: In older trees, bases of spines may persist as paired lumps on trunk. Edible fruit resembles guavas; food source for Aboriginal people.

Wildlife: Leaves — caterpillars of Striated Pearl-white, Southern Pearl-white and Caper White Butterflies.

Family: Capparaceae

Carissa ovata
Currant Bush, Carissa

Description: Shrub to 3 m, sometimes scrambling much higher into trees. Milky sap in branchlets and leaves. Leaves opposite; glossy green; ovate, 1–4 cm long; tip with sharp point; paired spines between leaf bases. White flowers with 5 petals; January–February. Fruit a glossy purplish-black berry; 1–1.5 cm across; ripe April–May.

Habitat and Range: In dry and subtropical rainforest, also in eucalypt and brigalow communities. Qld and NSW.

Notes: Flowers perfumed. Aboriginal people ate edible fruit. Similar to juvenile *Strychnos psilosperma* — lacks milky sap.

Wildlife: Fruit — Regent and Satin Bowerbirds; leaves — caterpillar of Common Crow Butterfly

Family: Apocynaceae

Castanospermum australe
Black Bean, Moreton Bay Chestnut

Description: Medium to large tree to 35 m. Trunk cylindrical, lacks buttresses or flanges. Branchlets with numerous raised lenticels and prominent leaf scars. Leaves alternate; large, pinnate, with 9–17 leaflets; dark glossy green above, paler below; leaflets oblong; 8–20 cm long; tip pointed; base more or less symmetrical; base of leaf stalk swollen. Flowers yellowish-red to orange; in racemes rising from scars of fallen leaves; 8–15 cm long; long stamens; October–December. Fruit a large brown, woody pod; 25 cm long and 5 cm across; contains 3–5 large, rounded seeds; ripe February–April.

Habitat and Range: Very common; often dominates dry riverine rainforest, also in subtropical rainforest on basalt plateaus. Qld and NSW, also New Guinea, Malesia and Asia.

Notes: Seeds poisonous to livestock and humans, but Aboriginal people ground and washed seeds to remove saponin. Alkaloid castanospermine used in trials to treat HIV. Timber hard and dark with attractive grain; used for veneers, wood turning and furniture.

Wildlife: Flowers — Rainbow Lorikeet, Noisy and Little Friarbird, Blue-faced, Mangrove and White-cheeked Honeyeaters, possums and bats; seed — Scaly-breasted Lorikeet; leaves — caterpillar of Common Pencilled-blue Butterfly.

Family: Fabaceae (Leguminosae).

Choricarpia subargentea
Giant Ironwood

Description: Medium to large tree to 30 m. Crown often open and sparse. Trunk buttressed in large trees; bark smooth, reddish-brown with patches of green and cream. Branchlets with rusty brown hairs. Leaves opposite; dark glossy green above, paler below; elliptical, 6–8 cm long; prominent veins; numerous small oil dots. Dense white, round flower heads; June–November. Brownish capsules clustered in dense globular heads; ripe February–October.

Habitat and Range: In dry rainforest and drier forms of subtropical rainforest. Qld and NSW.

Notes: Bark of this tree is as beautiful as that of exotic *Caesalpinia ferrea* (Leopard Tree) Similar to *Choricarpia leptopetala* (Brown Myrtle) — rough, dark brown persistent bark; lacks buttresses.

Family: Myrtaceae

Claoxylon australe
Brittlewood

Description: Shrub to small tree to 9 m. Branchlets greenish with pale lenticels. Leaves alternate; soft, thin, sometimes hairy below; elliptical to ovate, 6–15 cm long; tip with blunt point; edges bluntly toothed; leaf stalk 1–3 cm long, 2–5 raised glands on upper surface of leaf stalk. Cream flowers in racemes; September–November. Fruit a purplish-black capsule with 3 lobes; 4–5 mm wide; each lobe with bright red seed; ripe September–December.

Habitat and Range: Subtropical and dry rainforest and on edges. Qld and NSW.

Notes: Similar to some species of *Croton*, which have small stalked glands on either side of leaf stalk.

Wildlife: Fruit — Brown Cuckoo-dove, Lewin's Honeyeater and Australian King Parrot.

Family: Euphorbiaceae

Commersonia bartramia
Brown Kurrajong

Description: Shrub or small tree to 20 m. Crown of larger trees with characteristic, horizontally layered appearance. Older branchlets with prominent white raised lenticels; leaf buds and young branchlets with dense brown hairs. Leaves alternate; dark green above, pale yellowish below, covered with tiny star hairs; ovate to very broad-ovate, 2–14 cm long; finely toothed, sometimes almost entire. Small white flowers in broad clusters, producing a layered effect on branches; December–February. Fruit a brown capsule covered with long, soft bristles; 5–10 black seeds; 2 mm long; yellow aril; ripe March–June.

Habitat and Range: Common along smaller scrubby gullies, on rainforest edges and in regrowth of subtropical rainforest. Qld and NSW, also New Guinea, Malesia, Melanesia and Pacific Is.

Notes: Aboriginal people used tough fibrous bark to make kangaroo and fishing nets and lines. Similar to *Commersonia fraseri* — smaller; lacks obvious white lenticels on branchlets; coarsely toothed leaves grey rather than yellowish below; also on rainforest edges and in regrowth.

Wildlife: Leaves — caterpillar of Coral Jewel Butterfly.

Family: Sterculiaceae

Cordyline rubra
Red-fruited Palm Lily

Description: Low shrub to 3 m high. Leaves lanceolate, 15–50 cm long; tip with blunt point; base gradually tapers to stalk; leaf stalk 6–11 cm, flat to concave. White to mauve flowers in terminal panicles; September– October. Fruit a bright red berry; a few, glossy black seeds; ripe December– March.

Habitat and Range: Subtropical rainforest and adjacent wet eucalypt forest. Qld and NSW.

Notes: Similar to *Cordyline petiolaris* (Broad-leaved Palm Lily) — tall shrub to 5 m, leaves broad and elliptical; numerous parallel veins; leaf stalk long and narrow, 12–45 cm long, deeply channelled above. Also similar to *Cordyline congesta* — leaves narrower with rough toothed edges at base; common on rainforest edges and in wet eucalypt forest south of Brisbane.

Family: Dracaenaceae

Croton insularis
Silver Croton

Description: Shrub to small tree to 15 m high. Leaves alternate; dark green above, silvery below, dotted with small brown scales; two small raised glands at tip of leaf stalk. Old leaves often turn red or orange before falling. Cream to silvery-brown flowers in slender racemes; separate male and female flowers in same raceme; June– October. Fruit a small globular capsule, 6 mm across; seeds dark brown; ripe November– January.

Habitat and Range: In dry and sub-tropical rainforest, and in regrowth areas Qld and NSW; also Melanesia.

Notes: Similar to *Croton stigmatosus* — leaves have white star-hairs below, not silvery scales. Bark from this tree provides reddish-brown dye.

Wildlife: Leaves — caterpillar of Eastern Dusk-flat Butterfly.

Family: Euphorbiaceae

Cryptocarya glaucescens
Jackwood, Silver Sycamore

Description: Medium tree to 30 m. Bark brown, scaly. Leaves alternate; glossy green above, dull below with blotchy to almost even, ashy-green bloom; oblong-elliptical, 6–13 cm long; tip with blunt point; midvein broad and yellowish, fine net veins visible when leaf is held against light. Small creamish-green flowers in panicles; October–December. Fruit a black glossy drupe; round but somewhat flattened; 12–18 mm wide; single brown wrinkled seed; ripe March–June.

Habitat and Range: Generally on poorer soils in subtropical rainforest and adjacent wet eucalypt forest. Qld and NSW.

Notes: Similar to *Cryptocarya microneura* — Young leaves with greyish bloom on underside; narrowly elliptical; midvein white.

Family: Lauraceae

Cryptocarya laevigata
Glossy Laurel

Description: Shrub to 6 m high. Leaves alternate; glossy green, hairless; narrowly elliptic, 5–12 cm long; tip with blunt point; 3-veined from just above base to near tip, other lateral veins faint; leaf stalk short, 2–5 mm. Creamy-pink flowers in panicles; September–December. Fruit a fleshy drupe; usually red, sometimes orange-yellow; ovoid, 15 mm wide; ripe December–March.

Habitat and Range: On basaltic or alluvial soils in understorey of lowland subtropical rainforest. Qld and NSW.

Notes: Attractive glossy green leaves and red fruit; perfumed flowers. Suitable as an indoor plant.

Family: Lauraceae

Cryptocarya obovata
Pepperberry, White Walnut

Description: Large tree to 40 m. Trunk straight and cylindrical, buttressed at base. Bark brown and smooth, with patches or bands of greyish, finely wrinkled bark on older trees. Branchlets, terminal buds and leaf stalks with dense, soft brown hairs. Leaves alternate; glossy green above, dull below with uneven, ashy-green bloom, mostly with rusty hairs, especially on main veins; oblong to obovate, 6-13 cm long; blunt or rounded at tip. Juvenile leaves longer and pointed. White flowers in panicles; February–March. Fruit a black, globular drupe; single hard seed; ripe March–May.

Habitat and Range: On richer volcanic or alluvial soils in subtropical rainforest. Qld and NSW.

Family: Lauraceae

Cryptocarya triplinervis
Three-veined Cryptocarya

Description: Small to medium tree to 20 m high. Branchlets with dense hairs. Leaves alternate; dark green above, paler and often with dense hairs below; broadly lanceolate to elliptical, 3 veined from a little above base; 2 or more hairy domatia. Very small, yellowish-green flowers in panicles; October–January. Fruit a glossy black drupe; ovoid, to 12 mm long; ripe July–September.

Habitat and Range: Common. In dry and littoral rainforest and along scrubby gullies. Qld and NSW.

Notes: Excellent shade tree.

Wildlife: Fruit — Wompoo Fruit-dove, Topknot Pigeon, Crimson Rosella, Australian King Parrot and Lewin's Honeyeater.

Family: Lauraceae

Cupaniopsis anacardioides
Tuckeroo, Beach Tamarind

Description: Small tree to 10 m. Dense spreading crown. Branchlets grey and downy. Leaves alternate; consist of 4–11 leaflets; dark glossy green above, paler and dull below; obovate to oblong, 5–15 cm long; rounded and notched at tip; edges of leaflets entire. Greenish–white flowers in panicles; May–September. Fruit an orange-yellow capsule; 3 lobes, 1 shiny black seed in each lobe, enclosed in an orange aril; ripe July–December.

Habitat and Range: Littoral rainforest and coastal scrubs. Qld, NSW, NT, WA; also New Guinea.

Notes: Excellent shade or street tree near sea.

Wildlife: Fruit eaten by many species of birds.

Family: Sapindaceae

Cuttsia viburnea
Cuttsia

Description: Shrub or small tree to 20 m. Branchlets thick and fleshy, green or purple; smooth with small white lenticels. Leaves alternate; soft and thin; ovate–lanceolate to elliptical, 8–20 cm long; tip with fine point; edges prominently and evenly toothed; lateral veins curved. White flowers with 5 petals; in panicles; October–December. Fruit a small capsule, 3 mm long, opening at top with 4–5 valves; numerous red-brown seeds.

Habitat and Range: Subtropical and temperate rainforest, generally at higher altitudes, often on cliff tops and along watercourses. Qld and NSW.

Notes: Similar to *Abrophyllum ornans*, see p 237. Honey-scented flowers.

Family: Grossulariaceae

Cyathea cooperi
Straw Treefern

Description: Tall treefern to 10 m. Trunk slender and smooth with a pattern of oval scars where leaves have shed cleanly. Fronds large, divided 3 times; leaflet edges with shallow rounded teeth; base of leaf stalk red-brown, with small tubercles and a dense covering of long white and short red-brown scales.

Habitat and Range: In subtropical and littoral rainforest. Qld and NSW.

Notes: Similar to *Cyathea leichhardtiana* (Prickly Treefern) — to 7 m; trunk covered with prickly leaf bases; base of leaf stalk with many thin, sharp prickles and whitish, narrow scales. Also similar to *Cyathea australis* (Rough Treefern) — occasionally to 15–20 m; thick trunk; base of leaf stalk with many short, conical tubercles (not prickles) and long shiny brown scales.

Family: Cyatheaceae

Dendrocnide excelsa
Giant Stinging Tree

Description: Large tree, occasionally to 40 m. Trunk deeply fluted with large thick buttresses. Branchlets green and fleshy, covered with rigid stinging hairs. Leaves alternate; dull grey-green, both surfaces with scattered stinging hairs; round to heart-shaped, to 30 cm wide; edges toothed, fleshy leaf stalk, often with stinging hairs. Yellowish-green flowers in panicles; November–April. Fruit a cluster of swollen, dark pinkish, fleshy stalks; each with single, blackish seed; ripe April–August.

Habitat and Range: Subtropical and dry rainforest, especially following disturbance. Qld and NSW.

Notes: Juveniles similar to *Dendrocnide moroides*, (Gympie Stinger) — uncommon; shrub to 4 m; stalk attached inside edge of leaf blade, sting more severe.

Family: Urticaceae

Dendrocnide photinophylla
Shiny-leaved Stinging Tree, Mulberry Stinger

Description: Medium tree to 25 m. Often flanged or buttressed at base. Branchlets and leaf stalks often have few stinging hairs, especially in young growth. Soft glossy leaves; broad and ovate; base sometimes bluntly toothed; 3 veins at base, numerous oil-like dots and 2–4 domatia. Green flowers in short dense panicles; November–June. Cluster of swollen, greenish fleshy stalks, each with single, small dry fruit attached; ripe May–June.

Habitat and Range: Dry rainforest and subtropical rainforest. Qld and NSW.

Notes: Aboriginal people used fibre from timber to make cord, fishing nets and dilly bags.

Family: Urticaceae

Diospyros pentamera
Myrtle Ebony

Description: Medium to tall tree to 40 m. Small dense, dark conical crown. Trunk straight and fluted, lacks buttresses. Bark dark grey to black, rough and scaly, especially near base of trunk. Branchlets slightly zig-zag. Leaves alternate; dark green above, dull, greyish to yellowish-green, with small black dots below; lanceolate or narrowly elliptical, 3–8 cm long; fine point at tip. White flowers; single (female) or in clusters (male) on separate plants; October–November. Fruit a dull red to yellowish berry; enclosed at base in 5-lobed calyx; 2–5 light brown seeds; ripe April–December.

Habitat and Range: On wide range of soils in all types of rainforest. Qld and NSW.

Notes: Perfumed flowers. Important food tree for birds in winter– spring period, but may be several years between heavy crops.

Family: Ebenaceae

Diploglottis australis
Native Tamarind

Description: Medium to tall tree to 35 m. Trunk tall and straight, often fluted at base. Branchlets and new growth with dense rusty hairs. Leaves alternate; consist of 8–12 large leaflets; velvety brown hairs on both surfaces, denser below; leaflets elliptical to lanceolate, 15–30 cm long; tip rounded or bluntly pointed; unequal sides at base. Creamy-brown flowers in large panicles with dense rusty hairs; September–November. Fruit a yellow to brown, hairy capsule; 2–3 lobes, each with single pale brown seed enclosed in orange-yellow aril; ripe November–December.

Habitat and Range: Subtropical rainforest, also in dry rainforest. Qld and NSW.

Notes: Aril of fruit edible.

Family: Sapindaceae

Dissiliaria baloghioides
Lancewood, Hauer

Description: Medium to large tree to 30 m. Trunk buttressed; bark dark brown, shed in thin flakes or strips. Branchlets with raised pale spots. Leaves opposite or sometimes in groups of 3; hairless; glossy light green above and below; elliptical or ovate, 6–12 cm long, tip rounded or bluntly pointed; prominent lateral and net veins; new growth pink. Small creamy–brown flowers in panicles; separate male and female flowers on same plant; January–June. Woody capsule with rusty hairs; 10 mm wide; splits into 3 segments; ripe June–December.

Habitat and Range: Locally dominant in drier types of subtropical rainforest. Qld only.

Notes: Aboriginal people used wood to make spears, clubs and hunting sticks.

Family: Euphorbiaceae

Drypetes deplanchei
Yellow Tulip, Grey Boxwood

Description: Medium tree to 25 m. Trunk often fluted to base. Bark grey to brown, scaly on older trees; scales leave shallow depressions when shed. Branchlets covered with small pale lenticels. Leaves alternate; tough and leathery, glossy green; ovate to elliptical, 3–9 cm long; edges entire or toothed, often sharply toothed in young trees; prominent net veins. Flowers yellowish, single or in clusters; September–October. Fruit a fleshy, red to orange drupe; ovoid; single seed; ripe January–March.

Habitat and Range: Common in littoral and dry rainforest, also in drier subtropical rainforest. One of most widespread Australian rainforest trees; Qld, NSW and NT; also New Guinea and Melanesia.

Family: Euphorbiaceae

Duboisia myoporoides
Duboisia, Soft Corkwood

Description: Small tree to 6 m tall in coastal rainforest, to 20 m in moist high altitude forests. Bark pale brown; soft and corky; heavily fissured in older trees. Branchlets thick, purplish-green, hairless. Leaves alternate; dull pale green, soft and hairless; oblanceolate, 8–10 cm long; base tapering; midvein purplish. White flowers in panicles; June–October. Fruit a small black berry; 4–7 mm wide; 2–4, black seeds; ripe October–January.

Habitat and Range: Common at higher altitudes. Edges of, and regrowth areas within, littoral, dry and subtropical rainforest. Qld and NSW, also New Caledonia.

Notes: Leaves contain alkaloids hyoscine and hyoscamine, used extensively as a source of these compounds for motion sickness tablets and for dilating pupils in eye surgery.

Family: Solanaceae

Dysoxylum rufum
Hairy Rosewood, Rusty Mahogany

Description: Small to medium tree to 20 m. Trunk slightly fluted with short spur buttresses. Branchlets, leaf stalks and terminal buds with dense hairs. Leaves alternate; consist of 11–21 leaflets; soft, dull dark green above, paler and densely hairy below; leaflets entire, ovate to lanceolate, 9–20 cm long; tip pointed; unequal sides at base; small, often inconspicuous domatia in vein angles. White flowers with 5 petals; hairy; in long panicles; January–February. Fruit a yellow-orange capsule; about 2 cm wide; covered with dense short, stiff irritating hairs; opens to 4–5 valves; angular cream seeds; ripe June–September.

Habitat and Range: On fertile and relatively infertile soils in moister subtropical rainforest. Qld and NSW.

Notes: Attractive shade tree for large gardens and parks. Leaves similar to *Dysoxylum molissimum* subsp. *molle*, (Red Bean) — leaflets with very unequal sides at base and obvious domatia.

Wildlife: Fruit — Lewin's Honeyeater, Paradise Riflebird and Regent Bowerbird.

Family: Meliaceae

Elaeocarpus grandis
Blue Quandong, Cooloon

Description: Large tree o 35 m. Trunk cylindrical, to 2 m wide; large buttresses, whitish bark. Leaves alternate; glossy dark green, old leaves turn red before falling; oblong to elliptical, 10–18 cm long; tip bluntly pointed; base tapers to leaf stalk; edges with fine shallow teeth; numerous pit-like domatia in vein angles. Greenish-white, bell-shaped flowers with 5 fringed petals; in racemes from leaf scars along branchlets; March–June. Fruit a bright blue globular drupe; 2–3 cm wide; up to 5 seeds enclosed in hard stone; ripe September–November.

Habitat and Range: Beside rivers and creeks in subtropical rainforest. Qld, NSW and NT.

Notes: Timber highly valued; light, strong and bends well. Used for furniture, interior trim, flooring and racing skiffs and oars. Popular for farm forestry plantings. Fruit stones used for necklaces and earrings. Aboriginal people made edible paste from fruits.

Wildlife: Flowers — Rainbow Lorikeet; fruit — Eastern Tube-nosed Bat; Wompoo, Superb and Rose-crowned Fruit-doves, Topknot Pigeon, Double-eyed Fig Parrot, Crimson Rosella, Green Catbird, Pied Currawong; leaves — caterpillar of Bright Cornelian Butterfly.

Family: Elaeocarpaceae

Elaeocarpus kirtonii
White Quandong, Mowbullan Whitewood

Description: Large tree to 45 m. Trunk long and straight, buttressed at base. Bark whitish-grey. Branchlets with narrow black stipules at base of young leaves. Leaves alternate; narrowly, elliptical to oblong, 9–18 cm long; edges evenly and finely toothed; lateral veins numerous, net veins prominent; small hairy domatia usually present; slender leaf stalk 2–6 cm long with joint at tip. Old leaves turn red before falling. White bell shaped flowers; 5-petals, fringed; January–March. Fruit a pale blue ovoid drupe; 1–2 seeds in hard wrinkled stone; ripe November–January.

Habitat and Range: Cool subtropical and temperate rainforests, generally at higher altitudes. Qld and NSW.

Family: Elaeocarpaceae

Elaeocarpus obovatus
Hard Quandong

Description: Medium to large tree to 30 m. Trunk strongly buttressed in large trees. Branchlets brownish-grey with numerous pale lenticels. Leaves alternate; glossy green above, dull below; obovate or oblanceolate, 4–9 cm long (often much smaller in large trees); base tapers to short stalk, lacks a joint; edges with irregular blunt teeth, sometimes almost entire; 1–4 domatia present as flaps of tissue in vein angles. Creamy-white, bell-shaped flowers; 5 petals, fringed; September–November. Fruit a bright blue ovoid drupe; 1 seed in hard warty stone; ripe January–March.

Habitat and Range: Subtropical, dry and littoral rainforest. Qld and NSW.

Notes: Domatia sometimes difficult to find.

Wildlife: Fruit eaten by many species of birds.

Family: Elaeocarpaceae

Elaeodendron australe var. *australe*
Red Olive Plum

Description: Small tree to 8 m high. Small paired stipules on branchlets. Leaves opposite; smooth and thickish; light green; obovate to elliptical, 4–10 cm long; edges slightly toothed or crenate in upper part of blade; lateral veins faint, more obvious below. Small, pale green flowers with 4 petals, in slender clusters; male and female flowers on separate plants; August–November. Fruit an orange-red drupe; ovoid, 10 mm wide; inner hard 'stone'; 1–2 seeds; ripe March–July.

Habitat and Range: In dry, littoral and subtropical rainforest. Qld and NSW.

Notes: Previously known as *Cassine australis*. Ornamental appearance, particularly in heavy fruit.

Family: Celastraceae

Elattostacyhys xylocarpa
White Tamarind

Description: Small to medium tree to 25 m. Branchlets, leaf stalks and new growth with dense hairs. Leaves alternate; consist of 2–6 leaflets; dark green above, with fine hairs below, often with yellowish tinge; leaflets toothed, elliptical, 5–8 cm long; brown hair tuft domatia in vein-angles. Young leaves often bright red or orange. Small, white flowers; upper flowers male, lower bisexual; December–March. Fruit a yellowish, woody capsule; splits into 3 (rarely 4) valves; pinkish-red inside; each valve with 1 glossy black seed; small pink aril at base; ripe March–May.

Habitat and Range: In dry and drier subtropical rainforest. Qld and NSW.

Notes: Similar to *Elattostachys nervosa* (Green Tamarind) — narrow leaflets 7–15 cm long; lacks hair-tuft domatia; moister subtropical rainforest.

Family: Sapindaceae

Endiandra sieberi
Hard Corkwood

Description: Small to medium tree to 30 m. Bark grey, fissured and corky, becoming rough and scaly in larger trees. Branchlets, leaf stalks and terminal buds reddish. Leaves alternate, sometimes opposite; narrowly elliptical, 5–9 cm long; midvein broad and yellowish-white, numerous fine net veins; edges pale yellow and translucent; minute oil dots. White flowers in short panicles; June–October. Fruit a shiny, purplish-black drupe; ovoid; pale brown seed with longitudinal ridges; ripe March–August.

Habitat and Range: On sands and sandstone in littoral and subtropical rainforest, also wet eucalypt forest. Qld and NSW.

Notes: Leaves aromatic when crushed. Thick, corky bark allows this species to withstand periodic fires.

Family: Lauraceae

Eupomatia laurina
Bolwarra

Description: Shrub to small tree to 10 m. Branches long and arching, branchlets green and zig-zag; new growth bronze-red. Leaves alternate; soft glossy green; oblong, 6-12 cm long; tip blunt; numerous small oil dots. Creamy-white, daisy-like flowers; petals and sepals form a cap that is shed as flower opens; November–January. Fruit a soft greenish-yellow berry, 2 cm across; numerous seeds; ripe May–July.

Habitat and Range: All rainforests, except dry, also wet eucalypt forest. Qld, NSW and eastern Vic., also New Guinea.

Notes: Flowers strongly perfumed. Hardy, fast-growing shrub.

Wildlife: Flower parts eaten by small, brown, host-specific weevil, *Elleschodes hamiltoni*.

Family: Eupomatiaceae

Euroschinus falcata
Ribbonwood, Blush Cudgerie, Pink Poplar

Description: Medium to large tree to 40 m. Trunk buttressed in large trees. Bark brown, usually wrinkled and finely scaly. Branchlets pale brown with numerous lenticels; branchlets and leaf stalks exude clear sap that smells like mangoes. Leaves alternate; pinnate, with 4–10 leaflets; glossy green above, paler below, leaflets elliptical, 5–10 cm long; tip pointed; sides unequal at base; hair-tuft domatia in some vein angles. Pink or white flowers with 5 petals, in panicles; October–December. Fruit a black drupe; ovoid to 9 mm long; 1 seed; ripe December–January.

Habitat and Range: In subtropical, littoral and dry rainforest, also common on edges of rainforest. Qld and NSW.

Notes: Similar to *Toona ciliata*, (Red Cedar), see p. 299.

Wildlife: Fruit — Brown Cuckoo-dove, Topknot Pigeon, Rose-crowned Fruit-dove and Crimson Rosella; Lewin's Honeyeater, Silvereye, Paradise Riflebird, Green Catbird, Regent and Satin Bowerbirds.

Family: Anacardiaceae

Ficus coronata
Creek Sandpaper Fig

Description: Small to medium tree to 15 m. Branchlets brown, hairy and rough. Sap sparse, watery or slightly milky. Leaves rough and sandpapery above, less so below; ovate to oblong, 5–10 cm long; tip with blunt point; edges entire or toothed, especially in upper half. Fruit a purple-black fig; ovoid; 2 cm long; hairy with crown of bristles at top; ripe December–March.

Habitat and Range: In subtropical, littoral and dry rainforest, especially along creeks. Qld, NSW and eastern Vic.

Notes: Fruit sweet, edible if hairs removed. Leaves an effective substitute for sandpaper.

Wildlife: Fruit — many species of birds; leaves — caterpillars of Common Crow and Purple Moonbeam Butterflies.

Family: Moraceae

Ficus macrophylla
Moreton Bay Fig

Description: Large strangling fig to 50 m. Large, spreading crown. Massive dark brown trunk of coalesced roots; broad spreading buttresses; sap milky. Branchlets thick, brown, marked by scars of fallen stipules and leaves. Leaves alternate; thick, dark green above, brownish below; oblong or ovate-elliptical, 10–25 cm long; leaf stalk 5–10 cm long. Figs orange turning purple when ripe, with creamy-white spots; ripe February–May, also year-round.

Habitat and Range: Lowland subtropical rainforest, also dry rainforest. Qld and NSW.

Notes: Often planted in parks. Aboriginal people used root bark to make twine for dilly bags and fish nets. Edible fruit.

Wildlife: Fruit eaten by a wide range of rainforest birds.

Family: Moraceae

Ficus obliqua
Small-leaved Fig

Description: Large strangling fig to 50 m. Massive trunk of coalesced roots, buttressed at base; sap milky. Terminal bud enclosed in yellow-brown stipule, 3–4 cm long. Branchlets grey or brown, often marked with numerous pale lenticels. Leaves alternate; dark green above, paler below; elliptical to oblong, 3–6 cm long; lateral veins visible above, sometimes with 2 prominent veins at base; short leaf stalk. Figs in pairs, yellow turning orange when ripe in March–June, also year-round.

Habitat and Range: Lowland subtropical and littoral rainforest. Qld, NSW, NT and WA; also New Guinea, Malesia, Melanesia and Pacific Is.

Wildlife: Fruit eaten by a wide range of rainforest birds.

Family: Moraceae

Ficus rubiginosa
Rock Fig

Description: Small or medium tree to 30 m, often low and spreading. Sap milky. Branchlets with prominent scars left by fallen leaves and stipules. Leaves alternate; thick, dark green above, paler below; elliptical to obovate, 6–9 cm long; base of leaf drawn out into stalk. Figs in pairs, yellow, turning red when ripe; warty surface; ripe mainly March–July, also year-round.

Habitat and Range: In littoral, dry and subtropical rainforest, also on rocky sites in open forest. Qld and NSW.

Notes: Previously known as *Ficus platypoda*.

Wildlife: Fruit eaten by many species of birds.

Family: Moraceae

Ficus superba var. *henneana*
Deciduous Fig

Description: Large tree to 35 m. Massive trunk of 'strangler' roots, usually buttressed. Deciduous. Milky sap. Leaf buds enclosed in short yellowish stipules, 5–7 mm long. Leaves thin, hairless; ovate to elliptical, 8–12 cm long; base slightly heart-shaped with joint at tip of leaf stalk. Figs yellow, turning purple with paler spots; 2 cm wide; ripe November–January, also year-round.

Habitat and Range: Littoral, riverine, dry and subtropical rainforest. Qld, NSW and NT.

Wildlife: Fruit – Lewin's Honeyeater, Rose-crowned and Wompoo Fruit-doves, Topknot Pigeon, Crimson Rosella, Figbird and Yellow-eyed Cuckoo-shrike, Brown Cuckoo-dove, Green Catbird, Regent and Satin Bowerbirds, Common Koel.

Family: Moraceae

Ficus watkinsiana
Watkins Fig, Strangler Fig

Description: Large strangling fig to 45 m. Trunk of coalesced roots, widely buttressed at base; sap milky. Branchlets with prominent scars from fallen leaves and stipules. Leaves alternate; thick, glossy green above, pale below; elliptical, 10–25 cm long; tip pointed; base tapered; leaf stalk yellowish 4–7 cm long. Figs on thick stalks in pairs; purple-black with paler spots when ripe; ovoid; 3–4 cm long; ripe September–April, also year-round.

Habitat and Range: Subtropical rainforest from lowlands to higher altitudes. Qld and NSW.

Wildlife: Fruit – Regent and Satin Bowerbirds, Rose-crowned and Wompoo Fruit-doves, Topknot and White-headed Pigeons, Crimson Rosella, Green Catbird, Figbird and Pied Currawong.

Family: Moraceae

Flindersia australis
Crows Ash, Teak

Description: Medium to large tree to 40 m. Brown scaly bark; shed in irregular flakes leaving depressions. Branchlets often show leaf scars. Leaves alternate, crowded towards ends of branchlets; pinnate, with 5–9 leaflets; elliptical to narowly ovate, 5–13 cm long; often with unequal sides at base; glossy dark green above, paler below; prominent oil dots; terminal leaflet with stalk to 3 cm long; base of leaf stalk ridged on either side. White flowers 11 mm across, in branched panicles; September–February. Fruit a woody brown capsule with stout, blunt prickles; 7–10 cm long; splits into 5 boat-shaped valves that remain united at base; each valve with 2–3 flat winged seeds; ripe April–September.

Habitat and Range: Dry and drier subtropical rainforest. Qld and NSW.

Notes: Similar to *Flindersia bennettiana*, see opposite. Timber of this species highly durable; used for fencing in rainforest areas where eucalypt posts were scarce. Prized for dance floors; also used for ship-building, carriage and coach building. Excellent shade and street tree.

Wildlife: Fruit — White Cockatoos; seed – Wonga Pigeon; leaves — caterpillar of Orchard Swallowtail Butterfly.

Family: Rutaceae

Flindersia bennettiana
Bennett's Ash

Description: Tall tree to 40 m. Trunk straight and cylindrical, without prominent buttresses. Bark grey and wrinkled. Branchlets brown and wrinkled with pale lenticels and prominent leaf scars; young shoots green and finely downy. Leaves opposite; pinnate, with 3–9 leaflets; glossy dark green above, dull and paler below; ovate or elliptical, 8–15 cm long; almost equal sides at base; oil dots visible with hand lens; terminal leaflet stalk much longer (15–30 mm) than lateral leaflets stalks (1–4 mm). Creamy-white flowers in panicles; August–October. Fruit a dark brown, woody capsule with blunt prickles; 5–8 cm long; separates into 5 segments; 2-3 winged seeds per segment; ripe November– February.

Habitat and Range: Subtropical and littoral rainforest, more frequent on less fertile substrates, Qld and NSW.

Notes: Similar to *Flindersia australis*, see opposite.

Wildlife: Leaves — caterpillar of Orchard Swallowtail Butterfly.

Family: Rutaceae

Flindersia collina
Leopard Ash

Description: Medium tree to 25 m. Bark mottled grey and creamy-green. Branchlets with leaf scars, hairy towards ends. Leaves mostly opposite; pinnate, with 3–7 leaflets; leaflets tough, glossy green above, paler below; elliptical to obovate; 2–8 cm long; rounded or notched at tip; distinct venation and oil dots; main stem of leaf often winged, especially in juveniles. White flowers in panicles; 6 mm wide; September–October. Fruit a woody, dark brown capsule with short dense prickles; splits into 5 separate valves; 10 seeds, winged at both ends; ripe February–March.

Habitat and Range: Dry rainforest and inland vine thickets. Qld only.

Wildlife: Leaves — caterpillar of Orchard Swallowtail Butterfly.

Family: Rutaceae

Geissois benthamii
Red Carabeen

Description: Medium to large tree to 35 m. Trunk cylindrical, prominently buttressed. Branchlets green, smooth with circular scars left by stipules; stipules in pairs at base of leaf stalk, rounded, resemble a bow tie; new growth often bright red. Leaves opposite; consist of 3 leaflets; smooth, green and hairless; elliptical, 8–18 cm long; edges toothed; prominent lateral veins; leaflet stalks 5–20 mm long. Creamy-yellow flowers in slender racemes; November–January. Fruit a narrow 2-valved capsule; 10–15 mm long; numerous brown seeds 4 mm long; ripe May–August.

Habitat and Range: Common in cool subtropical and warm temperate rainforest. Qld and NSW.

Notes: Similar to *Pseudoweinmannia lachnocarpa*, (Mararie) see p 290.

Family: Cunoniaceae

Glochidion ferdinandi
Cheese Tree

Description: Small to medium tree to 20 m high, sometimes 35 m. Trunk crooked and flanged; bark dark brown, fissured, shed in longitudinal patches. Leaves alternate; glossy green, sometimes softly hairy below; elliptical to oblong 4–11 cm long; pairs of small, finely pointed stipules at bases of leaf stalk. Greenish-yellow flowers; single (female) or in clusters of 3 (male) on same plant; October–December. Fruit a green to red, ribbed capsule, 10–15 mm across; resembles a small pumpkin; seeds in 4–6 pairs, covered by red aril; ripe November–February.

Habitat and Range: Edges of subtropical, dry and littoral rainforest and along streams. Qld and NSW.

Notes: Similar to *Glochidion sumatranum* see below.

Family: Euphorbiaceae

Glochidion sumatranum
Umbrella Cheese Tree

Description: Small to medium tree to 15 m, sometimes reaching 30 m. Trunk crooked and fluted. Bark dark brown with loose grey flakes and scales on larger trees. Leaves alternate; glossy green, sometimes softly hairy below; elliptical or ovate, 5–22 cm long; pair of small pointed stipules at base of leaf stalk. Greenish-yellow flowers in clusters; October–December. Fruit a pinkish hairy capsule; splits into 5 cells, each with single orange-red seed; ripe April–September.

Habitat and Range: Edges of subtropical and littoral rainforest, also in swampy open-forest. Qld, NSW, NT and WA; also New Guinea and Malesia.

Notes: Perfumed flowers. Similar to *Glochidion ferdinandi,* see above.

Family: Euphorbiaceae

Gmelina leichhardtii
White Beech

Description: Very large, semi-deciduous tree to 40 m. Trunk cylindrical; flanged at base, sometimes extending length of bole. Bark light to dark grey, scaly in large trees. Leaves opposite; dark green above, pale-brown with dense hairs below; ovate or broadly ovate, 8–18 cm long; tip with blunt point; edges entire, except in juveniles, which may be lobed or toothed; main, lateral and net veins raised and prominent on lower surface. White flowers with purple and yellow markings, about 2 cm long; in large panicles; November–January. Fruit a succulent blue drupe; 15–20 mm wide; with persistent, enlarged calyx, 4 seeds encased in hard stone; ripe March–April.

Habitat and Range: On poor soils in subtropical rainforest, also on more fertile alluvial and volcanic soils. Qld and NSW.

Notes: Excellent shade tree with large attractive flowers and fruit. Timber straight-grained, soft and easy to work, but also durable and non-shrinking; highly sought after by boat-builders.

Wildlife: Fruit — Topknot Pigeon and Wompoo Fruit-dove.

Family: Lamiaceae (previously in family Verbenaceae)

Guioa semiglauca
Guioa, Wild Quince

Description: Small to medium tree to 25 m. Trunk cylindrical; flanged at base in large trees. Bark smooth, grey or slate-coloured, often spotted or patchy. Leaves alternate; pinnate, with 2–6 leaflets, dark green and glossy above, pale grey-green below, sometimes hairy; obovate to elliptical, 3–8 cm long; tip blunt or rounded, with small point. Yellowish-green flowers in panicles; September–November. Fruit a 2 or 3-lobed capsule, each lobe with 1 glossy brown or black seed with a thin aril; January–February.

Habitat and Range: All types of rainforest, except cool temperate; common in regrowth. Qld and NSW.

Wildlife: Fruit — Australian King Parrot and Crimson and Eastern Rosellas, Lewin's Honeyeater, Figbird, Olive-backed Oriole, Pied Currawong, Varied Triller.

Family: Sapindaceae

Harpullia alata
Wing-leaved Tulip

Description: Shrub or small tree to 5 m. Leaves alternate; pinnate, with 6–10 leaflets on prominently winged leaf axis; either hairless or with minute star hairs; lanceolate or oblanceolate, 8–16 cm long; tip pointed; edges coarsely toothed. White flowers with 5 petals, in panicles; April–May. Fruit a brownish-yellow 2-lobed capsule; 3–4 cm wide; red inside; 2–4 black seeds enclosed in orange aril; ripe June–August.

Habitat and Range: Moist subtropical rainforest, often at higher altitudes. Qld and NSW.

Family: Sapindaceae

Harpullia pendula
Tulipwood

Description: Small to medium tree to 25 m. Trunk irregular, often fluted. Bark grey, scaly, sheds in long irregular flakes. Branchlets light grey with numerous corky lenticels; young shoots finely hairy. Leaves alternate; pinnate, with 4–8 leaflets; glossy light green; elliptical, 5–10 cm long; bluntly pointed tip; 5–10 pairs of lateral veins; leaf stalk with fine hairs, swollen at base. Greenish-yellow flowers with 5 petals, in panicles; September–December. Fruit a yellow to red 2-lobed capsule; each lobe contains 1–2 glossy, dark brown or black seeds; ripe September–January.

Habitat and Range: Subtropical and dry rainforests. Qld and NSW.

Notes: Ornamental shade tree. Leaves similar to those of endangered *Diploglottis campbellii* — 15–25 pairs of lateral veins.

Wildlife: Fruit — Australian King Parrot; leaves — caterpillars of Speckled Line-blue and Bright Cornelian Butterflies.

Family: Sapindaceae

Hedraianthera porphyropetala

Description: Shrub to 6 m. Branchlets brownish, zig-zag. Leaves alternate; thick, hairless, pale or yellowish-green; often with 1–3 pale corky galls to 1 cm wide; lanceolate to narrowly elliptical, 6–10 cm long; blunt point. Very small purple or deep red flowers; single or in groups on long stalks up to 2.5 cm long; April–September. Fruit a brown ovoid capsule; splits into 5 valves; 2–3 dark brown seeds in each valve; white aril; April–September.

Habitat and Range: In subtropical and littoral rainforest, generally on less fertile soils. Qld and NSW.

Family: Celastraceae

Homalanthus nutans
Native Bleeding Heart

Description: Shrub or small tree to 6 m. Leaves alternate; soft, hairless, green above, pale grey-green below; broadly ovate to triangular, 6–20 cm long; tip with blunt point; raised gland at base of blade; leaf stalk slender, 2–9 cm long, reddish, with watery-milky sap; older leaves turn red before falling. Greenish-yellow flowers in racemes; September–December. Fruit a bluish-white, 2-lobed capsule; 2 seeds half enclosed in fleshy yellow aril; December–March.

Habitat and Range: Subtropical, warm temperate and dry rainforest; common in regrowth. Qld and NSW; also New Guinea and Melanesia.

Wildlife: Fruit — Brown Cuckoo-dove, Lewin's Honeyeater, Silvereye, Olive-backed Oriole and Mistletoe Bird.

Family: Euphorbiaceae

Hymenosporum flavum
Native Frangipani

Description: Medium tree to 20 m. Trunk and branches brittle and easily broken. Branchlets hairy towards ends; prominent leaf scars. Leaves alternate; clustered towards ends of branchlets; soft, dark green above, paler and sometimes slightly hairy below; oblanceolate, 6–15 cm long; pointed at tip; gradually taper to leaf stalk; juvenile leaves toothed. Creamy-yellow flowers in loose panicles; September–November. Fruit a brown capsule; splits into 2 segments; numerous flat, winged seeds; ripe December–April.

Habitat and Range: Subtropical, dry and riverine rainforest. Qld and NSW; also New Guinea.

Notes: Hardy, fast-growing tree with highly perfumed flowers.

Wildlife: Seed — Wonga Pigeon.

Family: Pittosporaceae

Jagera pseudorhus forma *pseudorhus*
Foam Bark Tree, Fern Tree

Description: Small tree to 15 m. Trunk smooth grey, with horizontal, raised ridges. Rusty hairs on branchlets and leaf stalks. Soft leaves alternate; pinnate, with 12–20 leaflets; soft, light green above, with rusty hairs below; lanceolate, 3–5 cm long, tip with sharp point; edges toothed. Small, yellowish-brown flowers in panicles; March–April. Fruit a yellow-brown capsule covered with stiff irritating hairs; splits into 3 valves; black seeds in fleshy aril; ripe August–September.

Habitat and Range: In dry, subtropical and littoral rainforest. Qld and NSW.

Notes: Hardy, ornamental tree, but fruit should not be handled without gloves because of irritant hairs. Aboriginal people used bark scrapings to poison fish.

Wildlife: Eaten by Lewin's Honeyeater, Paradise Riflebird, Regent and Satin Bowerbirds, and Noisy Miner.

Family: Sapindaceae

Macaranga tanarius
Macaranga

Description: Shrub or small tree to 6 m. Branchlets often blue-grey; prominent triangular stipules on young shoots. Leaves alternate; pale green to grey below, with short hairs; broadly ovate, 10–25 cm long; pointed tip; main veins reddish; leaf stalk long, 8–20 cm. Greenish-yellow flowers in panicles; November–January. Fruit a small yellow capsule; with soft prickles; 3 lobes; 3 glossy black seeds; January–February.

Habitat and Range: In disturbed littoral and subtropical rainforest. Qld, NSW and NT; also New Guinea, Malesia, Asia and Melanesia.

Wildlife: Flowers — Rainbow Lorikeet; fruit — Silvereye; Graceful Tree Frogs shelter under leaves.

Family: Euphorbiaceae

Mallotus claoxyloides
Green Kamala, Odour Bush, Smell-of-the-Bush

Description: Shrub or small tree to 8 m. Small stipules on branchlets at base of leaf-stalks. Leaves opposite; soft coating of fine, pale star-hairs below; broadly elliptical to obovate, 6–14 cm long; tip with blunt point; base slightly heart-shaped; edges entire or with a few shallow teeth; 2 glands at base of leaf-blade. Clusters of greenish-yellow flowers; October–November. Fruit a small brown, bristly capsule; splits into 2–3 segments each with 1 grey seed; ripe February–March.

Habitat and Range: Dry rainforest and drier subtropical rainforest, common in regrowth areas. Qld, NSW; also New Guinea

Notes: Plants have distinctive odour (reminiscent of possums or skunks), which can be smelt from several metres away, especially on humid summer evenings.

Family: Euphorbiaceae

Mallotus philippensis
Red Kamala

Description: Small to medium tree to 25 m. Large trees often fluted or flanged at base. Leaves alternate; green above, grey-green with numerous, minute red surface glands below; ovate to lanceolate, 5–15 cm long; 3-veined in lower half; often 2 raised glands at base; long, slender leaf stalks. Yellowish flowers in racemes; June– September. Fruit a 3-lobed capsule with red powdery covering; 6–9 mm wide; 3 black seeds; ripe September– December.

Habitat and Range: In subtropical and dry rainforests, also rainforest edges and along watercourses. Qld, NSW and NT; also New Guinea, Malesia and Asia.

Notes: Red dye known as kamala made from powdery covering on fruit.

Wildlife: Flowers — Mallotus Harlequin Bug

Family: Euphorbiaceae

Maytenus bilocularis
Orangebark

Description: Shrub to small tree to 12 m. Branchlets grey with fine vertical ridges, dotted with small lenticels; terminal buds scaly. Leaves alternate; tough; elliptical or narrowly elliptical, 4–9 cm long; edges toothed, especially in juvenile leaves; net veins and lateral veins obvious; leaf stalk short, 2–7 mm long. Yellowish-green flowers with 5 petals, in racemes; October– November. Fruit a small yellow capsule, 5 mm across, splits into 2 valves; 2 black seeds enclosed in orange aril; ripe March–October.

Habitat and Range: In dry rainforest and edges of subtropical rainforest. Qld and NSW.

Notes: Inner bark on stems and roots bright orange or orange-brown.

Wildlife: Fruit — Lewin's Honeyeater.

Family: Celastraceae

Melicope elleryana

Description: Medium tree to 25 m. Bark white, soft and corky. Leaves opposite; consist of 3 leaflets; soft, glossy green above, paler and sometimes sparsely hairy below; leaflets elliptical or ovate; 7–18 cm long; numerous minute oil dots; central leaflet longer than lateral ones. Numerous bright pink flowers in panicles; December–February. Fruit a small dark brown capsule; 2–4 almost separate lobes; each with single glossy black seed; ripe July–October.

Habitat and Range: Lowland subtropical rainforest and swampy open forest. Qld, NSW, NT and WA, also New Guinea, Malesia and Melanesia.

Notes: Previously known as *Euodia elleryana*. Planted as ornamental. Leaves often disfigured by brown galls. Similar to *Melicope vitiflora* (Coast Euodia) — white flowers; rare, subtropical and littoral rainforest.

Family: Rutaceae

Melicope micrococca
White Doughwood

Description: Small to medium tree to 30 m. Trunks of large trees sometimes corky and flanged at base. Branchlets reddish-brown, becoming green with fine hairs towards ends. Leaves opposite; consist of 3 leaflets; hairless or sometimes softly hairy below; elliptical or obovate, 5–13 cm long; conspicuous oil dots; stalk of terminal leaflet to 6 mm long, lateral leaflets lack stalk. White flowers in dense clusters; December–February. Fruit a small dry capsule; splits into 3–4 segments; 1 glossy black seed per segment; ripe March–June.

Habitat and Range: Subtropical and dry rainforests and along edges, common in regrowth. Qld and NSW.

Notes: Previously known as *Euodia micrococca*.

Family: Rutaceae

Neolitsea dealbata
White Bolly Gum

Description: Shrub or small tree to 15 m. Branchlets green with dense rusty-brown hairs. Leaves alternate, grouped in pseudo-whorls at ends of branchlets; glossy green above, pale grey or whitish below; elliptical to obovate, 8–20 cm long; 3-veined in lower half of leaf, numerous minute oil dots; leaf stalk 10 cm long, hairy. Cream to pale brown flowers in dense clusters, April–June. Fruit a purplish-black, globular drupe, 6–8 mm wide; 1 seed; ripe April–June.

Habitat and Range: Subtropical and warm temperate rainforest, also wet eucalypt forest. Qld and NSW; also New Guinea.

Notes: New foliage rusty-pink; perfumed flowers. Similar to *Neolitsea australiensis* (Green Bolly Gum) — hairless leaves, buds and branchlets, pale waxy bloom on leaf underside, not strongly whitish.

Family: Lauraceae

Niemeyera chartacea
Smooth-leaved Plum

Description: Small to medium tree to 20 m. Trunk slightly fluted, not buttressed. Branchlets with fine brown hairs; often with small lumps among and below leaves; milky sap in branchlets and leaf stalks. Leaves alternate; oblanceolate to elliptical, 7–14 cm long; tip with blunt point; midvein, lateral veins and net veins prominent below; sparse, widely spaced translucent dots. Small whitish flowers in dense clusters; January–September. Fruit a black berry; ovoid, 2–2.5 cm long. 1–2 smooth seeds with large elliptical scar; ripe May–November,

Habitat and Range: On less fertile soils in subtropical rainforest and wet eucalypt forest. Qld only.

Family: Sapotaceae

Nothofagus moorei
Antarctic Beech

Description: Medium to large tree to 25 m. Trunk crooked and leaning, swollen at base, often with several stems. Bark dark brown and scaly. Branchlets with brown hairs and scaly buds, reddish stipules on new shoots, falling as leaves expand; new growth deep red. Leaves opposite; thick and stiff, glossy; ovate, 4–12 cm long; tip with fine point; edges finely and evenly toothed; prominent lateral veins; leaf stalks hairy. Greenish flowers in catkins; August–October. Fruit a group of 3 angular, winged nuts enclosed in a hard prickly, 3 to 4-valved capsule; ripe December–January.

Habitat and Range: Cool temperate rainforest at high altitudes. Qld and NSW.

Family: Fagaceae

Olea paniculata
Native Olive, Maulwood

Description: Medium to large tree to 30 m. Trunk flanged, buttressed at base, often with small coppice stems. Bark grey to brown; numerous pale pustules, often in vertical rows. Branchlets with numerous small lenticels. Leaves opposite; glossy green above, paler below; elliptical, or ovate-elliptical 4–9 cm long; tip with narrow point; several hollow domatia in vein angles. Small pale green and white flowers in panicles; October–December. Fruit a bluish-black drupe; ovoid, 10–15 mm long; 1 creamy-brown seed; ripe May–October.

Habitat and Range: Subtropical, dry and littoral rainforest. Qld and NSW; also New Guinea and Melanesia.

Notes: Quick-growing and hardy tree, suitable for open sunny positions.

Family: Oleaceae

Pararchidendron pruinosum var. *pruinosum*
Snow-wood

Description: Small tree to 15 m tall. Bark dark reddish-brown; patterned with numerous corky pustules. Leaves alternate; bipinnate with 2–8 secondary leaf stalks and 20–60 leaflets. Leaflets soft, mostly hairy; lanceolate to rhomboid, 4–5 cm long; unequal sides at base; raised gland on main leaf stalk, 10–25 mm below first pair of leaf stalks, also occasionally below second pair. Pale greenish-white flowerheads, turning yellow with age; September–December. Fruit a twisted flat pod; yellowish outside, but orange-red inside; contains several glossy black seeds; ripe February– April.

Habitat and Range: Subtropical and dry rainforest. Qld and NSW; also New Guinea and Malesia.

Family: Mimosaceae

Pavetta australiensis
Pavetta

Description: Shrub to 4 m. Triangular stipules prominent on branchlets, persisting on stems. Terminal buds shiny. Leaves opposite; soft and thin, dark green; oblanceolate or narrowly elliptical, 6–14 cm long; prominent light coloured midvein and main lateral veins. Showy white flowers in clusters or heads; October–November. Fruit a small globular black berry; about 6 mm wide; 2 seeds; ripe February–March.

Habitat and Range: Dry rainforest. Qld and NSW.

Wildlife: Flowers — adult butterflies; leaves — Beehawk Moths.

Family: Rubiaceae

Pennantia cunninghamii
Brown Beech

Description: Medium tree to 30 m. Trunk crooked and leaning, flanged at base. Branchlets zig-zag, with numerous small brown lenticels. Leaves alternate; green and glossy; broadly elliptical, 7–15 cm long; edges wavy; hollow domatia present in upper forks of lateral veins near edges. White flowers in short dense panicles, generally shorter than leaves; separate male, female and bisexual flowers sometimes on same tree; November–January. Fruit a black drupe; ovoid, to 15 mm long; 1 seed; ripe October–July.

Habitat and Range: Moist subtropical rainforest, generally close to watercourses. Qld and NSW.

Wildlife: Fruit eaten by many species of birds.

Family: Icacinaceae

Pittosporum multiflorum
Orange Thorn

Description: Small shrub to 3 m tall. Branchlets rough with warty or scaly hair-bases. Leaves alternate; glossy dark green above and below; ovate or broadly elliptical, 4–12 mm long; edges toothed in upper half of leaf; sometimes sharp spines where leaf joins stem. Single white flowers with 5 petals; September–December. Fruit an orange berry, to 1 cm wide; a few to several seeds; ripe May–July.

Habitat and Range: In most types of rainforest. Qld and NSW.

Notes: Previously known as *Citriobatus pauciflorus*. Similar to *Pittosporum oreillyanum* — leaves entire; tip with short sharp point; at higher altitudes in cool temperate rainforest.

Family: Pittosporaceae

Pittosporum undulatum
Sweet Pittosporum

Description: Small to medium tree 25 m tall. Trunk often crooked, flanged at base. Bark brownish-grey, dotted with pale lenticels. Leaves alternate, clustered in pseudo-whorls near ends of branchlets; glossy green above, paler below, hairless; narrowly elliptical, 7–15 cm long; edges wavy; strong resinous smell when crushed. White flowers with 5 petals, in short clusters; September–October. Fruit, a yellow capsule, splitting into 2 valves, numerous dark red seeds, in an orange mucilage; ripe April–May

Habitat and Range: All types of rainforest and also moist gullies in open forest. Qld, NSW and eastern Vic.

Notes: Flowers perfumed. Attractive ornamental tree, but serious environmental weed around Sydney, Melbourne and Adelaide.

Family: Pittosporaceae

Podocarpus elatus
Brown Pine, Plum Pine

Description: Medium to large tree to 40 m. Trunk often irregularly fluted. Bark dark brown; fissured and scaly on large trees. Branchlets green with vertical ribs. Leaves alternate; oblong to linear, 4–18 cm long; stiff point at tip; midvein distinct, generally more prominent above. Male and female flowers on separate trees; males in spikes in clusters of 2–10; females single. Fruit consists of firm round seed on a swollen fleshy base that is blue-black and plum-like; to 2.5 cm wide; ripe March–June.

Habitat and Range: Subtropical and littoral rainforest. Qld and NSW.

Notes: Fruit edible; eaten by Aboriginal people; used for jam by European settlers.

Wildlife: Fruit — Green Catbird, Pied Currawong, Satin Bowerbird and Wompoo Fruit-dove.

Family: Podocarpaceae

Polyscias elegans
Celerywood, Silver Basswood

Description: Medium tree to 25 m. Young trees often unbranched with umbrella-shaped crown. Bark of larger trees fissured and scaly. Leaves alternate; very large; pinnate or bipinnate, with up to 55 leaflets; glossy and hairless; ovate, 4–13 cm long; swelling at each joint where leaflets meet stem. Very small purple flowers on large, branched panicle; February–March. Fruit a dark purple, flattened berry; 5 mm long; 2 seeds; ripe March–June.

Habitat and Range: Subtropical and dry rainforests, common in disturbed areas. Qld and NSW; also New Guinea.

Wildlife: Important food source for many rainforest birds; leaves —caterpillar of Dark Pencilled-blue Butterfly.

Family: Araliaceae

Polyscias murrayi
Pencil Cedar

Description: Medium tree to 20 m. Trunk straight and cylindrical, not buttressed. Young trees unbranched with tuft of long leaves; older trees moderately branched with umbrella-like crown. Leaves alternate; pinnate, with 13–51 soft leaflets; pale green, turning black when dry; elliptical to lanceolate, 8–15 cm long; often with unequal sides at base; edges entire or finely toothed; leaf stalk to 120 cm long; small gland between each pair of leaflets. Creamy-green flowers in large panicles; February–March. Fruit a pale blue drupe; 3 seeds; April–June.

Habitat and Range: Subtropical and littoral rainforest; common regrowth species. Qld and NSW only.

Wildlife: Eaten by many bird species including honeyeaters, bowerbirds and doves.

Family: Araliaceae

Pseudoweinmannia lachnocarpa
Mararie, Rose Marara

Description: Medium to large tree to 40 m. Trunk twisted, prominently buttressed. Branchlets with horizontal scars left by stipules. Leaves opposite; consist of 3 leaflets; hairless, glossy dark green; lanceolate, oblanceolate or narrowly elliptical, 6–15 cm long; mostly lack stalks; edges finely toothed. White flowers with fine hairs, in short racemes; September–November. Fruit a small capsule covered with soft brown hairs; opens in two valves; numerous seeds; ripe February–March.

Habitat and Range: On rich volcanic soils, subtropical and dry rainforest, also common in moist gullies. Qld and NSW.

Notes: May lose most of its foliage during severe dry seasons.

Family: Cunoniaceae

Psychotria daphnoides
Smooth Psychotria

Description: Shrub up to 5 m. Terminal buds enclosed in small paired stipules, lost as leaves expand, leaving scars between leaf bases. Leaves opposite; smooth, dark green above, paler below; oblanceolate, 1–4 cm long (5–8 cm in large-leaved form); tip round or bluntly pointed, tapering into base; domatia occasionally in vein angles. Small white flowers in clusters; October–January. Fruit a greenish, ellipsoid berry; 10 mm long; 2 ribbed seeds; ripe March–June.

Habitat and Range: Subtropical and dry rainforest, mostly at low altitudes, common on rainforest edges. Qld, NSW and NT.

Notes: Small-leaved and large-leaved forms occur in Greater Brisbane Region.

Family: Rubiaceae

Psychotria loniceroides
Hairy Psychotria

Description: Shrub up to 5 m high. Branchlets, leaf stalks and stipules with dense hairs; stipules lost as leaves expand. Leaves opposite; soft and hairy, light green above, paler below; oblanceolate to narrowly elliptical, 6–10 cm long; tip obtuse or barely pointed; small hairy domatia often in vein angles, midvein and lateral veins hairy, distinct on both surfaces, but particularly below. Yellowish-white flowers in clusters; February–April. Fruit a lemon-yellow berry; elliptical, 6–7 mm wide; ribbed when dry; often in pairs, 1 seed; ripe March–August.

Habitat and Range: All types of rainforest, also wet eucalypt forest. Qld, NSW and NT.

Wildlife: Fruit — Green Catbird.

Family: Rubiaceae

Quintinia verdonii
Grey Possumwood

Description: Medium tree to 20 m. Trunk often with coppice stems from base. Branchlets and leaf stalks often reddish. Leaves alternate; glossy green above, paler below, with numerous, minute pale surface glands; elliptical to obovate, 7–15 cm long; narrows to blunt point. Small creamy-white to yellow flowers in slender racemes; September–November. Fruit a brown capsule, 1–2 mm across; 3–5 cells, several tiny ovoid seeds per cell; ripe December–January.

Habitat and Range: Subtropical and warm temperate rainforest, mostly at higher altitudes. Qld and NSW.

Notes: Similar to *Quintinia sieberi* (Red Possumwood) — red-brown bark; reddish glands on leaf underside; flowers in panicles. Seeds of both species germinate and grow on bases of trunks of tree ferns.

Family: Grossulariaceae

Rhodamnia rubescens
Scrub Turpentine

Description: Small to medium tree to 10 m, but occasionally to 25 m. Reddish-brown fissured bark; papery-flaky. Leaves opposite; dark green above, pale or brownish and softly hairy below; ovate to elliptical, 5–11 cm long; tip pointed; 3-veined from near base; distinct oil dots. White flowers with 4 petals, in clusters; September–October. Fruit a red or black globular berry; 5 mm wide; ripe November–December.

Habitat and Range: In subtropical and dry rainforest, common on edges and in regrowth. Qld and NSW only.

Notes: Perfumed flowers.

Wildlife: Fruit — Brown Cuckoo-dove, Figbird and Green Catbird.

Family: Myrtaceae

Sarcopteryx stipata
Steelwood

Description: Small to medium tree to 25 m. Trunk often flanged at base in large trees; bark grey and wrinkled. Branchlets, leaf stalks and terminal buds with dense rusty hairs. Leaves alternate; pinnate, with 4–10 leaflets; glossy green above, paler with scattered brown hairs below; narrowly elliptical or ovate, 4–9 cm long; fine point at tip; leaf stalk swollen at base. Small, creamy-white flowers with 5 petals, in panicles; August–October. Fruit a red 3 to 4-lobed capsule; 3–4 black seeds, enclosed in yellow aril; ripe November–December.

Habitat and Range: Subtropical, warm temperate and littoral rainforest. Qld and NSW only.

Wildlife: Fruit — Lewin's Honeyeater and Green Catbird.

Family: Sapindaceae

Sloanea australis subsp. *australis*
Maiden's Blush, Blush Alder

Description: Small to medium tree to 30 m. Trunk often crooked and irregularly ridged; buttressed at base with numerous coppice shoots. Branchlets often dotted with narrow brown lenticels; new growth pinkish-red, small hairy stipules at base of leaf stalks, shed as leaves expand. Leaves alternate; hairless, dark glossy green above, paler below; obovate, 7–30 cm long; rounded or bluntly pointed at tip; narrowing and then heart-shaped at base; edges wavy and toothed; leaf stalk 6–25 mm long, with swollen joint at base of leaf blade. Creamy-white flowers with hairs; single or in small groups; October– November. Fruit a yellowish-brown capsule; covered with dense short brown hairs; 3–5 segments, glossy black seeds enclosed in orange-red aril; ripe February–June.

Habitat and Range: Common in moist subtropical rainforest, often close to watercourses. Qld and NSW only.

Notes: Foliage similar to *Sloanea woollsii* (Yellow Carabeen) — large canopy tree; prominent plank buttresses; leaf base tapered, not heart-shaped; hair-tuft domatia in vein angles.

Wildlife: Fruit — Brown Cuckoo-dove and Australian King Parrot, Lewin's Honeyeater, Figbird, Olive-backed Oriole, Paradise Rifle-bird, Regent Bowerbird.

Family: Elaeocarpaceae

S.woollsii   GL *S.woollsii*

Solanum aviculare
Kangaroo Apple

Description: Shrub to 4 m. Leaves alternate; soft, green and hairless; shape varies; to 20 cm long; tip pointed; edges entire or deeply lobed. Violet-blue flowers on slender stalks; flowers throughout year. Fruit an orange-red to scarlet berry; ellipsoid, 2 cm long; numerous flat seeds; ripe over several months of year.

Habitat and Range: Edges of subtropical and temperate rainforest, common in recently cleared areas. Qld, NSW, Vic. Tas.; also New Guinea and New Zealand.

Notes: Contains compounds used in synthesis of steroidal hormones, grown extensively in Russia.

Wildlife: Fruit — Brown Cuckoo-dove, Lewin's Honeyeater, Green Catbird, Regent and Satin Bowerbirds.

Family: Solanaceae

Stenocarpus sinuatus
Wheel of Fire Tree, Firewheel Tree

Description: Medium tree to 30 m. Leaves alternate; large, leathery to stiff texture; glossy dark green above, paler below; variable shape and size, juvenile leaves deeply lobed to 40 cm long, adult leaves without lobes or with shallow lobes to 25 cm long; leaf tip and lobes blunt or rounded. Large showy red flowers in wheel-shaped umbels; February–March. Fruit a cluster of large brown follicles; each contains numerous flattened, winged seeds; ripe April–September.

Habitat and Range: Subtropical, littoral and warm temperate rainforest. Qld and NSW; also New Guinea.

Notes: Popular ornamental. Juvenile leaves similar to *Grevillea hilliana* — silvery-white on underside.

Wildlife: Flowers — Red Wattlebird; leaves — caterpillar Bright Canadian Butterfly.

Family: Proteaceae

Sterculia quadrifida
Peanut Tree, Red-fruited Kurrajong

Description: Medium tree to 18 m. Deciduous during late winter–spring. Trunk cylindrical or slightly buttressed in large trees. Leaves alternate; clustered at end of branchlets; oblong to ovate, 5–12 cm long; base heart-shaped; leaf stalks slender, 1–5 cm long, with swelling at each end. Greenish, bell-shaped flowers in short racemes among outer leaves; November–January. Fruit a large red follicle; 5–7 cm long; splits to reveal several bluish-black seeds; ripe November–January.

Habitat and Range: In dry rainforest and littoral rainforest. NSW, Qld, NT; also New Guinea.

Notes: Perfumed flowers. Peanut-flavoured seeds may be eaten cooked or raw.

Family: Sterculiaceae

Streblus brunonianus
Whalebone Tree, Prickly Fig

Description: Small to medium tree to 15 m high. Crown often thin, somewhat drooping. Branchlets with scattered brown lenticels and scars left by fallen leaves and stipules; milky sap. Leaves alternate; smooth above, lower surface with fine rigid hairs, rough to touch; lanceolate to narrowly elliptical, 5–10 cm long; finely toothed. White to cream flowers in spikes; September–March. Fruit a small yellow berry; 5 mm wide; ripe March–November.

Habitat and Range: Subtropical and dry rainforest. Qld, NSW; also New Guinea and Melanesia.

Notes: Similar to *Aphananthe philippinensis* — see p.243. Aboriginal people used wood for boomerangs.

Wildlife: Fruit eaten by many species of birds.

Family: Moraceae

Synoum glandulosum
Scentless Rosewood

Description: Small to medium tree to 20 m. Bark dark brown with square scales, shedding in irregular patches. Leaves alternate; pinnate, with 5–9 leaflets; soft, dark green above, paler below; elliptical, 5–8 cm long; bluntly pointed at tip, equal-sided at base; small pale hair-tuft domatia in vein angles. Pinkish-white flowers with 4 petals, in panicles; February–June. Fruit a reddish 3-lobed capsule; 2 brown seeds in each segment, enclosed in fleshy red aril; ripe September–December.

Habitat and Range: Subtropical, littoral and dry rainforest; common on edges and in wet eucalypt forest. Qld and NSW.

Notes: Flowers with sweet perfume.

Wildlife: Fruit — Paradise Riflebird, Australian King Parrot and Green Catbird.

Family: Meliaceae

Syzygium australe
Scrub Cherry

Description: Small to medium tree to 25 m. Bark brown, softly scaly. Young branchlets 4-angled, reddish. Leaves opposite; soft, glossy green above, paler below; elliptical, oblanceolate or obovate, 2.5–8 cm long; tip blunt or narrowing to fine point; scattered, indistinct oil dots. White flowers with 4 petals in short panicles; December–June. Fruit a pinkish-red globular berry 15–25 mm long, single seed; ripe March–August.

Habitat and Range: Subtropical, littoral and dry rainforests and along moist, scrubby watercourses. Qld and NSW.

Notes: Fruit edible, crisp and slightly acidic. Similar to *Syzygium paniculatum* (Magenta Cherry) — restricted to central coast of NSW, but extensively planted around Brisbane; purple-red fruits and distinct oil dots.

Family: Myrtaceae

Syzygium crebrinerve
Purple Cherry

Description: Large tree to 40 m. Trunk prominently buttressed. Bark grey to light brown, with scaly fissures. Branchlets and leaf stalks red on upper surface; young leaves bright red. Leaves opposite; dark glossy green above, paler below; elliptical, 5–14 cm long; tip with narrow point; numerous, closely spaced lateral veins; oil dots obvious, widely spaced. White flowers with 4 petals and numerous stamens, in panicles; November–December. Fruit a purple berry, globular and flattened; single seed; ripe January–March.

Habitat and Range: Subtropical rainforest on alluvial soils and also on basaltic soils at higher altitudes. Qld and NSW.

Wildlife: Fruit — Rose-crowned Fruit-dove and Topknot Pigeon.

Family: Myrtaceae

Syzygium francisii
Giant Water Gum

Description: Medium to large tree to 45 m. Dense crown. Trunk 1.5 m wide; prominently buttressed. Bark light brown, smooth, shedding in reddish-brown patches. New growth pinkish red. Leaves opposite; dark green above, paler beneath; ovate–lanceolate or elliptical, 3–8 cm long; rounded point at tip; narrowed towards base; edges often wavy; net veins and intramarginal vein obvious below; scattered indistinct oil dots. Small white flowers with numerous stamens, in panicles; November–December. Fruit a bluish-purple berry; flattened and globular; 10–15 mm wide; ripe January–March.

Habitat and Range: Lowland subtropical rainforest in gullies and on alluvial flats. Qld and NSW.

Notes: Attractive tree with masses of ornamental fruit.

Family: Myrtaceae

Syzygium oleosum
Blue Lilly-pilly

Description: Small tree to 15 m. Trunk often crooked, bark reddish-brown, scaly. Branchlets and leaf stalks often red. Leaves opposite; dark glossy green above, paler below; oblong to elliptical or obovate, 4–10 cm long; tip with narrow point; numerous obvious oil dots. Creamy-white flowers with 4 petals, in panicles; November–January. Fruit a purplish-blue, globular berry; to 1.5 cm wide, single pinkish seed; ripe March–August.

Habitat and Range: On poorer soils, also rich volcanic soils, in littoral and subtropical rainforest and wet eucalypt forest. Qld and NSW.

Notes: Leaves sticky, aromatic when crushed. Fruit succulent and pleasant-tasting.

Family: Myrtaceae

Tasmannia insipida
Brush Pepperbush

Description: Shrub to 3 m. Terminal buds reddish, protected by scales. Leaves alternate, clustered in pseudowhorls; soft and thin, glossy green above and below; oblanceolate, 6–20 cm long; taper to a point at tip; gradually narrows to base, but rounded or slightly 2-lobed at junction with leaf stalk; minute oil dots. Creamy-white flowers on slender stalks, in umbels; separate male and female flowers on same plant; August–October. Fruit a dark purple to whitish berry; oblong to ovoid, 12–20 cm long; several seeds; ripe September–December.

Habitat and Range: All rainforest types except dry rainforest. Qld and NSW; also New Guinea.

Family: Winteraceae

Toona ciliata
Red Cedar

Description: Large deciduous tree to 45 m. Trunk up to 2 m wide; generally buttressed or flanged at base. Bark brown or grey with irregular scales. Leaves alternate; pinnate, with 20 leaflets, mostly opposite on leaf axis; ovate to lanceolate; often with unequal sides at base; small hairy domatia in vein angles. White flowers with 5 petals in large panicles; separate male and female flowers; October–November. Fruit a brown capsule to 2 cm long; splits into 5 segments each containing 4–5 winged seeds; ripe January to March.

Habitat and Range: Subtropical and riverine rainforests. Qld, NSW and Southeast Asia.

Notes: Originally common along most coastal rivers between Illawarra district, NSW and Gympie, Qld, but few large trees now remain. Deep red timber highly valued for furniture and cabinet work, being soft, light, beautifully figured and very easy to work. One of most durable of all timbers; logs lying for 50 years in forest have remained perfectly preserved. Trees are fully deciduous; new spring foliage is bright bronze-red, becoming green with age. In earlier years, the colour of new growth allowed cedar-getters to locate large trees easily within rainforest. Fast-growing, but young trees often damaged by caterpillars of Cedar Tip Moth. Flowers perfumed.

Family: Meliaceae

Trema tomentosa
Poison Peach

Description: Shrub or small tree to 6 m tall. Branchlets greyish, hairy, dotted with small pale lenticels. Leaves alternate; with short hairs, rough to touch; ovate to lanceolate, 4–9 cm long; tip with long point; edges finely toothed; 3-veined at base. Very small greenish flowers in short clusters; December–March. Fruit a small shiny black berry; 5–6 mm wide; ripe March–June.

Habitat and Range: Disturbed dry rainforest and subtropical rainforest, also common on rainforest edges. Qld, NSW, NT, also New Guinea, Malesia and Melanesia.

Notes: Leaves toxic to cattle.

Wildlife: Fruit — Lewin's Honeyeater, Figbird, Olive-backed Oriole, Brown Cuckoo-dove. Australian King Parrot; leaves — caterpillar of Speckled Line-blue Butterfly.

Family: Ulmaceae

Vitex lignum-vitae
Lignum Vitae, Satinwood

Description: Medium tree to 30 m. Trunk often fluted and slightly buttressed. Bark light brown; finely fissured and flaky. Branchlets hairy. Leaves opposite; elliptical to oblanceolate, 5–13 cm long; edges entire; small yellowish hairy domatia in vein angles; leaf stalk slightly enlarged just below junction with blade. Pinkish-purple flowers in short clusters; flowering irregular with peaks in April and December–January. Fruit a deep pink to red globular drupe; 8–12 mm wide; 4 seeds encased in round stone; ripe January–May.

Habitat and Range: Dry rainforest and subtropical rainforest. Qld and NSW.

Notes: Previously known as *Premna lignum-vitae*. Leaves turn black on drying. Dark wood hard and durable.

Family: Lamiaceae (previously in family Verbenaceae).

Waterhousea floribunda
Weeping Lilly-pilly

Description: Small to medium tree to 30 m. Bark dark grey and fissured; branches often drooping. Branchlets green. Leaves opposite; dark glossy green above, paler below; oblong–lanceolate to narrowly elliptical; 5–15 cm long; tip with fine point; edges wavy; numerous lateral veins, distinct intramarginal vein; numerous fine oil dots. Small white flowers in panicles; 2 mm wide, numerous stamens; October–December. Fruit a greenish-white berry; single large seed; ripe January–May.

Habitat and Range: Riverine rainforest, generally along banks and arching out over stream. Qld and NSW.

Notes: Occasional old red leaf in canopy.

Family: Myrtaceae

Wilkiea macrophylla
Large-leaved Wilkiea

Description: Shrub to 4 m. Branchlets smooth and hairless; terminal buds scaly; new growth red. Leaves opposite; thick and rigid, glossy green above, paler below; oblong–elliptical, 8–20 cm long; tip blunt; rounded at base; edges widely and sharply toothed, rarely entire; lateral veins distinct on both surfaces; numerous fine oil dots just visible, sometimes obscure. Yellowish-green flowers in clusters on short stalks; male and female flowers on separate plants; May–November. Fruit a black drupe on a hairless, fleshy base; ovoid, 12–15 mm long, ripe April–September.

Habitat and Range: Subtropical and littoral rainforest. Qld and NSW.

Notes: Similar to *Wilkiea austroqueenslandica* — silky-hairy terminal buds and inflorescences.

Family: Monimiaceae

Dave's Creek, Lamington National Park, GC

Plants of the Mountain heaths

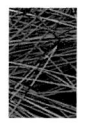

Heath is low, shrubby vegetation that usually grows on fairly infertile soils and is well known for its riot of colourful wildflowers during spring. Heathlands are characterised by a lack of continuous tree canopy. Some trees do grow in heaths, but usually as isolated specimens or in small clumps. Where this type of vegetation occurs on mountains it is referred to as montane heath.

The montane heaths are remnants of ancient times. The areas in which they grow have been subjected to geological and climatic changes and this has caused plant species to contract to the last remaining suitable soils. As a result, populations of some heath species are quite small.

Many of the mountains and ranges of the Greater Brisbane Region have areas of exposed rock that support montane heath and these include: the peaks around Mt Barney and Moogerah; Lamington National Park (mainly at Daves Creek); some of the Glasshouse Mountains; parts of Springbrook; restricted sections of Main Range; isolated peaks such as Mt French (near Boonah) and Glen Rock (near Esk); and the rocky outcrops of Diana's Bath and Mt Mee near Lake Somerset.

Although altitude, temperature and soil types differ significantly between montane and coastal heath (see p.61-63), the two vegetation communities share many common species. Montane heath plants are also similar to lowland heath species further west such as at Girraween, near Stanthorpe. Many of these same species reach their distribution limits in the montane heaths of the Greater Brisbane Region.

The soils in montane heaths are usually acidic, are often based on weathered volcanic rhyolite or trachyte, are very low in nitrogen and phosphorous and have low levels of organic material. They are kept cool by rocks and boulders and often accumulate as skeletal layers over rock platforms, or between and in boulders, rock outcrops and cliff faces. Where these soils occur, there can be an abrupt change in the vegetation from moist eucalypt forest or rainforest to montane heath. Drainage is usually good, although occasionally where soils are waterlogged, a unique mix of plants will occur.

The montane heaths are subject to extreme climatic conditions including frequent exposure to strong cold winds, low temperatures (even occasional snow on Mt Barney), fire and irregular rainfall, although moisture-laden clouds and mist are frequent. Many of the peaks experience relatively low rainfall, however Daves Creek averages around 150 cm a year.

Although soil fertility in montane heaths is low, plant species diversity is surprisingly high and it is usually dominated by plants in the following families:

Rutaceae (Boronias etc);

Myrtaceae (Tea-trees and Bottlebrushes etc);

Lamiaceae (Mint bushes etc);

Mimosaceae (Wattles);

Fabaceae (Peas);

Proteaceae (Grevilleas etc);

Epacridaceae (Epacris etc);

Xanthorrhoeaceae (Grass Trees);

Cyperaceae (Sedges); and

Orchidaceae (Orchids).

At ground level, mosses, lichens, some grasses and cryptic terrestrial orchids grow in the accumulated organically enriched soil.

Fire is an important influence in shaping heath communities. Species diversity reaches a peak about 10 years after fire and then declines. However, all heath plants have special adaptations to either survive fire or re-establish afterwards. They may possess a swollen, underground starchy root called a lignotuber from which the plant can re-shoot; there may be thick fire-resistant bark; or extremely tough oily leaves ('sclero-phyllous' leaves); or they may have specially adapted seeds that are only released or germinate after the heat of the fire.

In response to fire, some heath species develop multiple trunks. One species that exhibits this characteristic 'mallee' growth form is *Eucalyptus codonocarpa* (Bell-fruited Mallee), found on Mt Maroon. It has clustered thin trunks and rarely exceeds a few metres in height.

Restricted growth is characteristic of many

Dendrobium kingianum, BC

other montane heath species. In these harsh environments, where roots are often forced between rocks and confined to narrow crevices and cracks with little soil, plants can become stunted, attaining only a fraction of their potential height after many years. They often look like gnarled bonsai specimens.

Heath plants have developed other strategies to improve their ability to colonise low nutrient soils. Some, such as the Proteaceae, have highly effective, nutrient-seeking proteoid roots, which are clusters of rootlets that develop on plants in response to poor soils. Plants in the Rutaceae, Myrtaceae, Epacridaceae and Casuarinaceae groups have symbiotic fungi on their roots which enhance nutrient uptake. Similarly, plants of the Fabaceae family have bacteria in their roots to assist access to nitrogen. The insectivorous Droseras (sundews) absorb nutrients from insects trapped by the plant. All heath species exhibit at least some of the characteristics mentioned above.

While most heath plants need excellent root drainage, often preferring to grow on cliff faces and on skeletal porous soils, there are also many species that colonise and thrive in wet conditions where soils often become waterlogged. *Callistemon pallidus* (Lemon Bottlebrush) and *Baeckea linifolia* (Swamp Baeckea) are two species that favour these habitats.

Montane heath plants often flower profusely and are very colourful so as to attract insects, birds and some mammals (which assist in pollinisation). This flowering usually begins in late winter and intensifies through spring. The most floristically diverse heath in the region occurs at Daves Creek, a 12 km return walk from Binna Burra. Here, at an altitude of 900 m, the heathland covers nearly 300 ha of undulating ridges and precipitous cliffs. During spring, the variety of flowers can be stunning. Among the many species occurring here are white Leptospermums, yellow pea plants and Hibbertias, the mauve flowered Mint Bush, *Prostanthera phylicifolia*, and *Westringia blakeana*; thickets of *Acacia obtusifolia* (Blunt-leaved Wattle), stunted *Callitris monticola* (Mountain Cypress), and the rare *Banksia conferta* (Mountain Banksia).

Taller montane heath at Springbrook in the Gold Coast Hinterland is easily approached from Canyon Lookout and also occurs on the less accessible cliffs and escarpments in the area. Like Daves Creek, the rainfall here is high and fairly regular. *Leptospermum petersonii* (Lemon-scented Tea-tree), *Callistemon montanus* (Mountain Bottlebrush), *Platysace lanceolata* (Long-leaved Platysace), *Dendrobium kingianum* (Pink Rock Orchid), and *Doryanthes palmeri* (Spear Lily) can be found here.

Along the Main Range, montane heath occurs in a few separate areas. Mt Bangalore's rocky windswept pavements and Mt Cordeaux's stunning massed slopes and cliff faces of Spear Lilies are the most botanically interesting.

To visit other montane heaths in the Greater Brisbane Region, put on your hiking boots and backpack and be prepared for some steep, scrambling walks.

The upper slopes and summits of the Rathdowney peaks — Mt Maroon, Mt Ernest and Mt Barney — are exposed rocky areas with scattered heath vegetation. Mt Maroon is especially notable. A large, bowl-shaped depression below the north peak contains stands of *Eucalyptus codonocarpa*. On the surrounding rocky areas, gnarled and stunted shrubs include: stiff, pungently foliaged *Leucopogons*; delicate triggerplants; and the brilliant red pea bush *Bossiaea rupicola*.

The more physically challenging climbs in the Mt Barney area should not be attempted without reasonable levels of fitness and knowledge about your intended destination. Mt Barney is demanding and can be dangerous. The same cautionary warning applies to Mt Maroon and Mt Ernest. Dense vegetation, steep gorges and gullies, undulating ridges, sheer cliffs and a lack of defined tracks can all combine to disorient visitors.

Fortunately most of the peaks and ranges that support montane heath are protected in national parks or state forests, however threats still persist. If fires are too frequent, some species are unable to set seed between fires and so will die off. Trampling of sensitive areas can damage plant populations irreparably, particularly where heath areas are small and visitor numbers are high. Weeds can displace or choke heath plants.

However, because some montane heaths in the Greater Brisbane Region are relatively inaccessible, botanical exploration has been limited. A number of new species have recently been found and there are probably quite a few waiting to be discovered. — **Glenn Leiper**

Springbrook, GC

HERBS, GRASSES AND GROUNDCOVERS

Lobelia trigonocaulis
Forest Lobelia

Description: Weak-stemmed herb to 60 cm. Leaves alternate; heart-shaped with toothed edges; 40 mm long by 35 mm wide. Mauve-blue flowers to 15 mm wide; flowering stems to 60 cm; flowers throughout year.

Habitat and Range: Widespread. Ranges and mountains; also common in wet eucalypt forests and on rainforest edges, on volcanic soils. Some old records from The Gap, Brisbane. NSW to South-east, Central and Nth Qld.

Family: Campanulaceae

LILIES

Doryanthes palmeri
Spear Lily

Description: Spectacular ornate lily. Sword-shaped leaves to 3 m long, in large rosette clumps. Red or reddish-brown flowers to 6 cm; flower spike to 4 m; September–November.

Habitat and Range: In colonies along peaks and cliffs of Main Range and Springbrook; noticeable on eastern upper cliffs of Mt Cordeaux at Cunningham's Gap; also dense grove at Mt Cougal (Gold Coast hinterland). Coastal ranges that are part of the Mt Warning Caldera.

Note: Can take at least 10 years to flower. Possible to walk through groves. Queenslanders consider this plant superior to better known Gymea Lily (*Doryanthes excelsa*) from NSW.

Wildlife: Flowers — Noisy Miner.

Family: Agavaceae

ORCHIDS

Cryptostylis erecta
Bonnet Orchid

Description: Slender ground orchid. Erect green leathery leaves (sometimes a solitary leaf); purplish underneath; 20 cm long by 30 mm wide. Flower spike to about 50 cm with up to 12 green flowers with purplish spots; September–February.

Habitat and Range: Widespread. Moist, but well-drained soils; common on many peaks and ranges and along coastal sandmass. Vic. and NSW to Central Qld.

Notes: Flowers unusual because, unlike other orchids, they are upside down. Common name refers to purple-veined flower resembling a miniature bonnet. Aboriginal people probably ate underground stems.

Family: Orchidaceae

Corybas aconitiflorus
Spurred Helmet Orchid

Description: Tiny ground orchid. Easily overlooked; produces single, heart-shaped leaf to 35 mm; flat on ground among leaf litter. Leaf purplish on underside. Purplish flower to 15 mm; June–November.

Habitat and Range: Moist shaded conditions; various elevations around Greater Brisbane Region. Tas. to North Qld.

Notes: After setting seed, plant loses leaf and lies dormant with small underground tubers waiting to produce new foliage with onset of autumn rain. Sometimes forms dense colonies. Flowers pollinated by gnats.

Family: Orchidaceae

Dendrobium kingianum
Pink Rock Orchid

Description: Terrestrial or occasionally epiphytic orchid. Forms multi-stemmed dense clumps. Leaves alternate; 10 cm long by 20 mm wide; clustered at ends of stems which can reach 30 cm long. Flower spikes to 15 cm long with up to 15 pink flowers; August–October. Occasional white flowered forms.

Habitat and Range: Common. On exposed rock ledges, outcrops and platforms on most mountains and ranges of Greater Brisbane Region. Hunter River. NSW, to Central Qld.

Family: Orchidaceae

Thelymitra fragrans
Pink Sun Orchid

Description: Ground orchid. Solitary, shiny green, flaccid leaf; 30 cm long by 22 mm wide. Flower spike to 35 cm high; up to 11 fragrant pink or mauve flowers to 20 mm wide; September–November.

Habitat and Range: Uncommon. On some peaks in Mt Barney and Main Range areas, also Lamington NP. Often grows in clumps of *Dendrobium kingianum* (Pink Rock Orchids, see above); on sunny rock outcrops covered with lichens and mosses. Northern NSW to South-east Qld.

Notes: Aboriginal people probably ate underground stems.

Family: Orchidaceae

VINES AND CLIMBERS

Billardiera scandens
Apple Berry Vine

Description: Twining vine that climbs up shrubs to about 3 m. Leaves alternate; hairy with wavy edges; 6 cm long by 15 mm wide. Tubular white flowers to 20 mm (some forms age to pink); flowers throughout year. Green, oblong hairy fruit to 30 mm long; turns cream when it drops.

Habitat and Range: Widespread. At various altitudes in Greater Brisbane Region. Tas. to Central Qld.

Notes: Aboriginal people ate fallen ripe fruit.

Wildlife: Flowers — Eastern Spinebill and other birds; also favoured by some mammals.

Family: Pittosporaceae

Smilax glyciphylla
Sweet Sarsaparilla

Description: Thin wiry climber to 5 m long. Lacks prickles, but has coiling tendrils to assist climbing. Dark green leathery leaves; alternate; bluish-white on underside; 8 cm long by 40 mm wide; 3 obvious longitudinal veins. White flowers to 4 mm; September–February. Black berries to 10 mm.

Habitat and Range: Widespread on mountains, ranges, coastal sandmass and hills in Greater Brisbane Region, also common in eucalypt forests. Southern NSW to Nth Qld.

Notes: Early European settlers boiled leaves to produce bitter-sweet tea used as tonic and effective in prevention of scurvy when fresh fruit and vegetables were lacking.

Family: Smilacaceae

SHRUBS AND TREES

Acacia falciformis
Broad-leaved Hickory

Description: Shrub or small tree to 10 m. Curved bluish-green phyllodes; alternate; prominent mid-vein with fine lateral veins; 20 cm long by 5 cm wide; small gland on leaf edge up to 2.5 mm from base. Flowers to 10 mm wide; June–November. Flower stalk covered with small golden hairs. Seed pods flat and leathery; 5 cm long by 15 mm wide.

Habitat and Range: Mainly on volcanic soils in eucalypt forest. One record of species from Noosa Heads (1920). Vic. to North Qld.

Notes: Plants in Mt Barney–Main Range area bright yellow flowers; Glasshouse Mountains plants with white flowers and white coating on trunk.

Family: Mimosaceae

Allocasuarina rigida subsp. *rigida*
Rigid She-Oak

Description: Shrub or small tree to 5 m. Fine green, twig-like needles (branchlets) to 33 cm long, have whorls of 6–10 tiny scale-like 'leaves', giving impression of joints along branchlets. Separate male and female plants. Red female flowers on branches; orange-brown male flowers at tips of branchlets; flowers throughout year. Woody cones tapering at tip; 20 mm long by 12 mm wide.

Habitat and Range: On rocky exposed peaks of Main Range, Mt Barney region, Daves Creek and Springbrook.

Notes: *Casuarina* is derived from Latin *casuarius* meaning 'cassowary', drooping branches resemble feathers of bird. Common name *she-oak* may have been applied by European settlers disparagingly, referring to similarity, but inferiority of timber to that of European Oak; may also refer to similarity of timber to American Che-oak.

Family: Casuarinaceae

Banksia spinulosa var. *cunninghamii*
Hairpin Banksia

Description: Shrub to 5 m tall. Leaves narrow; alternate or scattered irregularly on branches; 7 cm long by 5 mm wide; a few teeth towards leaf tip. Golden flower spikes up to 20 cm long; styles yellow or black; March– August. Woody cones open with heat of fire, releasing papery seeds.

Habitat and Range: Prefers moist eucalypt forest with dense shrubby understorey. Daves Creek, Springbrook and Mt Barney region. Vic. to South-east Qld.

Notes: Flowers can have strong unpleasant smell.

Wildlife: Flowers — Honeyeaters and small mammals.

Family: Proteaceae

Bossiaea rupicola
Red Pea Bush

Description: Shrub to 2 m, usually with layered horizontal branches. Leaves alternate; greyish; 30 mm long by 7 mm wide. Stunning red, upright flowers (occasionally white); 20 mm long; crowded along branches; July–November.

Habitat and Range: Common understorey shrub on rocky acid, volcanic soils, especially on Moogerah Peaks, Mt French and peaks of Mt Barney area. Northern NSW to Central Qld.

Family: Fabaceae

Callistemon montanus
Mountain Bottlebrush

Description: Upright dense shrub to 5 m. New growth pinkish-brown. Pointed leaves; 10 cm long by 10 mm wide. Crimson flower spikes to about 5 cm long and 6 cm wide; mainly September–May. Woody seed capsules to 8 mm wide.

Habitat and Range: In dense shrubby heath near cliff edges where drainage is good. Springbrook and Daves Creek. Northern NSW to South-east Qld.

Wildlife: Flowers — Nectar-seeking birds and mammals.

Family: Myrtaceae

Callistemon pallidus
Lemon Bottlebrush

Description: Tall, upright bushy shrub to about 4 m. New growth usually soft, silky-hairy and silvery. Leaves pointed; alternate; conspicuous tiny glands on both surfaces; lateral veins barely visible; 7 cm long by 15 mm wide. Creamy-yellow flower spikes; 7 cm long by 40 mm wide; September–February. Woody seed capsules to 6 mm wide.

Habitat and Range: Near streams and damp rocky areas. Springbrook, Mt Barney region and Daves Creek. Tas. to South-east Qld.

Wildlife: Flowers — Nectar-seeking birds and mammals.

Family: Myrtaceae

Cassinia subtropica
Broad-leaved Cough Bush

Description: Upright shrub to 2.5 m. Leaves alternate; whitish or rusty-hairy underneath; 20 mm long by 7 mm wide; aromatic when crushed. Stems with fine woolly hairs. Pale straw-coloured flowers about 4 mm wide; clustered in panicles to 10 cm long; September–May.

Habitat and Range: Widespread; common in some areas. Usually on fertile soils in moist forests; various elevations around Greater Brisbane Region, also at lower altitudes; often on roadsides where bare soil promotes germination. Northern NSW to North Qld.

Family: Asteraceae

Comesperma esulifolium
Mountain Match-heads

Description: Shrub to 1 m tall. Branchlets often reddish. Leaves alternate; oblong to linear; 25 mm long by 4 mm wide; tip obtuse. Pink or mauve flowers (occasionally white) in racemes; each flower 2 petals; mainly September–November.

Habitat and Range: On acid volcanic soils in moist eucalypt forest with dense shrubby understorey. Mt Barney area, Ship's Stern, Daves Creek and Springbook. Central NSW to Central Qld.

Notes: Common name refers to shape of unopened flowers.

Family: Polygalaceae

Eucalyptus codonocarpa
Bell-fruited Mallee

Description: Small tree to about 6 m. Multiple trunks. Bark smooth; white or grey; shed in ribbons. Glossy green leaves; alternate; 12 cm long by 18 mm wide. Creamy-white flowers; about 15 mm wide; September–November. Woody fruit to 7 mm wide.

Habitat and Range: Rare. On rhyolitic soils. Daves Creek, Springbrook, Mt Maroon, Mt Barney. Northern NSW to South-east Qld.

Wildlife: Flowers — Nectar-seeking birds and mammals and also attracts insects.

Notes: Fire promotes more trunks on tree. Similar to *Eucalyptus curtisii* (see p. 329)

Family: Myrtaceae

Hakea salicifolia
Willow-leaved Hakea

Description: Erect shrub to 3 m. Leaves alternate; bluish-green; 11 cm long by 20 mm wide. White flowers in clusters; 15 mm wide; September–November. Woody fruits with warty surface; 30 mm wide.

Habitat and Range: In exposed positions on rocky ledges and platforms close to cliff edges at Springbrook; also understorey shrub in wet eucalypt forest. Jervis Bay, NSW, to Springbrook, Qld.

Wildlife: Flowers — Nectar-seeking birds and mammals and also attracts some insects.

Notes: Similar to *Hakea florulenta*, see p. 172.

Family: Proteaceae

Hibbertia hexandra
Tall Guinea Bush

Description: Tall shrub to 3 m. Branches with fine hairs. Leaves alternate; whitish underside; 6 cm long by 15 mm wide; rounded tip. Yellow flowers with 5 petals; 20 mm wide; mainly September–February.

Habitat and Range: Understorey shrub in wet eucalypt forest and adjoining heath in Daves Creek area of Lamington National Park. Limited distribution, Northern NSW to South-east Qld.

Family: Dilleniaceae

Keraudrenia hillii var. *hillii*
Mountain Keraudrenia

Description: Shrub to 2 m. Sparsely branched. Rusty hairs on stems and branches. Leaves dark green above, rusty hairs below; 9 cm long by 12 mm wide. Drooping purplish-pink flowers (occasionally white); usually 5 petals; 15 mm wide; September–February. Seed capsule covered in dense hairs; 15 mm wide.

Habitat and Range: On well-drained volcanic soils and sandstone, and rock outcrops. Mt Barney area, Moogerah Peaks, Main Range, Glasshouse Mountains and some Sunshine Coast peaks. Northern NSW to South-east Qld.

Family: Sterculiaceae

Leptospermum luehmannii
Glasshouse Mountains Tea-tree

Description: Shrub to 3 m tall. Multiple trunks. Smooth reddish-brown bark; shed in long thin strips. Shiny green leaves; alternate; 40 mm long by 10 mm wide. White flowers with 5 petals; 15 mm wide; December–February.

Habitat and Range: Rare. Restricted to Glasshouse Mountains on volcanic soils on rocky ledges, slopes and outcrops.

Wildlife: Flowers — Adult Caper White Butterfly.

Family: Myrtaceae

Leptospermum microcarpum
Small-fruited Tea-tree

Description: Shrub to 3 m tall. Papery fibrous bark. Small stiff, pointed leaves; alternate; 15 mm long by 4 mm wide. White flowers with 5 petals; about 12 mm wide (occasionally larger); June–November. Woody fruit to 4 mm.

Habitat and Range: Widespread. On rocky areas on volcanic soils and sandstone. many peaks and ranges in Brisbane Region; also Noosa Heads and Moggill. Northern NSW to South-east Qld.

Family: Myrtaceae

Leptospermum oreophilum
Mountain Tea-tree

Description: Shrub to about 3 m tall. Fibrous bark. Leaves alternate; 15 mm long by 4 mm wide. White flowers with 5 petals; 15 mm wide; September–November.

Habitat and Range: Rare. On volcanic soils on rocky slopes and outcrops. Glasshouse Mountains and Mt Coolum.

Notes: Leaves spicy and aromatic when crushed. Similar to *Leptospermum variabile* — common in Mt Barney and Moogerah areas, Springbrook and Main Range.

Family: Myrtaceae

Leptospermum petersonii
Lemon-scented Tea-tree

Description: Dense shrub to 6 m tall. Fibrous flaky bark. Leaves alternate; 30 mm long by 5 mm wide; strongly lemon-scented, but occasionally lack this fragrance. Profuse white flowers with 5 petals to 15 mm; December–February. Woody seed capsules to 6 mm diameter.

Habitat and Range: Rocky escarpments on volcanic soils; also in moist eucalypt forest and edges of rainforest. On many peaks in South-east Qld — Mt Cooroora, Mt Tinbeerwah, Mt Barney, Mt Maroon; also Springbrook and Main Range. Northern NSW to South-east Qld.

Notes: Common ornamental plant.

Wildlife: Flowers — adult Caper White Butterfly.

Family: Myrtaceae

Leucopogon neoanglicus
Rock Bearded Heath

Description: Shrub with tangled-stems. Two growth forms: Mt Barney area — dense dome-shaped, prostrate plant to 20 cm tall; Moogerah peaks — upright plant to almost 1 m. Stiff pointed leaves crowded on branches; alternate; 10 mm long by 4 mm wide; 3 central parallel veins and others diverging. White tubular flowers to 8 mm long; 5 petals; June–November. Brown fruit to 3 mm.

Habitat and Range: On acid volcanic soils on rocky pavements and slopes. Southern NSW to South-east Qld.

Notes: Several local *Leucopogon* species — all have small, white tubular flowers with tiny hairs on petals.

Family: Epacridaceae

Logania albiflora
Logania

Description: Erect shrub to 2.5 m. Dark green leaves, paler underside; opposite; 6 cm long by 15 mm wide; Nondescript plant for most of year; masses of tiny white flowers to 3 mm, in June–November. Separate male and female plants. Seed capsule to 9 mm long.

Habitat and Range: Elevated moist eucalypt forests and sometimes at lower altitudes. Vic. to North Qld.

Note: Strong flower perfume permeates forest.

Family: Loganiaceae

Platysace lanceolata
Long-leaved Platysace

Description: Erect shrub to 1.5 m tall. Branchlets fine, hairy. Dark green leaves; alternate; 7 cm long by 15 mm wide; tip pointed. Tiny white flowers in tight clusters about 25 mm wide; September–February. Furrowed fruit to 2 mm wide.

Habitat and Range: On volcanic soils in dense shrubby, moist eucalypt forest in higher areas, Springbrook and Mt Ballow; also on sandy soils at lower elevations on Sunshine Coast. Vic. to Central Qld.

Notes: Member of carrot family, crushed leaves smell like carrot.

Family: Apiaceae

Plectranthus graveolens
Sticky-leaved Plectranthus

Description: Strongly aromatic, brittle shrub to 1 m. Loosely branched with fine hairs on branches. Leaves opposite; dense hairs, edges serrated; 11 cm long by 8 cm wide. Leaves usually sticky to touch. Purple flowers; 1 cm long; flowers all year.

Habitat and Range: On rocky exposed ledges, outcrops and platforms amongst heath. Common on most peaks, plateaus and ranges of Greater Brisbane Region. Southern NSW to Far Nth Qld.

Notes: In exposed situations, leaves often turn brown or purplish.

Family: Lamiaceae

Pomaderris lanigera
Yellow Pomaderris

Description: Narrow shrub to 2 m. Rusty hairs on stems and leaves. Leaves alternate; green; 10 cm long by 30 mm wide. Golden yellow flowers in clusters to 5 cm wide; September–November.

Habitat and Range: On mountain tops or in exposed rocky areas; also understorey shrub in wet eucalypt forest. Common on peaks in Mt Barney area and at Springbrook; previously occurred at Mt Coot-tha. Southern NSW to Central Qld.

Family: Rhamnaceae

Stylidium laricifolium
Mountain Triggerplant

Description: Shrub to almost 1 m tall when in flower. Narrow leaves crowded along branchlets; alternate; 40 mm long by 1 mm wide. Pink flower spike to 45 cm long; flowers to 10 mm wide; June–November. Oblong seed capsule to 12 mm long.

Habitat and Range: On rocky outcrops and ledges on peaks in Mt Barney and Moogerah areas. Vic. to South-east Qld.

Notes: Flowers have 'spring' mechanism that acts as 'hammer' depositing pollen on visiting insects.

Family: Stylidiaceae

Xanthorrhoea glauca subsp. *glauca*
Blue Grass Tree

Description: To 4 m tall. Can be multi-trunked. Blue-green to grey foliage; each leaf four-sided in cross-section; to 5 mm wide. Tiny white flowers crowded on spike; flower spike always longer than stem that supports it; June–November. Fruit embedded in woody spike (flower base). Tiny black flattened seeds.

Habitat and Range: Variety of soils. Common on Main Range, especially Mt Mitchell, where it occurs in groves; also at Beechmont. Also in dry eucalypt forests at higher altitudes around Brisbane. Northern NSW to Central Qld.

Notes: Grass Trees are as typical of Australian bush as eucalypts and wattles.

Wildlife: Flowers — Noisy Miner, insects and small mammals.

Family: Xanthorrhoeaceae

New Farm Park, BC

Plants of the City Streets and Parks

Brisbane is one of Australia's greenest capital cities and its subtropical character owes much to its street and park plantings.

The vegetation in the built-up areas of Brisbane is a unique mosaic of:

- native bushland remnants;
- degraded remnant patches of rainforest along the Brisbane River and its many creeks;
- individual remnant eucalypt and fig trees among other native and exotic feature trees;
- parks and road reserves planted with trees and shrubs; and
- backyards, filled with a mixture of native and exotic plantings, that have been influenced by historical changes in garden design and city's outdoor lifestyle.

Early European botanists and landscape designers played a central role in determining the vegetation within the city today.

As Brisbane's original vegetation was being rapidly cleared for the expansion of the colony, Walter Hill, curator of the Botanic Gardens from 1855 to 1881, began acquiring colourful exotic tree species from other continents. His 'real work' was sourcing plants of economic potential for the colony. Thanks to Walter Hill's passion for amenity trees, parts of Brisbane are characterised by the flamboyant burst of red poincianas in Summer, the blue-mauve of jacarandas in Spring, mango trees in backyards, and huge shady fig trees.

Another major influence was Harry Oakman, Brisbane City Council's first Director of Parks and Gardens between 1946 and 1963. Harry's work transformed many Brisbane parks from overgrown grazing paddocks to places for people and showcases of sub-tropical landscaping. His work can be seen in the New Farm Park rose gardens, the Albert Park canna lily beds and the fig tree arboretum at McCaskie Oval, to name just a few. Harry Oakman also initiated the first major street tree plantings in Brisbane using a variety of native and exotic species in more than 150 streets. His landscape design philosophy for Brisbane was simple — colourful plants in every month of the year. The pink flowering trumpet trees (*Tabebuia* spp.) which

Jacaranda mimosaefolia (Jacaranda), GC

bloom in mid-Winter are examples of his colourful sub-tropical vision for the city.

Brisbane's parks and streets have become a lot greener in the past 50 years. Trees planted in parks and along footpaths have become a vital component of Brisbane's vegetation assets and grow closest to where we live, commute and relax. They provide benefits such as shade, colour, screening, cooling, improved property values, and a sense of place and time. In a city of almost one million people they enhance the quality of life of Brisbane's residents, add to the sub-tropical image of the city and support biodiversity values.

Although exotic species such as the Leopard Tree, *Caesalpinea ferrea*, were widely used in the 1970s and 80s, Brisbane's streetscapes are now an increasingly diverse mixture of native and exotic species, which help distinguish particular parts of the city from each other.

New and replacement plantings of street and park trees must continue to enhance and sustain the positive amenity values of Brisbane's 'urban forest'. At the same time they must balance other values, such as the potential of native species to add to the city's sub-tropical character while min-imising the risks to the people and property they grow amongst.

Trials of little-known native tree species are continuing to expand the street and park tree choices and more than 120 community groups now work in parks restoring indige-nous vegetation to improve habitats.

Colourful gardens and shady parks and streetscapes are now the signature of Brisbane's sub-tropical landscape and are an advantage to us all. — **Lyndal Plant with thanks to Kristen Sinden**

Delonix regia (Poinciana), GC

TREES

The tree species listed below represent those most commonly seen in Brisbane streets and parks. However, some of these trees are no longer recommended or planted by Brisbane City Council. Some are now recognised as weed species and this is noted in the species descriptions.

Agathis robusta
Queensland Kauri Pine

A stately conifer of large gardens and parks growing to 30 m in cultivation. It has large leathery leaves and interesting, brown flaking bark. Mature specimens can develop a massive trunk.

Araucaria bidwilli
Bunya Pine

A tall ornamental, dome-shaped conifer to 30 m or more in parks and large gardens. The very prickly green leaves are clustered towards the end of the tree's numerous horizontal branches. The Bunya Pine produces large cones weighing up to 4 kg each and should not be planted where falling cones might cause damage or injury.

Araucaria cunninghamii
Hoop Pine

A well known and widely planted Brisbane conifer growing to 30 m or more in cultivation. The dark green foliage is clustered in bunches towards the end of its branches, which arise in whorls from the trunk. The species is named after the explorer and botanist, Allan Cunningham. see p.244

Araucaria heterophylla
Norfolk Island Pine

This tall conifer is native to Norfolk Island and grows to 30 m. It has a very symmetrical cone-shaped canopy and soft dark green foliage. The Norfolk Island Pine is tolerant of salt spray and often planted as avenues in seaside locations.

Bauhinia variegata
Orchid Tree

This small deciduous tree to 6–8 m bears pink-purple, orchid-like flowers in late winter–spring after losing its leaves. The species was previously planted in Brisbane streets from the 1950s to the 1970s for its floral display.

Brachychiton rupestris
Bottle Tree

A semi-deciduous tree related to the Flame Tree, *Brachychiton acerifolius*, with a remarkable swollen, bottle-shaped trunk. It commonly grows to 8–10 m in cultivation, and bears inconspicuous yellow flowers. A well–known stand of this species can be found in Anzac Square, Brisbane.

Buckinghamia celsissima
Ivory Curl Flower

A rounded, dense foliaged tree native to North Queensland, growing to 6–8 m in Brisbane. In summer, the canopy is covered in masses of cream, scented flowers. Ivory Curl Flower is a useful street and home garden species in Brisbane.

Caesalpinia ferrea
Leopard Tree

An elegant tall deciduous tree to 10–15 m, with mottled cream and grey bark and a spreading vase-shaped canopy of finely divided dark green foliage. The Leopard Tree produces small yellow flowers in summer and the trees are distinctive features of Brisbane city streetscapes. A magnificent specimen can be seen in front of the Brisbane City Council library at New Farm.

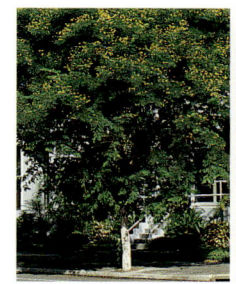

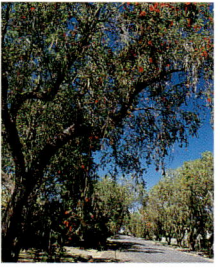

Callistemon viminalis
Weeping Bottlebrush

A weeping, small to medium–sized tree growing to 6 m or more. It has light green foliage and sprays of bright red bottlebrush flowers in spring and summer. Many cultivars have been developed from this species, which grows naturally along watercourses in the region.

Casuarina cunninghamiana
River She-oak

A large, fast growing she-oak to 15 m in cultivation with fine dark green foliage. It occurs naturally along watercourses and is often used in park and embankment plantings. See p.139

Corymbia citriodora subsp. *variegata*
Spotted Gum

This large, graceful eucalypt, which grows to 35 m or more, has a distinctive dimpled greyish–pink bark that sheds in small patches. It is a common bushland and park species often found on dry ridges. See p.141

Corymbia torelliana
Cadaghi

This large and fast growing tropical tree with its distinctive smooth green trunk is native to North Queensland and was planted widely in Brisbane in parks and home gardens in the late 1970s. It is now considered an undesirable species in the Brisbane region because it self-sows into natural areas, and is subject to sooty mould. The Cadaghi is listed as an **environmental weed** by Brisbane City Council.

Cupaniopsis anacardioides
Tuckeroo

A dense, shady, medium sized tree to 10 m with dark green foliage, Its orange fruits are attractive to birds and it is commonly used in street and home garden plantings. It occurs naturally in bushland areas in Brisbane. See p.258

Delonix regia
Poinciana

A magnificent ornamental tree with a spreading, umbrella-like crown and fern-like foliage. It is briefly deciduous before producing a canopy of bright scarlet-red blossoms in summer. The Poinciana is a significant element of the streetscape in older Brisbane suburbs such as Clayfield and New Farm, and is a popular park and home garden species.

Eucalyptus curtisii
Plunkett Mallee

A small multi–stemmed eucalypt that is indigenous to Brisbane. Plunkett's Mallee grows to 3–5 m and bears masses of pure white flowers in spring. It is frequently used in home gardens for its flowering qualities.

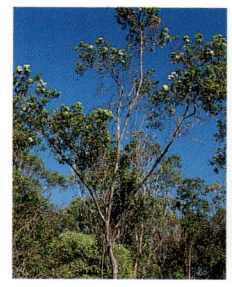

Eucalyptus microcorys
Tallowwood

A large majestic eucalypt that grows to 35 m and is found in bushland on more fertile soils. It has an attractive canopy with orange-brown, flaky bark. Tallowwoods provide habitat for a range of wildlife and are planted in parks for their aesthetic, shade and habitat values. See p.157

Ficus benjamina
Weeping Fig

This majestic shade tree is native to Asia and grows to 15–20 m tall with a spreading canopy of dense shiny weeping foliage. The small red fruits are attractive to birds. It is used extensively as a park tree in Brisbane and in selected locations as outstanding street specimens. A fine specimen planted in the 1920s extends over Lutwyche Rd, Windsor.

Ficus microcarpa var. *hilli*
Hill's Fig

A tall spreading shade tree to 18 m with glossy bright green leaves and a weeping habit in the upper branches. The fig is native to North Qld and was named after Walter Hill, the first curator of the Brisbane Botanic Gardens from 1855 to 1881. It is a popular park species in Brisbane.

Flindersia australis
Crow's Ash

A large, shady Brisbane rainforest tree with a dense rounded crown. Growing to about 15 m in cultivation, the Crow's Ash bears attractive cream flowers followed by striking woody fruits that are used in dried arrangements. It is used in street, park and home garden plantings. See p.272

Grevillea robusta
Southern Silky Oak

A tall ornamental tree that develops a pyramidal shape and has large, deep green fern-like foliage. In summer, it produces abundant combs of fiery golden-orange flowers that are very attractive to birds and flying foxes. It is an excellent specimen tree for large gardens or parks.

Harpullia pendula
Tulipwood

This native shade tree grows to 8–10 m and has glossy, light green leaves and small red or yellow berries that contain black shiny seeds. Tulipwood is used as a hardy and attractive street tree in Brisbane. It is also an ideal tree for home gardens and is in the same family as the Tuckeroo (Sapindaceae), see p.278

Jacaranda mimosifolia
Jacaranda

This large ornamental tree growing to 18 m has beautiful lace-like foliage that is deciduous immediately before a striking show of bluish-mauve, bell shaped flowers in October. It is an excellent ornamental species used in parks and street tree plantings.

Kigelia africana
Sausage Tree

One of the most unusual street trees in Brisbane, the Sausage Tree is named for its large pendulous fruit, which hang from long stalks and can weight up to 9 kg. The tree is native to Africa and can reach 18 m. It has reddish-orange flowers that open at night and which have a disagreeable odour.

Melaleuca bracteata
River Tea Tree

A fast growing tea-tree of Brisbane watercourses reaching 10–15 m, *Melaeuca bracteata* has grey furrowed bark and fine, dark green foliage. White flowers are borne in summer. The cultivars 'Revolution Green' and 'Revolution Gold' were developed from this species. See p.182

Plumeria rubra
Frangipani

A small deciduous tropical tree more commonly grown in Brisbane home gardens than in streets and parks. The frangipani has a short trunk and stubby, brittle branches bearing fragrant white and yellow flowers in summer. Pink and red flowering varieties are also available.

Spathodea campanulata
West African Tulip Tree

A native of West Africa, this tall tree growing up to 25 m, was a popular ornamental species once planted in Brisbane for its large orange-red tulip-shaped flowers. However, it is now listed as an **environmental weed** in the Brisbane city area. Other undesirable features are its brittle wood and suckering habit.

Syzygium luehmannii
Small-leafed Lilly-pilly

This dense, rounded to columnar tree reaches 10 m and has glossy dark green foliage and flushes of red-pink new growth. It bears fluffy white flowers followed by clusters of small, red fruit. The Lilly-pilly is often used as a street tree and screen species in home gardens.

Tabebuia chrysantha
Golden Trumpet Tree

A small to medium, open-crowned deciduous tree to 5 m with vivid yellow bell shaped flowers. It prefers drier sites.

Tabebuia rosea
Pink Trumpet Tree

A highly ornamental, semi-deciduous tree to 10 m, covered in pale pink, bell-shaped flowers in late winter.

Waterhousea floribunda
Weeping Lilly-pilly

An attractive shade tree with weeping dark green foliage to 8–10 m in cultivation. Small white flowers are produced in spring. Weeping Satinash grows along some Brisbane watercourses such as Enoggera and Downfall Creeks and it is now a popular home garden and street tree. See p.301

Downfall Creek, BC

Weeds

'Weed' is a word that dares you to define it and always eludes the attempt. But, weeds do have a common set of characteristics that include the ability to:

- grow profusely at the expense of native plants and their community;
- capitalise quickly on disturbance of an area;
- survive in a wide range of environments;
- produce seed prolifically; and
- cause adverse impacts on the natural environment, economic productivity, landscape character and/or human health.

Primarily, weeds are plants that are exotic to an area. Weeds can include plants that are not native to Australia (eg groundsel) or not native to an area (eg the Umbrella Tree from the northern rainforests is a weed in South-east Queensland). Many 'weed' introductions have been deliberate in an effort to 'acclimatise' an area. In the early days of European settlement, it was common practice to plant non-native species familiar to settlers, to 'enhance' the environment, add colour to ornamental gardens, or to improve the productivity of agricultural industries. A number of other plants have been unintentional 'hitchhikers', using their 'weedy' nature to 'immigrate' to the Greater Brisbane region.

The legacy of plant introductions, deliberate or accidental, is that these plants now seriously threaten the wild plants and their associated communities that are the focus of this book. Weeds also lead to high direct and indirect costs to the general community. In 2003–2004, Brisbane City Council will spend $2.2

Early botanists and acclimatisation societies are largely responsible for the introduced flora of the Greater Brisbane Region today. More than 1060 plant species have been introduced to Brisbane and become naturalised. Not all have invaded native vegetation or become environmental weeds, though there is still this potential for a large number of species. For example, *Cinnamomum camphora* (Camphor Laurel) was introduced into Australia from Asia in 1822. It was promoted as a shade and street tree. However, it grows and spreads rapidly and is now a declared pest. The invasion of pest species has continued unabated since European settlement, with an estimated 30 species arriving in South-east Queensland each year.

Cinnamomum camphora (Camphor laurel), GC

Cirsium vulgare (Scotch Thistle), BC

'The Impact of One Weed'

A sample of jam was awarded a prize at the Australasian Botanic and Horticultural Society meeting in Sydney in 1848. It was labelled 'jam from prickly pear'. Some 70 years later, ...*Opuntia stricta* (Common Prickly Pear) had spread to infest 24 million ha of land across southern Queensland and northern New South Wales, half of which was so densely covered that it could no longer be used for grazing or agriculture and was virtually abandoned by landholders. Government reports talked of a 'calamity befalling the land' and 'millions of acres of nothing but a veritable wilderness of pear' ... Such was the impact of one weed on the Australian landscape. — from '*Weeds and their Impact*', Brian M. Sindel in *Australian Weed Management Systems*, ed. Brian M. Sindel, R.G and F.J Richardson, Melbourne. 2000

million managing the impacts of weeds. Annually, pest species cost Queenslanders $600 million in lost production and control costs. This figure does not include the high costs to our natural environment.

The plants included here represent only a sample of the full array of weedy plants in Brisbane. They have been selected for their significant invasiveness and high likelihood of being seen on the fringes of any patch of bushland, wetland or waterway.

It is not possible to eradicate every weed species and it is not possible for the organisations responsible for weed control to manage each property individually. A strategic approach that integrates a number of actions is essential. These, depending on the extent of a weed infestation, range from:

- monitoring and preventing the entry of new species;
- eradication of recently introduced species before they spread;
- containment of those that cannot be eradicated; and
- management of species that cannot be contained.

The importance of weed management in our own backyards is essential and critical. At least 65% of the weed species in our wild places are garden escapees. Weed management can seem like a daunting task, but it is an essential for all landholders.

There are a number of interesting and fun ways to find out how to manage weeds in your garden. The Department of Natural Resources and Mines has a wide range of pest fact sheets available in hard copy or on their website http://www.nrm.qld.gov.au/pests/. They include suggested treatment techniques and information on how the plant came to be a pest. The *Suburban and Environmental Weeds* CD Rom is an interactive tool for identifying weeds and is available for purchase from the Naturally Queensland Shop or borrowing from Brisbane City Council's Mt Coot-tha Library.

Brisbane City Council has a section dedicated to just weeds in its *Green Garden Guide* publication. If you're still not sure of what to do, contact your local government pest management officer, or your local nursery.

It is hoped that this chapter has shown the perils of planting weeds and has provided the inspiration for eager gardeners to focus their creativity on the rich array of native plants available. — **Alan Barton and Dorean Hull, with thanks to Kristen Sinden**

HERBS, GRASSES AND GROUNDCOVERS

Ageratina riparia
Mist Flower, Creeping Crofton Weed

A perennial scrambling herb or shrub that is a weed of damp areas.

Amaranthus spinosus
Needleburr

An annual herb that grows to 1 m and has spines in the forks of the leaves.

Asparagus aethiopicus
Asparagus Fern

Prefers sandy or well-drained soils. Grows slowly until root system establishes and then spreads rapidly, smothering native groundcovers. Germinates and fruits year round.

Bidens pilosa
Cobbler's Pegs

Grows to 2 m. Yellow flowers. The hooked bristles of the seed attach to clothing fibres and animal fur.

Bryophyllum delagoense
Mother of Millions

Common on shady roadsides, along fence lines and rubbish dumps. Withstands extremely dry periods. Prevents growth of native vegetation.

Callisia fragans
Purple Succulent

Prefers shaded areas and is found in a variety of soils. Forms dense infestation smothering native groundcovers. Difficult to control.

Chloris gayana
Rhodes Grass

A weed of roadsides, footpaths, disturbed sites, railways and cultivation. Widely cultivated as a pasture grass.

Cirsium vulgare
Spear Thistle

Biennial plant, grows to 1.5 m. Pink flowers in summer. Found in gardens, along roadsides and in cultivated areas.

Eragrostis tenuifolia
Elastic Grass

Common and widespread weed of tended areas. It is a pest in lawns as the leaves are difficult to cut.

Heliotropium amplexicaule
Blue Heliotrope

Low-growing herb with coiled inflorescences and many small purple and yellow flowers arranged in two rows.

Hydrocotyle bonariensis
Pennywort

Small, hairy, creeping herb with lobed leaves, relatively long leaf stalks and clusters of tiny stalked flowers.

Found on sand dunes along coast.

Hypochaeris radicata
Flat Weed

A rosette-forming yellow-flowered herb resembling Dandelion (*Taraxacum officinale*), but can be distinguished by its branching flower stems.

Impatiens walleriana
Balsam

Common in disturbed areas along creekbanks. Prefers sheltered, moist and well-drained soils. Forms dense infestations that can suppress native seedlings.

Lantana montevidensis
Creeping Lantana

Common in grazed native pasture, dry eucalypt forest, dry ridge tops and gardens. Smothers native grasses, spreads quickly by seeds and runners; can germinate year round. **Serious environmental weed.**

Macroptilium atropurpureum
Siratro

A robust creeping or climbing plant, often seen on roadsides, or covering low shrubs, fences and grasses. Originally introduced as a pasture plant.

Macroptilium lathyroides
Phaseus Bean

Perennial, erect woody herb to 1 m tall it was introduced as a pasture legume, and is now a weed of disturbed areas.

Neonotonia wightii
White Glycine

Deep-rooting plant producing long, slender, trailing stems that root readily at branch nodes.

Nephrolepis cordifolia
Fishbone Fern

Grows in wide range of conditions, prefers shade to part shade. Can form dense infestations that may interfere with bush regeneration. Difficult and labour intensive to remove. **Serious environmental weed.**

Oxalis corniculata
Creeping Oxalis

A small creeping perennial herb with clover-like leaves and yellow funnel-shaped flowers. Its elastic fruit expel their seeds with some force when touched.

Rivina humilis
Coral Berry

Small woody herb found in damp and shady positions, particularly on forest edges. Produces spikes of small white flowers and glossy red berries.

Sansevieria trifasciata
Mother-in-law's Tongue

Prefers well-drained soils in shady areas and is able to tolerate dry periods. Spreads from dumped garden waste; displaces native groundcovers. **Serious environmental weed.**

Sphagneticola trilobata
Singapore Daisy

On coastal dunes, edges of rainforests and roads; prevalent along waterways, but can tolerate dry periods. Forms dense mats. **Serious environmental weed.**

Tradescantia albiflora
Wandering Jew

Fleshy perennial herb that grows in damp situations.

Urtica incisa
Scrub Nettle

Perennial herb. Stems and leaves have scattered stinging hairs. Avoid skin contact.

VINES AND CLIMBERS

Anredera cordifolia
Madeira Vine, Lamb's Tail

Climbing plant in coastal areas and rainforest edges. Reproduces by knobby tubers growing abundantly along stem. **Serious environmental weed.**

Aristolochia elegans
Dutchman's Pipe

Naturalised in high rainfall coastal areas. Leaves toxic to caterpillars of rare Richmond Birdwing Butterfly. **Serious environmental weed.**

Asparagus africanus
Climbing Asparagus Fern

Prickly. Invades bushland by climbing and smothering canopy; also along fence lines and roadsides where birds sit and deposit seeds. Difficult to remove.

Cardiospermum grandiflorum
Balloon Vine

Rampant vine found in bushland, along rivers and creekbanks. Smothers native trees, especially along waterways. **Serious environmental weed.**

Desmodium unicinatum
Silver-leaved Desmodium

Perennial vine that grows on fences and along roadsides. Distinctive silver stripe on the leaflets.

Ipomoea cairica
Mile-a-minute

Common in coastal forest, rainforest edges and cleared areas. Spreads quickly, smothering native vegetation. Grows in range of soil types.

Ipomoea indica
Morning Glory

In disturbed rainforest, along waterways, roadsides and neglected urban and rural areas. Invasive, quickly smothers and destroys native vegetation and habitats.

Macfadyena unguis-cati
Cat's-claw Creeper

Aggressive woody smothering vine with extensive thick root system. Has three-clawed tendrils that attach to objects. Difficult to remove. **Serious environmental weed.**

Passiflora foetida
Stinking Passionfriut

Stinking Passionfruit vine can be distinguished from two similar species, by its hairy leaves.

Passiflora suberosa
Wild Passionfruit, Corky Passion Vine

Common in gullies, rainforest edges and forests. Strangles native undergrowth. Leaves and fruit poisonous if eaten. Hand-pulling most reliable method of control.

Passiflora subpeltata
White Passion Flower

A vine or climber that is hairless with leaves that have heart-shaped stipules and three rounded lobes.

All parts poisonous.

SHRUBS AND TREES

Celtis sinensis
Chinese Elm

Common along cleared waterways. Large amounts of leaf drop may affect water quality. **Serious environmental weed.**

Cinnamomum camphora
Camphor Laurel

Aggressive, along waterways, forming dense infestations. Fruit toxic to birds. **Serious environmental weed.**

Gomphocarpus physocarpus
Balloon Cotton Bush

Small shrub with clusters of white flowers and distinctive balloon-like fruits. Care should be taken around this plant because the sap is poisonous.

Koelreuteria elegans
Golden Rain Tree

On fertile, well-drained soils in full sun. Extremely high percentage of seedling germination. **Serious environmental weed.**

Lantana camara
Lantana

Weed of national significance. Smothers native vegetation, increases fire risks, harbours vermin and is host to pathogens. Poisonous leaves, flowers and berries. **Serious environmental weed.**

Ligustrum lucidum
Large-leaved Privet

Prefers temperate areas. Colonises gullies, creek banks, bushland and pastures. Highly invasive. **Serious environmental weed.**

Ochna serrulata
Ochna

Occurs in range of soil types, common along watercourses and rainforest fringes. Spreads quickly, usually by birds. Difficult to remove. **Serious environmental weed.**

Physalis peruviana
Cape Gooseberry

Soft wooded shrub growing to 1 m tall with densely hairy stems and leaves. Yellow flowers and fruit are yellow berries enclosed within a papery structure.

Pinus spp.
Exotic Pines

Escapee from plantations. Invades bushland and roadsides; can dominate native forests.

Rhaphiolepis indica
Common Indian Hawthorn

Occurs on cleared sites in moist, sunny and open areas. Forms dense thickets, suppressing regeneration and growth of native species.

Ricinus communis
Castor Oil Plant

Perennial shrub to 3 m. Large red flowers on erect spikes in summer. Seeds capsules explode when ripe. Found on disturbed or cleared land and along creek banks.

Schefflera actinophylla
Umbrella Tree

Native to North Queensland. Invasive. Prefers fertile moist soils (eg. riparian areas, rainforest edges). Particular problem on Moreton Bay islands.

Schinus terebinthifolius
Broad-leaf Pepper Tree

Infests coastal wetlands, mangroves, disturbed sites, watercourses and other low-lying areas. Fruit toxic to birds and mammals. **Serious environmental weed.**

Senna pendula
Easter Cassia

In disturbed bushland, rainforest edges and untended backyards. Colonises bushland, prevents native regrowth. Produces masses of yellow flowers at Easter.

Solanum mauritianum
Wild Tobacco

A densely hairy large shrub or small tree with large leaves, purple star-shaped flowers and yellow globular fruit.

Syagrus romanzoffiana
Cocos Palm

Naturalised in urban bushland areas. Flying foxes are frequently injured by their fronds and fruit they consume can cause digestive problems, sometimes resulting in death.

AQUATIC PLANTS

Nymphaea caerulea subsp. *zanzibarensis*
Cape Waterlily

Floating aquatic plant. Purple-blue flowers have numerous yellow stamens and a purple tip above each yellow anther. Displaces native species, *Nymphaea gigantea*, which looks similar, but does not have a purple tip above each anther.

Hibiscus tiliaceus (Cotton Tree), BC

References

Introduction – Alan Barton

Adam, P. 1987. *New South Wales rainforests: the nomination for the world heritage list.* National Parks and Wildlife Service, Sydney.

Archer, M., Burnley, I., Dodson, J., Harding, R., Head, L. and Murphy, A. 1998, *From plesiosaurs to people: 10 million years of Australian environmental history*, Australia: State of the Environment Technical paper series (Portrait of Australia), Department of Environment, Canberra.

Batianoff, G. N. and Butler, D. W. 2002. *Assessment of invasive naturalised plants in south-east Queensland.* Queensland Environmental Protection Agency, Brisbane.

Beckman, G. G., Hubble, G. D., and Thompson, C. H. 1987. *The soil landscapes of Brisbane and South-eastern environs.* CSIRO, Melbourne.

Bernhardt, P. 1990. *Wily Violets and Underground Orchids, Revelations of a Botanist.* Allen and Unwin, Sydney.

Blake, S. T. and Roff, C. 1988. *The honey flora of Queensland.* Queensland Department of Primary Industries, Brisbane.

Bowman, D. M. J. S. 2002, Preface, Measuring and Imagining: Exploring Centuries of Australian Landscape Change. *Australian Journal of Botany*, 50, i-iii.

Brisbane City Council. 1992. *The Brisbane Conservation Atlas.* Environmental Management Branch, Brisbane City Council, Brisbane.

Brisbane City Council. 2003. *Draft Cunningham's Jute (Chorchorus cunninghamii) Conservation Action Statement.* Brisbane City Council, Brisbane.

Brisbane City Council. 1996, *State of the Environment Report 1 Brisbane 1996.* Brisbane City Council, Brisbane.

Brisbane City Council. 1998, *State of the Environment Report 2 Brisbane 1998.* Brisbane City Council, Brisbane.

Brisbane City Council. 2001, *State of the Environment Report 3 Brisbane 2001.* Brisbane City Council, Brisbane.

Burbidge, N. T. 1960. The phytogeography of the Australian region. *Australian Journal of Botany* 8, 75-212.

Cameron McNamara 1985. *An Inventory of Conservation Mapping Units in the City of Brisbane.* Prepared for Brisbane City Council. Cameron McNamara, Brisbane.

Catterall, C. P. 1990. *A Natural Area Conservation Strategy for Brisbane City.* Unpublished Report to the Brisbane Plan, Brisbane City Council.

Catterall, C. P. and Kingston, M. 1993. *Remnant Bushland of South East Queensland in the 1990's: it's distribution, loss, ecological consequences and future prospects.* Institute of Applied Ecological Research, Griffith University, Brisbane.

Clifford, H, T. and Specht, R.L. 1979. *The Vegetation of North Stradbroke Island.* University of Queensland Press, Brisbane.

Cole, J. 1984. *Shaping a city: Greater Brisbane 1925-1985.* William Brooks, Eagle Farm.

Commonwealth of Australia. 1999. *Comprehensive Regional Assessment World Heritage Sub-theme: Eucalypt-dominated vegetation.* Report of the Expert Workshop, Canberra, 8-9 March, 1999. Commonwealth Government of Australia, Canberra.

Davies, W. (ed).1983. *Wildlife of the Brisbane Area.* The Jacaranda Press, Milton.

DNRM (Department of Natural Resources and Mines). 2003. http://www.nrm.qld.gov.au/pests/. Queensland Government.

Dornan, D. and Cryle, D. 1992. *The Petrie Family: Building Colonial Brisbane.*

University of Queensland Press, St Lucia.

Environment Science and Services. 1989, *The Future of Brisbane's Bushland – A Discussion Paper*. Environment Science and Services, Brisbane.

EPA (Environmental Protection Agency) 1999. *State of the Environment, Queensland 1999*. Queensland Government.

EPA (Environmental Protection Agency). 2003. *Regional Nature Conservation Strategy for South East Queensland*. Queensland Government (in press).

Franks, D. M. 2000, *Weathering and Landscape Evolution, Southeast Queensland*. Thesis submitted in partial fulfilment of the requirements of the degree of Bachelor of Science with Honours in Earth Science. University of Queensland, Brisbane.

George, A. S. 1996. *The Banksia Book*. Kangaroo press, Kenthurst.

Hall, H. J. 1990, 20 000 Years of Human Impact on the Brisbane River and Environs. In *The Brisbane River A Source-book for the Future,* Ed. P Davie, E Stock and D Low Choy. Australian Littoral Society Incorporated, Brisbane.

Holliday, I. and Hill, R. 1983, *A Field Guide to Australian Trees*. Rigby, Adelaide.

Low, T. 2002. *The New Nature*. Penguin Books, Camberwell.

McInnes-King, D. 2002. *Tree Dinosaurs: Araucaria: The Masthead Species of Gondwanan Flora*. David McInnes-King, Larnook, NSW.

Monroe R and Stevens, N. C. (eds.) 1976. *The Border Ranges: A Land Use Conflict in Regional Perspective*. Proceedings of a Symposium by the Royal Society of Queensland and ANZAAS, Queensland division, Binna Burra Lodge, Lamington Plateau, 25th-27th June, 1976. Royal Society of Queensland, Brisbane.

Pryor, L.D. 1976, *The Biology of Eucalypts*. The Institute of Biology's Studies in Biology no. 61. Edward Arnold, London.

Riviere, M. S. 1998. *Discovery of the Brisbane River, 1823: Oxley, Uniacke and Pamphlet, 175 Years in Retrospect*. Royal Historical Society of Queensland, Brisbane.

Roberts, B. 1991. *Stories of the Southside*. Aussie Books, Archerfield.

Rolls, E. 1981. *A million wild acres*. Penguin Books, Ringwood.

Ryan, M. 1995. *Wildlife of Greater Brisbane*. Queensland Museum, Brisbane.

Solem, A. 1974. *The Shell Makers Introducing Mollusks*. John Wiley and Sons, New York.

Steele, J. G. 1972. *The explorers of the Moreton Bay district*. University of Queensland Press, St Lucia.

Symons, P. and Symons, S. 1994. *Bush Heritage: an introduction to the history of plant an animal use by Aboriginal people and colonists in the Brisbane and Sunshine Coast areas*. Pat and Sim Symons, Nambour.

Truswell, E. M. 1990. Australian rainforests: The 100 million year record. In *Australian Tropical Rainforests*. Ed. LJ Webb, J Kikkawa. CSIRO Publications, Melbourne.

White, M. E. 1990. *The Nature of Hidden Worlds*. REED, Chatswood.

Willmott W. F. and Stevens N. C. 1992. *Rocks and Landscapes of Brisbane and Ipswich*. Geological Society of Australia Incorporated (Queensland Division), Brisbane.

Yencken, D. and Wilson, D. 2000. *Resetting the Compass: Australia's Journey Towards Sustainability*. CSIRO Publishing, Collingwood.

Young, P. 1990, Vegetation of the Brisbane River. In *The Brisbane River A Source-book for the Future,* Ed. P Davie, E Stock and D Low Choy. Australian Littoral Society Incorporated, Brisbane.

Young, P. A. R., and Dillewaard, H. A. 1999. Southeast Queensland. In Sattler. P and Williams, R (eds). 1999, *Conservation Status of Queensland's Bioregional Ecosystems*. Environmental Protection Agency, Queensland Government.

Plants of the Coastal Dunes — Paul Donatiu
Additional Reading

Beach Protection Authority (1981) *Coastal Sand Dunes: Their Vegetation and Management*. Beach Protection Authority of Queensland, Brisbane.

Carolin R.C. and Clarke P. (1988) *Beach Plants of South Eastern Australia*. Sainty & Associates, Sydney.

Clarke P.J. (1994) Coastal dune vegetation. In *Australian Vegetation*. (Ed. R.H. Groves.) pp.501- 521. Cambridge University Press, Cambridge.

Hesp P.A. (1984) Foredune formation in Southeast Australia. In *Coastal Geomorphology in Australia*. (Ed. B.G. Thom.) pp. 69-97. Academic Press, Sydney.

Plants of the Eucalypt Forest – Robert Coutts

Coutts, R. H. (1994). *Plant community structure and dynamics on Aeolian sand dunes, Coomboo Lake area, Fraser Island*. Unpublished M. Phil Thesis, Griffith University, Brisbane.

Coutts, Bob (1984). Plant communities of the Brisbane Region. In: *Plant a tree: A working guide to the greening of southeast Queensland*. Ecos educational Publications, Nambour. Wally Davies (ed.)

McDonald, W. J. F., and Elsol, J. A. (1984). Moreton region vegetation map series: Summary report and check list for Caloundra, Brisbane, Beenleigh and Murwillumbah sheets. Botany branch, Queensland Department of Primary Industries, Brisbane.

Pryor, L. D. (1976). *Biology of the Eucalypts*. Studies in Biology no 61. Edward Arnold (Publishers) Limited, London.

Sattler, Paul. and Williams, Rebecca, (eds.) (1999). *The conservation status of Queensland bioregional ecosystems*. Enviromental Protection Agency, Queensland Government, Brisbane.

Symons, Pat and Sim. (1994). *Bush Heritage: An introduction to the history of plant and animal use by aboriginal people in the Brisbane and Sunshine Coast areas*. Pat and Sim Symons, Nambour.

Plant description references:

Catterall, C. P. and Wallace, C. J. (1987). *An island in suburbia: The natural and social history of Toohey Forest*. Institute of Applied Environmental Research, Griffith University, Brisbane.

Coutts, R. H. and Catterall, C. P., (1982). *Identifying the plants of Toohey Forest*. Ecos Educational Publications, Nambour.

Clifford, H. T. (1978). *Eucalypts of the Brisbane Region*. Queensland Museum Booklet No 6, Brisbane.

Harden, G.J.(ed.) (2000). *Flora of New South Wales*. Volume 1 Revised edition. University of New South Wales Press Ltd, Sydney.

Harden, G. J. (ed.) (2002). *Flora of New South Wales*. Volume 2 Revised edition, University of New South Wales Press Ltd, Sydney.

Harden, G. J. (ed.) (2002). *Flora of New South Wales*. Volume 3 Reprint, University of New South Wales Press Ltd, Sydney.

Harden, G. J. (ed.) (1993). *Flora of New South Wales*. Volume 4. University of New South Wales Press Ltd, Sydney.

Henderson, R. F., (ed.) (2002). *Names and distribution of Queensland plants, algae and lichens*. Queensland Herbarium, Environmental Protection Agency, Brisbane Botanic Gardens, Mt.Coot-tha, Toowong.

Jessup, L.W. (2002). *Flora of South-eastern Queensland*. Volume 2: Changes to names or status of taxa. Queensland Herbarium, Environmental Protection Agency, Brisbane Botanic Gardens, Mt.Coot-tha, Toowong.

Jessup, L.W. (2003). *Flora of South-eastern Queensland*. Volume 1: Changes to names or status of taxa. Queensland Herbarium, Environmental Protection Agency, Brisbane Botanic Gardens Mt.Coot-tha, Toowong.

Lebler, Beryl, A., (1977). *Wild flowers of South-eastern Queensland*. Volume 1. Botany branch, Department of Primary Industries. S. R. Hampson Government Printer, Brisbane.

Stanley, T. D. and Ross, E.M. (1983). *Flora of South-eastern Queensland*. Volume1. Queensland Department of Primary Industries, Brisbane.

Stanley, T. D. and Ross, E.M. (2002). *Flora of South-eastern Queensland*. Reprint of Volume 2. Queensland Department of Primary Industries, Brisbane.

Stanley, T. D. and Ross, E.M. (1989). *Flora of South-eastern Queensland*. Volume 3 Queensland Department of Primary Industries, Brisbane.

Authors and Acknowledgements

Authors

Alan Barton is the Principal Program Officer of Conservation Land Management at Brisbane City Council. His role is to develop and coordinate policies, strategies and programs for the management and enhancement of the natural, cultural and recreational values of natural areas in Brisbane City. Alan has more than 17 years experience in natural resources and is dedicated to biodiversity conservation and protecting Brisbane's natural areas.

David Barnes is an ecologist and landscape architect. He has been involved in bushland regeneration projects and is particularly interested in native plants, their use in horticulture and their usefulness to local fauna. He is co-author of *The Fauna Friendly Plants of South East Queensland*. David and his wife, Margery, have established a native 'habitat' garden in Bracken Ridge, which is part of Australia's Open Garden Scheme and shows what can be achieved in suburban back yards.

Bob Coutts is a botanist, who has been working at Griffith University since 1975. Initially Bob was a research assistant studying Brisbane's forest parks and he is now a scientific officer in the faculty of Environmental Sciences where he sets up laboratory classes for undergraduates in the plant ecology and soils area. His job as a research assistant started a continuing interest in the distribution patterns of plant communities in the Greater Brisbane Region.

Paul Donatiu is Ecoregion Program Manager for the World Wide Fund for Nature. Before commencing with WWF in May 2003, Paul worked for Greening Australia, providing extension support to vegetation management groups, and working on such projects as the SEQ Fire and Biodiversity Consortium and the SEQ Rainforest Recovery Project. He has a background in vegetation management, restoration ecology, training and community education.

Glenn Leiper is the Principal of the Jacobs Well Environmental Education Centre. He has a life-long interest in natural history with extensive bushwalking and club memberships. To date he has co-authored two plant books, *Mutooroo* (Aboriginal Plant Usage) and *Mangroves to Mountains*, a field guide to the plants of South-east Queensland. Fortunately, his long-suffering family tolerates his insatiable obsession with native plants.

Janet Hauser is a botanical artist with a lifelong interest in natural history and a passion for botanizing. Janet has been involved in conservation for many years and has enjoyed a lifetime of bush wandering, during which she has gained an extensive knowledge of our native flora.

Bill McDonald is a Principal Botanist at Queensland Herbarium, where he has been employed since 1977 as a vegetation surveyor and ecologist. Bill has worked in a wide range of ecosystems from semi-arid grasslands and Acacia woodlands in Central-western Queensland to moist eucalypt forests and rainforests in South-eastern Queensland.

Lyndal Plant is the Principal Program Officer for the Landscape Amenity Section of Brisbane City Council's Environment and Parks Branch. She describes her role as an 'urban forester'; responsible for the management of Brisbane's amenity tree resources including street and park trees. Lyndal was a Churchill Fellow and has worked in local government tree management for 14 years. Previously she worked for 7 years with the Queensland Department of Forestry.

Kathy Stephens is a senior botanist at Queensland Herbarium. She has undertaken mapping, vegetation monitoring, and applied ecology projects in coastal wetlands and heathlands in South-east Queensland, and is especially interested in water plants. Kathy is the author of *Wetland Plants of Queensland — a Field Guide* and lectures at the University of Queensland. Her detailed mapping of the wetlands of south-east Queensland has formed the basis of the regional coastal management plan.

Acknowledgements

This book could not have been published without the generous support and assistance of the following organisations and individuals:

Griffith University
John Oxley Library
Staff of the Queensland Herbarium

Tony Bean, Queensland Herbarium
Chris Burwell, Queensland Museum
Philip Cameron, Mt Cooth-tha Botanic Gardens
Alex Cook, Queensland Museum
Greg Czechura, Queensland Museum,
Dan Daly, Brisbane City Council
Martin Fingland, Brisbane Forest Park
Primrose Gamble, Fairhill Native Plants
Gordon Guymer, Queensland Herbarium
Barbara Henderson, Wallum Study Group
Laurence Herron, Hawkins Home and Garden
Alison Hill, Hawkins Home and Garden
Dorean Hull, Brisbane City Council
Laurie Jessup, Queensland Herbarium
Michelle Marshall, Queensland Herbarium
Ken McClymont, Brisbane City Council
Ric Natrass, environmental consultant
Bruce Noble, Brisbane Forest Park
Don Perrin, Redcliffe Botanical Gardens
Graham Phegan, Brisbane City Council
Klaus Querengasser, Brisbane Forest Park
Kristen Sinden, Brisbane City Council
Jan Sked, Society for Growing Australian Plants
Anne Spooner
Pam Usher, Greening Australia
John Ward, Wallum Action Group

Brisbane City Council

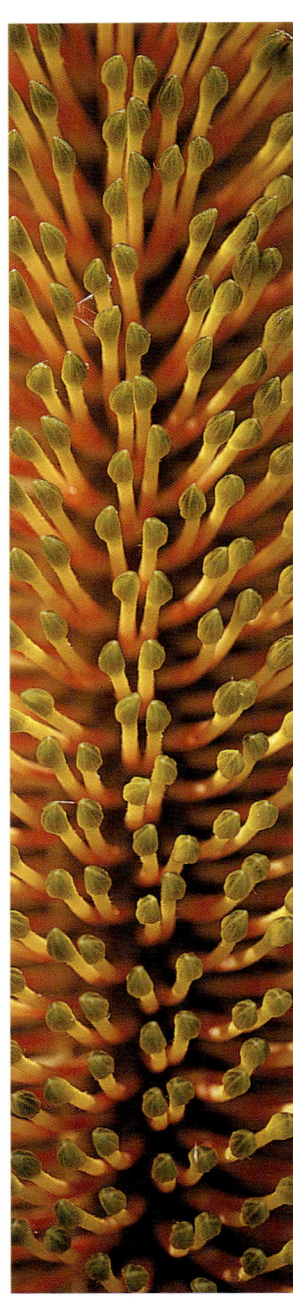

Brisbane City Council is committed to managing the City's natural heritage and has developed a comprehensive range of local government environmental programs. These initiatives aim to protect and enhance Brisbane's biodiversity and will assist in achieving Council's *Living in Brisbane* 2010 strategy and its vision for Brisbane as a 'clean and green' city.

Conserving Council and Privately Owned Natural Areas

Council began a significant bushland acquisition program in 1991. A total of $77 million has been spent through the Bushland Preservation Levy to acquire 1688 ha of significant natural habitats. Council aims to secure 2500 ha by 2010.

A major focus of the Bushland Acquisition Program in recent years has been the consolidation and linking of core habitat areas. As a result, Brisbane now contains a significant number of large bushland and wetland reserves in public ownership, including Karawatha Forest, Tinchi Tamba Wetlands, Boondall Wetlands, White's Hill Reserve, Seven Hills Reserve, Brisbane Koala Bushlands, Bayside Parklands, Mt Coot-tha Forest, Toohey Forest and the Anstead Bushlands.

Brisbane City's statutory planning scheme, *City Plan*, is a key mechanism in delivering ecologically sustainable development within the City and protecting significant natural assets. It achieves this through a framework of Desired Environmental Outcomes, Codes and development assessment processes.

The Natural Assets Local Law 2003 has evolved from the former Vegetation Protection Ordinances (VPOs) introduced in 1991. Protected vegetation coverage has been expanded by 60% to include approximately 50 000 hectares of publicly and privately owned land.

Involving the Community

Council supports biodiversity conservation through community partnerships. *The Habitat Brisbane* program brings Council and the community together to protect and enhance biodiversity at a local level. There are well over a hundred bushcare groups actively participating with Council to restore bushland, wetland and waterway habitat across Brisbane.

Other initiatives include conservation partnerships with private landowners, such as *Land for Wildlife* and *Voluntary Conservation Agreement* programs and guidelines for managing our biodiversity.

Community Advisory Committees have been established to partner with Council in targeting and progressing its environmental programs. This brings local people into the decision-making process and facilitates community education, appreciation and participation in wildlife conservation.

Council also provides direct funding to community groups through its environmental grants program to undertake practical, hands-on activities that protect biodiversity, raise community awareness and develop stronger community partnerships.

Managing Threatening Processes

Weeds are the second highest threat to biodiversity after land clearing. Pest animals (e.g. Red Imported Fire Ants) vandalism, illegal fires, habitat loss & fragmentation, recreation and pollution are just a few of the other threats to Brisbane's natural heritage that require on-going, active management.

Management of identified pest vegetation is also required under the Natural Assets Local Law and the Land Protection (Pest Stock Route Management) Act 2002. Reducing the level of weed infestations protects the integrity of our unique biodiversity. A new program has begun across Brisbane to restore and rehabilitate remnant bushland. Brisbane City Council invests significant resources annually on weed management.

Local laws protect significant vegetation from indiscriminate clearing, illegal dumping, and the impacts of declared and noxious weeds.

Improving Knowledge

Council recognises that effective biodiversity conservation must be underpinned by the best available knowledge and information. Through a co-operative biodiversity research program, Council undertakes flora and fauna surveys and investigations with community and industry partners to better understand and manage the City's biodiversity.

Greening Brisbane Naturally

This initiative focuses on enhancing the quantity and quality of vegetation cover in Brisbane and has several components including:

- *One Million Trees* program;
- *Greening the Gaps*;
- *Wipeout Weeds* Program;
- Cultural and Corridor Links; and the
- *Green Garden* Guide.

Further information:

Brisbane City Council
GPO Box 1434
Brisbane Qld 4001
Phone: 07 3403 8888
www.brisbane.qld.gov.au

The Queensland Herbarium

The Queensland Herbarium, part of the Environmental Protection Agency, is the centre for information and research on Queensland plants and plant communities. It is responsible for discovering, describing, monitoring, modelling, surveying, naming and classifying Queensland's plant and ecosystem diversity.

The Queensland Herbarium collection of 680,000 specimens of plants, algae and fungi, form the basis for botanical research and knowledge of the State's flora. The collections contain many historical specimens, including some collected by Joseph Banks and Daniel Solander, the botanists who accompanied Captain Cook in 1770. In recent times, more than 30 species new to science have been discovered and described each year.

The Queensland Herbarium is accumulating data on the rare and threatened plant species listed under the Schedule of the Queensland Nature Conservation Act 1992. Knowledge of the distribution, population size, genetic diversity, ecology and habitat needs of these plants is essential to enable their effective conservation and the management.

The Vegetation Survey and Mapping program aims to provide a comprehensive 1:100,000 scale vegetation and regional ecosystem information base across Queensland. Vegetation and regional ecosystem maps now exists for 60% of the State. The maps are an essential component of the administration of the Vegetation Management Act 1999 and are an important tool for land management, and conservation planning.

Ecological research at the Queensland Herbarium is concentrated in coastal communities, rainforests, serpentine areas, grasslands, artesian springs and wetlands, as well as on the possible effects of changes in vegetation structure over time. This research provides essential information for the conservation and management of Queensland's plant communities and ecosystems.

Environmental weeds are a significant threat to the conservation of the State's plant species diversity. Herbarium research focuses on prioritising environmental weed species for all regions of Queensland and understanding the invasion process.

The Queensland Herbarium identifies plants and provides information on poisonous properties, distribution, weediness and conservation status on request. The Queensland Herbarium's journal, Austrobaileya and other publications on Queensland plants and vegetation are available on request.

The Queensland Herbarium is located in the Brisbane Botanic Gardens, Mt Coot-tha. Visiting hours are 9:00am to 5:00pm, Monday to Friday. Tours of the Herbarium are available for groups by prior arrangement. Information on events and seminars are available on our web site: www.epa.qld.gov.au/herbarium or phone 3896 9326.

Queensland Government
Environmental Protection Agency

Greening Australia

Greening Australia is an apolitical, not-for-profit, membership-based organisation dedicated to managing and repairing native vegetation. GA works in partnership with landholders and other members of the community, government and business in local and regional Queensland to tackle environmental degradation. The organisation's guiding principles are based on economic, social, and ecological considerations.

Greening Australia operates in 16 locations throughout Queensland and employs more than 85 staff. In South-east Queensland alone, there are more than 650 volunteers who dedicate their time to the work of Greening Australia.

The organisation has 21 years of experience specialising in native vegetation management and nature conservation, and it is committed to training, educating and contributing to the development of skills and knowledge in the community.

In 2002/2003 Greening Australia worked with 7088 volunteers, planted or transplanted 799,427 trees, collected 151 kg of seed and removed 3156 m3 of weeds.

Greening Australia has a demonstrated track record of involving communities in the repair and conservation of their own environments. The organisation's strong representation in local and regional Queensland allows them to work closely with communities to identify their needs and implement responses. GA's Training Services have helped to build bridges between communities, industries and research centres to promote learning and environmental action.

Greening Australia's reputation and on-ground achievements across all sectors of the community bear testament to its ability to develop strong community network structures in which it operates.

*Greening **Australia***
Queensland (Inc.)

Glossary

Achene — A dry fruit that does not open at maturity; formed from a single carpel; has 1 seed.

Alternate — Leaves are alternate when the point of attachment alternates from one side of the stem to the other and is at different levels along the stem, not directly opposite; includes spiral leaf arrangements.

Annual — A plant that completes its lifecycle within one season or one year.

Anther — The part of the plant that produces the pollen, see p.357

Aquatic — Growing in water.

Aril — An expansion of the seed stalk into an often brightly coloured, fleshy or membranous appendage, sometimes partially or completely enclosing the seed.

Awn — An elongated, bristle-like appendage.

Axil — The upper angle between the stem and a leaf.

Axillary — Describes a bud or flower stem arising in the upper angle (axil) between the stem and leaf.

Basal — At the base of the plant.

Beak — A pointed projection or protuberance.

Berry — A succulent fruit that does not split open when ripe and which consists of a skin and a pulp, usually contains a number of seeds; see drupe.

Bipinnate — A compound leaf with leaflets divided twice pinnately into pinnules. At each node on the stem, there are 2 branches opposite one another, each with the leaflets arranged like a pinnate leaf (ie in 2 rows along a rachis); eg jacaranda leaves.

Bisexual — When both the stamens (male) and the carpels (female) occur on the same flower.

Blade (Lamina) — The expanded portion of a leaf.

Bract — A leaf-like structure or scale at the base of a flower or inflorescence.

Bristle — A stiff hair.

Bulb — A storage organ usually underground, composed of a stem and leaf bases.

Buttress — A flange, or relatively flat, variously shaped outgrowth protruding from the lower trunk in many rainforest species. A buttress gives strength and support to the tree.

Calyx — The outer whorl of flower parts that consist of free or fused, leaf-like sepals that protect the flower bud; is usually green.

Canopy — The branches and foliage of a tree, sometimes used as a collective term for the crowns of trees in a forest.

Capsule — A dry fruit that opens when ripe to release seeds; derived from 2 or more carpels; opens in different ways in eucalypt capsules valves at top open releasing seed.

Carpel — The female part of the flower, consisting of the ovary (containing ovules), usually with a style and stigma attached; a flower may have one or several carpels that may be separate or fused.

Common Name — A popular name applied to a particular species in certain areas or districts, often varying from one area to another.

Compound Leaf — A compound leaf consists of a number of leaflets arranged about a main stalk.

Coppice — Shoots arising from the base of the tree trunk.

Corolla — The second whorl of flower parts, consisting of free or fused, often brightly coloured conspicuous petals.

Crown —The part of a tree of shrub above the level of the lowest branch.

Crenate — A leaf edge with shallow, rounded teeth.

Cupule — Small and cup-shaped.

Deciduous — A plant that loses its leaves for part of the year.

Disc — A circular zone of tissue between the point of attachment of a 2-lidded operculum and the ring of stamens and valves of a eucalypt capsule.

Domatia — Projections in the vein/axils of a leaf.

Drupe — A succulent fruit that does not split open when ripe, consists of a skin, a fleshy layer, and a hard stony layer enclosing the seed or seeds.

Elliptical — A two-dimensional shape; shaped like an ellipse.

Ellipsoidal — The 3-dimensional equivalent of elliptical.

Emergent —Rising above the main canopy of eucalypt or rainforest (eg *Araucaria cunninghamii*, Hoop Pine, is sometimes an emergent in dry rainforest communities).

Entire leaf — Without any incision or division along the length of the leaf edge.

Epipyhte — A plant attached to another plant, but not as a parasite, often found above ground level (eg Crows Nest Fern).

Evergreen — A plant that does not lose its leaves; opposite of deciduous.

Exserted — The valves of some eucalypts are projected above the rim of the capsule (eg *Eucalyptus resinifera*, Red Mahogany).

Family — A taxonomic grouping of closely related genera and species usually distinct from other groups, in plants ending in aceae. For example, the myrtle family Myrtaceae contains a number of genera, including *Eucalyptus Melaleuca* and *Syzygium*

Ferns — A group of primitive vascular plants generally found in moist, shaded habitats. Composed of fronds (leaves) and an underground stem (rhizome) Reproducing by means of spores. When first developed, the frond is rolled up like a shepherd's crook in a structure called a 'crozier' that distinguishes the plant as a fern.

Filament — The stalk of a stamen.

Fissure —Long narrow cracks or grooves in tree bark.

Floret — A small, modified flower.

Flower — The reproductive structure of flowering plants. It may consist of all of the following parts: sepals (calyx), petals (corolla) stamens and carpels. Some parts may be fused or modified in some way.

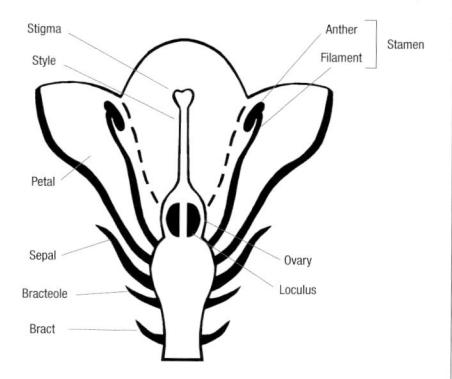

Diagram of flower showing: Stigma, Style, Petal, Sepal, Bracteole, Bract, Anther, Filament, Stamen, Ovary, Loculus

Follicle — A dry fruit formed from a single carpel that opens along one side at maturity.

Frond — The leaf of ferns, cycads and palms that consists of the blade (lamina) and the stalk (stipe). The blade may be flat and leaf-like or sometimes much divided or very narrow and linear in outline.

Funicle — The seed or ovule stalk.

Fused — Joined and growing together.

Gall — An outgrowth of plant tissue, sometimes resembling the reproductive structures of the host plant, but growing around eggs and larvae of a range of insects.

Genus — A taxonomic grouping of closely related species.

Glabrous — Lacks hairs, smooth.

Gland — A structure on the surface or within a plant often secreting substances such as oils.

Glandular Hairs — Hairs with a swollen gland-like tip.

Glume — One of usually two bracts that enclose a grass spikelet; also used in Cyperaceae family for the bracts that enclose flowers.

Grass — A plant belonging to the Poaceae family; herbaceous, tufted and sometimes with runners and a modified flower (Floret). Grasses may be separated from the sedges by the presence of a ligule at the junction of the leaf blade and the open sheath partly enclosing the grass stem.

Groundcovers — The lowermost layer of a plant community covering the soil and consisting of a variety of generally low-growing plants that may include grasses, sedges, orchids, creepers or ferns.

Hastate — Spear-shaped; when a leaf has a narrow pointed blade with 2 basal lobes spreading almost at right angles to the stalk.

Heads — A dense cluster of flowers or florets, usually with very short or no stalks.

Herb — A plant that does not produce a woody stem although it may be woody at the base.

Hybrid — The offspring of two different species.

Hypanthium —A cup-like or tubular structure that forms the lower half of a flower bud (as in eucalypt capsules).

Inflorescence — A collective term for the arrangement of groups of flowers, including the stalks and branches bearing them. Spikes, racemes and panicles are types of inflorescences.

Keel — The 2 partially joined, lowest petals of a pea flower, enclosing the stamens and carpel.

Labellum — The distinctive middle petal of an orchid flower (family Orchidaceae) usually differing in size and shape from the petals on either side.

Lanceolate — Shaped like a lance; leaves that are 3 or 6 times longer than broad and broadest below the middle, usually tapering to a point at the tip.

Lateral veins — Veins arising from each side of the midvein of the leaf.

Leaflet — One of the ultimate (top) segments of a compound leaf, sometimes called a pinna or pinnule.

Lenticel — A small raised, corky spot or line appearing on young bark through which gaseous exchange occurs.

Lignotuber — A woody swelling at the base of the stem or trunk partly or more commonly wholly underground, bearing latent buds as in many eucalypts.

Ligule — A membranous or hairy outgrowth at the junction of the grass leaf sheath and the leaf blade.

Linear — Long and narrow with parallel edges.

Lithophyte — A plant that grows on rocks – as in some orchids.

Littoral — On or growing near the seashore.

Lobe — The incomplete division of a leaf into almost separate parts or leaflets; often rounded and formed by a natural incision in the leaf, often to about halfway to the midrib.

Mallee — A growth form in which many stems arise from a lignotuber, usually applied to eucalypts, also used to describe a plant community dominated by mallee eucalypts.

Membranous — Thin and translucent, like a membrane.

Midrib (Midvein) — The central vein of a leaf.

Net veins — The veins forming a network in the leaf blade.

Node — The point of a stem at which leaves or branches begin to grow.

Numerous — In a flower, refers to more than 10 stamens.

Nut — A dry fruit that doesn't open at maturity; single seed; derived from 2 or more carpels.

Oblong — Rectangular, longer than broad with parallel sides.

Obovate — Ovate, with the broadest part above the middle.

Obtuse — Blunt or rounded at the end.

Oil glands or oil dots — Small structures embedded in a leaf or other organs that secrete a volatile oil. Mostly visible as small translucent dots (hand lens a help) against a strong light; usually make the leaf aromatic when crushed.

Operculum (calyptra) — The cap-like cover of a eucalypt flower bud; formed from fused perianth parts consisting of 1 or 2 caps depending on species; if 2, the outer is shed some time before the inner cap.. The shape of the operculum is often a good diagnostic character to help identify eucalypt species.

Opposite — Opposite leaves are arranged on opposite sides of the stem at the same level.

Orchids — Herbaceous plants of the family Orchidaceae, with petals and stamens of flowers modified for particular pollinators (eg see labellum).

Ovary — The base portion of the carpel or fused carpels enclosing the ovules that become seeds after fertilisation.

Ovate — Shaped like an egg, but usually tapering to a point at the tip; about twice as long as broad.

Ovoid — The 3-dimensional equivalent of ovate; egg-shaped.

Palms — A group of single stemmed plants with feather-like or fan-shaped leaves. Palms belong to the group of flowering plants known as monocotyledons, which usually have one seed leaf (cotyledon).

Panicle — A much-branched flower spike with the youngest flowers at the top.

Parasite — An organism growing and feeding on another organism (the host).

Peduncle – The common stalk of an inflorescence.

Penniveined — When the lateral veins are conspicuous and numerous, and are more or less parallel to one another, as in a feather.

Perennial — A plant that lives for more than 1 growing season or year.

Perianth — The sepals (calyx) and petals (corolla), particularly when they are similar. See p.357

Petal — One of the segments forming the second whorl of flower parts or corolla; often brightly coloured and conspicuous. See p.357

Petiole — A leaf stalk.

Phyllode — A flattened, modified leaf stalk; leaf-like in shape and function, often with a marginal gland as in many wattles (Acacia spp.). The true leaf is bipinnate and only seen on seedlings.
Parasite - An organism growing and feeding on another organism (the host).

Pinna — The primary division or segment of a pinnately divided lamina

Pinnate — A pinnate leaf is a compound leaf, in which the leaflets are arranged in two rows on opposite sides of a common stalk.

Pinnule — the leaflet of a bipinnate leaf.

Pod — A fruit that splits open at maturity along two sides to release the seeds.

Prickle — A hard sharp outgrowth from the surface of a plant, similar to a spine or thorn.

Prostrate — Flat on the ground.

Pseudo — Apparently like, but not genuine. 'Pseudowhorled' describes leaves clustered together in a whorl-like arrangement.

Pseudobulb — A thickened bulb-like stem of a sympodial orchids, with one or several internodes. The growing point terminates in an inflorescence or dies each year, the growth being continued a new lateral branch.

Raceme — A non-branching flower stalk with the youngest flowers at the top.

Rachis — The main stalk of a compound leaf or inflorescence.

Rhizome — An underground stem.

Seed — The fertilised ovule of a plant containing an embryonic plant and stored food material.

Sedges — Grass-like plants of the sedge family, Cyperaceae; annual or perennial tufted or creeping grass-like or rush-like herbs, sometimes with underground or above-ground creeping stems.

Sepal — One of the segments forming the outer whorl of flower parts, usually green and leaf like. surrounding the corolla and fertile parts of the flower (calyx).

Sessile — Flowers or leaves without a stalk.

Sheath — A tubular or rolled part of a plant organ (eg lower part of the leaf in most grasses).

Shrub — A much-branched woody plant with no distinct trunk, usually with the main branches arising near ground level and usually less than 8 m tall.

Simple Leaf — A leaf not divided into leaflets and with an axillary bud between leaf stalk and the stem.

Sorus (plural. sori) — A discrete aggregate of sporangia in the ferns often arranged in a particular fashion on back of fern frond.

Spathe —A large bract that initially encloses a spike-like inflorescence, but which may become more open at maturity. The inflorescence has a thickened, often succulent axis.

Species — The smallest taxonomic unit commonly used. For many animals and plants a species is a group of individuals potentially capable of interbreeding to produce fertile offspring for a number of generations.

Spike — A simple inflorescence of flowers that lack stalks, with the youngest at the top.

Spikelet — A unit of the grass (Poaceae), sedge family (Cyperaceae) and the Restionaceae family; composed of an axis, usually bearing two or more glumes that enclose one or more small flowers.

Spine (thorn) — A hard sharp outgrowth of a plant organ; similar to a prickle in appearance and effect.

Spores — Usually microscopic single-celled or several-celled reproductive units.

Sporangium (plural Sporangia) — A structure in which the spores are produced as in the ferns.

Stamen — The anther and the stalk on which it is borne. The male organ of the flower consisting of the anther, which produces the pollen, and a filament or stalk. See p.357

Sterile — Lacking reproductive structures, not producing spores, seeds or pollen. In the case of spores, seeds of pollen not capable of reproduction.

Stigma — The usually expanded terminal part of the style, adapted to receive the pollen of carpel.

Stipule — One or a pair of leaf-like, membranous or spine-like appendages at the base of the leaf stalk in some flowering plants.

Succulent — Juicy, fleshy, a plant with a fleshy texture.

Taxon — A term used to describe a member of any taxonomic category (e.g. genus, species). Plural taxa.

Taxonomy — The study of the principles and practices of classification and the establishment and defining of relationships between organisms.

Tendril — Tendril: An elongated slender coiled modified plant part that is sensitive to contact aiding in climbing by coiling around objects.

Terrestrial — Growing on the ground.

Thorn — See spine.

Tree — A woody plant with usually a single trunk branching well above ground, and is at least 5m tall at maturity.

Trifoliate — Having three leaflets.

Trunk — The stem of a tree ending in a crown of leaves. The part of the trunk to the first branch is sometimes called the bole.

Umbel — An inflorescence where all the flowers or flowers stalks (pedicels) arise from the top of a common stalk (peduncle).

Valve — A segment formed by the splitting on certain fruits when they are ripe. A lid or segment of an anther or capsule which opens or separates at maturity to release pollen or seeds; as in the teeth-like segments of the eucalypt capsule.

Variety — A taxonomic category below that of species and subspecies that differentiates variable populations.

Venation — The arrangement of the veins of the leaf.

Vines — Plants that climb, twine or creep over the ground or other plants by means of modified stems or leaf parts (eg twining stems and tendrils).

Whorl — A group of three or more segments or organs around a stem at the same level.

Wing — A membranous expansion of a seed or fruit that aids in its dispersal.

Winged — When there is a distinct layer of tissue along each side of the more-or-less cylindrical stem.

Information courtesy of Robert Coutts

Index of Scientific Names

Abrophyllum ornans	237, 258	
Abrus prectorius	223	
Acacia baueri subsp. baueri	68	
Acacia complanata	116	
Acacia concurrens	117	
Acacia disparrima subsp. disparrima	118	
Acacia falciformis	310	
Acacia fimbriata	119	
Acacia implexa	120	
Acacia irrorata subsp. irrorata	121	
Acacia leiocalyx	121	
Acacia maidenii	238	
Acacia melanoxylon	238	
Acacia penninervis var. longiracemosa	122	
Acacia perangusta	122	
Acacia podalyriifolia	123	
Acacia sophorae	26	
Acacia suaveolens	69	
Acacia ulicifolia	69	
Acmena ingens	238	
Acmena smithii	239	
Acronychia imperforata	239	
Acronychia laevis	240	
Acronychia littoralis	239	
Acronychia oblongifolia	240	
Acronychia pauciflora	240	
Acrostichum speciosum	42	
Acrotriche aggregata	123	
Adiantum aethiopicum	216	
Adiantum atroviride	216	
Adiantum hispidulum	217	
Adiantum silvaticum	217	
Aegiceras corniculatum	42	
Agathis robusta	325	
Ageratina riparia	337	
Alchornea ilicifolia	241	
Alectryon coriaceus	241	
Alectryon subdentatus	242	
Alectryon tomentosus	242	
Allocasuarina littoralis	124	
Allocasuarina rigida subsp. rigida	310	
Allocasuarina torulosa	125	
Alocasia brisbanensis	214	
Alphitonia excelsa	126	
Alpinia arundelliana	214	
Alpinia caerulea	214	
Alyxia magnifolia	242	
Alyxia ruscifolia	242	
Amaranthus spinosus	337	
Amyema congener	127	
Angophora floribunda	128	
Angophora leiocarpa	129	
Angophora subvelutina	130	
Angophora woodsiana	131	
Anopterus macleayanus	243	
Anredera cordifolia	341	
Aotus ericoides	70	
Aotus lanigera	70	
Aphananthe philippinensis	243	
Araucaria bidwillii	325	
Araucaria cunninghamii	244, 325	
Araucaria heterophylla	326	
Archontophoenix alexandrae	236	
Archontophoenix cunninghamiana	236	
Argyrodendron actinophyllum subsp. actinophyllum	244	
Argyrodendron sp.	245	
Argyrodendron trifoliolatum	245	
Aristolochia elegans	341	
Arthropteris beckleri	217	
Arthropteris tenella	217	
Asparagus aethiopicus	337	
Asparagus africanus	341	
Asplenium australasicum	218	
Asplenium harmanii	218	
Astrotricha latifolia	132	
Astrotricha longifolia	70	
Atractocarpus chartaceus	246	
Auranticarpa rhombifolia	246	
Austromyrtus dulcis	132	
Austrosteenisia blackii	224	
Austrosteenisia glabristyla	224	
Avicennia marina subsp. australasica	43	
Baeckea frutescens	71	
Baloghia inophylla	247	
Baloskion pallens	48	
Baloskion tetraphyllum	49	
Banksia aemula	71	
Banksia integrifolia subsp. compar	133	
Banksia integrifolia subsp. monticola	133	
Banksia integrifolia subsp. integrifolia	26	
Banksia oblongifolia	72	
Banksia robur	57	
Banksia serrata	71	
Banksia spinulosa var. collina	134	
Banksia spinulosa var. cunninghamii	311	
Banksia spinulosa var. spinulosa	134	
Bauhinia variegata	326	
Baumea rubiginosa	49	
Bidens pilosa	337	
Billardiera scandens	309	
Blandfordia grandiflora	64	
Blechnum cartilagineum	201	
Blechnum indicum	56	
Blechnum patersonii	218	
Bolboschoenus caldwellii	50	
Bolboschoenus fluviatilis	50	
Boronia falcifolia	72	
Boronia parviflora	135	
Boronia polygalifolia	135	
Boronia rosmarinifolia	135	
Bossiaea rupicola	311	
Brachychiton acerifolius	248	
Brachychiton australis	249	
Brachychiton discolor	249	
Brachychiton populneus	136	
Brachychiton rupestris	326	
Breynia oblongifolia	137	
Bruguiera gymnorhiza	43	
Bryophyllum delagoense	337	
Buckinghamia celsissima	326	
Burchardia umbellata	64	
Bursaria incana	137	
Bursaria spinosa	137	
Caesalpinia ferrea	327	
Calamus muelleri	224	
Calanthe triplicata	222	
Callerya australis	217	
Callerya megasperma	225	
Callicarpa pedunculata	250	
Callisia fragrans	337	
Callistemon montanus	312	
Callistemon pallidus	312	
Callistemon salignus	138	
Callistemon viminalis	327	
Callitris columellaris	27	
Callitris glaucophylla	27	
Calochlaena dubia	110	
Calotis lappulacea	94	
Canavalia rosea	24	
Canthium coprosmoides	250	
Canthium odoratum	250	
Capparis arborea	251	
Cardiospermum grandiflorum	341	
Carissa ovata	251	
Carpobrotus glaucescens	22	
Cassine australis	266	
Cassinia subtropica	313	
Cassytha pubescens	68	
Castanospermum australe	252	
Casuarina cunninghamiana	139, 327	
Casuarina equisetifolia subsp. incana	28	
Casuarina glauca	58	
Caustis blakei		

SCIENTIFIC NAMES INDEX

subsp. *blakei* 94	*Daviesia villifera* 147	*Endiandra sieberi* 267
Caustis recurvata 65	*Daviesia wyattiana* 148	*Epacris microphylla* 74
Cayratia clematidea 113	*Dawsonia longifolia* 215	*Epacris obtusifolia* 74
Celastrus australis 225	*Dawsonia polytrichoides* 215	*Epacris pulchella* 74
Celastrus subspicata 225	*Dawsonia superba* 215	*Eragrostis tenuifolia* 338
Celtis sinensis 343	*Delonix regia* 328	*Eucalyptus acmenoides* 149
Ceriops tagal 44	*Dendrobium kingianum* 308	*Eucalyptus baileyana* 150
Chloris gayana 338	*Dendrobium speciosum* 222	*Eucalyptus biturbinata* 151
Choricarpia leptopetala 253	*Dendrocnide excelsa* 259	*Eucalyptus carnea* 152
Choricarpia subargentea 253	*Dendrocnide moroides* 259	*Eucalyptus codonocarpa* 314
Chrysocephalum apiculatum 95	*Dendrocnide photinophylla* 260	*Eucalyptus crebra* 153
Cinnamomum camphora 343	*Derris involuta* 224	*Eucalyptus curtisii* 329
Cirsium vulgare 338	*Desmodium rhytidophyllum* 96	*Eucalyptus dura* 154
Cissus antarctica 226	*Desmodium unicinatum* 341	*Eucalyptus eugenioides* 169
Cissus hypoglauca 226	*Dianella caerulea* var. *caerula* 97	*Eucalyptus fibrosa* 154
Cissus sterculiifolia 226	*Dianella caerulea*	*Eucalyptus grandis* 203
Cladium procerum 50	var. *producta* 97	*Eucalyptus helidonica* 149
Claoxylon australe 253	*Dianella congesta* 22	*Eucalyptus major* 155
Clematis glycinoides 227	*Dianella revoluta* var. *revoluta* 98	*Eucalyptus melanophloia* 156
Clematis pickeringii 227	*Dicranopteris linearis*	*Eucalyptus microcorys* 157, 329
Clerodendrum floribundum 140	var. *linearis* 66	*Eucalyptus moluccana* 158
Clerodendrum inerme 140	*Dillwynia retorta*	*Eucalyptus pilularis* 159
Clerodendrum tomentosum 140	var. *retorta* 73	*Eucalyptus planchoniana* 160
Comesperma esulifolium 313	*Dioscorea transversa* 227	*Eucalyptus propinqua* 161
Commelina diffusa 95	*Diospyros pentamera* 260	*Eucalyptus psammitica* 162
Commersonia bartramia 254	*Diploglottis australis* 261	*Eucalyptus racemosa* 163
Commersonia fraseri 254	*Diploglottis campbellii* 278	*Eucalyptus resinifera* 164
Conospermum taxifolium 73	*Dipodium hamiltonianum* 112	*Eucalyptus robusta* 165
Cordyline congesta 255	*Dipodium punctatum* 112	*Eucalyptus saligna* 204
Cordyline petiolaris 255	*Dipodium variegatum* 112	*Eucalyptus seeana* 166
Cordyline rubra 255	*Dissiliaria baloghioides* 261	*Eucalyptus siderophloia* 167
Corybas aconitiflorus 307	*Dockrillia linguiformis* 112	*Eucalyptus tereticornis* 168
Corymbia citriodora	*Dodonaea triquetra* 148	*Eucalyptus tindaliae* 169
subsp. *citriodora* 141	*Dodonaea viscosa* 148	*Eupomatia laurina* 267
Corymbia citriodora	*Doryanthes excelsa* 306	*Euroschinus falcata* 268
subsp. *variegata* 141, 327	*Doryanthes palmeri* 306	*Eustrephus latifolius* 113
Corymbia gummifera 142	*Drosera binata* 51	*Excoecaria agallocha* 44
Corymbia henryi 143	*Drosera peltata* 51	*Exocarpos cupressiformis* 170
Corymbia intermedia 144	*Drosera spatulata* 52	*Exocarpos latifolius* 170
Corymbia tessellaris 145	*Drynaria rigidula* 110	*Ficus benjamina* 329
Corymbia torelliana 328	*Drypetes deplanchei* 262	*Ficus coronata* 269
Corymbia trachyphloia	*Duboisia myoporoides* 262	*Ficus microcarpa* var. *hilli* 330
subsp. *trachyphloia* 146	*Dysoxylum molissimum*	*Ficus macrophylla* 269
Crinum pedunculatum 36	subsp. *molle* 263	*Ficus obliqua* 270
Croton insularis 255	*Dysoxylum rufum* 263	*Ficus rubiginosa* 270
Cryptocarya glaucescens 256	*Egragrostis tenuifolia* 38	*Ficus superba*
Cryptocarya laevigata 256	*Einadia hastata* 36	var. *henneana* 271
Cryptocarya microneura 256	*Einadia nutans* 37	*Ficus watkinsiana* 271
Cryptocarya obovata 257	*Elaeocarpus grandis* 264	*Fieldia australis* 228
Cryptocarya triplinervis 257	*Elaeocarpus kirtonii* 265	*Flindersia australis* 272, 330
Cryptostylis erecta 307	*Elaeocarpus obovatus* 265	*Flindersia bennettiana* 273
Cupaniopsis anacardioides 258, 328	*Elaeocarpus reticulatus* 74	*Flindersia collina* 274
Cuttsia viburnea 258	*Elaeodendron australe*	*Gahnia aspera* 98
Cyathea australis 259	var. *australe* 266	*Geissois benthamii* 274
Cyathea cooperi 259	*Elatostema reticulatum* 215	*Geitonoplesium cymosum* 114
Cyathea leichhardtiana 259	*Elatostema stipitatum* 215	*Geranium solanderi*
Cymbopogon refractus 96	*Elattostachys nervosa* 266	var. *solanderi* 200
Daviesia umbellulata 147	*Elattostachys xylocarpa* 266	*Gleichenia dicarpa* 67
Daviesia ulicifolia 147	*Enchylaena tomentosa* 45	*Gleicheria mendellii* 67

Glochidion ferdinandi	275	
Glochidion sumatranum	275	
Gmelina leichhardtii	276	
Gomphocarpus physocarpus	343	
Gompholobium latifolium	171	
Gompholobium pinnatum	171	
Gompholobium virgatum var. *virgatum*	75	
Goodenia hederacea	99	
Goodenia rotundifolia	99	
Grevillea hilliana	294	
Grevillea robusta	330	
Guioa semiglauca	277	
Haemodorum austroqueenslandicum	100	
Haemodorum tenuifolium	100	
Hakea florulenta	172	
Hakea plurinervia	173	
Hakea salicifolia	314	
Halosarcia indica	37	
Hardenbergia violacea	114	
Harpullia alata	277	
Harpullia pendula	278, 331	
Hedraianthera porphyropetala	278	
Heliotropium amplexicaule	338	
Hibbertia aspera	173	
Hibbertia hexandra	315	
Hibbertia scandens	25	
Hibbertia stricta	174	
Hibbertia vestita	174	
Hibiscus diversifolius	175	
Hibiscus heterophyllus	175	
Hibiscus splendens	175	
Hibiscus tiliaceus	28	
Homalanthus nutans	279	
Homoranthus virgatus	75	
Hovea acutifolia	176	
Hovea heterophylla	176	
Hybanthus monopetalus	100	
Hybanthus stellarioides	100	
Hydrocotyle bonariensis	338	
Hymenosporum flavum	279	
Hypochaeris radicata	338	
Impatiens walleriana	339	
Imperata cylindrica	101	
Ipomoea cairica	341	
Ipomoea indica	342	
Ipomoea pes-caprae	25	
Isolepis inundata	38	
Jacaranda mimosifolia	331	
Jacksonia scoparia	177	
Jacksonia stackhousii	76	
Jagera pseudorhus forma *pseudorhus*	280	
Jasminum didymum subsp. *didymum*	228	
Jasminum didymum subsp. *racemosum*	228	
Juncus kraussii	38
Kennedia rubicunda	115
Keraudrenia hillii var. *hillii*	315
Kigelia africana	331
Koelreuteria elegans	343
Lantana camara	343
Lantana montevidensis	339
Lastreopsis decomposita	219
Lastreopsis microsora subsp. *microsora*	219
Lastreopsis silvestris	219
Laxmannia compacta	101
Laxmannia gracilis	101
Legnephora moorei	229
Lepidosperma laterale var. *angustum*	102
Lepidosperma laterale var. *laterale*	102
Lepidosperma laterale var. *majus*	102
Lepidozamia peroffskyana	205
Lepironia articulata	52
Leptomeria acida	76
Leptospermum liversidgei	77
Leptospermum luehmannii	316
Leptospermum microcarpum	316
Leptospermum oreophilum	317
Leptospermum petersonii	317
Leptospermum polygalifolium	77
Leptospermum semibaccatum	78
Leptospermum variabile	317
Leucopogon biflorus	178
Leucopogon juniperinus	178
Leucopogon margarodes	179
Leucopogon neoanglicus	318
Leucopogon pimeleoides	78
Ligustrum lucidum	343
Linospadix monostachya	237
Livistona australis	202
Lobelia gibbosa	102
Lobelia purpurascens	102
Lobelia trigonocaulis	306
Logania albiflora	318
Lomandra confertifolia subsp. *confertifolia*	103
Lomandra confertifolia subsp. *pallida*	103
Lomandra hystrix	103
Lomandra longifolia	103
Lomandra multiflora	104
Lomatia arborescens	205
Lomatia silaifolia	179
Lophostemon confertus	206
Lophostemon suaveolens	180
Ludwigia octovalvis	53
Lumnitzera racemosa	45
Lycopodiella cernua	67
Lysiana maritima	181
Lysiana subfalcata	181	
Macaranga tanarius	281	
Macfadyena unguis-cati	342	
Macroptilium atropurpureum	339	
Macroptilium lathyroides	339	
Macrozamia lucida	207	
Macrozamia macleayi	207	
Mallotus claoxyloides	281	
Mallotus phillippensis	282	
Marsdenia longiloba	229	
Marsdenia rostrata	229	
Maytenus bilocularis	282	
Maytenus silvestris	182	
Melaleuca bracteata	182, 331	
Melaleuca linariifolia	183	
Melaleuca nodosa	183	
Melaleuca quinquenervia	59	
Melaleuca thymifolia	79	
Melaleuca trichostachya	183	
Melastoma affine	208	
Melichrus adpressus	184	
Melichrus procumbens	184	
Melichrus urceolatus	184	
Melicope elleryana	283	
Melicope micrococca	283	
Melicope vitiflora	283	
Melodorum leichhardtii	230	
Microsorum pustulatum	219	
Microsorum scandens	219	
Monotoca scoparia	185	
Monotoca sp.	185	
Morinda canthoides	230	
Morinda jasminoides	230	
Murdannia graminea	104	
Myoporum acuminatum	46	
Neolitsea australiensis	284	
Neolitsea dealbata	284	
Neonotonia wightii	339	
Nephrolepis cordifolia	339	
Niemeyera chartacea	284	
Nothofagus moorei	285	
Nymphaea caerulea subsp. *zanzibarensis*	345	
Nymphoides indica	48	
Ochna serrulata	344	
Oenothera drummondii subsp. *drummondii*	23	
Olearia hygrophila	53	
Olea paniculata	285	
Oxalis corniculata	340	
Ozothamnus diosmifolius	185	
Palmeria scandens	231	
Pandanus tectorius	29	
Pararchidendron pruinosum var. *pruinosum*	286	
Parsonsia longipetiolata	229	
Parsonsia straminea	57	
Passiflora aurantia	231	

Passiflora foetida	342	
Passiflora herbertiana		
subsp. *herbertiana*	231	
Passiflora suberosa	342	
Passiflora subpeltata	342	
Patersonia fragilis	65	
Patersonia glabrata	65	
Patersonia sericea		
var. *sericea*	65	
Pavetta australiensis	286	
Pennantia cunninghamii	287	
Persicaria decipiens	54	
Persoonia cornifolia	186	
Persoonia stradbrokensis	186	
Persoonia virgata	79	
Petalostigma pubescens	187	
Petalostigma triloculare	187	
Petrophile canescens	80	
Phaius australis	56	
Phebalium woombye	80	
Phyllota phylicoides	81	
Physalis peruviana	344	
Pilidiostigma glabrum	208	
Pilidiostigma rhytispermum	208	
Pimelea linifolia		
subsp. *linifolia*	188	
Pimelea neo-anglica	188	
Pinus spp.	344	
Piper novae-hollandiae	232	
Pittosporum multiflorum	287	
Pittosporum oreillyanum	287	
Pittosporum revolutum	189	
Pittosporum undulatum	288	
Platycerium bifurcatum		
subsp. *bifurcatum*	220	
Platycerium superbum	220	
Platysace ericoides	81	
Platysace lanceolata	319	
Plectranthus graveolens	319	
Plectranthus nitidus	216	
Plectranthus parviflorus	216	
Plumeria rubra	332	
Poa labillardieri		
var. *labillardieri*	105	
Podocarpus elatus	288	
Podolobium aciculiferum	190	
Podolobium ilicifolium	190	
Polyscias elegans	289	
Polyscias murrayi	289	
Pomaderris argyrophylla		
subsp. *argyrophylla*	191	
Pomaderris ferruginea	191	
Pomaderris lanigera	320	
Pomax umbellata	105	
Portulaca oleracea	39	
Pothos longipes	232	
Premna lignum-vitae	300	
Pseuderanthemum variabile	200	
Pseudoweinmannia		
lachnocarpa	290	
Psilotum nudum	111
Psychotria daphnoides	290
Psychotria loniceroides	291
Pultenaea euchila	192
Pultenaea myrtoides	82
Pultenaea paleacea	82
Pultenaea petiolaris	192
Pultenaea retusa	194
Pultenaea villosa	193
Pyrrosia confluens	
var. *confluens*	221
Pyrrosia rupestris	221
Quintinia sieberi	291
Quintinia verdonii	291
Rapanea variabilis	194, 291
Rhapiolepis indica	344
Rhizophora stylosa	46
Rhodamnia rubescens	292
Ricinocarpos pinifolius	83
Ricinus cummunis	344
Ripogonum album	233
Ripogonum brevifolium	233
Ripogonum elseyanum	233
Rivina humilis	340
Rubus rosifolius var. *rosifoluis*	234
Rubus rosifolius	
var. *commersonii*	234
Sansevieria trifasciata	340
Sarcochilus falcatus	223
Sarcocornia quinqueflora	39
Sarcopteryx stipata	292
Scaevola calendulacea	23
Schefflera actinophylla	344
Schinus terebinthifolia	345
Schoenoplectus validus	54
Senna pendula	345
Sesuvium portulacastrum	40
Sloanea australis	
subsp. *australis*	293
Sloanea woollsii	293
Smilax australis	115
Smilax glyciphylla	309
Solanum aviculare	294
Solanum mauritianum	345
Sowerbaea juncea	66
Spathodea campanulata	332
Sphagneticola trilobata	340
Spinifex sericeus	24
Sporobolus virginicus	40
Sprengelia sprengelioides	83
Stenocarpus sinuatus	294
Sterculia quadrifida	295
Sticherus flabellatus	
var. *flabellatus*	201
Strangea linearis	84
Streblus brunonianus	295
Strychnos psilosperma	251
Stylidium debile	106
Stylidium graminifolium	106
Stylidium laricifolium	320
Suaeda arbusculoides	41
Suaeda australis	41
Swainsona galegifolia	195
Swainsona queenslandica	195
Syagrus romanzoffiana	345
Synoum glandulosum	296
Syzygium australe	296
Syzygium crebrinerve	297
Syzygium francisii	297
Syzygium luehmannii	332
Syzygium oleosum	298
Syzygium paniculatum	296
Tabebula chrysantha	333
Tabebula rosea	333
Tasmannia insipida	298
Tetragonia tetragonioides	41
Tetrastigma nitens	234
Thelymitra fragrans	308
Themeda triandra	107
Thysanotus tuberosus	107
Toona ciliata	299
Tradescantia albiflora	340
Trema tomentosa	300
Tricoryne anceps	
subsp. *pterocaulon*	108
Tricoryne elatior	108
Trochocarpa laurina	208
Trophis scandens	
subsp. *scandens*	235
Urtica incisa	340
Viola betonicifolia	
subsp. *betonicifolia*	109
Viola hederacea	55
Vitex lignum-vitae	300
Wahlenbergia gracilis	109
Wahlenbergia stricta	109
Waterhousea floribunda	301, 333
Westringia eremicola	196
Westringia blakeana	196
Westringia fruticosa	196
Westringia grandifolia	196
Westringia rupicola	196
Westringia sericea	196
Westringia tenuicaulis	196
Wikstroemia indica	209
Wilkiea macrophylla	301
Wilkiea austroqueenslandica	301
Woollsia pungens	84
Xanthorrhoea fulva	85
Xanthorrhoea glauca	321
Xanthorrhoea johnsonii	197
Xanthorrhoea latifolia	
subsp. *latifolia*	198
Xanthorrhoea macronema	198
Xyris juncea	55
Xyris complanata	55
Zehneria cunninghamii	235

Index of Common Names

Alexandra Palm	236	Bottle-brush Grass Tree	198	Coffee Bush	137
Anchor Vine	231	Bribie Island Pine	27	Common Acronychia	240
Angular Pigface	22	Brisbane Golden Wattle	119	Common Hovea	176
Antarctic Beech	285	Brittlewood	253	Common Indian Hawthorn	344
Apple Berry Vine	309	Broadleaf Apple	130	Common Milk Vine	229
Asparagus Fern	337	Broad-leaf Pepper Tree	345	Conesticks	80
Australian Bluebell	109	Broad-leaved Banksia	57	Cooloon	264
Austral Sarsaparilla	115	Broad-leaved Cough Bush	313	Coral Berry	340
Bailey's Stringybark	150	Broad-leaved Hickory	310	Coral Fern	67
Balloon Cotton Bush	343	Broad-leaved Ironbark	154	Corky Passion Vine	342
Balloon Vine	341	Broad-leaved Native Cherry	170	Cotton Tree	28
Balsam	339	Broad-leaved Paperbark	59	Crab's Eye	223
Bangalow	236	Broad-leaved		Creek Sandpaper Fig	269
Barbed Wire Grass	96	White Mahogany	152	Creeping Crofton Weed	337
Basket Fern	110	Brown Beech	287	Creeping Lantana	339
Beach Acronychia	239	Brown Bloodwood	146	Creeping Oxalis	340
Beach Alectryon	241	Brown Kurrajong	254	Creeping Shield Fern	219
Beach Morning Glory	25	Brown Pine	288	Crinkle Bush	179
Beach Primrose	23	Brown Tulip Oak	245	Crow's Ash	272, 330
Beach Spinifex	24	Brush Bloodwood	247	Crows Nest Fern	218
Beach Tamarind	258	Brush Box	206	Cunjevoi	214
Beadweed	39	Brush Caper Berry	251	Curly Wig	65
Bell-fruited Mallee	314	Brush Pepperbush	298	Curracabah	117
Bennett's Ash	273	Bungwall Fern	56	Currant Bush	76, 251
Berry Saltbush	36	Bunya Pine	325	Cuttsia	258
Bird's Nest Fern	218	Burny Vine	235	Cycad Flower	205
Bitter Bark	187	Cabbage Tree Palm	202	Darling Pea	195
Bitter Pea	147	Cadaghi	328	Deciduous Fig	271
Black Bean	252	Callicarpa	250	Devil's Rice	73
Black Booyong	244	Camphor Laurel	343	Dodder Laurel	68
Black Mangrove	45	Cape Gooseberry	344	Dogwood	177
Black She-oak	124	Cape Waterlily	345	Duboisia	262
Black Tea Tree	182	Carissa	251	Dutchman's Pipe	341
Black Thistle	338	Carrabeen	145	Dwarf Banksia	72
Black Wattle	117, 121	Castor Oil Plant	344	Dwarf Boronia	135
Blackbutt	159	Cat's Claw Creeper	342	Easter Cassia	345
Blackwood	238	Celerywood	289	Elastic Grass	338
Blady Grass	101	Chain Fruit	242	Elkhorn	220
Blind-your-eye	44	Cheese Tree	275	Eprapah Wattle	122
Bloodroot	100	Chinese Elm	343	Exotic Pines	344
Blood Vine	224	Christmas Bells	64	Feathered Yellow-eye	55
Blue Flax Lily	22, 97	Christmas Orchid	222	Fern Tree	280
Blue Grass Tree	321	Climbing Asparagus Fern	341	Fieldia	228
Blue Heliotrope	338	Climbing Guinea Flower	25	Firewheel Tree	294
Blue Lilly-pilly	298	Coast Banksia	26, 133	Fishbone Fern	339
Blue Murdannia	104	Coast Cypress Pine	27	Five-leaf Water Vine	226
Blue Quandong	264	Coastal Boobialla	46	Flame Kurrajong	248
Blueberry Ash	74	Coastal Geebung	186	Flame Tree	248
Blueberry Lily	97	Coastal Jack Bean	24	Flat Weed	338
Blush Alder	293	Coastal Rosemary	196	Flat-stemmed Wattle	116
Blush Cudgerie	268	Coastal Screw Pine	29	Flax Leaf Paperbark	183
Blush Tulip Oak	244	Coastal She-oak	28	Flax Lily	98
Bolwarra	267	Coastal Wattle	26	Flooded Gum	203
Bonnet Orchid	307	Cobbler's Pegs	337	Foam Bark Tree	280
Bottle Tree	326	Cocos Palm	345	Forest Boronia	135

Forest Hop Bush	148	Hickory Wattle	118	Midyim	132
Forest Lobelia	306	Hill's Fig	330	Mile-a-minute	341
Forest Red Gum	168	Holly Wood	246	Milk Maids	64
Forest She-oak	125	Hoop Pine	244, 325	Milky Mangrove	44
Forked Sundew	51	Horseshoe Felt Fern	221	Mist Flower	337
Foxtails	94	Horse-tail She-oak	28	Mistletoe	127
Fragrant Fern	219	Hyacinth Orchid	112	Monkey Rope	57
Frail Trigger Plant	106	Illawarra Flame Tree	248	Moreton Bay Ash	145
Frangipani	332	Ivory Curl Flower	326	Moreton Bay Chestnut	252
Fringed Lily	107	Ivy-leaved Violet	55	Moreton Bay Fig	269
Fringed Wattle	119	Jacaranda	331	Morning Glory	342
Geebung	79	Jackwood	256	Mother of Millions	337
Giant Blood Vine	224	Jam Tarts	184	Mother-in-law's Tongue	340
Giant Ironwood	253	Juniper Wattle	69	Mountain Bottlebrush	312
Giant Moss	215	Kangaroo Apple	294	Mountain Bracken	110
Giant Pepper Vine	232	Kangaroo Fern	219	Mountain Hickory	122
Giant Stinging Tree	259	Kangaroo Grass	107	Mountain Keraudrenia	315
Giant Water Gum	297	Kangaroo Vine	226	Mountain Match-heads	313
Giant Water Vine	226	Kerosene Bush	193	Mountain Tea-tree	317
Gidee-Gidee	223	King Orchid	222	Mountain Triggerplant	320
Glasshouse Mountains		Kurrajong	136	Mowbullan	265
Tea-tree	316	Lacebark	249	Mulberry Stinger	260
Glossy Acronychia	240	Ladies Slipper	100	Muttonwood	194
Glossy Laurel	256	Lamb's Tail	341	Myrtle Ebony	260
Golden Candlesticks	134	Lancewood	261	Narrow-leaved Gardenia	246
Golden Glory Pea	171	Lantana	343	Narrow-leaved Ironbark	153
Golden Rain Tree	343	Large-leaved Privet	343	Narrow-leaved Orangebark	182
Golden Trumpet Tree	333	Large-leaved Spotted Gum	143	Narrow-leaved Red Gum	166
Grass Tree	197, 198	Large-leaved Wilkiea	301	Native Bleeding Heart	279
Grass Trigger Plant	106	Lawyer Vine	224	Native Cherry	170
Green Kamala	281	Leafy Twigrush	50	Native Desmodium	96
Green Wattle	121	Lemon Bottlebrush	312	Native Frangipani	279
Grey Boxwood	262	Lemon-scented Tea-tree	317	Native Geranium	200
Grey Gum	151, 155, 161	Leopard Ash	274	Native Ginger	214
Grey Handlewood	243	Leopard Tree	327	Native Gorse	147
Grey Ironbark	167	Lightwood	120	Native Grape	226
Grey Mangrove	43	Lignum Vitae	300	Native Holly	190, 241
Grey Possumwood	291	Lilly-pilly	239	Native Hydrangea	237
Grey Sedge	52	Logania	318	Native Jasmine	228
Gristle Fern	201	Lolly Bush	140	Native Olive	285
Ground Berry	123	Long Yam	227	Native Passionfruit	231
Guinea Flower	174	Long-leaf Bitter Bark	187	Native Rosella	175
Guioa	277	Long-leaved Bitter Pea	148	Native Sarsaparilla	114
Gum-topped Box	158	Long-leaved Platysace	319	Native Seaberry	37
Gum-topped Ironbark	154	Macaranga	281	Native Spinach	215
Hairpin Banksia	311	Macleay Laurel	243	Native Tamarind	261
Hairy Alectryon	242	Madeira Vine	341	Native Violet	55
Hairy Bird's Eye	242	Maidenhair Fern	216	Native Wistaria	225
Hairy Bush Pea	193	Maiden's Blush	293	Native Yam	227
Hairy Psychotria	291	Maiden's Wattle	238	Needleburr	337
Hairy Rosewood	263	Mangrove Fern	42	New Zealand Spinach	41
Hairy Supplejack	233	Many-flowered Mat Rush	104	Norfolk Island Pine	326
Hard Aspen	240	Mararie	290	Northern Bitter Pea	147
Hard Corkwood	267	Marsh Clubrush	42	Ochna	344
Hard Quandong	265	Mat Rush	103	Odour Bush	281
Hatpins	55	Maulwood	285	Orange Blossom Orchid	223
Hauer	261	Midgenbil	237	Orange Mangrove	43
Headache Vine	227	Midgin	132	Orange Pultenaea	192

Orange Thorn	287	*Red Ironbark*	153	*Silver Basswood*	289
Orangebark	282	*Red Kamala*	282	*Silver Croton*	255
Orchid Tree	326	*Red Kennedy Pea*	115	*Silver Leaf Ironbark*	156
Pandanus	29	*Red Mahogany*	164	*Silver Sycamore*	256
Paperbark Tea-tree	59	*Red Mangrove*	46	*Silver-leaved Desmodium*	341
Paroo Lily	97	*Red Olive Plum*	266	*Singapore Daisy*	340
Pavetta	286	*Red Pea Bush*	311	*Siratro*	339
Peanut Tree	295	*Red-fruited Kurrajong*	295	*Slender Cucumber*	235
Pencilwood	289	*Red-fruited Palm Lily*	255	*Slender Grape*	225
Pennywort	338	*Rhodes Grass*	338	*Slender Grapefruit*	113
Pepperberry	257	*Ribbonwood*	268	*Slender Knotweed*	54
Phaseus Bean	339	*Rigid She-oak*	310	*Slender Rice Flower*	188
Piccabeen Palm	236	*River Clubrush*	54	*Slender Westringia*	196
Pigweed	39	*River Mangrove*	42	*Slug Herb*	104
Pineapple Palm	205	*River She-oak*	139, 327	*Small-leafed Lilly-pilly*	332
Pineapple Zamia	207	*River Tea Tree*	174, 331	*Small-fruited Tea-tree*	316
Pink-bearded Heath	179	*Rock Bearded Heath*	318	*Small-leaved Fig*	270
Pink Bloodwood	144	*Rock Felt Fern*	221	*Small-leaved Plum Myrtle*	208
Pink Poplar	268	*Rock Fig*	270	*Smell-of-the-Bush*	281
Pink Rock Orchid	308	*Rock Orchid*	222	*Smooth Darling Pea*	195
Pink Sun Orchid	308	*Rose Marara*	290	*Smooth Psychotria*	290
Pink Trumpet Tree	333	*Rose She-oak*	125	*Smooth-leaved Plum*	284
Planchon's Stringybark	160	*Rose-leaf Bramble*	234	*Smudgee*	131
Plum Pine	288	*Rough-barked Apple*	128	*Snake Vine*	25
Plunkett Mallee	329	*Rough-leaved Elm*	243	*Snow-wood*	286
Poinciana	328	*Round Leaf Vine*	229	*Snow-in-summer*	183
Pointed-leaved Hovea	176	*Ruby Saltbush*	45	*Soap Tree*	126
Poison Peach	300	*Running Postman*	115	*Soapy Ash*	126
Poison Pimelea	188	*Rush Lily*	66	*Soft Corkwood*	262
Pomax	105	*Rusty Gum*	129	*Soft Twigrush*	49
Poor-man's Gold	171	*Rusty Mahogany*	263	*Southern Silky Oak*	330
Pothos	232	*Rusty Tic-trefoil*	96	*Spade Flower*	100
Pouched Coral Fern	67	*Rusty Tulip Oak*	245	*Spear Lily*	306
Prickly Bearded Heath	178	*Sago Flower*	185	*Spear Thistle*	338
Prickly Broom Heath	185	*Saltwater Couch*	40	*Spider Lily*	36
Prickly Fig	295	*Samphire*	37, 39	*Spiny Shaggy Pea*	190
Prickly Leaf Paperbark	183	*Sandstone Mahogany*	162	*Spiny-headed Mat Rush*	102
Prickly Moses	69	*Satinwood*	300	*Spoon Lily*	214
Prickly Pine	137	*Sausage Tree*	331	*Spoon-leaf Sundew*	52
Prickly Shaggy Pea	190	*Saw Sedge*	98	*Spotted Gum*	141, 327
Purple Cherry	297	*Saw-edged Grass Tree*	198	*Spotted Mangrove*	46
Purple Succulent	337	*Saw-leaf*	98	*Spurred Helmet Orchid*	307
Purple Violet	109	*Scanty Rice Flower*	188	*Staff Vine*	225
Purslane	39	*Scented Fan Flower*	23	*Staghorn*	220
Queensland Hakea	173	*Scentless Rosewood*	296	*Star Goodenia*	99
Queensland Kauri Pine	325	*Scrambling Clerodendrum*	140	*Steelwood*	292
Queensland Silver Wattle	123	*Scrambling Lily*	114	*Sticky-leaved Plectranthus*	319
Queensland White Mahogany	152, 169	*Scribbly Gum*	163	*Stiff Canthium*	250
Queensland White Stringybark	169	*Scrub Cherry*	296	*Stinking Passionfruit*	342
		Scrub Nettle	340	*Strangler Fig*	271
Rayed Bush Pea	192	*Scrub Turpentine*	292	*Strap Water Fern*	218
Red Apple	238	*Scurvy Weed*	95	*Straw Tree-fern*	259
Red Ash	126	*Sea Purslane*	40	*Swamp Banksia*	57
Red Bean	263	*Sea Rush*	38	*Swamp Boronia*	135
Red Bloodwood	142	*Seablite*	41	*Swamp Box*	180
Red Carabeen	274	*Shiny Fan Fern*	201	*Swamp Club Rush*	38
Red Cedar	299	*Shiny-leaved Canthium*	250	*Swamp Daisy*	53
		Shiny-leaved Stinging Tree	260	*Swamp Grass Tree*	85

COMMON NAMES INDEX

Swamp Hibiscus	175
Swamp Lily	36
Swamp Mahogany	165
Swamp Orchid	56
Swamp She-oak	58
Swamp Water Fern	56
Sweet Morinda	230
Sweet Pittosporum	288
Sweet Sarsaparilla	309
Sweet Susie	280
Sweet Wattle	69
Sword Grass	98
Sydney Blue Gum	204
Tall Bluebell	109
Tall Guinea Bush	315
Tall Sundew	51
Tallowwood	157, 329
Teak	272
Tea-tree	77, 78
Thin-leaved Stringybark	169
Three-leaf Water Vine	234
Three-veined Cryptocarya	257
Thumbnail Orchid	112
Thyme Honey Myrtle	79
Tick Orchid	112
Tie Bush	209
Tongue Orchid	112
Trailing Guinea Flower	173
Tree Heath	208
Tree Lomatia	205
Tuckeroo	258, 328
Tulipwood	278, 331
Tussock Grass	105
Twin-flowered Bearded Heath	178
Umbrella Cheese Tree	275
Umbrella Tree	344
Vanilla Lily	66
Veiny Morinda	230
Variable Swordsedge	102
Wait-a-while	224
Walking Stick Palm	237
Wallum Banksia	71
Wallum Boronia	72
Wallum Dogwood	76
Wallum Heath	74
Wallum Wedge Pea	75
Wandering Jew	95
Water Bush	46
Water Snowflake	48
Water Vine	226
Watkin's Fig	271
Wedding Bush	83
Wedge Pea	171
Weeping Baeckea	71
Weeping Bottlebrush	327
Weeping Fig	329
Weeping Lilly-pilly	301, 333
Weeping Satinash	333
West African Tulip Tree	332
Whalebone Tree	295
Wheel of Fire Tree	294
White Acronychia	240
White Beech	276
White Bolly Gum	284
White Booyong	245
White Bottlebrush	138
White Cypress	27
White Doughwood	283
White Glycine	339
White Mahogany	149
White Passion Flower	342
White Quandong	265
White Root	102
White Supplejack	233
White Tamarind	266
White Walnut	257
Whitewood	265
Wild May	77
Wild Passionfruit	342
Wild Quince	277
Wild Tobacco	345
Willow Primrose	53
Willow-leaved Hakea	314
Wing-leaved Tulip	277
Wire Lily	101
Wombat Berry	113
Yellow Burr Daisy	94
Yellow Buttons	95
Yellow Hyacinth Orchid	112
Yellow Mangrove	44
Yellow Pittosporum	189
Yellow Pomaderris	320
Yellow Rush Lily	108
Yellow Stringybark	149
Yellow Tulip	262
Zig-zag Vine	230

List of Wildlife Species

Common Names	Scientific Names
Australian King Parrot	Alisteris scapularis
Australian Painted Lady Butterfly	Vanessa kershawi
Bell Miner	Manorina melanophrys
Black Jezebel Butterfly	Delias nigrina
Black-ringed Ochre Butterfly	Trapezites petalia
Blue-banded Bee	Amegilla pulchra
Blue-faced Honeyeater	Entomyzon cyanotis
Bright Copper Butterfly	Paralucia aurifer
Bright Cornelian Butterfly	Deudorix epijarbas
Bronze Flat Butterfly	Netrocoryne repanda
Brown Antechinus	Antechinus stuartii
Brown Cuckoo-dove	Macropygia ambionensis
Brown Honeyeater	Lichmera indistincta
Brown Ochre Butterfly	Trapezites iacchus
Brush Bronzewing Butterfly	Phaps elegans
Australian Brush Turkey	Alectura lathami
Common Brushtail Possum	Trichosurus vulpecula
Caper White Butterfly	Belenois java teutonia
Channel-billed Cuckoo	Scythrops novaehollandiae
Chequered Grass-skipper Butterfly	Anisynta tillyardi
Chequered Swallowtail Butterfly	Papilio demoleus
Common Brown Butterfly	Heteronympha merope
Common Crow Butterfly	Euploea core
Common Grass-blue Butterfly	Zizina labradus
Common Koel	Eudynamys scolopacea
Common Pencilled-blue Butterfly	Candalides absimilis
Coral Jewel Butterfly	Hypochrysops miskini
Crested Pigeon	Ocyphaps lophotes
Crimson Rosella	Platycercus elegans
Cyane Jewel Butterfly	Hypochrysops cyane
Dark Pencilled-blue Butterfly	Candalides consimilis goodingi
Dark Purple Azure Butterfly	Ogyris abrata
Diamond Dove	Geopelia cuneata
Double-eyed Fig Parrot	Cyclopsitta diophthalma
Dusky Honeyeater	Myzomela obscura
Dusky Flat Butterfly	
Eastern Dusky Flat Butterfly	(Eastern Flat? Netrocoryne repanda?)
Eastern Pygmy Possum	Cercaertus nanus
Eastern Rosella	Platyercus eximius
Eastern Spinebill	Acanthorhynchus tenuirostris
Eastern Tube-nosed Fruit Bat	Nyctimene robinsoni
Emerald Dove	Chalcophaps indica
Emerald Hairstreak Butterfly	
Evening Brown Butterfly	Nelanitis leda
Feathertail Glider	Acrovates pygmaeus
Fiery Copper Butterfly	Lycaena theris
Fiery Jewel Butterfly	Hypochrysops ignita
Figbird	Specotheres virides
Flame Sedge Skipper	Hesperillo idothea clara
Fuscous Honeyeater	Meliphaga fusca
Glistening Blue Butterfly	Sahulana scintillata
Greater Glider	Petauroides volans
Green Catbird	Ailuroedus crassirostris
Green Darter Butterfly	Telicora ancilla
Grey Kangaroo	Macropus giganteus
Grey-headed Flying Fox	Pteropus poliocephalus
Hairy Line-blue Butterfly	Erysichton lineata
Heath Ochre Butterfly	Trapezites phigalia
Hibiscus Harlequin Bug	Tectocoris diophthalmus
Imperial Hairstreak Butterfly	Jalmenus evagoras
Imperial Jezebel Butterfly	Delias harpalyce
Jezebel Nymph Butterfly	Mynes geoffroyi
Joseph's Coat Moth	Agarista agricola
Koala	Phascolarctos cinereus
Large Grass-yellow Butterfly	Eurema hecabe
Large Purple Line-blue Butterfly	Nacaduba berenice
Lewin's Honeyeater	Meliphaga lewinii
Little Friarbird	Philemon citreogularis
Little Lorikeet	Glossopsitta pusilla
Little Red Flying Fox	Pteropus scapulatus
Mallotus Harlequin Bug	Cantao parentum
Mangrove Honeyeater	Meliphaga fasciogularis
Mangrove Jewel Butterfly	Hypochrysops epicurus
Marbled Xenica Butterfly	Geitoneura klugii
Meadow Argus Butterfly	Junonia villida
Mistletoe Bird	Dicaeum hirundinaceum
Moonlight Jewel Butterfly	Hypochrysops delica delos
Musk Lorikeet	Glossopsitta concinna
New Holland Honeyeater	Phylidonyris novaehollandiae
Noisy Friarbird	Philemon corniculatus
Noisy Miner	Manorina melanocephala
Olive-backed Oriole	Oriolus sagittatus
Orange Ochre Butterfly	Trapezites eliena
Orange Palm Dart Butterfly	|ephrenes augiands sperthias
Orange Ringlet Butterfly	Hypocysta adiante
Orchard Swallowtail Butterfly	Papilio aegeus
Ornate Ochre Butterfly	Trapezites genevieveae
Pale-headed Rosella	Platycercus adscitus
Paradise Riflebird	Ptiloris paradiseus
Pied Currawong	Strepera graculina
Plumed Whistling Duck	Dendrocygna eytoni
Purple Cerulean Butterfly	Jamides phaseli
Purple Line-blue Butterfly	Prosotas dubiosa
Purple Moonbeam Butterfly	Philiris innotatus
Queensland Blossom Bat	Syconycteris australis
Rainbow Lorikeet	Trichoglussus haematodus
Red-rumped Parrot	Psephotus haematonotus
Red-tailed Black Cockatoo	Calyptorhynchus banksii
Regent Bowerbird	Sericulus chrysocephalus
Regent Honeyeater	Xanthomyza phrygia
Richmond Birdwing Butterfly	Ornithoptera richmondia
Ringed Xenica Butterfly	Geitoneura acantha ocrea

Common Names	Scientific Names	Common Names	Scientific Names
Rose-crowned Fruit Dove	*Ptilinopus regina*	Queensland Tube-nosed Fruit Bat	*Nyctimeme robinsoni*
Saltbush Blue Butterfly	*Theclinessthes serpentata*	Turquoise Parrot	*Neophema pulchella*
Samphire Blue Butterfly	*Theclinessthes sulpitius*	Two-spotted Line Blue Butterfly	*Nacaduba biocellata*
Satin Azure Butterfly	*Ogyris amaryllis meridionalis*	Varied Sedge Skipper	*Hesperilla donnysa*
Satin Bowerbird	*Ptilinorhynchus violaceus*	Varied Sword-grass Brown Butterfly	*Tisiphone abeona alloifascia*
Scaly-breasted Lorikeet	*Trichoglossus chlorolepidotus*	Variegated Fairy Wren	*Malurus lambertii*
Scarlet Honeyeater	*Myzomela sanguinolenta*	Wandering Whistling Duck	*Dendrocygna arcuata*
Silvereye	*Zosterops lateralis*	White Cockatoo	*Cacatua galerita*
Small Green-banded Blue Butterfly	*Danis hymetus*	White-banded Line Blue Butterfly	*Nacaduba kurava*
Small-tailed Line Blue Butterfly	*Prosotas felderi*	White-banded Plane Butterfly	*Phaedyma shepherdi*
Southern Pearl-white Butterfly	*Elodina angulipennis*	White-banded Blue-line Butterfly	*Nacaduba kurava*
Southern Purple Azure Butterfly	*Ogyris genoveva araxes*	White-cheeked Honeyeater	*Phylidonyris nigra*
Speckled Line Blue Butterfly	*Catopyrops floribunda araxes*	White-naped Honeyeater	*Melithreptus lunatus*
Spiny-cheeked Honeyeater	*Acanthogenuys rufogularis*	White-throated Honeyeater	*Melithreptus albogularis*
Splendid Ochre Butterfly	*Tropezites symmomus soma*	White-throated Treecreeper	*Cormobates leucophaea*
Spotted Jezebel Butterfly	*Delias aganippe*	Wompoo Fruit Dove	*Ptilinopus magnificus*
Spotted Sedge Skipper	*Hesperilla ornata*	Wonga Pigeon	*Leucosarcia melanoleuca*
Squirrel Glider	*Petaurus norfolcensis*	Yellow Palm-dart Butterfly	*Cephrenes trichopepla*
Stencilled Hairstreak Butterfly	*Jalmenus ictinus*	Yellow-bellied Glider	*Petaurus australis*
Striated Pearl-white Butterfly	*Elodina parthia*	Yellow-eyed Cuckoo-shrike	*Cocacina lineata*
Sugar Glider	*Petaurus breviceps*	Yellow-faced Honeyeater	*Lichenostomus chrysops*
Swift Parrot	*Lathamus discolor*	Yellow-spotted Blue Butterfly	*Candalides xanthospilos*
Tailed Emperor Butterfly	*Polyura sempronius*	Yellow-tailed Black Cockatoo	*Calyptorhynchus funereus*
Topknot Pigeon	*Lopholaimus antarcticus*	Yellow-tufted Honeyeater	*Lichenostomus melanops*
Trident Pencilled-blue Butterfly	*Candalides margarita*		

The Queensland Museum is the State's leading publisher of natural and cultural heritage books. Best-selling titles include:

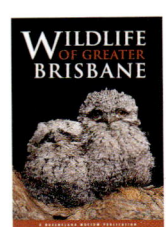

Wildlife of Greater Brisbane

This colourful identification guide is a comprehensive introduction to more than 600 animals with which we share our diminishing wilderness, sprawling urban environs and even the intimacy of our homes. Snails, spiders, insects, other vertebrates, fish, frogs, reptiles, mammals and more than 100 birds are include in easy-to-read entries that describe the physical appearance of each animal and where it is most likely to be found. 384 pages.

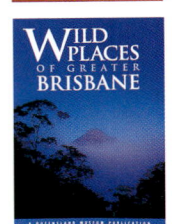

Wild Places of Greater Brisbane

The Greater Brisbane Region encompasses some of the most diverse and beautiful natural environments in Australia — beaches, wetlands, forests and mountains. This full colour guide invites you to explore and discover more than 30 of the region's outstanding 'wild places', including national parks, state forests and conservation reserves. 224 pages.

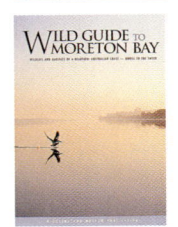

Wild Guide to Moreton Bay

Moreton Bay, in South-east Queensland, is one of Australia's most important natural areas. It is a place of great beauty and variety on the edge of one of Australia's largest cities. From mangroves to mudflats, to rocky shores and pristine sandy beaches, Moreton Bay supports an enormous diversity of life. To the people of South-east Queensland, the Bay is an integral part of their lives. An essential handbook for residents and visitors alike. 432 pages.

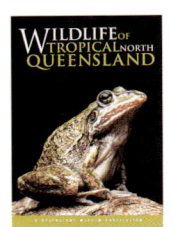

Wildlife of Tropical Queensland

Each year, thousands of tourists from across Australia and overseas are drawn to Tropical North Queensland to experience for themselves the lure of the region's spectacular landscapes and astonishing wildlife. *Wildlife of Tropical North Queensland* is the fourth volume in the Museum's successful *Wild Guide* series.

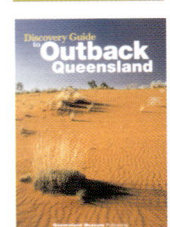

Discovery Guide to Outback Queensland

Outback Queensland encompasses a broad sweep of Australia's early history set against an incomparable landscape. This full colour guide leads travellers through a diverse environment with its sometimes curious animals and plants and a history of human endeavour that reaches back more than 17,000 years. Keep this book close by as you make your own journey of discovery through Outback Queensland. 350 pages.

Museum books are available from all good booksellers.

Inquiries:
The Museum Explorer Shop
PO Box 3300
South Brisbane Q 4101
Phone: 07 3840 77 29
Fax: 07 3846 1918

Or
Queensland Museum Wholesale Division
Phone: 07 3840 7645
Fax: 07 3812 9192

Field Notes

When attempting to identify plants in the field, it is helpful to look for unusual characteristics, such as spines, oil dots in leaves, the shape of stems and the arrangement and shape of leaves along the stem.

When collecting plant material for later identification, keep the following points in mind:
- specimens pressed between sheets of newspaper are easier to identify than shrivelled, loose pieces;
- collect flowers and/ or fruit whenever possible; and
- collect sufficient leaves to show their arrangement along stem.

It is also helpful to note the type of plant (eg herb, shrub or tree), its growth habit, its height, and the habitat in which the plant was collected. In the case of eucalypts, note the bark type.

Subjective characteristics, such as colour, texture or fruit shape, are a guide only because many plant species show considerable variation and these features may not seem the same to everyone.

Field Notes